FREE RV Camping

Ultimate Campgrounds

American Heartland

Discover 1,784 places where you can camp for free!

Published by:

Roundabout Publications
P.O. Box 569
LaCygne, KS 66040

Phone: 800-455-2207
Internet: www.RoundaboutPublications.com

Library of Congress Control Number: 2020940376
ISBN-10: 1-885464-78-9
ISBN-13: 978-1-885464-78-1

Table of Contents

Introduction

About the Ultimate Public Campground Project

The Ultimate Public Campground Project was conceived in 2008 to provide a consolidated and comprehensive source for public campgrounds of all types. It all began with a simple POI (Point of Interest) list of GPS coordinates and names, nothing more, totaling perhaps 5,000 locations. As the list grew in size and information provided, a website was designed to display the data on a map. Next came mobile apps, first iOS and Mac apps and more recently Android versions.

Ultimate Campgrounds is NOT the product of some large company with deep pockets. We are a team of three, all working on this as a part-time avocation: Ted is the founder of Ultimate Campgrounds and its Data Meister, Bill is our iOS and Mac developer and Geoff is our Android guy. Both Ted and Bill have been camping for many years and Ultimate Campgrounds reflects their interest in accurate and useful campground information.

Please note that despite our best efforts, there will always be errors to be found in the data. With over 43,000 records in our database, it is impossible to ensure that each one is always up-to-date. Ted tries to work his way through the data at least once a year to pick up things like increased fees and URL's that always seem to be changing. On an annual basis, it requires reviewing over 115 locations each and every day of the year – that's a pretty tall order.

Thus we always appreciate input from users who have found errors…or would like to submit a new location. Our goal is accuracy and we will gratefully accept any and all input.

We decided some years ago to focus on just one thing, publicly-owned camping locations, and try to be the best at it.

You can find a lot more information about Ultimate Campgrounds on our website: www.ultimatecampgrounds.com.

Feel free to address any questions or comments to us at info@ultimatecampgounds.com.

Happy Camping!

About This Guide

State Maps

Each state begins with a map of that state. The towns shown on the map indicate that camping areas are nearby. Lines of latitude and longitude are also indicated on each map, which can help in locating the camping areas.

Abbreviations Chart

Following each state map is a list, in chart form, showing the abbreviations used in the camping area names for that state.

Camping Area Details

Free camping areas in each state are listed alphabetically under a town name. The towns within the state are also presented in alphabetical order.

Details of each camping area include most or all of the information listed below using the following "headings" and in the same order as shown:

- Name of the camping area
- Agency: managing agency or organization
- Tel: phone number for information
- Location: miles from camping area to town
- GPS: latitude and longitude coordinates
- Open: the season of operation
- Stay Limit: restrictions on length of stay
- Total Sites: number of sites or "dispersed" camping
- RV Sites: number of sites or "undefined" for dispersed
- Max RV Length: any known length limits
- RV Fee: all are free but some will accept donations
- Electric Sites: number of sites with hookups
- Water: comment on availability
- Toilet: comment on availability and type
- Notes: area specific comments
- Activities: list of the popular activities
- Elevation: camping area elevation

Using This Guide

You have the opportunity to discover many wonderful and scenic areas ranging from small remote settings offering peace and quiet to larger lakeside recreation areas complete with all the sights and sounds of people in motion. Knowing how to use this guide will help you receive the most from it.

Camping Area Locations

Only towns with camping areas nearby are shown on the state maps. Town selection was based on the roads traveled to reach the camping area and not a straight line aerial path. When possible, towns that offer services for the traveler were chosen over towns with no services. So the referenced town will not always be the closest town to the camping area.

Keep in mind that lakes, rivers, mountains and access roads can make the camping area a greater distance away (in miles) from town than it would appear on a map. Sometimes camping areas can be fairly close to each other but have different reference towns because of the access roads used to reach each location.

Getting There

This guide is best used in conjunction with Google Maps or similar mapping programs that can provide detailed driving directions. Satellite images can also be helpful in showing the surrounding area and the type of camping experience available.

We have attempted to omit locations with access roads that require a 4x4 vehicle or similar challenging road conditions but it is always advisable to inquire locally with any concerns about your specific rig setup.

Helpful Tips

In the descriptions for each camping area, nearby towns with limited or no services available for the traveler have been tagged with "limited services" and a second nearby town with more traveler services is provided.

A wide variety of camping areas are offered and many are located around or near water. Some are in or near a population center and many are in remote locations. Always plan ahead for a safe and enjoyable visit.

Agencies

This directory includes camping areas managed and operated by a variety of agencies including federal, state, local, and others. Below is a list of the abbreviations used when identifying the various agencies.

Abbreviation	Description
BLM	Bureau of Land Management
BR	US Bureau of Reclamation
COE	Corps of Engineers
CP	County/Regional Park
FWS	US Fish & Wildlife Service
IND	Indian Reservation
MISC	Miscellaneous
MU	Municipal
NP	National Park Service
PRIV	Non-profit, such as museums or conservation groups
ST	State
TVA	Tennessee Valley Authority
USFS	US Forest Service
UT	Utility Company

Arkansas

Arkansas — Camping Areas

Abbreviation	Description
NF	National Forest
NR	National River
NWR	National Wildlife Refuge
WMA	Wildlife Management Area

Altheimer

George H. Dunklin Jr. Bayou Meto WMA - Longbell Road • Agency: State • Tel: 877-367-3559 • Location: 10 miles SE of Altheimer (limited services), 22 miles NE of Pine Bluff • GPS: Lat 34.278181 Lon -91.691129 • Open: All year • Total sites: Dispersed • RV sites: Undefined (several sites along the road) • RV fee: Free • No water • No toilets • Activities: Hiking • Elevation: 181

Arkadelphia

Big Timber WMA 4 • Agency: State • Tel: 877-836-4612 • Location: 7 miles E of Arkadelphia • GPS: Lat 34.095117 Lon -92.966934 • Open: All year • Total sites: Dispersed • RV sites: Undefined • RV fee: Free • No water • No toilets • Activities: Fishing, hunting • Elevation: 192

Arkansas City

Freddie Black Choctaw Island WMA - Ole Miss Trial • Agency: State • Tel: 877-367-3559 • Location: 2 miles NE of Arkansas City (limited services), 13 miles E of McGehee • GPS: Lat 33.624429 Lon -91.179545 • Open: All year • Total sites: 7 • RV sites: 7 • RV fee: Free • No water • No toilets • Activities: Fishing, power boating, hunting • Elevation: 134

Freddie Black Choctaw Island WMA - Thane Rd • Agency: State • Tel: 877-367-3559 • Location: 2 miles E of Arkansas City (limited services), 13 miles E of McGehee • GPS: Lat 33.605006 Lon -91.166506 • Open: All year • Total sites: Dispersed • RV sites: Undefined • RV fee: Free • No water • No toilets • Activities: Fishing, power boating, hunting • Elevation: 126

Freddie Black Choctaw Island WMA - The Chute • Agency: State • Tel: 877-367-3559 • Location: 2 miles E of Arkansas City (limited services), 13 miles E of McGehee • GPS: Lat 33.601541 Lon -91.167098 • Open: All year • Total sites: 6 • RV sites: 6 • RV fee: Free • No water • No toilets • Activities: Fishing, power boating, hunting • Elevation: 130

Ash Flat

Harold E. Alexander Spring River WMA - Spurlock Hollow • Agency: State • Tel: 877-297-4331 • Location: 11 miles E of Ash Flat • GPS: Lat 36.213592 Lon -91.463672 • Open: All year • Total sites: 10 • RV sites: 10 • RV fee: Free • No water • No toilets • Activities: Hiking, hunting • Elevation: 592

Harold E. Alexander Spring River WMA - White Tail Road • Agency: State • Tel: 877-297-4331 • Location: 12 miles SE of Ash Flat • GPS: Lat 36.188767 Lon -91.477755 • Open: All year • Total sites: 10 • RV sites: 10 • RV fee: Free • No water • No toilets • Activities: Hiking, hunting • Elevation: 778

Ashdown

Pond Creek NWR - Ashley's Camp • Agency: US Fish & Wildlife • Tel: 870-289-2126 • Location: 12 miles N of Ashdown • GPS: Lat 33.783715 Lon -94.144343 • Stay limit: 14 days • Total sites: Dispersed • RV sites: Undefined • RV fee: Free • No water • No toilets • Elevation: 275

Pond Creek NWR - River Road • Agency: US Fish & Wildlife • Tel: 870-289-2126 • Location: 10 miles N of Ashdown • GPS: Lat 33.806295 Lon -94.164021 • Stay limit: 14 days • Total sites: Dispersed • RV sites: Undefined • RV fee: Free • No water • No toilets • Elevation: 315

Avant

Buckville (Ouachita Lake) • Agency: Corps of Engineers • Tel: 501-767-2101 • Location: 3 miles S of Avant (limited services), 25 miles W of Hot Springs Village • GPS: Lat 34.612958 Lon -93.342172 • Open: All year • Total sites: 30 • RV sites: 30 • Max RV Length: 20 • RV fee: Free • Central water • Vault toilets • Activities: Swimming, power boating, non-power boating • Elevation: 663

Bald Knob

Henry Gray Hurricane Lake WMA - Big Bell Lake • Agency: State • Tel: 877-734-4581 • Location: 14 miles SE of Bald Knob • GPS: Lat 35.211618 Lon -91.432415 • Open: All year • Total sites: Dispersed • RV sites: Undefined • RV fee: Free • No water • No toilets • Notes: Easily floods • Activities: Fishing, power boating, hunting, non-power boating • Elevation: 195

Henry Gray Hurricane Lake WMA - Big Hurricane Lake • Agency: State • Tel: 877-734-4581 • Location: 17 miles SE of Bald Knob • GPS: Lat 35.240987 Lon -91.440805 • Open: All year • Total sites: Dispersed • RV sites: Undefined • RV fee: Free • No water • No toilets • Notes: Easily floods • Activities: Fishing, power boating, hunting, non-power boating • Elevation: 197

Henry Gray Hurricane Lake WMA - Bollie Pond • Agency: State • Tel: 877-734-4581 • Location: 8 miles SE of Bald Knob • GPS: Lat 35.261105 Lon -91.475269 • Open: All year • Total sites: Dispersed • RV sites: Undefined • RV fee: Free • No water • No toilets • Notes: Easily floods • Activities: Fishing, hunting • Elevation: 189

Henry Gray Hurricane Lake WMA - Glaise Creek 1 • Agency: State • Tel: 877-734-4581 • Location: 9 miles SE of Bald Knob • GPS: Lat 35.230802 Lon -91.481629 • Open: All year • Total sites: Dispersed • RV sites: Undefined • RV fee: Free • No water • No toilets • Notes: Easily floods • Activities: Fishing, power boating, hunting, non-power boating • Elevation: 202

Henry Gray Hurricane Lake WMA - Glaise Creek 2 • Agency: State • Tel: 877-734-4581 • Location: 10 miles SE of Bald Knob • GPS: Lat 35.226392 Lon -91.476869 • Open: All year • Total sites: Dispersed • RV sites: Undefined • RV fee: Free • No water • No toilets • Notes: Easily floods • Activities: Fishing, power boating, hunting, non-power boating • Elevation: 199

Henry Gray Hurricane Lake WMA - Glaise Creek 3 • Agency: State • Tel: 877-734-4581 • Location: 12 miles SE of Bald Knob • GPS: Lat 35.210478 Lon -91.452573 • Open: All year • Total sites: Dispersed • RV sites: Undefined • RV fee: Free • No water • No toilets • Notes: Easily floods • Activities: Fishing, power boating, hunting, non-power boating • Elevation: 195

Henry Gray Hurricane Lake WMA - Glaise Creek 4,5 • Agency: State • Tel: 877-734-4581 • Location: 10 miles SE of Bald Knob • GPS: Lat 35.223804 Lon -91.461882 • Open: All year • Total sites: Dispersed • RV sites: Undefined • RV fee: Free • No water • No toilets • Notes: Easily floods • Activities: Fishing, power boating, hunting, non-power boating • Elevation: 200

Henry Gray Hurricane Lake WMA - Glaise Creek 5-8 • Agency: State • Tel: 877-734-4581 • Location: 12 miles SE of Bald Knob • GPS: Lat 35.203941 Lon -91.449707 • Open: All year • Total sites: Dispersed • RV sites: Undefined • RV fee: Free • No water • No toilets • Notes: Easily floods • Activities: Fishing, power boating, hunting, non-power boating • Elevation: 195

Henry Gray Hurricane Lake WMA - Honey Lake • Agency: State • Tel: 877-734-4581 • Location: 13 miles SE of Bald Knob • GPS: Lat 35.197704 Lon -91.438238 • Open: All year • Total sites: Dispersed • RV sites: Undefined • RV fee: Free • No water • No toilets • Notes: Easily floods • Activities: Fishing, power boating, hunting, non-power boating • Elevation: 195

Henry Gray Hurricane Lake WMA - Little Red River • Agency: State • Tel: 877-734-4581 • Location: 15 miles SE of Bald Knob • GPS: Lat 35.188291 Lon -91.446404 • Open: All year • Total sites: Dispersed • RV sites: Undefined • RV fee: Free • No water • No toilets • Notes: Easily floods • Activities: Fishing, power boating, hunting, non-power boating • Elevation: 195

Henry Gray Hurricane Lake WMA - Mallard Pond • Agency: State • Tel: 877-734-4581 • Location: 17 miles SE of Bald Knob • GPS: Lat 35.196953 Lon -91.469055 • Open: All year • Total sites: Dispersed • RV sites: Undefined • RV fee: Free • No water • No toilets • Notes: Easily floods • Activities: Fishing, power boating, hunting, non-power boating • Elevation: 195

Henry Gray Hurricane Lake WMA - Three Sisters • Agency: State • Tel: 877-734-4581 • Location: 10 miles SE of Bald Knob • GPS: Lat 35.227193 Lon -91.469576 • Open: All year • Total sites: Dispersed • RV sites: Undefined • RV fee: Free • No water • No toilets • Notes: Easily floods • Activities: Fishing, power boating, hunting, non-power boating • Elevation: 201

Henry Gray Hurricane Lake WMA - Whirl Lake 1 • Agency: State • Tel: 877-734-4581 • Location: 14 miles SE of Bald Knob • GPS: Lat 35.206234 Lon -91.431143 • Open: All year • Total sites: Dispersed • RV sites: Undefined • RV fee: Free • No water • No toilets • Notes: Easily floods • Activities: Fishing, power boating, hunting, non-power boating • Elevation: 195

Henry Gray Hurricane Lake WMA - Whirl Lake 2,3 • Agency: State • Tel: 877-734-4581 • Location: 13 miles SE of Bald Knob • GPS: Lat 35.199962 Lon -91.433031 • Open: All year • Total sites: Dispersed • RV sites: Undefined • RV fee: Free • No water • No toilets • Notes: Easily floods • Activities: Fishing, power boating, hunting, non-power boating • Elevation: 195

Henry Gray Hurricane Lake WMA - Whirl Lake 4 • Agency: State • Tel: 877-734-4581 • Location: 14 miles SE of Bald Knob • GPS: Lat 35.196843 Lon -91.429734 • Open: All year • Total sites: Dispersed • RV sites: Undefined • RV fee: Free • No water • No toilets • Notes: Easily floods • Activities: Fishing, power boating, hunting, non-power boating • Elevation: 195

Henry Gray Hurricane Lake WMA - White River • Agency: State • Tel: 877-734-4581 • Location: 14 miles SE of Bald Knob • GPS: Lat 35.194888 Lon -91.428327 • Open: All year • Total sites: Dispersed • RV sites: Undefined • RV fee: Free • No water • No toilets • Notes: Easily floods • Activities: Fishing, power boating, hunting, non-power boating • Elevation: 195

Henry Gray Hurricane Lake WMA - Willow Pond • Agency: State • Tel: 877-734-4581 • Location: 18 miles SE of Bald Knob • GPS: Lat 35.247496 Lon -91.428686 • Open: All year • Total sites: Dispersed • RV sites: Undefined • RV fee: Free • No water • No toilets • Notes: Easily floods • Activities: Fishing, hunting • Elevation: 182

Bismarck

Lenox Marcus (Degray Lake) • Agency: Corps of Engineers • Tel: 870-246-5501 • Location: 6 miles SW of Bismarck (limited services), 17 miles SW of Lake Hamilton • GPS: Lat 34.267116 Lon -93.217566 • Open: All year • Total sites: Dispersed • RV sites: Undefined • RV fee: Free • Central water • Vault toilets • Activities: Power boating, non-power boating • Elevation: 433

Blue Springs

Cedar Fourche (Ouachita Lake) • Agency: Corps of Engineers • Tel: 501-767-2101 • Location: 14 miles W of Blue Springs (limited services), 30 miles NW of Hot Springs • GPS: Lat 34.662625 Lon -93.283621 • Open: All year • Total sites: 30 • RV sites: 30 • RV fee: Free • No water • Vault toilets • Activities: Fishing, power boating, non-power boating • Elevation: 614

Booneville

Jack Creek (Ouachita NF) • Agency: US Forest Service • Tel: 479-637-4174 • Location: 10 miles SE of Booneville • GPS: Lat 35.033855 Lon -93.845912 • Open: Apr-Nov • Total sites: 5 • RV sites: 5 • RV fee: Free • No water • Vault toilets • Activities: Hiking, fishing, swimming • Elevation: 699

Bradley

Layafette County WMA • Agency: State • Tel: 877-777-5580 • Location: 5 miles E of Bradley (limited services), 45 miles SE of Texarkana • GPS: Lat 33.103884 Lon -93.601614 • Open: All year • Total sites: Dispersed • RV sites: Undefined • RV fee: Free • No toilets • Activities: Hunting • Elevation: 259

Calion

Lock and Dam No. 8 (Calion Pool) • Agency: Corps of Engineers • Tel: 601-631-5000 • Location: 14 miles SE of Calion (limited services), 26 miles NE of El Dorado • GPS: Lat 33.300169 Lon -92.461527 • Open: All year • Total sites: 7 • RV sites: 7 • RV fee: Free • No water • Vault toilets • Activities: Fishing, power boating, non-power boating • Elevation: 95

Cedarville

Lee Creek • Agency: State • Location: 11 miles N of Cedarville (limited services), 19 miles N of Van Buren • GPS: Lat 35.702296 Lon -94.328095 • Total sites: Dispersed • RV sites: Undefined • RV fee: Free • No water • No toilets • Activities: Fishing, non-power boating • Elevation: 766

Crossett

Casey Jones WMA - 4A • Agency: State • Tel: 877-367-3559 • Location: 3 miles SE of Crossett • GPS: Lat 33.108674 Lon -91.907462 • Open: All year • Total sites: Dispersed • RV sites: Undefined • RV fee: Free • No water • No toilets • Activities: Hunting • Elevation: 163

Casey Jones WMA - 4B • Agency: State • Tel: 877-367-3559 • Location: 3 miles SW of Crossett • GPS: Lat 33.098969 Lon -91.995968 • Open: All year • Total sites: Dispersed • RV sites: Undefined • RV fee: Free • No water • No toilets • Activities: Hunting • Elevation: 138

Felsenthal NWR - Old Beer Joint (Hogan Tract) • Agency: US Fish & Wildlife • Tel: 870-364-3167 • Location: 8 miles W of Crossett • GPS: Lat 33.157609 Lon -92.111868 • Total sites: Dispersed • RV sites: Undefined • RV fee: Free • No water • No toilets • Activities: Fishing, power boating, non-power boating • Elevation: 68

Delaplaine

Dave Donaldson Black River WMA - Green Rd • Agency: State • Tel: 877-972-5438 • Location: 4 miles NW of Delaplaine (limited services), 13 miles E of Pocahontas • GPS: Lat 36.253396 Lon -90.778055 • Open: All year • Total sites: Dispersed • RV sites: Undefined • RV fee: Free • No water • No toilets • Activities: Fishing, power boating, hunting, non-power boating • Elevation: 269

Dave Donaldson Black River WMA - Lake Ashbaugh • Agency: State • Tel: 877-972-5438 • Location: 5 miles NW of Delaplaine (limited services), 13 miles E of Pocahontas • GPS: Lat 36.253039 Lon -90.771971 • Open: All year • Total sites: Dispersed • RV sites: Undefined • RV fee: Free • No water • No toilets • Activities: Fishing, power boating, hunting, non-power boating • Elevation: 263

Dermott

Casey Jones WMA - 2A • Agency: State • Tel: 877-367-3559 • Location: 13 miles SE of Dermott • GPS: Lat 33.463165 Lon -91.570629 • Open: All year • Total sites: Dispersed • RV sites: Undefined • RV fee: Free • No water • No toilets • Activities: Hunting • Elevation: 170

Casey Jones WMA - 2B • Agency: State • Tel: 877-367-3559 • Location: 14 miles SE of Dermott • GPS: Lat 33.447709 Lon -91.572243 • Open: All year • Total sites: Dispersed • RV sites: Undefined • RV fee: Free • No water • No toilets • Activities: Hunting • Elevation: 160

Des Arc

Bayou Des Arc WMA • Agency: State • Tel: 877-734-4581 • Location: 4 miles N of Des Arc • GPS: Lat 35.019884 Lon -91.515944 • Open: All year • Total sites: 10 • RV sites:

10 • RV fee: Free • No water • Vault toilets • Activities: Fishing, power boating, non-power boating • Elevation: 201

DeWitt

George H. Dunklin Jr. Bayou Meto WMA - Buckingham Flats • Agency: State • Tel: 877-367-3559 • Location: 24 miles SW of DeWitt • GPS: Lat 34.211768 Lon -91.590506 • Open: All year • Total sites: Dispersed • RV sites: Undefined • RV fee: Free • No water • No toilets • Activities: Fishing, power boating, non-power boating • Elevation: 179

George H. Dunklin Jr. Bayou Meto WMA - Cox Cypress 1 • Agency: State • Tel: 877-367-3559 • Location: 16 miles W of DeWitt • GPS: Lat 34.289407 Lon -91.619993 • Open: All year • Total sites: Dispersed • RV sites: Undefined • RV fee: Free • No water • No toilets • Activities: Fishing, power boating, non-power boating • Elevation: 180

George H. Dunklin Jr. Bayou Meto WMA - Cox Cypress 2 • Agency: State • Tel: 877-367-3559 • Location: 17 miles W of DeWitt • GPS: Lat 34.296338 Lon -91.628243 • Open: All year • Total sites: Dispersed • RV sites: Undefined • RV fee: Free • No water • No toilets • Activities: Fishing, power boating, non-power boating • Elevation: 185

George H. Dunklin Jr. Bayou Meto WMA - Cox Cypress 3 • Agency: State • Tel: 877-367-3559 • Location: 16 miles W of DeWitt • GPS: Lat 34.289896 Lon -91.612959 • Open: All year • Total sites: Dispersed • RV sites: Undefined • RV fee: Free • No water • No toilets • Activities: Fishing, power boating, non-power boating • Elevation: 184

George H. Dunklin Jr. Bayou Meto WMA - Duck Lane • Agency: State • Tel: 877-367-3559 • Location: 17 miles W of DeWitt • GPS: Lat 34.304867 Lon -91.631045 • Open: All year • Total sites: Dispersed • RV sites: Undefined • RV fee: Free • No water • No toilets • Activities: Fishing, power boating, non-power boating • Elevation: 192

George H. Dunklin Jr. Bayou Meto WMA - Grand Lake Lane 1 • Agency: State • Tel: 877-367-3559 • Location: 17 miles W of DeWitt • GPS: Lat 34.275928 Lon -91.629054 • Open: All year • Total sites: Dispersed • RV sites: Undefined (several sites along the road) • RV fee: Free • No water • No toilets • Activities: Fishing, power boating, non-power boating • Elevation: 179

George H. Dunklin Jr. Bayou Meto WMA - Grand Lake Lane 2 • Agency: State • Tel: 877-367-3559 • Location: 19 miles W of DeWitt • GPS: Lat 34.260981 Lon -91.641477 • Open: All year • Total sites: Dispersed • RV sites: Undefined • RV fee: Free • No water • No toilets • Activities: Fishing, power boating, non-power boating • Elevation: 187

George H. Dunklin Jr. Bayou Meto WMA - Wrapa Road • Agency: State • Tel: 877-367-3559 • Location: 23 miles SW of DeWitt • GPS: Lat 34.205455 Lon -91.582738 • Open: All year • Total sites: Dispersed • RV sites: Undefined • RV fee: Free • No water • No toilets • Elevation: 178

Little Bayou Meto (Arkansas River) • Agency: Corps of Engineers • Tel: 870-548-2291 • Location: 21 miles SW of DeWitt • GPS: Lat 34.134197 Lon -91.579016 • Open: All year • Total sites: Dispersed • RV sites: Undefined • RV fee: Free • No water • Vault toilets • Activities: Fishing, power boating • Elevation: 181

Diercks

Howard County WMA • Agency: State • Tel: 877-777-5580 • Location: 15 miles NW of Diercks • GPS: Lat 34.246721 Lon -94.144264 • Open: All year • Total sites: Dispersed • RV sites: Undefined (numerous sites) • RV fee: Free • No water • No toilets • Activities: Hunting • Elevation: 860

Ellizabeth

Kerley Point (Lake Noorfolk) • Agency: Corps of Engineers • Tel: 870-425-2700 • Location: 6 miles SW of Ellizabeth (limited services), 24 miles SE of Mountain Home • GPS: Lat 36.30617 Lon -92.15691 • Total sites: Dispersed • RV sites: Undefined • RV fee: Free • No water • No toilets • Notes: Permit required • Activities: Fishing • Elevation: 558

Fouke

Sulphur River WMA - Crabtree Landing • Agency: State • Tel: 877-777-5580 • Location: 6 miles SW of Fouke (limited services), 20 miles SE of Texarkana • GPS: Lat 33.211269 Lon -93.937233 • Total sites: Dispersed • RV sites: Undefined • RV fee: Free • No water • No toilets • Activities: Fishing • Elevation: 226

Sulphur River WMA - Lower Mound • Agency: State • Tel: 877-777-5580 • Location: 15 miles SW of Fouke (limited services), 28 miles SE of Texarkana • GPS: Lat 33.167584 Lon -93.938411 • Total sites: Dispersed • RV sites: Undefined • RV fee: Free • No water • No toilets • Activities: Fishing • Elevation: 233

Fountain Hill

Casey Jones WMA - 5D • Agency: State • Tel: 877-367-3559 • Location: 11 miles NW of Fountain Hill (limited services), 17 miles SE of Warren • GPS: Lat 33.451372 Lon -91.969083 • Open: All year • Total sites: Dispersed • RV sites: Undefined • RV fee: Free • No water • No toilets • Activities: Hunting • Elevation: 106

Casey Jones WMA - 5E • Agency: State • Tel: 877-367-3559 • Location: 10 miles NW of Fountain Hill (limited services), 18 miles SE of Warren • GPS: Lat 33.430436 Lon -91.964753 • Open: All year • Total sites: Dispersed • RV sites: Undefined • RV fee: Free • No water • No toilets • Activities: Hunting • Elevation: 112

Casey Jones WMA - 5F • Agency: State • Tel: 877-367-3559 • Location: 8 miles NW of Fountain Hill (limited services), 20 miles SW of Monticello • GPS: Lat 33.404787 Lon -91.963731 • Open: All year • Total sites: Dispersed • RV sites: Undefined • RV fee: Free • No water • No toilets • Activities: Hunting • Elevation: 108

Casey Jones WMA - 5G • Agency: State • Tel: 877-367-3559 • Location: 8 miles NW of Fountain Hill (limited services), 20 miles SW of Monticello • GPS: Lat 33.379396 Lon -91.929464 • Open: All year • Total sites: Dispersed • RV sites: Undefined • RV fee: Free • No water • No toilets • Activities: Hunting • Elevation: 113

Fulton

Dr. Lester Sitzes III Bois D'Arc WMA - Road 6 • Agency: State • Tel: 877-777-5580 • Location: 7 miles SE of Fulton (limited services), 19 miles SE of Hope • GPS: Lat 33.566512 Lon -93.734969 • Open: All year • Total sites: Dispersed • RV sites: Undefined • RV fee: Free • No water • No toilets • Activities: Hunting • Elevation: 291

Gillett

Big Bayou Meto (Arkansas River) • Agency: Corps of Engineers • Tel: 870-548-2291 • Location: 6 miles SW of Gillett (limited services), 18 miles SW of DeWitt • GPS: Lat 34.081947 Lon -91.441684 • Total sites: Dispersed • RV sites: Undefined • RV fee: Free • No water • Vault toilets • Activities: Fishing, power boating • Elevation: 171

Moore Bayou (Arkansas River) • Agency: Corps of Engineers • Tel: 870-548-2291 • Location: 7 miles S of Gillett (limited services), 19 miles S of DeWitt • GPS: Lat 34.025611 Lon -91.362056 • Open: All year • Total sites: Dispersed • RV sites: Undefined • RV fee: Free • No water • Vault toilets • Activities: Fishing, power boating • Elevation: 164

Trusten Holder WMA - Arkansas Post Canal • Agency: State • Tel: 877-367-3559 • Location: 19 miles SE of Gillett (limited services), 24 miles SE of DeWitt • GPS: Lat 34.022212 Lon -91.224419 • Total sites: Dispersed • RV sites: Undefined • RV fee: Free • No water • No toilets • Activities: Hunting • Elevation: 152

Trusten Holder WMA - Benzal Bridge • Agency: State • Tel: 877-367-3559 • Location: 23 miles SE of Gillett (limited services), 28 miles SE of DeWitt • GPS: Lat 33.998234 Lon -91.160904 • Total sites: Dispersed • RV sites: Undefined • RV fee: Free • No water • No toilets • Activities: Hunting • Elevation: 146

Trusten Holder WMA - White River 1,2 • Agency: State • Tel: 877-367-3559 • Location: 23 miles SE of Gillett (limited services), 28 miles SE of DeWitt • GPS: Lat 34.003225 Lon -91.162869 • Total sites: Dispersed • RV sites: Undefined • RV fee: Free • No water • No toilets • Activities: Hunting • Elevation: 138

Wild Goose Bayou (Arkansas River) • Agency: Corps of Engineers • Tel: 870-548-2291 • Location: 20 miles SE of Gillett (limited services), 25 miles SE of DeWitt • GPS: Lat 34.021014 Lon -91.188577 • Open: All year • Total sites: Dispersed • RV sites: Undefined • RV fee: Free • No water • Vault toilets • Activities: Fishing, power boating • Elevation: 142

Gurdon

Big Timber WMA 2 • Agency: State • Tel: 877-836-4612 • Location: 7 miles SW of Gurdon • GPS: Lat 33.877319 Lon -93.242977 • Open: All year • Total sites: Dispersed • RV sites: Undefined • RV fee: Free • No water • No toilets • Activities: Fishing, hunting • Elevation: 206

Big Timber WMA 3 • Agency: State • Tel: 877-836-4612 • Location: 7 miles SW of Gurdon • GPS: Lat 33.860067 Lon -93.222341 • Open: All year • Total sites: Dispersed • RV sites: Undefined • RV fee: Free • No water • No toilets • Activities: Fishing, hunting • Elevation: 199

Big Timber WMA 5 • Agency: State • Tel: 877-836-4612 • Location: 12 miles NE of Gurdon • GPS: Lat 34.001565 Lon -93.049806 • Open: All year • Total sites: Dispersed • RV sites: Undefined • RV fee: Free • No water • No toilets • Activities: Fishing, hunting • Elevation: 195

Hardy

Harold E. Alexander Spring River WMA - Headquarters • Agency: State • Tel: 877-297-4331 • Location: 7 miles SE of Hardy • GPS: Lat 36.238617 Lon -91.433325 • Open: All year • Total sites: Dispersed • RV sites: Undefined • RV fee: Free • No water • No toilets • Activities: Hiking, hunting • Elevation: 609

Harold E. Alexander Spring River WMA - North Trailer • Agency: State • Tel: 877-297-4331 • Location: 6 miles SE of Hardy • GPS: Lat 36.265059 Lon -91.455798 • Open: All year • Total sites: 10 • RV sites: 10 • RV fee: Free • No water • No toilets • Activities: Hiking, hunting • Elevation: 678

Harold E. Alexander Spring River WMA - River Launch • Agency: State • Tel: 877-297-4331 • Location: 9 miles SE of Hardy • GPS: Lat 36.254103 Lon -91.408988 • Open: All year • Total sites: 10 • RV sites: 10 • RV fee: Free • No water • No toilets • Activities: Hiking, fishing, hunting, non-power boating • Elevation: 326

Harrison

Buffalo NR - Erbie Horse Camp • Agency: National Park Service • Tel: 870-439-2502 • Location: 16 miles SW of Harrison • GPS: Lat 36.081269 Lon -93.232818 • Open: All year • Total sites: Dispersed • RV sites: Undefined • RV fee: Free • No water • Vault toilets • Activities: Equestrian area • Elevation: 990

Hermitage

Felsenfal NWR - Eagle Lake • Agency: US Fish & Wildlife • Tel: 870-364-3167 • Location: 16 miles S of Hermitage (limited services), 27 miles S of Warren • GPS: Lat 33.241285 Lon -92.164823 • Total sites: Dispersed • RV sites: Undefined • RV fee: Free • No water • No toilets • Elevation: 108

Hope

Dr. Lester Sitzes III Bois D'Arc WMA - Finger Point Landing • Agency: State • Tel: 877-777-5580 • Location: 10 miles SE of Hope • GPS: Lat 33.561397 Lon -93.700214 • Total sites: Dispersed • RV sites: Undefined • RV fee: Free • No toilets • Activities: Fishing, power boating, hunting, non-power boating • Elevation: 276

Dr. Lester Sitzes III Bois D'Arc WMA.- Hatfield Landing • Agency: State • Tel: 877-777-5580 • Location: 10 miles SW of Hope • GPS: Lat 33.564939 Lon -93.700996 • Total sites: Dispersed • RV sites: Undefined • RV fee: Free • Vault toilets • Activities: Fishing, power boating, hunting, non-power boating • Elevation: 325

Dr. Lester Sitzes III Bois D'Arc WMA.- Spillway Landing • Agency: State • Tel: 877-777-5580 • Location: 13 miles SW of Hope • GPS: Lat 33.543964 Lon -93.700594 • Total sites: Dispersed • RV sites: Undefined • RV fee: Free • No toilets • Activities: Fishing, power boating, hunting, non-power boating • Elevation: 276

Horatio

Pond Creek NWR - Gillahand Sholes • Agency: US Fish & Wildlife • Tel: 870-289-2126 • Location: 13 miles SE of Horatio (limited services), 20 miles SE of De Queen • GPS: Lat 33.821079 Lon -94.269029 • Stay limit: 14 days • Total sites: Dispersed • RV sites: Undefined • RV fee: Free • No water • No toilets • Elevation: 331

Pond Creek NWR - Nobles Mound Rd • Agency: US Fish & Wildlife • Tel: 870-289-2126 • Location: 13 miles SE of Horatio (limited services), 20 miles SE of De Queen • GPS: Lat 33.837656 Lon -94.234861 • Stay limit: 14 days • Total sites: Dispersed • RV sites: Undefined • RV fee: Free • No water • No toilets • Elevation: 322

Pond Creek NWR - Red Lake • Agency: US Fish & Wildlife • Tel: 870-289-2126 • Location: 15 miles SE of Horatio (limited services), 22 miles SE of De Queen • GPS: Lat 33.816123 Lon -94.236804 • Stay limit: 14 days • Total sites: Dispersed • RV sites: Undefined • RV fee: Free • No water • No toilets • Elevation: 325

Pond Creek NWR - Stag Lake • Agency: US Fish & Wildlife • Tel: 870-289-2126 • Location: 14 miles SE of Horatio (limited services), 21 miles SE of De Queen • GPS: Lat 33.830636 Lon -94.239405 • Stay limit: 14 days • Total sites: Dispersed • RV sites: Undefined • RV fee: Free • No water • No toilets • Elevation: 289

Pond Creek NWR - Yellow Banks • Agency: US Fish & Wildlife • Tel: 870-289-2126 • Location: 13 miles SE of Horatio (limited services), 19 miles S of De Queen • GPS: Lat 33.824783 Lon -94.302355 • Stay limit: 14 days • Total sites: Dispersed • RV sites: Undefined • RV fee: Free • No water • No toilets • Elevation: 302

Hot Springs

Cedar Glades • Agency: County • Tel: 501-623-2854 • Location: 3 miles NW of Hot Springs • GPS: Lat 34.539074 Lon -93.087426 • Total sites: Dispersed • RV sites: Undefined • RV fee: Free • No water • Vault toilets • Activities: Hiking, mountain biking, disc golf • Elevation: 568

Houston

Cypress Creek (Arkansas River) • Agency: Corps of Engineers • Tel: 501-329-2986 • Location: 3 miles NW of Houston (limited services), 16 miles W of Conway • GPS: Lat 35.068675 Lon -92.717199 • Open: Mar-Oct • Total sites: 9 • RV sites: 9 • Max RV Length: 40 • RV fee: Free • Central water • Vault toilets • Activities: Power boating, non-power boating • Elevation: 331

Humphrey

George H. Dunklin Jr. Bayou Meto WMA - Tipton Lane • Agency: State • Tel: 877-367-3559 • Location: 8 miles SE of Humphrey (limited services), 15 miles SW of Stuttgart • GPS: Lat 34.349891 Lon -91.649608 • Open: All year • Total sites: Dispersed • RV sites: Undefined • RV fee: Free • No water • No toilets • Elevation: 177

Jacksonville

Holland Bottoms WMA • Agency: State • Tel: 877-734-4581 • Location: 5 miles NE of Jacksonville • GPS: Lat 34.897872 Lon -92.070033 • Open: All year • Total sites: Dispersed • RV sites: Undefined • RV fee: Free • No water • No toilets • Activities: Fishing, hunting • Elevation: 250

Jasper

Buffalo NR - Erbie • Agency: National Park Service • Tel: 870-439-2502 • Location: 8 miles N of Jasper (limited services), 20 miles SW of Harrison • GPS: Lat 36.071318 Lon -93.215626 • Open: Mar-Nov • Total sites: 16 • RV sites: 14 • RV fee: Free • No water • Vault toilets • Activities: Hiking, fishing, non-power boating • Elevation: 857

Kirby

Bear Creek (Greeson Lake) • Agency: Corps of Engineers • Tel: 870-285-2151 • Location: 2 miles SW of Kirby (limited services), 11 miles SW of Glenwood • GPS: Lat 34.237305 Lon -93.667969 • Open: All year • Total sites: 19 • RV sites: 9 • RV fee: Free • Central water • Vault toilets • Activities: Hiking, mountain biking, fishing • Elevation: 636

Star of the West (Greeson Lake) • Agency: Corps of Engineers • Tel: 870-285-2151 • Location: 12 miles W of Kirby (limited services), 21 miles SW of Glenwood • GPS: Lat 34.239014 Lon -93.825195 • Open: All year • Total sites: 21 • RV sites: 21 • RV fee: Free • Central water • Vault toilets • Activities: Fishing • Elevation: 614

Knobel

Dave Donaldson Black River WMA - Mill Lake • Agency: State • Tel: 877-972-5438 • Location: 3 miles SW of Knobel (limited services), 17 miles SW of Corning • GPS: Lat 36.335541 Lon -90.636577 • Open: All year • Total sites: Dispersed • RV sites: Undefined • RV fee: Free • No water • No toilets • Activities: Fishing, power boating, hunting, non-power boating • Elevation: 278

Magazine

Ashley Creek • Agency: Corps of Engineers • Tel: 479-947-2372 • Location: 7 miles SE of Magazine (limited services), 13 miles SE of Booneville • GPS: Lat 35.107422 Lon -93.709229 • Open: All year • Total sites: 10 • RV sites: 10 • RV fee: Free • Central water • Vault toilets • Activities: Fishing, power boating, non-power boating • Elevation: 443

Hise Hill • Agency: Corps of Engineers • Tel: 479-947-2372 • Location: 10 miles SE of Magazine (limited services), 12 miles SE of Booneville • GPS: Lat 35.083449 Lon -93.773086 • Total sites: 9 • RV sites: 9 • RV fee: Free • Central water • Vault toilets • Activities: Fishing, power boating, non-power boating • Elevation: 430

Lease Three (Blue Mountain Lake) • Agency: Corps of Engineers • Tel: 501-324-5551 • Location: 16 miles SE of Magazine (limited services), 17 miles SE of Booneville • GPS: Lat 35.089622 Lon -93.698288 • Total sites: Dispersed • RV sites: Undefined • RV fee: Free • No water • Vault toilets • Notes: Permit required • Activities: Fishing, non-power boating • Elevation: 396

Lick Creek • Agency: Corps of Engineers • Tel: 479-947-2372 • Location: 16 miles SE of Magazine (limited services), 21 miles SE of Booneville • GPS: Lat 35.093015 Lon -93.68804 • Total sites: 7 • RV sites: 7 • RV fee: Free • Central water • Vault toilets • Activities: Fishing, power boating, non-power boating • Elevation: 459

Persimmion Point #1 (Blue Mountain Lake) • Agency: Corps of Engineers • Tel: 501-324-5551 • Location: 8 miles SE of Magazine (limited services), 13 miles SE of Booneville • GPS: Lat 35.093176 Lon -93.737098 • Total sites: Dispersed • RV sites: Undefined • RV fee: Free • No water • Vault toilets • Notes: Permit required • Activities: Fishing, non-power boating • Elevation: 410

Persimmion Point #2 (Blue Mountain Lake) • Agency: Corps of Engineers • Tel: 501-324-5551 • Location: 7 miles SE of Magazine (limited services), 12 miles SE of Booneville • GPS: Lat 35.104876 Lon -93.739768 • Total sites: Dispersed • RV sites: Undefined • RV fee: Free • No water • Vault toilets • Notes: Permit required • Activities: Fishing, non-power boating • Elevation: 391

Persimmion Point #3 (Blue Mountain Lake) • Agency: Corps of Engineers • Tel: 501-324-5551 • Location: 6 miles SE of Magazine (limited services), 12 miles SE of Booneville • GPS: Lat 35.107413 Lon -93.742663 • Total sites: Dispersed • RV sites: Undefined • RV fee: Free • No water • Vault toilets • Notes: Permit required • Elevation: 419

Persimmion Point #4 (Blue Mountain Lake) • Agency: Corps of Engineers • Tel: 501-324-5551 • Location: 6 miles SE of Magazine (limited services), 12 miles SE of Booneville • GPS: Lat 35.107288 Lon -93.746492 • Total sites: Dispersed • RV sites: Undefined • RV fee: Free • No water • Vault toilets • Notes: Permit required • Elevation: 418

Manila

Big Lake WMA • Agency: State • Tel: 877-972-5438 • Location: 5 miles E of Manila • GPS: Lat 35.873577 Lon -90.100357 • Open: All year • Total sites: Dispersed • RV sites: Undefined • RV fee: Free • No toilets • Elevation: 236

Marshall

Buffalo NR - South Maumee • Agency: National Park Service • Tel: 870-439-2502 • Location: 12 miles N of Marshall • GPS: Lat 36.039606 Lon -92.635726 • Open: All year • Total sites: 5 • RV sites: 5 • RV fee: Free • No water • Vault toilets • Activities: Hiking, fishing, non-power boating • Elevation: 568

Monticello

Casey Jones WMA - 1A • Agency: State • Tel: 877-367-3559 • Location: 12 miles E of Monticello • GPS: Lat 33.613008 Lon -91.578682 • Open: All year • Total sites: Dispersed • RV sites: Undefined • RV fee: Free • No water • No toilets • Activities: Hunting • Elevation: 167

Casey Jones WMA - 1B • Agency: State • Tel: 877-367-3559 • Location: 12 miles E of Monticello • GPS: Lat 33.604468 Lon -91.596404 • Open: All year • Total sites: Dispersed • RV sites: Undefined • RV fee: Free • No water • No toilets • Activities: Hunting • Elevation: 162

Mountain Home

Calamity Beach (Norfork Lake) • Agency: Corps of Engineers • Tel: 870-425-2700 • Location: 16 miles NE of Mountain Home • GPS: Lat 36.476575 Lon -92.258567 • Total sites: Dispersed • RV sites: Undefined • RV fee: Free • No water • No toilets • Notes: Permit required • Activities: Fishing, swimming, power boating, non-power boating • Elevation: 614

Mt Ida

Hickory Nut Mountain (Ouachita Lake) • Agency: US Forest Service • Tel: 870-867-2101 • Location: 16 miles E of Mt Ida • GPS: Lat 34.561521 Lon -93.422959 • Open: All year • Total sites: 8 • RV sites: 8 • RV fee: Free • No water • Vault toilets • Elevation: 1220

Mt Judea

Gene Rush WMA - Pokeberry Rd • Agency: State • Tel: 866-253-2506 • Location: 11 miles E of Mt Judea (limited services), 40 miles SE of Harrison • GPS: Lat 35.941557 Lon -92.936426 • Open: All year • Total sites: Dispersed • RV sites: Undefined • RV fee: Free • No water • No toilets • Activities: Hiking, hunting, equestrian area • Elevation: 1347

Gene Rush WMA - Road 239 • Agency: State • Tel: 866-253-2506 • Location: 13 miles NE of Mt Judea (limited services), 42 miles SE of Harrison • GPS: Lat 35.970763

Lon -92.947374 • Open: All year • Total sites: Dispersed • RV sites: Undefined • RV fee: Free • No water • No toilets • Activities: Hiking, hunting, equestrian area • Elevation: 1186

Gene Rush WMA - Road 250 • Agency: State • Tel: 866-253-2506 • Location: 9 miles NE of Mt Judea (limited services), 25 miles S of Harrison • GPS: Lat 35.979252 Lon -93.013975 • Open: All year • Total sites: Dispersed • RV sites: Undefined • RV fee: Free • No water • No toilets • Activities: Hiking, hunting, equestrian area • Elevation: 1076

Gene Rush WMA - Road 251 • Agency: State • Tel: 866-253-2506 • Location: 9 miles NE of Mt Judea (limited services), 28 miles SE of Harrison • GPS: Lat 35.982206 Lon -92.976457 • Open: All year • Total sites: Dispersed • RV sites: Undefined • RV fee: Free • No water • No toilets • Activities: Hiking, hunting, equestrian area • Elevation: 1218

Gene Rush WMA - Road 252 • Agency: State • Tel: 866-253-2506 • Location: 14 miles NE of Mt Judea (limited services), 43 miles SE of Harrison • GPS: Lat 35.966969 Lon -92.959672 • Open: All year • Total sites: Dispersed • RV sites: Undefined • RV fee: Free • No water • No toilets • Activities: Hiking, hunting, equestrian area • Elevation: 710

Gene Rush WMA - Road 39 • Agency: State • Tel: 866-253-2506 • Location: 10 miles NE of Mt Judea (limited services), 26 miles SE of Harrison • GPS: Lat 35.976394 Lon -93.001446 • Open: All year • Total sites: Dispersed • RV sites: Undefined • RV fee: Free • No water • No toilets • Activities: Hiking, hunting, equestrian area • Elevation: 786

Murfreesboro

Buckhorn (Greeson Lake) • Agency: Corps of Engineers • Tel: 870-285-2151 • Location: 14 miles NW of Murfreesboro • GPS: Lat 34.1786 Lon -93.7307 • Open: All year • Total sites: 9 • RV sites: 4 • RV fee: Free • No water • Vault toilets • Activities: Hiking, fishing • Elevation: 620

Pikeville (Greeson Lake) • Agency: Corps of Engineers • Tel: 870-285-2151 • Location: 12 miles NW of Murfreesboro • GPS: Lat 34.169189 Lon -93.729248 • Open: All year • Total sites: 12 • RV sites: 12 • RV fee: Free • No water • Vault toilets • Activities: Hiking • Elevation: 591

Norman

Crystal (Ouachita NF) • Agency: US Forest Service • Tel: 870-356-4186 • Location: 4 miles NE of Norman (limited services), 11 miles S of Mt Ida • GPS: Lat 34.479411 Lon -93.638484 • Open: All year • Total sites: 9 • RV sites: 9 (no large RV's) • RV fee: Free • No water • Vault toilets • Activities: Hiking, swimming • Elevation: 1034

Pine Bluff

George H. Dunklin Jr. Bayou Meto WMA - Cannon Break • Agency: State • Tel: 877-367-3559 • Location: 24 miles E of Pine Bluff • GPS: Lat 34.208742 Lon -91.631914 • Open: All year • Total sites: Dispersed • RV sites: Undefined (several sites along the road) • RV fee: Free • No water • No toilets • Activities: Fishing, power boating, non-power boating • Elevation: 177

George H. Dunklin Jr. Bayou Meto WMA - Vallier • Agency: State • Tel: 877-367-3559 • Location: 22 miles E of Pine Bluff • GPS: Lat 34.237577 Lon -91.669412 • Open: All year • Total sites: Dispersed • RV sites: Undefined • RV fee: Free • No water • No toilets • Elevation: 188

Trulock (Arkansas River) • Agency: Corps of Engineers • Tel: 870-534-0451 • Location: 9 miles E of Pine Bluff • GPS: Lat 34.210039 Lon -91.832913 • Open: Mar-Oct • Total sites: Dispersed • RV sites: Undefined • RV fee: Free • Central water • Vault toilets • Activities: Fishing, power boating, non-power boating • Elevation: 223

Scranton

Cane Creek (Dardanelle Lake) • Agency: Corps of Engineers • Tel: 479-968-5008 • Location: 5 miles NE of Scranton (limited services), 14 miles S of Clarksville • GPS: Lat 35.388359 Lon -93.502854 • Open: Mar-Oct • Total sites: 9 • RV sites: 9 • RV fee: Free • No water • Vault toilets • Activities: Fishing, power boating, non-power boating • Elevation: 371

Searcy

Henry Gray Hurricane Lake WMA - Cypert Bluff Road • Agency: State • Tel: 877-734-4581 • Location: 17 miles SE of Searcy • GPS: Lat 35.177491 Lon -91.467075 • Open: All year • Total sites: Dispersed • RV sites: Undefined • RV fee: Free • No water • No toilets • Notes: Easily floods • Activities: Fishing, power boating, hunting, non-power boating • Elevation: 206

Henry Gray Hurricane Lake WMA - Deep Bank Slough • Agency: State • Tel: 877-734-4581 • Location: 16 miles SE of Searcy • GPS: Lat 35.121337 Lon -91.447543 • Open: All year • Total sites: Dispersed • RV sites: Undefined • RV fee: Free • No water • No toilets • Activities: Fishing, power boating, hunting, non-power boating • Elevation: 195

Henry Gray Hurricane Lake WMA - Georgetown Access • Agency: State • Tel: 877-734-4581 • Location: 16 miles SE of Searcy • GPS: Lat 35.127347 Lon -91.449081 • Open: All year • Total sites: Dispersed • RV sites: Undefined • RV fee: Free • No water • No toilets • Activities: Fishing, power boating, hunting, non-power boating • Elevation: 195

Snyder

Little Bayou WMA • Agency: State • Tel: 877-367-3559 • Location: 9 miles NE of Snyder (limited services), 18 miles SW of Dermott • GPS: Lat 33.346501 Lon -91.568875 • Open: All year • Total sites: Dispersed • RV sites: Undefined • RV fee: Free • No water • No toilets • Activities: Fishing, hunting • Elevation: 133

Southside

Jamestown Independence County WMA • Agency: State • Tel: 877-267-4331 • Location: 8 miles SW of Southside (limited services), 11 miles SW of Batesville • GPS: Lat 35.670045 Lon -91.726023 • Open: All year • Total sites: Dispersed • RV sites: Undefined • RV fee: Free • No water • No toilets • Activities: Fishing, hunting • Elevation: 1001

St Joe

Buffalo NR - Woolum • Agency: National Park Service • Tel: 870-439-2502 • Location: 7 miles SW of St Joe (limited services), 21 miles NW of Marshall • GPS: Lat 35.970919 Lon -92.879962 • Open: All year • Total sites: Dispersed • RV sites: Undefined • RV fee: Free • No toilets • Activities: Hiking, fishing, non-power boating • Elevation: 669

Story

Irons Fork (Ouachita Lake) • Agency: Corps of Engineers • Tel: 501-984-5313 • Location: 9 miles E of Story (limited services), 23 miles NE of Mt Ida • GPS: Lat 34.686299 Lon -93.372717 • Open: All year • Total sites: 5 • RV sites: 5 • RV fee: Free • No water • Vault toilets • Activities: Power boating, non-power boating • Elevation: 627

Washita (Ouachita Lake) • Agency: Corps of Engineers • Tel: 501-767-2101 • Location: 3 miles S of Story (limited services), 10 miles NE of Mt Ida • GPS: Lat 34.649691 Lon -93.531228 • Open: All year • Total sites: 70 • RV sites: 70 • RV fee: Free • No water • Vault toilets • Activities: Fishing, power boating, non-power boating • Elevation: 614

Texarkana

Hervey Access Camping • Agency: County • Tel: 870-774-1501 • Location: 14 miles E of Texarkana • GPS: Lat 33.497915 Lon -93.769645 • Total sites: Dispersed • RV sites: Undefined • RV fee: Free • No water • No toilets • Activities: Power boating, non-power boating • Elevation: 240

Wabbaseka

George H. Dunklin Jr. Bayou Meto WMA - Mulberry Grove • Agency: State • Tel: 877-367-3559 • Location: 6 miles E of Wabbaseka (limited services), 20 miles SW of Stuttgart • GPS: Lat 34.344725 Lon -91.704734 • Open: All year • Total sites: Dispersed • RV sites: Undefined • RV fee: Free • No water • No toilets • Activities: Fishing, power boating, non-power boating • Elevation: 186

Walmut Ridge

Shirey Bay Rainey Brake WMA - Shirey Bay • Agency: State • Tel: 877-972-5438 • Location: 18 miles SW of Walmut Ridge • GPS: Lat 35.957663 Lon -91.181084 • Total sites: 1 • RV sites: 1 • RV fee: Free • No water • No toilets • Activities: Fishing, power boating, hunting, non-power boating • Elevation: 243

Warren

Casey Jones WMA - 5A • Agency: State • Tel: 877-367-3559 • Location: 13 miles SE of Warren • GPS: Lat 33.524728 Lon -91.972231 • Open: All year • Total sites: Dispersed • RV sites: Undefined • RV fee: Free • No water • No toilets • Activities: Hunting • Elevation: 119

Casey Jones WMA - 5B • Agency: State • Tel: 877-367-3559 • Location: 13 miles SE of Warren • GPS: Lat 33.524961 Lon -91.955152 • Open: All year • Total sites: Dispersed • RV sites: Undefined • RV fee: Free • No water • No toilets • Activities: Hunting • Elevation: 123

Casey Jones WMA - 5C • Agency: State • Tel: 877-367-3559 • Location: 15 miles SE of Warren • GPS: Lat 33.498455 Lon -91.971088 • Open: All year • Total sites: Dispersed • RV sites: Undefined • RV fee: Free • No water • No toilets • Activities: Hunting • Elevation: 122

Weiner

Earl Buss Bayou DeView WMA - Flag Slough • Agency: State • Tel: 877-972-5438 • Location: 6 miles SW of Weiner (limited services), 20 miles W of Harrisburg • GPS: Lat 35.594475 Lon -90.962531 • Open: All year • Total sites: Dispersed • RV sites: Undefined • RV fee: Free • No water • No toilets • Activities: Hunting • Elevation: 223

Earl Buss Bayou DeView WMA - Lake Hogue • Agency: State • Tel: 877-972-5438 • Location: 5 miles SW of Weiner (limited services), 16 miles W of Harrisburg • GPS: Lat 35.589818 Lon -90.959155 • Open: All year • Total sites: Dispersed • RV sites: Undefined • RV fee: Free • No water • No toilets • Activities: Hunting • Elevation: 226

Earl Buss Bayou DeView WMA - Martin Tract • Agency: State • Tel: 877-972-5438 • Location: 11 miles NW of Weiner (limited services), 24 miles SW of Jonesboro • GPS: Lat 35.676954 Lon -90.932227 • Open: All year • Total sites: Dispersed • RV sites: Undefined • RV fee: Free • No water • No toilets • Activities: Hunting • Elevation: 234

Earl Buss Bayou DeView WMA - Thompson Tract • Agency: State • Tel: 877-972-5438 • Location: 4 miles W of Weiner (limited services), 18 miles NW of Harrisburg • GPS: Lat 35.625019 Lon -90.951205 • Open: All year • Total sites: Dispersed • RV sites: Undefined • RV fee: Free • No water • No toilets • Activities: Hunting • Elevation: 234

Iowa

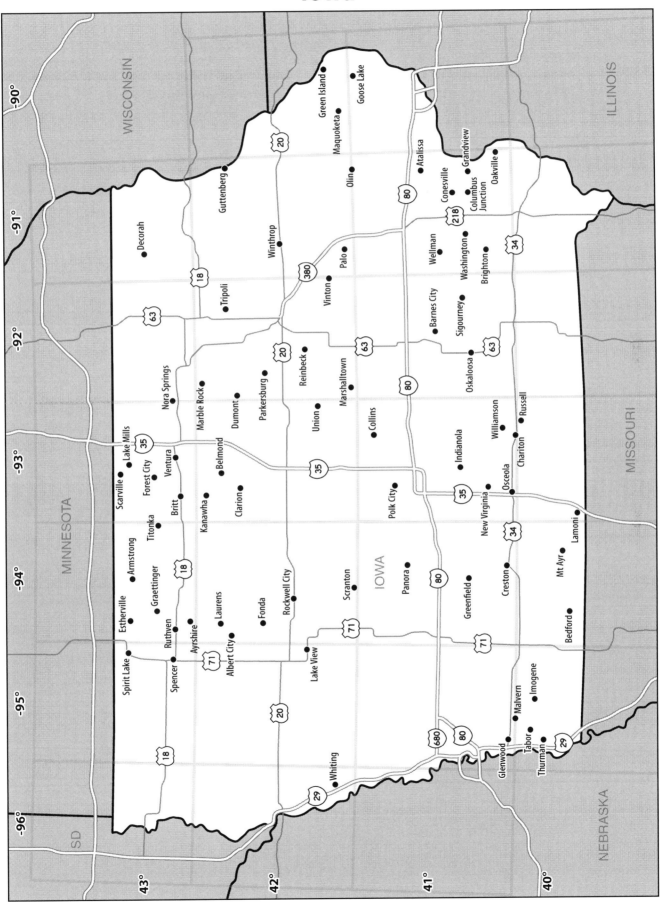

Iowa — Camping Areas

Abbreviation	Description
DNR	Department of Natural Resources
WMA	Wildlife Management Area

Albert City

Little Clear Lake Recreation Area • Agency: County • Location: 6 miles SE of Albert City (limited services), 15 miles W of Pocahontas • GPS: Lat 42.733163 Lon -94.908223 • Total sites: Dispersed • RV sites: Undefined • RV fee: Free • Central water • Vault toilets • Elevation: 1295

Armstrong

Goose Lake (Kossuth) WMA • Agency: State • Tel: 712-260-1003 • Location: 10 miles NE of Armstrong (limited services), 13 miles SE of Fairmont, MN • GPS: Lat 43.484747 Lon -94.404338 • Total sites: Dispersed • RV sites: Undefined • RV fee: Free • No water • No toilets • Activities: Fishing • Elevation: 1158

Okamanpeedan WMA • Agency: State • Location: 12 miles NW of Armstrong (limited services), 17 miles NE of Estherville • GPS: Lat 43.490129 Lon -94.587114 • Total sites: Dispersed • RV sites: Undefined • RV fee: Free • No water • No toilets • Elevation: 1224

Atalissa

Wiese Slough WMA • Agency: State • Location: 4 miles SE of Atalissa (limited services), 9 miles SE of West Liberty • GPS: Lat 41.548845 Lon -91.132353 • Total sites: Dispersed • RV sites: Undefined • RV fee: Free • No water • No toilets • Elevation: 650

Ayrshire

Silver Lake WMA • Agency: State • Location: 2 miles W of Ayrshire (limited services), 15 miles SW of Emmetsburg • GPS: Lat 43.037561 Lon -94.876138 • Total sites: Dispersed • RV sites: Undefined • RV fee: Free • No water • No toilets • Elevation: 1322

Barnes City

Hawthorn Lake WMA • Agency: State • Location: 2 miles S of Barnes City (limited services), 10 miles SE of Montezuma • GPS: Lat 41.484635 Lon -92.469962 • Total sites: Dispersed • RV sites: Undefined • RV fee: Free • No water • No toilets • Activities: Fishing • Elevation: 850

Bedford

Ross • Agency: County • Tel: 712-542-3864 • Location: 16 miles SW of Bedford • GPS: Lat 40.609053 Lon -94.963779 • Total sites: Dispersed • RV sites: Undefined • RV fee: Free • No water • No toilets • Activities: Hiking, mountain biking, fishing • Elevation: 1010

Belmond

Morse Lake - DNR • Agency: State • Location: 5 miles W of Belmond • GPS: Lat 42.835603 Lon -93.691022 • Total sites: Dispersed • RV sites: Undefined • RV fee: Free • No water • No toilets • Elevation: 1207

Brighton

Brighton Boat Access • Agency: County • Tel: 641-472-4421 • Location: 1 mile N of Brighton (limited services), 9 miles SW of Washington • GPS: Lat 41.193997 Lon -91.807231 • Total sites: Dispersed • RV sites: Undefined • RV fee: Free • No water • Vault toilets • Activities: Fishing, non-power boating • Elevation: 614

Brinton Timber • Agency: County • Tel: 319-657-2400 • Location: 4 miles NW of Brighton (limited services), 15 miles SW of Washington • GPS: Lat 41.223691 Lon -91.849773 • Total sites: Dispersed • RV sites: Undefined • RV fee: Free • No water • Vault toilets • Activities: Hiking • Elevation: 722

McKain's River Access • Agency: County • Tel: 641-472-4421 • Location: 6 miles NW of Brighton (limited services), 14 miles SW of Washington • GPS: Lat 41.226218 Lon -91.888318 • Total sites: Dispersed • RV sites: Undefined • RV fee: Free • No water • Vault toilets • Activities: Fishing, non-power boating • Elevation: 633

Britt

Eagle Lake WMA • Agency: State • Tel: 641-425-0823 • Location: 6 miles NE of Britt • GPS: Lat 43.137785 Lon -93.729466 • Total sites: Dispersed • RV sites: Undefined • RV fee: Free • No water • No toilets • Elevation: 1207

Chariton

Morris Lake WMA • Agency: State • Location: 3 miles E of Chariton • GPS: Lat 41.015784 Lon -93.252068 • Total sites: Dispersed • RV sites: Undefined • RV fee: Free • No water • No toilets • Elevation: 981

Clarion

Big Wall Lake WMA - North • Agency: State • Tel: 641-425-0823 • Location: 11 miles SE of Clarion • GPS: Lat

42.629934 Lon -93.644177 • Total sites: Dispersed • RV sites: Undefined • RV fee: Free • No water • No toilets • Activities: Fishing, power boating • Elevation: 1217

Big Wall Lake WMA - South • Agency: State • Tel: 641-425-0823 • Location: 12 miles SE of Clarion • GPS: Lat 42.615488 Lon -93.646224 • Total sites: Dispersed • RV sites: Undefined • RV fee: Free • No water • No toilets • Activities: Fishing, power boating • Elevation: 1236

Elm Lake WMA • Agency: State • Tel: 641-425-0823 • Location: 5 miles NE of Clarion • GPS: Lat 42.774325 Lon -93.686092 • Total sites: Dispersed • RV sites: Undefined • RV fee: Free • No water • No toilets • Elevation: 1201

Collins

Hendrickson Marsh - DNR • Agency: State • Location: 6 miles NE of Collins (limited services), 20 miles SW of Marshalltown • GPS: Lat 41.937149 Lon -93.232386 • Total sites: Dispersed • RV sites: Undefined • RV fee: Free • No water • No toilets • Elevation: 951

Columbus Junction

River Forks Access • Agency: County • Tel: 319-523-8381 • Location: 2 miles E of Columbus Junction • GPS: Lat 41.283004 Lon -91.345213 • Total sites: Dispersed • RV sites: Undefined • RV fee: Free • No water • No toilets • Activities: Fishing, power boating, non-power boating • Elevation: 591

Conesville

Cone Marsh WMA - North • Agency: State • Tel: 563-260-1223 • Location: 6 miles NW of Conesville (limited services), 19 miles S of Iowa City • GPS: Lat 41.399475 Lon -91.406508 • Total sites: Dispersed • RV sites: Undefined • RV fee: Free • No water • No toilets • Activities: Fishing, power boating • Elevation: 602

Cone Marsh WMA - South • Agency: State • Tel: 563-260-1223 • Location: 3 miles W of Conesville (limited services), 20 miles S of Iowa City • GPS: Lat 41.383808 Lon -91.400909 • Total sites: Dispersed • RV sites: Undefined • RV fee: Free • No water • No toilets • Activities: Fishing, power boating • Elevation: 597

Creston

Summitt Lake - DNR • Agency: State • Location: 1 mile W of Creston • GPS: Lat 41.070758 Lon -94.391491 • Total sites: Dispersed • RV sites: Undefined • RV fee: Free • No water • No toilets • Elevation: 1257

Twelve Mile Creek WMA • Agency: State • Location: 5 miles E of Creston • GPS: Lat 41.081484 Lon -94.284091 • Total sites: Dispersed • RV sites: Undefined • RV fee: Free • No water • No toilets • Elevation: 1194

Decorah

Chimney Rock • Agency: County • Tel: 563-735-5786 • Location: 12 miles NW of Decorah • GPS: Lat 43.423024 Lon -91.939008 • Open: May-Oct • Total sites: Dispersed • RV sites: Undefined • RV fee: Free • Electric sites: 20 • No water • Vault toilets • Activities: Fishing, non-power boating • Elevation: 1030

Dumont

Dumont Park - South Fork Access • Agency: County • Tel: 319-278-4237 • Location: 1 mile SW of Dumont (limited services), 11 miles E of Hampton • GPS: Lat 42.743837 Lon -92.986931 • Total sites: Dispersed • RV sites: Undefined • RV fee: Free • No water • No toilets • Activities: Fishing, non-power boating • Elevation: 984

Estherville

Swan Lake - DNR • Agency: State • Location: 8 miles NW of Estherville • GPS: Lat 43.464016 Lon -94.946419 • Total sites: Dispersed • RV sites: Undefined • RV fee: Free • No water • No toilets • Elevation: 1378

West Swan Lake WMA • Agency: State • Location: 11 miles SE of Estherville • GPS: Lat 43.350683 Lon -94.676888 • Total sites: Dispersed • RV sites: Undefined • RV fee: Free • No water • No toilets • Elevation: 1250

Fonda

Sunken Grove WMA • Agency: State • Location: 6 miles NW of Fonda (limited services), 20 miles E of Storm Lake • GPS: Lat 42.632038 Lon -94.899418 • Total sites: Dispersed • RV sites: Undefined • RV fee: Free • No water • No toilets • Elevation: 1234

Forest City

Myre Slough WMA • Agency: State • Location: 8 miles NW of Forest City • GPS: Lat 43.297222 Lon -93.765704 • Total sites: Dispersed • RV sites: Undefined • RV fee: Free • No water • No toilets • Elevation: 1257

Glenwood

Keg Creek WMA • Agency: State • Location: 5 miles SW of Glenwood • GPS: Lat 40.987229 Lon -95.805336 • Total sites: Dispersed • RV sites: Undefined • RV fee: Free • No water • No toilets • Activities: Fishing, non-power boating • Elevation: 945

Goose Lake

Goose Lake WMA - East • Agency: State • Tel: 563-357-1078 • Location: 1 mile W of Goose Lake (limited services), 13 miles NW of Clinton • GPS: Lat 41.965496 Lon -90.396751 • Total sites: Dispersed • RV sites: Undefined • RV fee: Free • No water • No toilets • Activities: Fishing • Elevation: 663

Goose Lake WMA - West • Agency: State • Tel: 563-357-1078 • Location: 2 miles W of Goose Lake (limited services), 15 miles NW of Clinton • GPS: Lat 41.967611 Lon -90.407002 • Total sites: Dispersed • RV sites: Undefined • RV fee: Free • No water • No toilets • Activities: Fishing • Elevation: 663

Graettinger

Burr Oak Lake WMA • Agency: State • Tel: 712-260-1009 • Location: 4 miles N of Graettinger (limited services), 10 miles SE of Estherville • GPS: Lat 43.287356 Lon -94.753092 • Total sites: Dispersed • RV sites: Undefined • RV fee: Free • No water • No toilets • Activities: Fishing, power boating • Elevation: 1240

Ingham Lake WMA • Agency: State • Location: 9 miles NE of Graettinger (limited services), 12 miles SE of Estherville • GPS: Lat 43.324202 Lon -94.693726 • Total sites: Dispersed • RV sites: Undefined • RV fee: Free • No water • No toilets • Elevation: 1273

Jim Hall Habitat WMA • Agency: State • Location: 2 miles N of Graettinger (limited services), 10 miles S of Estherville • GPS: Lat 43.262765 Lon -94.766491 • Total sites: Dispersed • RV sites: Undefined • RV fee: Free • No water • No toilets • Elevation: 1230

Grandview

Klum Lake WMA • Agency: State • Location: 5 miles E of Grandview (limited services), 9 miles NE of Wapello • GPS: Lat 41.260347 Lon -91.137525 • Total sites: Dispersed • RV sites: Undefined • RV fee: Free • No water • No toilets • Elevation: 538

Green Island

Green Island Lake - DNR • Agency: State • Location: 2 miles E of Green Island (limited services), 14 miles NE of Preston • GPS: Lat 42.150599 Lon -90.275961 • Total sites: Dispersed • RV sites: Undefined • RV fee: Free • No water • No toilets • Elevation: 600

Greenfield

Meadow Lake - DNR • Agency: State • Location: 7 miles N of Greenfield • GPS: Lat 41.387334 Lon -94.435395 • Total sites: Dispersed • RV sites: Undefined • RV fee: Free • No water • No toilets • Activities: Fishing, power boating, non-power boating • Elevation: 1273

Guttenberg

Frenchtown • Agency: County • Tel: 563-245-1516 • Location: 4 miles N of Guttenberg • GPS: Lat 42.846606 Lon -91.106496 • Total sites: 3 • RV sites: 3 • RV fee: Free • No water • No toilets • Activities: Fishing, power boating, non-power boating • Elevation: 617

Imogene

Imogene Trailhead • Agency: Municipal • Tel: 515-210-0269 • Location: In Imogene (limited services), 10 miles N of Shenandoah • GPS: Lat 40.879578 Lon -95.429381 • Total sites: 6 • RV sites: 2 • RV fee: Free • Electric sites: 2 • Central water • Flush toilets • Elevation: 1050

Indianola

Hooper Pond WMA • Agency: State • Location: 6 miles S of Indianola • GPS: Lat 41.277383 Lon -93.588769 • Total sites: Dispersed • RV sites: Undefined • RV fee: Free • No water • No toilets • Activities: Fishing, power boating, non-power boating • Elevation: 925

Kanawha

East Twin Lake - DNR • Agency: State • Tel: 641-425-0823 • Location: 5 miles E of Kanawha (limited services), 15 miles SW of Garner • GPS: Lat 42.936228 Lon -93.698065 • Total sites: Dispersed • RV sites: Undefined • RV fee: Free • No water • No toilets • Elevation: 1194

West Twin Lake - DNR • Agency: State • Location: 3 miles E of Kanawha (limited services), 17 miles SW of Garner • GPS: Lat 42.937571 Lon -93.728727 • Total sites: Dispersed • RV sites: Undefined • RV fee: Free • No water • No toilets • Elevation: 1214

Lake Mills

Elk Creek Marsh WMA • Agency: State • Tel: 641-425-0828 • Location: 5 miles E of Lake Mills • GPS: Lat 43.412383 Lon -93.438542 • Total sites: Dispersed • RV sites: Undefined • RV fee: Free • No water • No toilets • Elevation: 1224

Elk Creek Marsh WMA - East • Agency: State • Tel: 641-425-0828 • Location: 8 miles E of Lake Mills • GPS: Lat

43.406532 Lon -93.401515 • Total sites: Dispersed • RV sites: Undefined • RV fee: Free • No water • No toilets • Activities: Fishing, power boating • Elevation: 1215

Rice Lake Access - DNR • Agency: State • Location: 5 miles SE of Lake Mills • GPS: Lat 43.384346 Lon -93.488431 • Total sites: Dispersed • RV sites: Undefined • RV fee: Free • No water • No toilets • Elevation: 1230

Lake View

Black Hawk Marsh WMA - North • Agency: State • Tel: 712-661-9237 • Location: 2 miles S of Lake View • GPS: Lat 42.278086 Lon -95.049222 • Total sites: Dispersed • RV sites: Undefined • RV fee: Free • No water • No toilets • Activities: Fishing, power boating • Elevation: 1224

Black Hawk Marsh WMA - South • Agency: State • Tel: 712-661-9237 • Location: 2 miles S of Lake View • GPS: Lat 42.273523 Lon -95.050765 • Total sites: Dispersed • RV sites: Undefined • RV fee: Free • No water • No toilets • Activities: Fishing, power boating • Elevation: 1236

Lamoni

Lake LeShane WMA • Agency: State • Location: 2 miles NW of Lamoni • GPS: Lat 40.637315 Lon -93.967599 • Total sites: Dispersed • RV sites: Undefined • RV fee: Free • No water • No toilets • Elevation: 1099

Laurens

Pickeral Lake WMA • Agency: State • Location: 7 miles NW of Laurens (limited services), 25 miles SW of Emmetsburg • GPS: Lat 42.909666 Lon -94.920361 • Total sites: Dispersed • RV sites: Undefined • RV fee: Free • No water • No toilets • Elevation: 1335

Rush Lake WMA • Agency: State • Location: 7 miles N of Laurens (limited services), 19 miles SW of Emmetsburg • GPS: Lat 42.950343 Lon -94.860621 • Total sites: Dispersed • RV sites: Undefined • RV fee: Free • No water • No toilets • Elevation: 1322

Malvern

Willow Slough WMA • Agency: State • Location: 12 miles NE of Malvern (limited services), 19 miles NE of Glenwood • GPS: Lat 41.098394 Lon -95.464482 • Total sites: Dispersed • RV sites: Undefined • RV fee: Free • No water • No toilets • Elevation: 1020

Maquoketa

Joinerville • Agency: County • Tel: 563-652-3783 • Location: 5 miles W of Maquoketa • GPS: Lat 42.079303

Lon -90.751315 • Total sites: Dispersed • RV sites: Undefined • RV fee: Free • No water • No toilets • Notes: Permit required • Activities: Fishing, power boating, non-power boating • Elevation: 705

Marble Rock

Gates Bridge Access • Agency: County • Tel: 641-756-3490 • Location: 3 miles SE of Marble Rock (limited services), 17 miles SW of Charles City • GPS: Lat 42.934913 Lon -92.850906 • Total sites: 6 • RV sites: 6 • RV fee: Free • No water • No toilets • Activities: Fishing, power boating, non-power boating • Elevation: 954

Marble Rock City Park • Agency: Municipal • Tel: 641-315-2621 • Location: In Marble Rock (limited services), 16 miles SW of Charles City • GPS: Lat 42.967583 Lon -92.869647 • Open: All year • Stay limit: 3 days • Total sites: 6 • RV sites: 6 • RV fee: Free (donation appreciated) • Electric sites: 6 • Central water • Elevation: 1015

Marshalltown

Sand Lake WMA • Agency: State • Location: 1 mile E of Marshalltown • GPS: Lat 42.051618 Lon -92.862876 • Total sites: Dispersed • RV sites: Undefined • RV fee: Free • No water • Vault toilets • Elevation: 850

Mt Ayr

Walnut Creek Lake - DNR • Agency: State • Location: 6 miles W of Mt Ayr • GPS: Lat 40.694729 Lon -94.333022 • Total sites: Dispersed • RV sites: Undefined • RV fee: Free • No water • No toilets • Elevation: 1070

New Virginia

Hickory Hills • Agency: County • Tel: 515-961-6169 • Location: 8 miles E of New Virginia (limited services), 14 miles S of Indianola • GPS: Lat 41.179848 Lon -93.610551 • Stay limit: 14 days • Total sites: Dispersed • RV sites: Undefined • RV fee: Free • No water • Vault toilets • Elevation: 1020

Nora Springs

Shellrock River County Preserve • Agency: County • Tel: 641-423-5309 • Location: 3 miles NW of Nora Springs (limited services), 9 miles E of Mason City • GPS: Lat 43.173632 Lon -93.043611 • Open: All year • Total sites: Dispersed • RV sites: Undefined • RV fee: Free • No water • Vault toilets • Activities: Equestrian area • Elevation: 1096

Oakville

Cappy Russell Access • Agency: County • Tel: 319-523-8381 • Location: 6 miles N of Oakville (limited services), 17 miles E of Wapello • GPS: Lat 41.162222 Lon -91.014285 • Total sites: Dispersed • RV sites: Undefined • RV fee: Free • No water • No toilets • Activities: Fishing, power boating, non-power boating • Elevation: 551

Ferry Landing (Mississippi River) • Agency: Corps of Engineers • Tel: 563-263-7913 • Location: 6 miles N of Oakville (limited services), 17 miles E of Wapello • GPS: Lat 41.162472 Lon -91.009086 • Open: All year • Total sites: 22 • RV sites: 22 • RV fee: Free • No toilets • Activities: Fishing, power boating, non-power boating • Elevation: 532

Olin

Muskrat Slough WMA • Agency: State • Location: 6 miles SW of Olin (limited services), 11 miles SE of Anamosa • GPS: Lat 41.986716 Lon -91.204649 • Total sites: Dispersed • RV sites: Undefined • RV fee: Free • No water • No toilets • Elevation: 784

Osceola

West Lake - DNR • Agency: State • Location: 3 miles W of Osceola • GPS: Lat 41.030887 Lon -93.805243 • Total sites: Dispersed • RV sites: Undefined • RV fee: Free • No water • Vault toilets • Elevation: 1089

Oskaloosa

Glendale Access • Agency: County • Tel: 641-673-9327 • Location: 4 miles NE of Oskaloosa • GPS: Lat 41.342843 Lon -92.592081 • Total sites: Dispersed • RV sites: Undefined • RV fee: Free • No water • Activities: Fishing, power boating, non-power boating • Elevation: 702

Palo

Chain-O-Lakes WMA • Agency: State • Tel: 319-350-2863 • Location: 1 mile SE of Palo (limited services), 6 miles NW of Cedar Rapids • GPS: Lat 42.049358 Lon -91.775799 • Total sites: Dispersed • RV sites: Undefined • RV fee: Free • No water • No toilets • Activities: Fishing, power boating • Elevation: 722

Panora

Bays Branch WMA • Agency: State • Tel: 712-250-0061 • Location: 5 miles NE of Panora • GPS: Lat 41.731731 Lon -94.321235 • Total sites: Dispersed • RV sites: Undefined • RV fee: Free • No water • No toilets • Activities: Fishing, power boating • Elevation: 1055

Parkersburg

Big Marsh WMA - East • Agency: State • Tel: 319-240-8033 • Location: 6 miles N of Parkersburg • GPS: Lat 42.661322 Lon -92.791125 • Total sites: Dispersed • RV sites: Undefined • RV fee: Free • No water • No toilets • Activities: Fishing, power boating • Elevation: 933

Big Marsh WMA - West • Agency: State • Tel: 319-240-8033 • Location: 7 miles N of Parkersburg • GPS: Lat 42.658664 Lon -92.819711 • Total sites: Dispersed • RV sites: Undefined • RV fee: Free • No water • No toilets • Activities: Fishing, power boating • Elevation: 948

Polk City

Big Creek Lake WMA • Agency: State • Location: 4 miles NW of Polk City • GPS: Lat 41.818997 Lon -93.756089 • Stay limit: 14 days • Total sites: Dispersed • RV sites: Undefined • RV fee: Free • No water • No toilets • Activities: Fishing, power boating • Elevation: 978

Reinbeck

Gutknecht Roadside Park • Agency: County • Tel: 319-345-2688 • Location: 2 miles NW of Reinbeck (limited services), 7 miles SE of Grundy Center • GPS: Lat 42.333702 Lon -92.632197 • Total sites: 5 • RV sites: 5 • RV fee: Free • Central water • No toilets • Elevation: 922

Rockwell City

South Twin Lake WMA • Agency: State • Location: 6 miles N of Rockwell City • GPS: Lat 42.453251 Lon -94.647148 • Total sites: Dispersed • RV sites: Undefined • RV fee: Free • No water • No toilets • Elevation: 1217

Russell

North Colyn Marsh WMA • Agency: State • Location: 6 miles S of Russell (limited services), 11 miles SE of Chariton • GPS: Lat 40.924033 Lon -93.192878 • Total sites: Dispersed • RV sites: Undefined • RV fee: Free • No water • No toilets • Elevation: 948

South Colyn Marsh WMA • Agency: State • Location: 6 miles S of Russell (limited services), 11 miles SE of Chariton • GPS: Lat 40.920244 Lon -93.198057 • Total sites: Dispersed • RV sites: Undefined • RV fee: Free • No water • No toilets • Elevation: 932

Ruthven

Barringer Slough WMA • Agency: State • Tel: 712-260-1004 • Location: 6 miles NW of Ruthven (limited services), 13 miles E of Spencer • GPS: Lat 43.146647 Lon -94.941621 • Total sites: Dispersed • RV sites: Undefined • RV fee: Free • No water • No toilets • Elevation: 1345

Elk Lake WMA • Agency: State • Tel: 712-260-1004 • Location: 5 miles SW of Ruthven (limited services), 14 miles SE of Spencer • GPS: Lat 43.082517 Lon -94.932917 • Total sites: Dispersed • RV sites: Undefined • RV fee: Free • No water • No toilets • Activities: Fishing, power boating, non-power boating • Elevation: 1384

Virgin Lake WMA • Agency: State • Location: 2 miles S of Ruthven (limited services), 14 miles E of Spencer • GPS: Lat 43.105765 Lon -94.892684 • Total sites: Dispersed • RV sites: Undefined • RV fee: Free • No water • No toilets • Elevation: 1401

Scarville

Harmon Lake WMA • Agency: State • Location: 4 miles W of Scarville (limited services), 12 miles NW of Lake Mills • GPS: Lat 43.463682 Lon -93.694499 • Total sites: Dispersed • RV sites: Undefined • RV fee: Free • No water • No toilets • Elevation: 1237

Scranton

Dunbar Slough WMA • Agency: State • Tel: 515-432-2545 • Location: 8 miles SW of Scranton (limited services), 15 miles SW of Jefferson • GPS: Lat 41.973818 Lon -94.610616 • Total sites: Dispersed • RV sites: Undefined • RV fee: Free • No water • Vault toilets • Elevation: 1118

Sigourney

Chacauqua River Access • Agency: County • Tel: 641-622-3757 • Location: 2 miles S of Sigourney • GPS: Lat 41.302907 Lon -92.205212 • Total sites: Dispersed • RV sites: Undefined • RV fee: Free • No water • No toilets • Elevation: 673

Manhattan Bridge Access • Agency: County • Tel: 641-472-4421 • Location: 11 miles SE of Sigourney • GPS: Lat 41.238884 Lon -92.107734 • Total sites: Dispersed • RV sites: Undefined • RV fee: Free • No water • Vault toilets • Activities: Fishing • Elevation: 679

South River Access • Agency: County • Tel: 641-472-4421 • Location: 11 miles S of Sigourney • GPS: Lat 41.236054 Lon -92.186667 • Total sites: Dispersed • RV sites: Undefined • RV fee: Free • No water • No toilets • Activities: Fishing, non-power boating • Elevation: 676

Spencer

Dan Green Slough WMA • Agency: State • Tel: 712-260-1004 • Location: 11 miles NE of Spencer • GPS: Lat 43.214821 Lon -95.010479 • Total sites: Dispersed • RV sites: Undefined • RV fee: Free • No water • No toilets • Activities: Fishing, power boating • Elevation: 1348

Spirit Lake

Center Lake - DNR • Agency: State • Tel: 712-260-1017 • Location: 3 miles W of Spirit Lake • GPS: Lat 43.413059 Lon -95.141885 • Total sites: Dispersed • RV sites: Undefined • RV fee: Free • No water • No toilets • Activities: Fishing, power boating • Elevation: 1411

East Hottes - DNR • Agency: State • Tel: 712-260-1017 • Location: 4 miles N of Spirit Lake • GPS: Lat 43.481567 Lon -95.126737 • Total sites: Dispersed • RV sites: Undefined • RV fee: Free • No water • No toilets • Elevation: 1398

Grover's Marsh WMA • Agency: State • Location: 10 miles NW of Spirit Lake • GPS: Lat 43.497231 Lon -95.165422 • Total sites: Dispersed • RV sites: Undefined • RV fee: Free • No water • No toilets • Elevation: 1401

Hale Slough WMA • Agency: State • Location: 5 miles NE of Spirit Lake • GPS: Lat 43.475714 Lon -95.068068 • Total sites: Dispersed • RV sites: Undefined • RV fee: Free • No water • No toilets • Elevation: 1391

Little Spirit Lake WMA • Agency: State • Location: 5 miles N of Spirit Lake • GPS: Lat 43.491603 Lon -95.130279 • Total sites: Dispersed • RV sites: Undefined • RV fee: Free • No water • No toilets • Elevation: 1417

Tabor

Forney's Lake WMA - North • Agency: State • Tel: 712-520-0506 • Location: 7 miles SW of Tabor (limited services), 17 miles S of Glenwood • GPS: Lat 40.858084 Lon -95.765391 • Total sites: Dispersed • RV sites: Undefined • RV fee: Free • No water • No toilets • Activities: Fishing • Elevation: 947

Forney's Lake WMA - South • Agency: State • Tel: 712-520-0506 • Location: 7 miles SW of Tabor (limited services), 17 miles S of Glenwood • GPS: Lat 40.854023 Lon -95.766678 • Total sites: Dispersed • RV sites: Undefined • RV fee: Free • No water • No toilets • Activities: Fishing • Elevation: 943

Thurman

Scott WMA • Agency: State • Location: 5 miles NW of Thurman (limited services), 15 miles S of Glenwood • GPS:

Lat 40.861851 Lon -95.799392 • Total sites: Dispersed • RV sites: Undefined • RV fee: Free • No water • No toilets • Activities: Fishing • Elevation: 938

Titonka

Union Slough (Smith Pool) - DNR • Agency: State • Location: 6 miles W of Titonka (limited services), 16 miles NE of Algona • GPS: Lat 43.250072 Lon -94.142142 • Total sites: Dispersed • RV sites: Undefined • RV fee: Free • No water • No toilets • Elevation: 1125

Tripoli

Martens Lake - DNR • Agency: State • Location: 2 miles E of Tripoli (limited services), 18 miles NE of Waverly • GPS: Lat 42.815053 Lon -92.229358 • Total sites: Dispersed • RV sites: Undefined • RV fee: Free • No water • No toilets • Activities: Fishing, power boating, non-power boating • Elevation: 1001

Sweet Marsh WMA • Agency: State • Location: 5 miles NE of Tripoli (limited services), 22 miles NE of Waverly • GPS: Lat 42.830696 Lon -92.219289 • Total sites: Dispersed • RV sites: Undefined • RV fee: Free • No water • No toilets • Elevation: 1020

Union

David Bates Memorial Park • Agency: County • Tel: 641-648-4361 • Location: 3 miles N of Union (limited services), 21 miles NW of Marshalltown • GPS: Lat 42.261779 Lon -93.057902 • Total sites: Dispersed • RV sites: Undefined • RV fee: Free • Central water • Vault toilets • Activities: Fishing, power boating, non-power boating • Elevation: 948

Ventura

Ventura Marsh WMA • Agency: State • Location: 1 mile S of Ventura (limited services), 5 miles W of Clear Lake • GPS: Lat 43.117692 Lon -93.487307 • Total sites: Dispersed • RV sites: Undefined • RV fee: Free • No water • No toilets • Elevation: 1224

Vinton

Dudgeon Lake WMA • Agency: State • Tel: 319-350-2871 • Location: 2 miles N of Vinton • GPS: Lat 42.192677 Lon -92.024091 • Total sites: Dispersed • RV sites: Undefined • RV fee: Free • No water • No toilets • Activities: Fishing, power boating • Elevation: 787

Washington

Clemons Creek Recreation Area • Agency: County • Tel: 319-657-2400 • Location: 3 miles W of Washington • GPS: Lat 41.304553 Lon -91.744558 • Total sites: Dispersed • RV sites: Undefined • RV fee: Free • No water • No toilets • Activities: Hiking, mountain biking, fishing • Elevation: 692

Wellman

Foster Woods • Agency: County • Tel: 319-657-2400 • Location: 1 mile SW of Wellman (limited services), 9 miles SW of Kalona • GPS: Lat 41.449366 Lon -91.849465 • Total sites: Dispersed • RV sites: Undefined • RV fee: Free • No water • Vault toilets • Activities: Hiking, mountain biking, fishing • Elevation: 718

Whiting

Badger Lake WMA - North • Agency: State • Tel: 712-420-1486 • Location: 5 miles NW of Whiting (limited services), 12 miles NW of Onawa • GPS: Lat 42.154868 Lon -96.223217 • Total sites: Dispersed • RV sites: Undefined • RV fee: Free • No water • No toilets • Activities: Fishing, power boating • Elevation: 1061

Badger Lake WMA - South • Agency: State • Tel: 712-420-1486 • Location: 5 miles W of Whiting (limited services), 12 miles NW of Onawa • GPS: Lat 42.130289 Lon -96.223131 • Total sites: Dispersed • RV sites: Undefined • RV fee: Free • No water • No toilets • Activities: Fishing, power boating • Elevation: 1059

Williamson

Williamson Pond WMA • Agency: State • Location: 2 miles NE of Williamson (limited services), 8 miles NE of Chariton • GPS: Lat 41.097313 Lon -93.215228 • Total sites: Dispersed • RV sites: Undefined • RV fee: Free • No water • No toilets • Activities: Fishing, power boating, non-power boating • Elevation: 984

Winthrop

Buffalo Creek Wildlife Area • Agency: County • Location: 2 miles E of Winthrop (limited services), 10 miles E of Independence • GPS: Lat 42.471243 Lon -91.687339 • Total sites: Dispersed • RV sites: Undefined • RV fee: Free • No water • Vault toilets • Activities: Fishing, hunting, disc golf • Elevation: 1017

Kansas

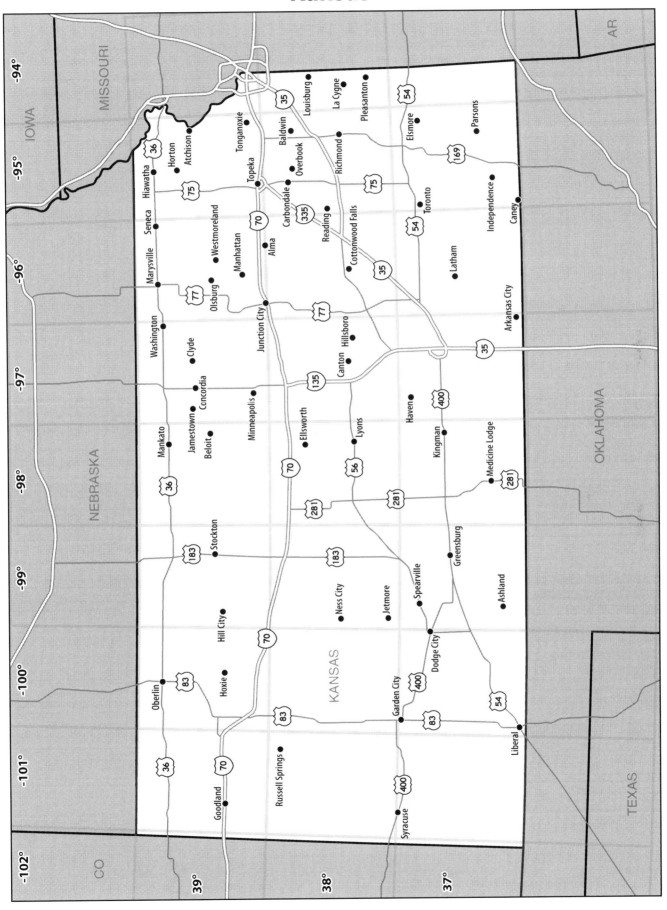

Kansas — Camping Areas

Abbreviation	Description
KDWPT	Kansas Department of Wildlife, Parks and Tourism
SWA	State Wildlife Area

Alma

McKnight City Park • Agency: Municipal • Tel: 785-765-3922 • Location: In Alma • GPS: Lat 39.009628 Lon -96.285862 • Total sites: 3 • RV sites: 3 • RV fee: Free (donation appreciated) • Electric sites: 3 • Water at site • Flush toilets • Notes: Near RR tracks • Elevation: 1060

Arkansas City

Cowley State Fishing Lake • Agency: State • Tel: 620-876-5730 • Location: 13 miles E of Arkansas City • GPS: Lat 37.102966 Lon -96.797154 • Total sites: Dispersed • RV sites: Undefined • RV fee: Free • No water • Vault toilets • Activities: Fishing, power boating, non-power boating • Elevation: 1214

Ashland

Clark County State Lake • Agency: State • Tel: 620-227-8609 • Location: 18 miles N of Ashland • GPS: Lat 37.394415 Lon -99.783429 • Total sites: Dispersed • RV sites: Undefined • RV fee: Free • No water • Vault toilets • Activities: Fishing, power boating, non-power boating • Elevation: 2313

Atchison

Atchison State Fishing Lake • Agency: State • Tel: 913-367-7811 • Location: 6 miles NW of Atchison • GPS: Lat 39.633079 Lon -95.175223 • Total sites: Dispersed • RV sites: Undefined • RV fee: Free • Central water • Vault toilets • Activities: Fishing, power boating, hunting, non-power boating • Elevation: 906

Baldwin

Douglas State Fishing Lake • Agency: State • Tel: 913-845-2665 • Location: 2 miles NE of Baldwin • GPS: Lat 38.799901 Lon -95.163771 • Total sites: Dispersed • RV sites: Undefined • RV fee: Free • No water • Vault toilets • Activities: Hiking, mountain biking, fishing, power boating, non-power boating • Elevation: 961

Beloit

Chautauqua Park • Agency: Municipal • Tel: 785-738-2270 • Location: In Beloit • GPS: Lat 39.455071 Lon -98.113568 • Stay limit: 10 days • Total sites: 30 • RV sites: 30 • RV fee: Free (donation appreciated) • Electric sites: 30 • Water at site • Activities: Fishing, swimming, power boating • Elevation: 1384

Caney

Copan SWA • Agency: State • Tel: 620-331-6820 • Location: 1 mile W of Caney • GPS: Lat 37.010232 Lon -95.950343 • Total sites: Dispersed • RV sites: Undefined • RV fee: Free • No water • No toilets • Elevation: 732

Canton

McPherson State Fishing Lake (Canton Lake) • Agency: State • Tel: 620-628-4592 • Location: 10 miles NW of Canton (limited services), 15 miles NE of McPherson • GPS: Lat 38.478647 Lon -97.470919 • Total sites: Dispersed • RV sites: Undefined • RV fee: Free • Activities: Fishing • Elevation: 1437

Carbondale

Osage State Fishing Lake • Agency: State • Tel: 620-699-3372 • Location: 4 miles S of Carbondale (limited services), 17 miles S of Topeka • GPS: Lat 38.763157 Lon -95.675306 • Total sites: Dispersed • RV sites: Undefined • RV fee: Free • No water • Vault toilets • Activities: Fishing • Elevation: 1092

Clyde

Clyde City Park • Agency: Municipal • Location: In Clyde (limited services), 14 miles E of Concordia • GPS: Lat 39.595075 Lon -97.404719 • Open: All year • Total sites: 2 • RV sites: 2 • RV fee: Free • Electric sites: 6 • Central water • No toilets (toilets/showers at nearby pool) • Elevation: 1302

Concordia

Airport Park • Agency: Municipal • Tel: 785-243-2670 • Location: 1 mile S of Concordia • GPS: Lat 39.546371 Lon -97.656963 • Open: All year • Total sites: 12 • RV sites: 12 • RV fee: Free (donation appreciated) • Electric sites: 9 • Water at site • No toilets • Elevation: 1473

Cottonwood Falls

Chase State Fishing Lake • Agency: State • Tel: 620-767-5900 • Location: 3 miles W of Cottonwood Falls • GPS: Lat 38.366611 Lon -96.592274 • Total sites: Dispersed • RV sites: Undefined • RV fee: Free • No water • Vault toilets • Activities: Fishing • Elevation: 1296

Dodge City

Ford County State Fishing Lake • Agency: State • Tel: 620-895-6446 • Location: 8 miles NE of Dodge City • GPS: Lat 37.821307 Lon -99.920393 • Total sites: 12 • RV sites: 12 • RV fee: Free • Activities: Fishing • Elevation: 2470

Ellsworth

Boldt Bluff (Lake Kanapolis) • Agency: Corps of Engineers • Location: 20 miles SE of Ellsworth • GPS: Lat 38.633119 Lon -98.005323 • Total sites: Dispersed • RV sites: Undefined • RV fee: Free • No water • No toilets • Activities: Fishing • Elevation: 1480

Yankee Run (Lake Kanapolis) • Agency: Corps of Engineers • Tel: 785-546-2294 • Location: 20 miles SE of Ellsworth • GPS: Lat 38.643798 Lon -98.014438 • Open: All year • Total sites: Dispersed • RV sites: Undefined • RV fee: Free • No water • Vault toilets • Elevation: 1506

Elsmore

Bourbon State Fishing Lake • Agency: State • Tel: 620-449-2539 • Location: 5 miles E of Elsmore (limited services), 25 miles W of Fort Scott • GPS: Lat 37.796495 Lon -95.068275 • Total sites: Dispersed • RV sites: Undefined • RV fee: Free • Central water • Vault toilets • Activities: Fishing • Elevation: 961

Garden City

Concannon State Fishing Lake • Agency: State • Tel: 620-276-8886 • Location: 17 miles NE of Garden City • GPS: Lat 38.069097 Lon -100.556767 • Total sites: Dispersed • RV sites: Undefined • RV fee: Free • No water • Vault toilets • Activities: Fishing, power boating, non-power boating • Elevation: 2710

Goodland

Smoky Gardens State Fishing Lake • Agency: State • Tel: 785-899-4800 • Location: 13 miles S of Goodland • GPS: Lat 39.186935 Lon -101.756715 • Total sites: Dispersed • RV sites: Undefined • RV fee: Free • Central water • Vault toilets • Activities: Fishing • Elevation: 3619

Greensburg

Kiowa County State Lake • Agency: State • Tel: 620-895-6446 • Location: In Greensburg • GPS: Lat 37.612942 Lon -99.299327 • Total sites: Dispersed • RV sites: Undefined • RV fee: Free • No water • Vault toilets • Activities: Fishing • Elevation: 2251

Haven

Cheney Wildlife Area - DeWeese - KDWPT • Agency: State • Tel: 620-459-6922 • Location: 11 miles SW of Haven (limited services), 16 miles S of Hutchinson • GPS: Lat 37.821047 Lon -97.895534 • Total sites: Dispersed • RV sites: Undefined • RV fee: Free • No water • Vault toilets • Activities: Fishing • Elevation: 1434

Cheney Wildlife Area - Fish Cove - KDWPT • Agency: State • Tel: 620-459-6922 • Location: 11 miles SW of Haven (limited services), 16 miles S of Hutchinson • GPS: Lat 37.801968 Lon -97.866372 • Total sites: Dispersed • RV sites: Undefined • RV fee: Free • No water • Vault toilets • Activities: Fishing • Elevation: 1437

Hiawatha

Brown County State Lake • Agency: State • Tel: 785-273-6740 • Location: 10 miles E of Hiawatha • GPS: Lat 39.849082 Lon -95.376867 • Total sites: Dispersed • RV sites: Undefined • RV fee: Free • No water • No toilets • Activities: Fishing • Elevation: 1037

Hill City

Hill City Roadside Park • Agency: Municipal • Tel: 785-421-5621 • Location: In Hill City • GPS: Lat 39.364527 Lon -99.856727 • Total sites: Dispersed • RV sites: Undefined • RV fee: Free • Elevation: 2238

Hillsboro

Marion Reservoir - Durham Cove - KDWPT • Agency: State • Tel: 620-241-7669 • Location: 7 miles NE of Hillsboro • GPS: Lat 38.437646 Lon -97.162787 • Total sites: Dispersed • RV sites: Undefined • RV fee: Free • Vault toilets • Activities: Fishing • Elevation: 1375

Horton

Atchison County Lake • Agency: County • Tel: 913-804-6120 • Location: 6 miles SE of Horton • GPS: Lat 39.636707 Lon -95.456072 • Total sites: Dispersed • RV sites: Undefined • RV fee: Free • Central water • Vault toilets • Notes: Permit required • Activities: Fishing, power boating, hunting, non-power boating • Elevation: 1087

Hoxie

Sheridan State Fishing Lake • Agency: State • Location: 11 miles E of Hoxie • GPS: Lat 39.360428 Lon -100.231912 • Open: All year • Total sites: 12 • RV sites: 12 • RV fee: Free • No water • Vault toilets • Activities: Fishing, power boating, non-power boating • Elevation: 2477

Independence

Buffalo Ranch SWA • Agency: State • Tel: 620-331-6820 • Location: 14 miles W of Independence • GPS: Lat 37.189016 Lon -95.963322 • Total sites: Dispersed • RV sites: Undefined • RV fee: Free • No water • Vault toilets • Notes: No open fires • Elevation: 873

Montgomery State Fishing Lake • Agency: State • Tel: 620-331-6820 • Location: 5 miles S of Independence • GPS: Lat 37.164727 Lon -95.689697 • Total sites: Dispersed • RV sites: Undefined • RV fee: Free • No water • Vault toilets • Activities: Fishing, power boating, non-power boating • Elevation: 791

Jamestown

Jamestown SWA • Agency: State • Tel: 785-753-4971 • Location: 7 miles NW of Jamestown (limited services), 17 miles NW of Concordia • GPS: Lat 39.662166 Lon -97.904794 • Open: Sep-Apr • Total sites: Dispersed • RV sites: Undefined • RV fee: Free • No water • Vault toilets • Elevation: 1401

Jetmore

Hodgeman State Lake • Agency: State • Tel: 620-276-8886 • Location: 6 miles SE of Jetmore (limited services), 29 miles NE of Dodge City • GPS: Lat 38.049913 Lon -99.826343 • Total sites: Dispersed • RV sites: Undefined • RV fee: Free • No water • Vault toilets • Activities: Fishing • Elevation: 2310

Junction City

Geary State Fishing Lake • Agency: State • Tel: 785-238-3014 • Location: 8 miles S of Junction City • GPS: Lat 38.904429 Lon -96.861065 • Total sites: Dispersed • RV sites: Undefined • RV fee: Free • No water • Vault toilets • Activities: Fishing, power boating, non-power boating • Elevation: 1257

Kingman

Kingman State Fishing Lake • Agency: State • Tel: 620-532-3242 • Location: 8 miles W of Kingman • GPS: Lat 37.650642 Lon -98.254937 • Total sites: Dispersed • RV sites: Undefined • RV fee: Free • No water • Vault toilets • Activities: Fishing • Elevation: 1631

La Cygne

La Cygne SWA • Agency: State • Tel: 913-352-8941 • Location: 10 miles NE of La Cygne (limited services), 17 miles S of Louisburg • GPS: Lat 38.402365 Lon -94.654955 • Total sites: Dispersed • RV sites: Undefined • RV fee: Free • No water • Vault toilets • Activities: Fishing, power boating, non-power boating • Elevation: 850

Miami State Fishing Lake • Agency: State • Tel: 913-783-4507 • Location: 6 miles N of La Cygne (limited services), 16 miles SE of Osawatomie • GPS: Lat 38.421549 Lon -94.782913 • Total sites: 14 • RV sites: 14 • RV fee: Free • No water • Vault toilets • Activities: Fishing • Elevation: 922

Latham

Butler State Fishing Lake • Agency: State • Tel: 316-683-8069 • Location: 4 miles NW of Latham (limited services), 18 miles E of Douglas • GPS: Lat 37.546253 Lon -96.692473 • Total sites: Dispersed • RV sites: Undefined • RV fee: Free • Central water • Vault toilets • Activities: Fishing • Elevation: 1463

Liberal

Mary Frame City Park • Agency: Municipal • Tel: 620-626-2206 • Location: In Liberal • GPS: Lat 37.031759 Lon -100.919282 • Total sites: 3 • RV sites: 3 • RV fee: Free • Central water • Flush toilets • Notes: 1-night limit • Elevation: 2851

Louisburg

Louisburg Middle Creek State Fishing Lake • Agency: State • Tel: 913-783-4507 • Location: 9 miles S of Louisburg • GPS: Lat 38.51064 Lon -94.673572 • Total sites: 10 • RV sites: 10 • RV fee: Free • No water • Vault toilets • Activities: Fishing • Elevation: 1001

Lyons

Chase Roadside Park • Agency: Municipal • Location: 4 miles W of Lyons • GPS: Lat 38.347321 Lon -98.297758 • Total sites: Dispersed • RV sites: Undefined • RV fee: Free • No water • No toilets • Elevation: 1680

Lyons City Campground • Agency: Municipal • Tel: 620-257-2320 • Location: In Lyons • GPS: Lat 38.340201 Lon -98.210389 • Open: All year • Stay limit: 5 days • Total sites: 18 • RV sites: 18 • RV fee: Free • Electric sites: 18 • Central water • Flush toilets • Elevation: 1709

Manhattan

Pottawatomie State Fishing Lake #2 • Agency: State • Tel: 785-539-9999 • Location: 5 miles NE of Manhattan • GPS: Lat 39.229041 Lon -96.529662 • Total sites: Dispersed • RV sites: Undefined • RV fee: Free • No water • Vault toilets • Activities: Fishing • Elevation: 1152

Mankato

Jewell Lake State Fishing Area • Agency: State • Tel: 785-545-3345 • Location: 10 miles SW of Mankato • GPS: Lat 39.698735 Lon -98.282244 • Total sites: Dispersed • RV sites: Undefined • RV fee: Free • No water • Vault toilets • Activities: Fishing • Elevation: 1683

Marysville

Marysville City Park • Agency: Municipal • Tel: 785-562-3101 • Location: In Marysville • GPS: Lat 39.838691 Lon -96.646568 • Total sites: 4 • RV sites: 4 • RV fee: Free • Electric sites: 4 • Central water • Activities: Swimming • Elevation: 1145

Medicine Lodge

Barber County State Lake • Agency: State • Tel: 620-895-6446 • Location: In Medicine Lodge • GPS: Lat 37.299574 Lon -98.579925 • Total sites: Dispersed • RV sites: Undefined • RV fee: Free • No water • Vault toilets • Activities: Fishing, power boating, non-power boating • Elevation: 1545

Medicine Lodge City Park • Agency: Municipal • Tel: 620-895-6446 • Location: In Medicine Lodge • GPS: Lat 37.278614 Lon -98.574837 • Total sites: 4 • RV sites: 4 • Max RV Length: 40 • RV fee: Free • Electric sites: 4 • Central water • No toilets • Notes: 2-night limit • Elevation: 1464

Minneapolis

Ottowa County State Fishing Lake • Agency: State • Tel: 785-658-2465 • Location: 8 miles E of Minneapolis • GPS: Lat 39.111575 Lon -97.567241 • Total sites: Dispersed • RV sites: Undefined • RV fee: Free • Central water • Vault toilets • Activities: Fishing, power boating, non-power boating • Elevation: 1302

Ness City

Goodman State Fishing Lake • Agency: State • Tel: 620-276-8886 • Location: 8 miles SE of Ness City • GPS: Lat 38.387267 Lon -99.853839 • Total sites: Dispersed • RV sites: Undefined • RV fee: Free • No water • Vault toilets • Activities: Fishing, power boating, non-power boating • Elevation: 2224

Oberlin

Sappa City Park • Agency: Municipal • Tel: 785-475-3441 • Location: 2 miles NE of Oberlin • GPS: Lat 39.839189 Lon -100.495291 • Total sites: 14 • RV sites: 14 • RV fee: Free • Electric sites: 14 • No water • Vault toilets • Activities: Hiking, fishing, disc golf • Elevation: 2543

Olsburg

Carnahan Creek County Park (Tuttle Creek Lake) • Agency: County • Tel: 785-539-7941 • Location: 7 miles S of Olsburg (limited services), 14 miles N of Manhattan • GPS: Lat 39.337167 Lon -96.627127 • Total sites: 4 • RV sites: 4 • RV fee: Free • No water • Vault toilets • Activities: Hiking, equestrian area • Elevation: 1152

Overbrook

Cedar Park (Pomona Lake) • Agency: Corps of Engineers • Tel: 785-453-2201 • Location: 9 miles SW of Overbrook (limited services), 24 miles NW of Ottawa • GPS: Lat 38.693403 Lon -95.609254 • Open: All year • Total sites: 8 • RV sites: 8 • RV fee: Free • No water • Vault toilets • Elevation: 1007

Parsons

Neosho State Fishing Lake • Agency: State • Tel: 620-449-2539 • Location: 9 miles NE of Parsons • GPS: Lat 37.423501 Lon -95.197521 • Total sites: 3 • RV sites: 3 • RV fee: Free • No water • Vault toilets • Activities: Fishing • Elevation: 916

Pleasanton

Marais des Cygnes SWA - Unit A East • Agency: State • Tel: 913-352-8941 • Location: 12 miles N of Pleasanton (limited services), 31 miles S of Louisburg • GPS: Lat 38.246868 Lon -94.689093 • Total sites: Dispersed • RV sites: Undefined • RV fee: Free • No water • No toilets • Activities: Hiking, fishing • Elevation: 791

Marais des Cygnes SWA - Unit A North • Agency: State • Tel: 913-352-8941 • Location: 11 miles N of Pleasanton (limited services), 30 miles S of Louisburg • GPS: Lat 38.253328 Lon -94.701796 • Total sites: Dispersed • RV sites: Undefined • RV fee: Free • No water • No toilets • Activities: Hiking, fishing • Elevation: 791

Reading

Lyon County State Lake • Agency: State • Tel: 620-699-3372 • Location: 7 miles NW of Reading (limited services), 13 miles NE of Emporia • GPS: Lat 38.547813 Lon -96.061548 • Total sites: Dispersed • RV sites: Undefined • RV fee: Free • No water • Vault toilets • Activities: Fishing, power boating, non-power boating • Elevation: 1191

Richmond

Richmond City Lake • Agency: Municipal • Tel: 785-835-6425 • Location: 2 miles SE of Richmond (limited services), 9 miles N of Garnett • GPS: Lat 38.392109 Lon

-95.223836 • Total sites: Dispersed • RV sites: Undefined • RV fee: Free • No water • Vault toilets • Elevation: 981

Russell Springs

Logan County Lake • Agency: County • Location: 4 miles NW of Russell Springs (limited services), 30 miles SW of Oakley • GPS: Lat 38.932864 Lon -101.234829 • Total sites: Dispersed • RV sites: Undefined • RV fee: Free • No water • No toilets • Activities: Fishing • Elevation: 3025

Seneca

Nemaha SWA • Agency: State • Tel: 785-363-7316 • Location: 6 miles S of Seneca • GPS: Lat 39.767191 Lon -96.028168 • Total sites: Dispersed • RV sites: Undefined • RV fee: Free • Central water • Vault toilets • Elevation: 1184

Spearville

Hain State Fishing Lake • Agency: State • Tel: 620-895-6446 • Location: 6 miles W of Spearville (limited services), 12 miles NE of Dodge City • GPS: Lat 37.85484 Lon -99.85961 • Total sites: Dispersed • RV sites: Undefined • RV fee: Free • No water • No toilets • Activities: Fishing • Elevation: 2411

Stockton

Rooks State Fishing Lake • Agency: State • Tel: 785-425-6775 • Location: 4 miles SW of Stockton • GPS: Lat 39.397294 Lon -99.317581 • Total sites: Dispersed • RV sites: Undefined • RV fee: Free • No water • Vault toilets • Activities: Fishing • Elevation: 1844

Syracuse

Hamilton State Fishing Lake • Agency: State • Tel: 620-227-8609 • Location: 6 miles NW of Syracuse • GPS: Lat 38.031693 Lon -101.822164 • Total sites: Dispersed • RV sites: Undefined • RV fee: Free • No water • Vault toilets • Notes: No open fires • Activities: Fishing • Elevation: 3346

Tonganoxie

Leavenworth State Fishing Lake • Agency: State • Tel: 913-845-2665 • Location: 4 miles NW of Tonganoxie (limited services), 17 miles NE of Lawrence • GPS: Lat 39.126607 Lon -95.143585 • Total sites: Dispersed • RV sites: Undefined • RV fee: Free • No water • Vault toilets • Activities: Fishing • Elevation: 1030

Topeka

Shawnee State Fishing Lake • Agency: State • Tel: 913-845-2665 • Location: 13 miles N of Topeka • GPS: Lat 39.203261 Lon -95.800981 • Total sites: Dispersed • RV sites: Undefined • RV fee: Free • No water • Vault toilets • Activities: Fishing • Elevation: 1043

Toronto

Woodson State Lake • Agency: State • Tel: 620-637-2748 • Location: 7 miles E of Toronto (limited services), 12 miles SW of Yates Center • GPS: Lat 37.796685 Lon -95.847219 • Total sites: 30 • RV sites: 30 • RV fee: Free • Central water • Vault toilets • Activities: Fishing • Elevation: 997

Washington

Washington State Fishing Lake • Agency: State • Tel: 785-461-5402 • Location: 11 miles NW of Washington • GPS: Lat 39.928353 Lon -97.118037 • Total sites: Dispersed • RV sites: Undefined • RV fee: Free • No water • Vault toilets • Activities: Fishing • Elevation: 1421

Westmoreland

Pottawatomie State Fishing Lake #1 • Agency: State • Tel: 785-539-9999 • Location: 6 miles N of Westmoreland (limited services), 20 miles N of Wamego • GPS: Lat 39.473642 Lon -96.412691 • Total sites: Dispersed • RV sites: Undefined • RV fee: Free • No water • Vault toilets • Activities: Fishing • Elevation: 1421

Louisiana

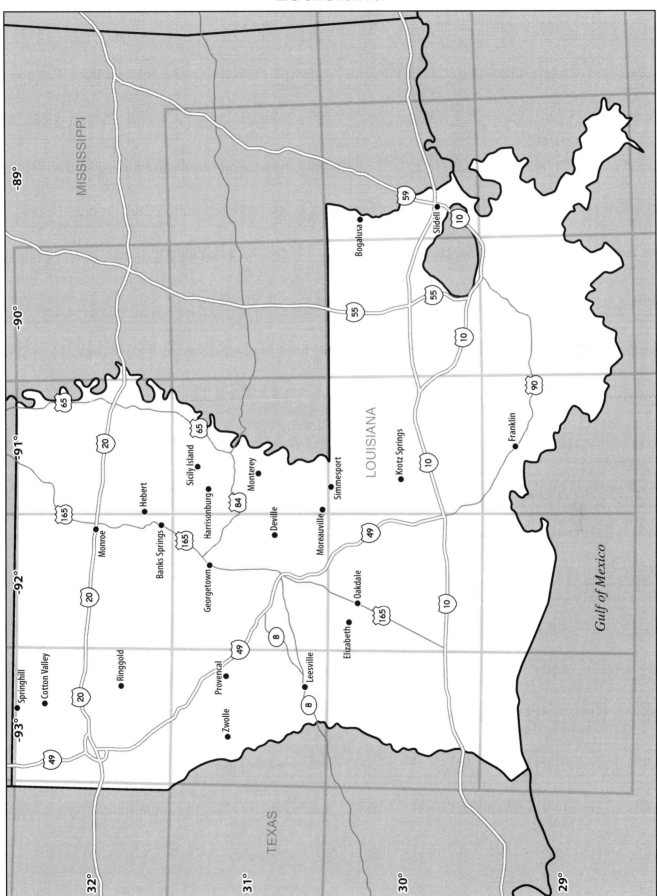

Louisiana — Camping Areas

Abbreviation	Description
NF	National Forest
WMA	Wildlife Management Area

Banks Springs

Boeuf WMA-Big Ridge Rd • Agency: State • Tel: 318-343-2417 • Location: 12 miles SE of Banks Springs • GPS: Lat 32.052648 Lon -91.953459 • Open: All year • Total sites: Dispersed • RV sites: Undefined • RV fee: Free • No water • No toilets • Activities: Hiking, hunting • Elevation: 72

Fort Necessity • Agency: Corps of Engineers • Tel: 318-322-6391 • Location: 12 miles E of Banks Springs • GPS: Lat 32.074044 Lon -91.927618 • Total sites: 10 • RV sites: 6 • RV fee: Free • No water • Vault toilets • Elevation: 59

Cotton Valley

Bodcau WMA - Corner of the Old Field (Bayou Bodcau Reservoir) • Agency: Corps of Engineers • Tel: 318-371-3050 • Location: 8 miles SW of Cotton Valley (limited services), 20 miles S of Springhill • GPS: Lat 32.78773 Lon -93.47464 • Open: All year • Total sites: Dispersed • RV sites: Undefined • RV fee: Free • No water • No toilets • Activities: Power boating, non-power boating • Elevation: 173

Bodcau WMA - Ivan Lake (Bayou Bodcau Reservoir) • Agency: Corps of Engineers • Tel: 318-322-6391 • Location: 5 miles W of Cotton Valley (limited services), 17 miles S of Springhill • GPS: Lat 32.831431 Lon -93.493306 • Open: All year • Total sites: 4 • RV sites: 4 • RV fee: Free • No water • Vault toilets • Activities: Fishing, power boating, non-power boating • Elevation: 240

Deville

Dewey Wills WMA - Duck Bayou • Agency: State • Tel: 318-487-5885 • Location: 16 miles E of Deville (limited services), 33 miles E of Alexandria • GPS: Lat 31.346987 Lon -91.989775 • Total sites: Dispersed • RV sites: Undefined • RV fee: Free • No water • No toilets • Elevation: 44

Dewey Wills WMA - Saline Bayou • Agency: State • Tel: 318-487-5885 • Location: 8 miles NE of Deville (limited services), 21 miles NE of Alexandria • GPS: Lat 31.456572 Lon -92.119426 • Total sites: Dispersed • RV sites: Undefined • RV fee: Free • No water • No toilets • Elevation: 43

Dewey Wills WMA-Larto Lake • Agency: State • Tel: 318-487-5885 • Location: 22 miles E of Deville (limited services), 34 miles E of Alexandria • GPS: Lat 31.351828 Lon -91.945853 • Open: All year • Total sites: Dispersed • RV sites: Undefined • RV fee: Free • No water • No toilets • Activities: Hiking, hunting • Elevation: 56

Dewey Wills WMA-Muddy Bayou • Agency: State • Tel: 318-487-5885 • Location: 9 miles NE of Deville (limited services), 24 miles E of Alexandria • GPS: Lat 31.391071 Lon -92.053453 • Open: All year • Total sites: Dispersed • RV sites: Undefined • RV fee: Free • No water • No toilets • Activities: Hiking, hunting • Elevation: 82

Elizabeth

West Bay WMA - Wolfs Bay • Agency: State • Tel: 337-491-2575 • Location: 5 miles SW of Elizabeth (limited services), 15 miles NW of Oakdale • GPS: Lat 30.835592 Lon -92.854212 • Open: All year • Total sites: Dispersed • RV sites: Undefined • RV fee: Free • No water • No toilets • Activities: Hiking, hunting • Elevation: 187

Franklin

Attakapas Island WMA - Millet Point • Agency: State • Location: 8 miles NE of Franklin • GPS: Lat 29.876957 Lon -91.455432 • Open: All year • Total sites: 12 • RV sites: 12 • RV fee: Free • Central water • No toilets • Activities: Hiking, hunting • Elevation: 13

Georgetown

Little River WMA - Doughty Bluff • Agency: State • Tel: 318-487-5885 • Location: 9 miles S of Georgetown (limited services), 25 miles W of Jena • GPS: Lat 31.658978 Lon -92.369747 • Open: All year • Total sites: Dispersed • RV sites: Undefined • RV fee: Free • No water • No toilets • Notes: Permit required • Elevation: 49

Little River WMA - Fish Creek • Agency: State • Tel: 318-487-5885 • Location: 12 miles S of Georgetown (limited services), 28 miles W of Jena • GPS: Lat 31.640169 Lon -92.367254 • Open: All year • Total sites: Dispersed • RV sites: Undefined • RV fee: Free • No water • No toilets • Notes: Permit required • Activities: Fishing, power boating • Elevation: 47

Harrisonburg

J.C. "Sonny" Gilbert WMA - South • Agency: State • Tel: 318-757-4571 • Location: 5 miles NE of Harrisonburg (limited services), 15 miles N of Jonesville • GPS: Lat 31.802013 Lon -91.761364 • Open: All year • Total sites: Dispersed • RV sites: Undefined • RV fee: Free • No toilets • Notes: Permit required • Activities: Hiking, hunting • Elevation: 176

Hebert

Boeuf WMA-Morengo Lake • Agency: State • Tel: 318-343-2417 • Location: 5 miles SE of Hebert (limited services), 15 miles NE of Banks Springs • GPS: Lat 32.135916 Lon -91.936863 • Open: All year • Total sites: Dispersed • RV sites: Undefined • RV fee: Free • No water • No toilets • Activities: Hiking, hunting • Elevation: 105

Boeuf WMA-Tempelton Bend • Agency: State • Tel: 318-343-2417 • Location: 4 miles SE of Hebert (limited services), 13 miles NE of Banks Springs • GPS: Lat 32.139306 Lon -91.970551 • Open: All year • Total sites: Dispersed • RV sites: Undefined • RV fee: Free • No water • No toilets • Activities: Hiking, hunting • Elevation: 85

Krotz Springs

Sherburn WMA - Gun Range • Agency: State • Tel: 337-948-0255 • Location: 5 miles SE of Krotz Springs (limited services), 23 miles E of Opelousas • GPS: Lat 30.514103 Lon -91.711885 • Open: All year • Total sites: Dispersed • RV sites: Undefined • RV fee: Free • No toilets • Notes: Permit required • Activities: Hiking, hunting • Elevation: 29

Sherburn WMA - South campground • Agency: State • Tel: 337-948-0255 • Location: 10 miles S of Krotz Springs (limited services), 25 miles NE of Breaux Bridge • GPS: Lat 30.457749 Lon -91.72839 • Open: All year • Total sites: Dispersed • RV sites: Undefined • RV fee: Free • No toilets • Notes: Permit required • Activities: Hiking, hunting • Elevation: 72

Leesville

Clear Creek WMA • Agency: State • Tel: 337-491-2575 • Location: 12 miles SW of Leesville • GPS: Lat 31.051217 Lon -93.401463 • Open: All year • Total sites: Dispersed • RV sites: Undefined • RV fee: Free • No water • No toilets • Notes: Permit required • Elevation: 264

Monroe

Russell Sage WMA • Agency: State • Tel: 318-343-4044 • Location: 9 miles SW of Monroe • GPS: Lat 32.374116 Lon -92.041529 • Open: All year • Total sites: Dispersed • RV sites: Undefined • RV fee: Free • No water • No toilets • Notes: Permit required • Activities: Hiking, fishing, power boating, hunting, equestrian area • Elevation: 60

Russell Sage WMA - US 80 • Agency: State • Tel: 318-343-4044 • Location: 8 miles E of Monroe • GPS: Lat 32.511743 Lon -91.936178 • Open: All year • Total sites: Dispersed • RV sites: Undefined • RV fee: Free • No water • No toilets • Notes: Permit required • Activities: Hiking, fishing, power boating, hunting, equestrian area • Elevation: 60

Monterey

Richard K. Yancey WMA - Red River • Agency: State • Tel: 337-948-0255 • Location: 30 miles S of Monterey (limited services), 36 miles SW of Vidalia • GPS: Lat 31.197262 Lon -91.677779 • Open: All year • Total sites: Dispersed • RV sites: Undefined • RV fee: Free • No toilets • Activities: Hiking, hunting • Elevation: 66

Richard K. Yancey WMA - Upper Sunk Lake • Agency: State • Tel: 337-948-0255 • Location: 27 miles S of Monterey (limited services), 41 miles SW of Vidalia • GPS: Lat 31.216623 Lon -91.746193 • Open: All year • Total sites: Dispersed • RV sites: Undefined • RV fee: Free • No toilets • Activities: Hiking, hunting • Elevation: 44

Richard K. Yancey WMA - Yakey Road • Agency: State • Tel: 337-948-0255 • Location: 16 miles SE of Monterey (limited services), 23 miles SW of Vidalia • GPS: Lat 31.314832 Lon -91.614875 • Open: All year • Total sites: Dispersed • RV sites: Undefined • RV fee: Free • No toilets • Activities: Hiking, hunting • Elevation: 40

Moreauville

Pomme de Terre WMA • Agency: State • Tel: 337-948-0255 • Location: 8 miles E of Moreauville (limited services), 16 miles SE of Marksville • GPS: Lat 31.03567 Lon -91.872413 • Open: All year • Total sites: Dispersed • RV sites: Undefined • RV fee: Free • No water • No toilets • Notes: Permit required • Activities: Hiking, fishing, power boating, hunting • Elevation: 49

Spring Bayou WMA - Old River • Agency: State • Tel: 337-948-0255 • Location: 10 miles NE of Moreauville (limited services), 17 miles SE of Marksville • GPS: Lat 31.091341 Lon -91.959657 • Open: All year • Total sites: Dispersed • RV sites: Undefined • RV fee: Free • No water • No toilets • Notes: Permit required • Activities: Fishing, power boating • Elevation: 45

Oakdale

West Bay WMA - Spikes Campsite • Agency: State • Tel: 337-491-2575 • Location: 9 miles SW of Oakdale • GPS: Lat 30.746344 Lon -92.739585 • Open: All year • Total sites: Dispersed • RV sites: Undefined • RV fee: Free • No water • No toilets • Activities: Hiking, hunting • Elevation: 118

Provencal

Dogwood (Kisatchie NF) • Agency: US Forest Service • Tel: 318-473-7160 • Location: 12 miles S of Provencal (limited services), 22 miles SW of Natchitoches • GPS: Lat 31.493239 Lon -93.193046 • Open: All year • Total sites: 16 • RV sites: 16 • Max RV Length: 20 • RV fee: Free • Central water • No toilets • Elevation: 213

Ringgold

Loggy Bayou WMA - PAR 511 • Agency: State • Tel: 318-371-3050 • Location: 10 miles W of Ringgold (limited services), 24 miles SE of Bossier City • GPS: Lat 32.313643 Lon -93.421792 • Open: All year • Total sites: Dispersed • RV sites: Undefined • RV fee: Free • No water • No toilets • Activities: Hiking, hunting • Elevation: 158

Loggy Bayou WMA - Poole Road • Agency: State • Tel: 318-371-3050 • Location: 15 miles SW of Ringgold (limited services), 24 miles SE of Bossier City • GPS: Lat 32.266094 Lon -93.429116 • Open: All year • Total sites: Dispersed • RV sites: Undefined • RV fee: Free • No water • No toilets • Notes: Permit required • Elevation: 145

Sicily Island

J.C. "Sonny" Gilbert WMA - North • Agency: State • Tel: 318-757-4571 • Location: 6 miles NW of Sicily Island (limited services), 22 miles NE of Jonesville • GPS: Lat 31.866838 Lon -91.743504 • Open: All year • Total sites: Dispersed • RV sites: Undefined • RV fee: Free • No water • No toilets • Notes: Permit required • Activities: Fishing, power boating • Elevation: 253

Simmesport

Richard K. Yancey WMA - Carrs Point Lake • Agency: State • Tel: 337-948-0255 • Location: 14 miles E of Simmesport • GPS: Lat 31.009493 Lon -91.645764 • Open: All year • Total sites: Dispersed • RV sites: Undefined • RV fee: Free • No water • No toilets • Activities: Hiking, hunting • Elevation: 89

Richard K. Yancey WMA - Shell Road • Agency: State • Tel: 337-948-0255 • Location: 24 miles NE of Simmesport • GPS: Lat 31.081906 Lon -91.625844 • Open: All year • Total sites: Dispersed • RV sites: Undefined • RV fee: Free • Central water • Vault toilets • Activities: Hiking, hunting • Elevation: 56

Slidell

Pearl River WMA - Crawford Landing • Agency: State • Tel: 985-543-4777 • Location: In Slidell • GPS: Lat 30.302263 Lon -89.707658 • Open: All year • Total sites: Dispersed • RV sites: Undefined • RV fee: Free • No water • No toilets • Notes: Permit required • Activities: Hiking, fishing, power boating, hunting • Elevation: 26

Springhill

Bodcau WMA - Teague Lake (Bayou Bodcau Reservoir) • Agency: Corps of Engineers • Location: 4 miles W of Springhill • GPS: Lat 33.018774 Lon -93.521408 • Total sites: Dispersed • RV sites: Undefined • RV fee: Free • No toilets • Elevation: 199

Zwolle

Sabine WMA • Agency: State • Tel: 318-371-3050 • Location: 4 miles SE of Zwolle • GPS: Lat 31.606118 Lon -93.569102 • Open: All year • Total sites: Dispersed • RV sites: Undefined • RV fee: Free • No toilets • Activities: Hiking, hunting • Elevation: 308

Minnesota

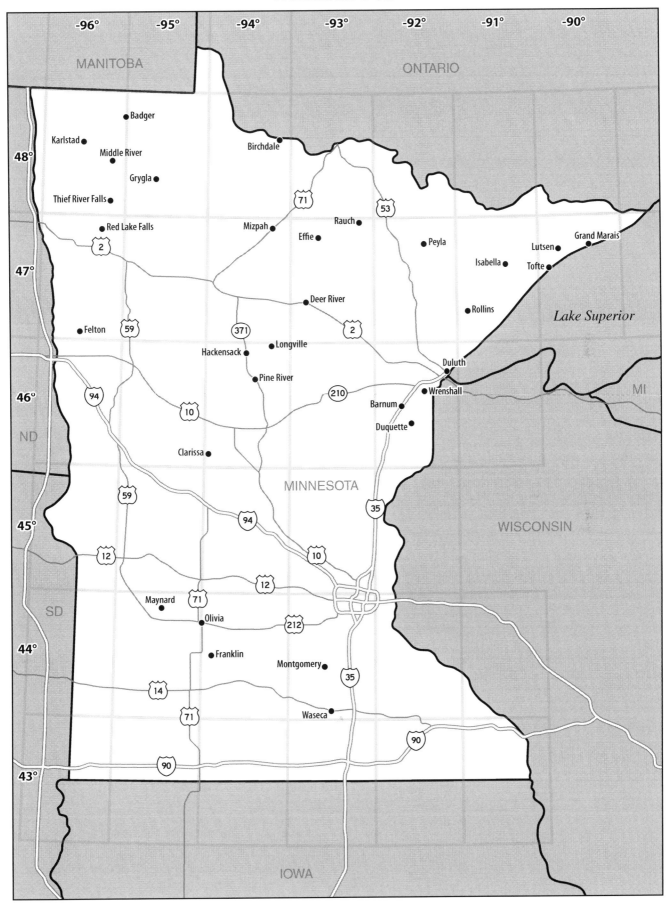

Minnesota — Camping Areas

Abbreviation	Description
DNR	Department of Natural Resources
NF	National Forest
WMA	Wildlife Management Area

Badger

Roseau River WMA • Agency: State • Tel: 218-463-1130 • Location: 14 miles N of Badger (limited services), 19 miles NW of Roseau • GPS: Lat 48.978584 Lon -96.019943 • Total sites: Dispersed • RV sites: Undefined • RV fee: Free • Central water • Vault toilets • Activities: Hiking, mountain biking, fishing, power boating, hunting, non-power boating • Elevation: 1057

Barnum

Blackhoof River WMA #3 • Agency: State • Location: 11 miles NE of Barnum (limited services), 17 miles S of Scanlon • GPS: Lat 46.525833 Lon -92.467822 • Total sites: Dispersed • RV sites: Undefined • RV fee: Free • No water • Vault toilets • Activities: Hiking, fishing, hunting • Elevation: 954

Birchdale

Nelson Park - DNR • Agency: State • Location: 1 mile N of Birchdale (limited services), 27 miles SE of Baudette • GPS: Lat 48.643856 Lon -94.101957 • Open: Apr-Nov • Total sites: 10 • RV sites: 6 • RV fee: Free • Central water • Vault toilets • Activities: Fishing, power boating, non-power boating • Elevation: 1056

Clarissa

Clarissa City Park • Agency: Municipal • Tel: 218-756-2450 • Location: In Clarissa • GPS: Lat 46.131093 Lon -94.949606 • Open: May-Sep • Total sites: 5 • RV sites: 5 • RV fee: Free (donation appreciated) • Electric sites: 5 • Water at site • No toilets • Notes: 1 week free - then $5/day • Elevation: 1319

Deer River

Bowstring State Forest - Cottonwood Lake • Agency: State • Tel: 218-743-3362 • Location: 11 miles NE of Deer River • GPS: Lat 47.427682 Lon -93.697866 • Total sites: 10 • RV sites: 10 • RV fee: Free • Central water • Vault toilets • Activities: Fishing, power boating, non-power boating • Elevation: 1342

Duluth

Cloquet Valley State Forest • Agency: State • Tel: 218-878-5640 • Location: 24 miles N of Duluth • GPS: Lat 47.067302 Lon -92.232702 • Total sites: Dispersed • RV sites: Undefined • RV fee: Free • No water • Vault toilets • Elevation: 1439

Cloquet Valley State Forest - Cloquet River Water Camp • Agency: State • Tel: 218-878-5640 • Location: 27 miles N of Duluth • GPS: Lat 47.115768 Lon -92.025063 • Total sites: Dispersed • RV sites: Undefined • RV fee: Free • No water • Vault toilets • Elevation: 1427

Duquette

Jackie Berger Park • Agency: Municipal • Location: In Duquette (limited services), 15 miles SE of Moose Lake • GPS: Lat 46.372333 Lon -92.555371 • Total sites: 6 • RV sites: 6 • RV fee: Free (donation appreciated) • Electric sites: 6 • No water • Vault toilets • Notes: Near RR tracks • Activities: Hiking • Elevation: 1135

Effie

Little American Falls • Agency: County • Tel: 218-283-1127 • Location: 7 miles N of Effie (limited services), 37 miles E of Northome • GPS: Lat 47.920624 Lon -93.620262 • Total sites: 5 • RV sites: 5 • RV fee: Free • No water • Vault toilets • Elevation: 1319

Felton

Felton WMA • Agency: State • Tel: 218-739-7576 • Location: 5 miles SE of Felton (limited services), 24 miles NE of Fargo • GPS: Lat 47.049839 Lon -96.44216 • Total sites: Dispersed • RV sites: Undefined • RV fee: Free • No water • No toilets • Activities: Hiking, hunting • Elevation: 985

Franklin

Franklin City Campground - Ball Park • Agency: Municipal • Tel: 507-557-2259 • Location: In Franklin (limited services), 16 miles E of Redwood Falls • GPS: Lat 44.530027 Lon -94.879352 • Open: May-Oct • Total sites: 3 • RV sites: 3 • RV fee: Free • Electric sites: 3 • Central water • Flush toilets • Notes: 3-night limit • Elevation: 1010

Franklin City Campground - Landing • Agency: Municipal • Tel: 507-557-2259 • Location: 1 mile S of Franklin (limited services), 13 miles E of Redwood Falls • GPS: Lat 44.518319 Lon -94.884679 • Open: May-Oct • Total sites: Dispersed • RV sites: Undefined • RV fee: Free • No water • No toilets • Notes: 7-night limit • Activities: Fishing, power boating, non-power boating • Elevation: 869

Grand Marais

Cascade River (Superior NF) • Agency: US Forest Service • Tel: 218-387-1750 • Location: 16 miles NW of Grand Marais • GPS: Lat 47.833646 Lon -90.530676 • Total sites: 4 • RV sites: 1 • RV fee: Free • No water • Vault toilets • Activities: Fishing • Elevation: 1631

Grand Portage State Forest - Devilfish Lake • Agency: State • Tel: 218-387-3039 • Location: 35 miles NE of Grand Marais • GPS: Lat 47.990731 Lon -90.095206 • Total sites: 5 • RV sites: 5 • RV fee: Free • No water • Vault toilets • Activities: Hiking, fishing, swimming • Elevation: 1880

Grand Portage State Forest - Esther Lake • Agency: State • Tel: 218-387-3039 • Location: 36 miles NE of Grand Marais • GPS: Lat 47.981739 Lon -90.108114 • Total sites: 3 • RV sites: 3 • RV fee: Free • No water • Vault toilets • Activities: Hiking, fishing, swimming, power boating, non-power boating • Elevation: 1975

Grand Portage State Forest - McFarland Lake • Agency: State • Tel: 218-387-3039 • Location: 35 miles NE of Grand Marais • GPS: Lat 48.045519 Lon -90.057883 • Total sites: 5 • RV sites: 5 • RV fee: Free • No water • Vault toilets • Activities: Fishing, swimming, power boating, non-power boating • Elevation: 1529

Lichen Lake Canoe Camp (Superior NF) • Agency: US Forest Service • Tel: 218-663-8060 • Location: 28 miles NW of Grand Marais • GPS: Lat 47.850391 Lon -90.712627 • Open: Apr-Sep • Total sites: 1 • RV sites: 1 • RV fee: Free • No water • Vault toilets • Activities: Hiking, fishing, non-power boating • Elevation: 1808

Grygla

Wolf Trail WMA • Agency: State • Tel: 218-219-8587 • Location: 14 miles SE of Grygla (limited services), 43 miles NE of Thief River Falls • GPS: Lat 48.237447 Lon -95.401725 • Total sites: Dispersed • RV sites: Undefined • RV fee: Free • No water • No toilets • Activities: Hiking • Elevation: 1223

Hackensack

Diamond Lake - DNR • Agency: State • Location: 8 miles NE of Hackensack • GPS: Lat 46.996592 Lon -94.454595 • Total sites: Dispersed • RV sites: Undefined • RV fee: Free • No water • No toilets • Activities: Fishing, non-power boating • Elevation: 1385

Isabella

Eighteen Lake (Superior NF) • Agency: US Forest Service • Tel: 218-323-7722 • Location: 3 miles N of Isabella (limited services), 30 miles N of Silver Bay • GPS: Lat 47.643759 Lon -91.344178 • Total sites: 3 • RV sites: 3 • RV fee: Free • No water • Vault toilets • Activities: Hiking, fishing, non-power boating • Elevation: 1926

Hogback Lake (Superior NF) • Agency: US Forest Service • Tel: 218-323-7722 • Location: 12 miles E of Isabella (limited services), 35 miles N of Silver Bay • GPS: Lat 47.644385 Lon -91.136046 • Total sites: 3 • RV sites: 3 • RV fee: Free • No water • Vault toilets • Activities: Hiking, fishing, non-power boating • Elevation: 1775

Section 29 Lake (Superior NF) • Agency: US Forest Service • Tel: 218-323-7722 • Location: 12 miles NE of Isabella (limited services), 39 miles N of Silver Bay • GPS: Lat 47.741338 Lon -91.241822 • Total sites: 3 • RV sites: 3 • RV fee: Free • No water • Vault toilets • Activities: Fishing, non-power boating • Elevation: 1627

Silver Island Lake • Agency: US Forest Service • Tel: 218-323-7722 • Location: 17 miles NE of Isabella (limited services), 44 miles N of Silver Bay • GPS: Lat 47.727398 Lon -91.149167 • Total sites: 8 • RV sites: 8 • RV fee: Free • No water • Vault toilets • Activities: Fishing, power boating, non-power boating • Elevation: 1640

Karlstad

East Park WMA • Agency: State • Tel: 218-436-2427 • Location: 12 miles SE of Karlstad (limited services), 21 miles SW of Greenbush • GPS: Lat 48.493339 Lon -96.348576 • Total sites: Dispersed • RV sites: Undefined • RV fee: Free • No water • No toilets • Activities: Hiking, hunting • Elevation: 1107

Twin Lakes WMA Site 1 • Agency: State • Tel: 218-436-2427 • Location: 3 miles NE of Karlstad • GPS: Lat 48.591734 Lon -96.470196 • Total sites: Dispersed • RV sites: Undefined • RV fee: Free • No water • No toilets • Activities: Hiking, power boating, hunting, non-power boating • Elevation: 1059

Twin Lakes WMA Site 2 • Agency: State • Tel: 218-436-2427 • Location: 4 miles NE of Karlstad • GPS: Lat 48.601608 Lon -96.452088 • Total sites: Dispersed • RV sites: Undefined • RV fee: Free • No water • No toilets • Activities: Hiking, power boating, hunting, non-power boating • Elevation: 1063

Twin Lakes WMA Site 3 • Agency: State • Tel: 218-436-2427 • Location: 4 miles NE of Karlstad • GPS: Lat 48.615107 Lon -96.447574 • Total sites: Dispersed • RV sites: Undefined • RV fee: Free • No water • No toilets • Activities: Hiking, power boating, hunting, non-power boating • Elevation: 1057

Twin Lakes WMA Site 4 • Agency: State • Tel: 218-436-2427 • Location: 5 miles NE of Karlstad • GPS: Lat 48.601463 Lon -96.417101 • Total sites: Dispersed • RV sites: Undefined • RV fee: Free • No water • No toilets • Activities:

Hiking, power boating, hunting, non-power boating • Elevation: 1059

Twin Lakes WMA Site 6 • Agency: State • Tel: 218-436-2427 • Location: 8 miles NE of Karlstad • GPS: Lat 48.642849 Lon -96.398116 • Total sites: Dispersed • RV sites: Undefined • RV fee: Free • No water • No toilets • Activities: Hiking, power boating, hunting, non-power boating • Elevation: 1062

Longville

Moccasin Lake - DNR • Agency: State • Location: 8 miles W of Longville • GPS: Lat 46.992263 Lon -94.356091 • Total sites: Dispersed • RV sites: Undefined • RV fee: Free • No water • No toilets • Activities: Fishing, non-power boating • Elevation: 1368

Lutsen

Clara Lake (Superior NF) • Agency: US Forest Service • Tel: 218-663-8060 • Location: 13 miles N of Lutsen (limited services), 27 miles W of Grand Marais • GPS: Lat 47.774354 Lon -90.752134 • Total sites: 3 • RV sites: 1 • RV fee: Free • No water • Vault toilets • Activities: Fishing, non-power boating • Elevation: 1726

Poplar River (Superior NF) • Agency: US Forest Service • Tel: 218-663-8060 • Location: 11 miles NW of Lutsen (limited services), 26 miles W of Grand Marais • GPS: Lat 47.738693 Lon -90.777797 • Total sites: 4 • RV sites: 2 • Max RV Length: 20 • RV fee: Free • No water • Vault toilets • Elevation: 1572

White Pine Lake (Superior NF) • Agency: US Forest Service • Tel: 218-663-8060 • Location: 10 miles NW of Lutsen (limited services), 25 miles W of Grand Marais • GPS: Lat 47.738251 Lon -90.752428 • Total sites: 3 • RV sites: 2 • Max RV Length: 20 • RV fee: Free • No water • Vault toilets • Activities: Fishing, non-power boating • Elevation: 1618

Maynard

Maynard Lions Park • Agency: Municipal • Tel: 320-367-2140 • Location: 1 mile S of Maynard (limited services), 10 miles NE of Granite Falls • GPS: Lat 44.901969 Lon -95.464868 • Total sites: 5 • RV sites: 5 • RV fee: Free (donation appreciated) • Flush toilets • Elevation: 1017

Middle River

Thief Lake WMA Site 1 • Agency: State • Tel: 218-222-3747 • Location: 16 miles NE of Middle River (limited services), 22 miles SE of Greenbush • GPS: Lat 48.518594 Lon -95.947511 • Total sites: Dispersed • RV sites: Undefined • RV fee: Free • No water • Activities: Hiking, fishing, hunting, non-power boating • Elevation: 1171

Thief Lake WMA Site 2 • Agency: State • Tel: 218-222-3747 • Location: 20 miles NE of Middle River (limited services), 27 miles SE of Greenbush • GPS: Lat 48.502757 Lon -95.860801 • Total sites: Dispersed • RV sites: Undefined • RV fee: Free • No water • Vault toilets • Activities: Hiking, fishing, hunting, non-power boating • Elevation: 1165

Thief Lake WMA Site 3 • Agency: State • Tel: 218-222-3747 • Location: 21 miles NE of Middle River (limited services), 28 miles SE of Greenbush • GPS: Lat 48.491302 Lon -95.841136 • Total sites: Dispersed • RV sites: Undefined • RV fee: Free • No water • No toilets • Activities: Hiking, fishing, hunting, non-power boating • Elevation: 1165

Thief Lake WMA Site 4 • Agency: State • Tel: 218-222-3747 • Location: 15 miles NE of Middle River (limited services), 29 miles SE of Greenbush • GPS: Lat 48.470944 Lon -95.881247 • Total sites: Dispersed • RV sites: Undefined • RV fee: Free • No water • Activities: Hiking, fishing, hunting, non-power boating • Elevation: 1165

Thief Lake WMA Site 5 • Agency: State • Tel: 218-222-3747 • Location: 21 miles NE of Middle River (limited services), 29 miles SE of Greenbush • GPS: Lat 48.478078 Lon -95.925159 • Total sites: Dispersed • RV sites: Undefined • RV fee: Free • No water • Activities: Hiking, fishing, hunting, non-power boating • Elevation: 1165

Mizpah

Seretha Lake Access • Agency: County • Location: 8 miles NE of Mizpah (limited services), 13 miles NE of Northwood • GPS: Lat 48.008043 Lon -94.102726 • Total sites: 1 • RV sites: Undefined • RV fee: Free • No water • Vault toilets • Elevation: 1296

Montgomery

Clear Lake • Agency: County • Tel: 507-237-4330 • Location: 6 miles W of Montgomery • GPS: Lat 44.442454 Lon -93.702328 • Open: May-Oct • Total sites: 4 • RV sites: 4 • RV fee: Free • Central water • Vault toilets • Notes: Must call the Sibley County Sheriff's office at 507-237-4330 to obtain permission • Activities: Hiking, fishing, power boating, non-power boating • Elevation: 1034

Olivia

Olivia Memorial Park • Agency: Municipal • Tel: 320-523-2361 • Location: In Olivia • GPS: Lat 44.775905 Lon -95.006561 • Open: Apr-Oct • Total sites: 6 • RV sites: 6 • RV fee: Free (donation appreciated) • Central water • Flush toilets • Notes: 3-day limit • Activities: Swimming • Elevation: 1070

Peyla

Big Rice Lake (Superior NF) • Agency: US Forest Service • Tel: 218-229-8800 • Location: 11 miles SW of Peyla (limited services), 17 miles N of Virginia • GPS: Lat 47.704199 Lon -92.498842 • Total sites: 3 • RV sites: 3 • Max RV Length: 20 • RV fee: Free • No water • Vault toilets • Activities: Fishing, power boating, hunting, non-power boating • Elevation: 1466

Pine River

Foothills State Forest • Agency: State • Tel: 218-947-3232 • Location: 12 miles W of Pine River • GPS: Lat 46.721759 Lon -94.61837 • Total sites: Dispersed • RV sites: Undefined • RV fee: Free • No water • Activities: Hiking • Elevation: 1425

Rauch

Samuelson • Agency: County • Location: 3 miles E of Rauch (limited services), 24 miles NW of Cook • GPS: Lat 47.948508 Lon -93.099205 • Total sites: 1 • RV sites: Undefined • RV fee: Free • No water • Vault toilets • Activities: Non-power boating • Elevation: 1222

Red Lake Falls

Old Crossing Treaty Park • Agency: County • Tel: 218-253-2684 • Location: 9 miles W of Red Lake Falls • GPS: Lat 47.861346 Lon -96.425523 • Open: All year • Total sites: 10 • RV sites: 10 • RV fee: Free • Central water • Vault toilets • Activities: Power boating, non-power boating • Elevation: 899

Rollins

Cloquet Valley State Forest - Bear Lake • Agency: State • Tel: 218-878-5640 • Location: 7 miles SW of Rollins (limited services), 37 miles NE of Duluth • GPS: Lat 47.206438 Lon -91.921768 • Total sites: Dispersed • RV sites: Undefined • RV fee: Free • No water • Vault toilets • Activities: Non-power boating • Elevation: 1502

Thief River Falls

Elm Lake WMA • Agency: State • Location: 18 miles NE of Thief River Falls • GPS: Lat 48.262167 Lon -96.017753 • Total sites: Dispersed • RV sites: Undefined • RV fee: Free • No water • No toilets • Elevation: 1143

Tofte

Baker Lake (Superior NF) • Agency: US Forest Service • Tel: 218-663-8060 • Location: 23 miles N of Tofte (limited services), 36 miles NW of Grand Marais • GPS: Lat 47.844528 Lon -90.817046 • Total sites: 5 • RV sites: 5 • RV fee: Free • Central water • Vault toilets • Activities: Fishing, power boating, non-power boating • Elevation: 1749

Fourmile Lake • Agency: US Forest Service • Tel: 218-663-8060 • Location: 17 miles NW of Tofte (limited services), 40 miles NW of Silver Bay • GPS: Lat 47.702262 Lon -90.963536 • Total sites: 4 • RV sites: 2 • RV fee: Free • No water • Vault toilets • Activities: Fishing, non-power boating • Elevation: 1670

Harriet Lake (Superior NF) • Agency: US Forest Service • Tel: 218-663-8060 • Location: 18 miles NW of Tofte (limited services), 35 miles N of Silver Bay • GPS: Lat 47.656881 Lon -91.115144 • Total sites: 4 • RV sites: 2 • RV fee: Free • No water • Vault toilets • Elevation: 1772

Kawishiwi Lake Rustic (Superior NF) • Agency: US Forest Service • Tel: 218-663-8060 • Location: 33 miles NW of Tofte (limited services), 57 miles NW of Grand Marais • GPS: Lat 47.838663 Lon -91.102413 • Total sites: 5 • RV sites: 5 • Max RV Length: 25 • RV fee: Free • No water • Vault toilets • Activities: Fishing, non-power boating • Elevation: 1656

Toohey Lake (Superior NF) • Agency: US Forest Service • Tel: 218-663-8060 • Location: 20 miles N of Tofte (limited services), 40 miles NE of Silver Bay • GPS: Lat 47.712827 Lon -90.953511 • Total sites: 5 • RV sites: 3 • RV fee: Free • No water • Vault toilets • Activities: Fishing, non-power boating • Elevation: 1690

Whitefish Lake (Superior NF) • Agency: US Forest Service • Tel: 218-663-8060 • Location: 20 miles NW of Tofte (limited services), 43 miles NE of Silver Bay • GPS: Lat 47.719106 Lon -91.045364 • Total sites: 3 • RV sites: 2 • RV fee: Free • No water • Vault toilets • Activities: Fishing, non-power boating • Elevation: 1700

Wilson Lake (Superior NF) • Agency: US Forest Service • Tel: 218-663-8060 • Location: 16 miles NW of Tofte (limited services), 34 miles NE of Silver Bay • GPS: Lat 47.660068 Lon -91.062459 • Total sites: 4 • RV sites: 3 • RV fee: Free • No water • Vault toilets • Activities: Fishing, non-power boating • Elevation: 1713

Windy Lake (Superior NF) • Agency: US Forest Service • Tel: 218-663-8060 • Location: 26 miles NW of Tofte (limited services), 42 miles NE of Silver Bay • GPS: Lat 47.743903 Lon -91.087007 • Total sites: 1 • RV sites: 1 • RV fee: Free • No water • Vault toilets • Activities: Fishing, non-power boating • Elevation: 1680

Waseca

Red Lake State Forest - Waskish • Agency: State • Tel: 218-647-8592 • Location: In Waseca (limited services), 40 miles S of Baudette • GPS: Lat 48.164737 Lon -94.508666 • Open: May-Oct • Total sites: Dispersed • RV sites: Undefined • RV fee: Free • No water • Vault toilets • Elevation: 1178

Wrenshall

Blackhoof River WMA #1 • Agency: State • Location: 7 miles S of Wrenshall (limited services), 13 miles S of Scanlon • GPS: Lat 46.532491 Lon -92.415547 • Total sites: Dispersed • RV sites: Undefined • RV fee: Free • No water • Vault toilets • Activities: Hiking, fishing, hunting • Elevation: 925

Blackhoof River WMA #2 • Agency: State • Location: 10 miles SW of Wrenshall (limited services), 14 miles S of Scanlon • GPS: Lat 46.527562 Lon -92.464167 • Total sites: Dispersed • RV sites: Undefined • RV fee: Free • No water • Vault toilets • Activities: Hiking, fishing, hunting • Elevation: 916

Mississippi

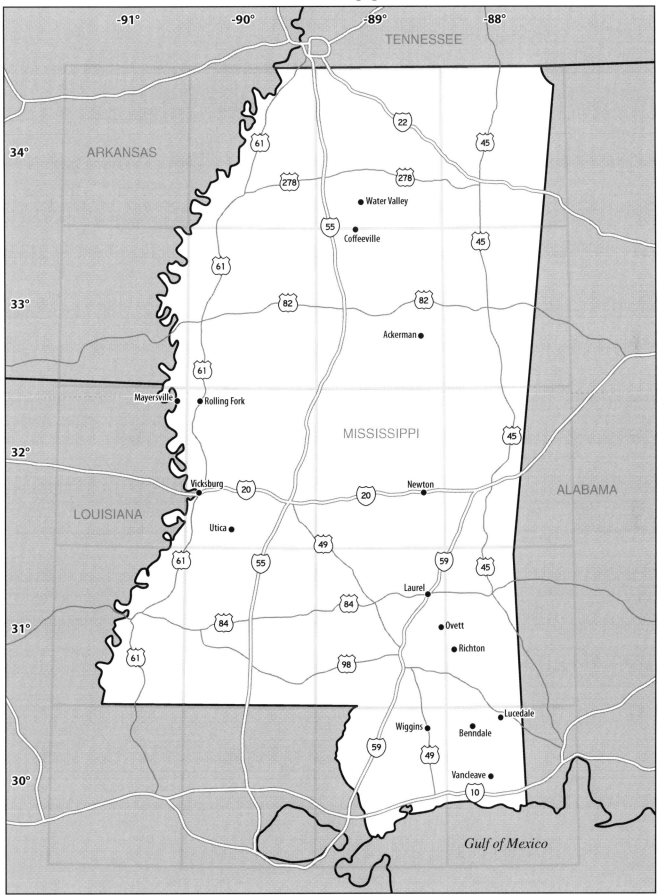

Mississippi — Camping Areas

Abbreviation	Description
NF	National Forest
NP	National Park
WMA	Wildlife Management Area

Ackerman

Natchez Trace NP - Jeff Busby • Agency: National Park Service • Tel: 800-305-7417 • Location: 11 miles NW of Ackerman • GPS: Lat 33.416691 Lon -89.266241 • Open: All year • Total sites: 24 • RV sites: 24 • RV fee: Free • Central water • Flush toilets • Elevation: 459

Benndale

Leaf River WMA - FR-309 #1 • Agency: State • Tel: 601-598-2323 • Location: 14 miles NW of Benndale (limited services), 21 miles NE of Wiggins • GPS: Lat 30.978574 Lon -88.908468 • Total sites: Dispersed • RV sites: Undefined • Max RV Length: 18 • RV fee: Free • No toilets • Elevation: 278

Leaf River WMA - FR-309 #2 • Agency: State • Tel: 601-598-2323 • Location: 15 miles NW of Benndale (limited services), 19 miles NE of Wiggins • GPS: Lat 30.991628 Lon -88.923789 • Total sites: Dispersed • RV sites: Undefined • Max RV Length: 18 • RV fee: Free • No toilets • Elevation: 281

Leaf River WMA - FR-309A • Agency: State • Tel: 601-598-2323 • Location: 15 miles NW of Benndale (limited services), 22 miles NE of Wiggins • GPS: Lat 30.969402 Lon -88.889217 • Total sites: Dispersed • RV sites: Undefined • Max RV Length: 25 • RV fee: Free • No toilets • Elevation: 218

Leaf River WMA - FR-315-G • Agency: State • Tel: 601-598-2323 • Location: 17 miles NW of Benndale (limited services), 24 miles NE of Wiggins • GPS: Lat 31.004562 Lon -88.925496 • Total sites: Dispersed • RV sites: Undefined • Max RV Length: 18 • RV fee: Free • No toilets • Elevation: 249

Leaf River WMA - FR-322 • Agency: State • Tel: 601-598-2323 • Location: 9 miles NW of Benndale (limited services), 19 miles NE of Wiggins • GPS: Lat 30.931719 Lon -88.899228 • Total sites: Dispersed • RV sites: Undefined • Max RV Length: 18 • RV fee: Free • No toilets • Elevation: 261

Leaf River WMA - FR-353 • Agency: State • Tel: 601-598-2323 • Location: 19 miles NW of Benndale (limited services), 26 miles NE of Wiggins • GPS: Lat 31.013775 Lon -88.878881 • Total sites: Dispersed • RV sites: Undefined • Max RV Length: 16 • RV fee: Free • No toilets • Elevation: 201

Pascagoula River WMA - Davis Eddy • Agency: State • Tel: 228-588-3878 • Location: 5 miles NE of Benndale (limited services), 14 miles W of Lucedale • GPS: Lat 30.903467 Lon -88.747436 • Total sites: Dispersed • RV sites: Undefined • Max RV Length: 18 • RV fee: Free • No toilets • Activities: Hunting • Elevation: 43

Pascagoula River WMA - Hutson Lake • Agency: State • Tel: 228-588-3878 • Location: 2 miles E of Benndale (limited services), 10 miles SW of Lucedale • GPS: Lat 30.875343 Lon -88.760904 • Total sites: Dispersed • RV sites: Undefined • Max RV Length: 18 • RV fee: Free • No toilets • Activities: Hunting • Elevation: 34

Pascagoula River WMA - Lower Rice Lake • Agency: State • Tel: 228-588-3878 • Location: 8 miles SE of Benndale (limited services), 20 miles SW of Lucedale • GPS: Lat 30.803594 Lon -88.732884 • Total sites: Dispersed • RV sites: Undefined • Max RV Length: 18 • RV fee: Free • No toilets • Activities: Hunting • Elevation: 34

Pascagoula River WMA - Wilkerson Ferry #1 • Agency: State • Tel: 228-588-3878 • Location: 6 miles SE of Benndale (limited services), 18 miles SW of Lucedale • GPS: Lat 30.815411 Lon -88.747301 • Total sites: Dispersed • RV sites: Undefined • Max RV Length: 18 • RV fee: Free • No toilets • Activities: Hunting • Elevation: 33

Pascagoula River WMA #1 • Agency: State • Tel: 228-588-3878 • Location: 13 miles SE of Benndale (limited services), 25 miles SW of Lucedale • GPS: Lat 30.750171 Lon -88.704644 • Total sites: Dispersed • RV sites: Undefined • Max RV Length: 16 • RV fee: Free • No toilets • Activities: Hunting • Elevation: 21

Bogalusa

Old River WMA Dispersed 1 • Agency: State • Tel: 228-588-3878 • Location: 13 miles SE of Bogalusa • GPS: Lat 30.692435 Lon -89.805929 • Total sites: Dispersed • RV sites: Undefined • RV fee: Free • No water • No toilets • Elevation: 62

Coffeeville

Skuna - Turkey Creek (Grenada Lake) • Agency: Corps of Engineers • Tel: 662-226-5911 • Location: 12 miles S of Coffeeville • GPS: Lat 33.878066 Lon -89.689229 • Open: All year • Total sites: 6 • RV sites: 6 • Max RV Length: 20 • RV fee: Free • Central water • Vault toilets • Activities: Power boating, non-power boating • Elevation: 207

Laurel

Chickasawhay WMA - Road 201/SR 536 • Agency: State • Tel: 601-344-0600 • Location: 12 miles NE of

Laurel • GPS: Lat 31.581998 Lon -88.99577 • Total sites: Dispersed • RV sites: Undefined • Max RV Length: 16 • RV fee: Free • No toilets • Elevation: 292

Lucedale

Pascagoula River WMA - GMR Road • Agency: State • Tel: 228-588-3878 • Location: 11 miles W of Lucedale • GPS: Lat 30.912688 Lon -88.728431 • Total sites: Dispersed • RV sites: Undefined • Max RV Length: 16 • RV fee: Free • No toilets • Activities: Hunting • Elevation: 43

Pascagoula River WMA - Indian Creek • Agency: State • Tel: 228-588-3878 • Location: 15 miles SW of Lucedale • GPS: Lat 30.744581 Lon -88.658252 • Total sites: Dispersed • RV sites: Undefined • Max RV Length: 18 • RV fee: Free • No toilets • Activities: Hunting • Elevation: 27

Pascagoula River WMA - Pierce Lake • Agency: State • Tel: 228-588-3878 • Location: 11 miles SW of Lucedale • GPS: Lat 30.843847 Lon -88.742029 • Total sites: Dispersed • RV sites: Undefined • Max RV Length: 18 • RV fee: Free • No toilets • Activities: Hunting • Elevation: 38

Pascagoula River WMA - Plum Bluff • Agency: State • Tel: 228-588-3878 • Location: 11 miles SW of Lucedale • GPS: Lat 30.799929 Lon -88.700728 • Total sites: Dispersed • RV sites: Undefined • Max RV Length: 20 • RV fee: Free • No toilets • Activities: Hunting • Elevation: 29

Pascagoula River WMA - Wilkerson Ferry #2 • Agency: State • Tel: 228-588-3878 • Location: 10 miles SW of Lucedale • GPS: Lat 30.833831 Lon -88.734971 • Total sites: Dispersed • RV sites: Undefined • Max RV Length: 25 • RV fee: Free • No toilets • Activities: Hunting • Elevation: 37

Mayersville

Shipland WMA Dispersed 1 • Agency: State • Tel: 662-873-6958 • Location: 12 miles SW of Mayersville (limited services), 23 miles SW of Rolling Fork • GPS: Lat 32.769911 Lon -91.143307 • Stay limit: 14 days • Total sites: Dispersed • RV sites: Undefined • Max RV Length: 20 • RV fee: Free • No water • No toilets • Elevation: 114

Shipland WMA Dispersed 2 • Agency: State • Tel: 662-873-6958 • Location: 12 miles SW of Mayersville (limited services), 23 miles SW of Rolling Fork • GPS: Lat 32.767938 Lon -91.139733 • Stay limit: 14 days • Total sites: Dispersed • RV sites: Undefined • RV fee: Free • No water • No toilets • Elevation: 115

Newton

Tallahala WMA - Cedar Creek • Agency: State • Tel: 601-859-3425 • Location: 16 miles SW of Newton • GPS: Lat 32.195242 Lon -89.311322 • Total sites: Dispersed • RV sites: Undefined • Max RV Length: 16 • RV fee: Free • No toilets • Elevation: 402

Tallahala WMA - Road 25 • Agency: State • Tel: 601-859-3425 • Location: 13 miles SW of Newton • GPS: Lat 32.195368 Lon -89.228306 • Total sites: Dispersed • RV sites: Undefined • Max RV Length: 16 • RV fee: Free • No water • No toilets • Elevation: 450

Tallahala WMA - Shopping Center Road • Agency: State • Tel: 601-859-3425 • Location: 18 miles SW of Newton • GPS: Lat 32.23151 Lon -89.325758 • Total sites: Dispersed • RV sites: Undefined • Max RV Length: 16 • RV fee: Free • No toilets • Elevation: 464

Ovett

Chickasawhay WMA - Old Culpepper Road #1 • Agency: State • Tel: 601-344-0600 • Location: 8 miles NE of Ovett (limited services), 17 miles N of Richton • GPS: Lat 31.546474 Lon -88.954752 • Total sites: Dispersed • RV sites: Undefined • Max RV Length: 18 • RV fee: Free • No toilets • Elevation: 246

Chickasawhay WMA - Old Culpepper Road #2 • Agency: State • Tel: 601-344-0600 • Location: 7 miles NE of Ovett (limited services), 17 miles N of Richton • GPS: Lat 31.542153 Lon -88.955143 • Total sites: Dispersed • RV sites: Undefined • Max RV Length: 18 • RV fee: Free • No toilets • Elevation: 231

Richton

Chickasawhay WMA - FR 205 • Agency: State • Tel: 601-344-0600 • Location: 9 miles N of Richton • GPS: Lat 31.476524 Lon -88.950573 • Total sites: Dispersed • RV sites: Undefined • Max RV Length: 18 • RV fee: Free • No toilets • Elevation: 257

Rolling Fork

Sunflower WMA Dispersed 35 • Agency: State • Tel: 662-873-6958 • Location: 15 miles SE of Rolling Fork • GPS: Lat 32.765152 Lon -90.793499 • Total sites: Dispersed • RV sites: Undefined • Max RV Length: 16 • RV fee: Free • No water • No toilets • Elevation: 109

Sunflower WMA Dispersed 39 • Agency: State • Tel: 662-873-6958 • Location: 24 miles SE of Rolling Fork • GPS: Lat 32.727117 Lon -90.793525 • Total sites: Dispersed • RV sites: Undefined • Max RV Length: 16 • RV fee: Free • No water • No toilets • Elevation: 109

Sunflower WMA Dispersed 43 • Agency: State • Tel: 662-873-6958 • Location: 22 miles SE of Rolling Fork • GPS: Lat 32.716231 Lon -90.783594 • Total sites: Dispersed • RV sites: Undefined • Max RV Length: 16 • RV fee: Free • No water • No toilets • Elevation: 95

Sunflower WMA Dispersed 45 • Agency: State • Tel: 662-873-6958 • Location: 20 miles SE of Rolling Fork • GPS: Lat 32.736583 Lon -90.758925 • Total sites: Dispersed • RV sites: Undefined • Max RV Length: 16 • RV fee: Free • No water • No toilets • Elevation: 100

Sunflower WMA Dispersed 51-52 (Delta NF) • Agency: State • Tel: 601-661-0294 • Location: 26 miles SE of Rolling Fork • GPS: Lat 32.678585 Lon -90.792728 • Total sites: Dispersed • RV sites: Undefined • RV fee: Free • No water • Vault toilets • Elevation: 170

Sunflower WMA Dispersed 60 • Agency: State • Tel: 662-873-6958 • Location: 28 miles SE of Rolling Fork • GPS: Lat 32.662513 Lon -90.760499 • Total sites: Dispersed • RV sites: Undefined (8 sites along the road) • Max RV Length: 16 • RV fee: Free • No water • No toilets • Elevation: 93

Sunflower WMA Dispersed 64 • Agency: State • Tel: 662-873-6958 • Location: 17 miles E of Rolling Fork • GPS: Lat 32.896666 Lon -90.707394 • Total sites: Dispersed • RV sites: Undefined • Max RV Length: 18 • RV fee: Free • No water • No toilets • Elevation: 106

Sunflower WMA Dispersed 65 (Delta NF) • Agency: State • Tel: 601-661-0294 • Location: 25 miles SE of Rolling Fork • GPS: Lat 32.698427 Lon -90.699147 • Stay limit: 14 days • Total sites: Dispersed • RV sites: Undefined (numerous sites along road) • RV fee: Free • No water • No toilets • Elevation: 111

Sunflower WMA Dispersed 8 (Delta NF) • Agency: State • Tel: 601-661-0294 • Location: 9 miles SE of Rolling Fork • GPS: Lat 32.835807 Lon -90.810895 • Total sites: Dispersed • RV sites: Undefined • RV fee: Free • No water • No toilets • Elevation: 88

Twin Oaks WMA - Fort Creek Rd #1 • Agency: State • Tel: 601-661-0294 • Location: 7 miles SE of Rolling Fork • GPS: Lat 32.852182 Lon -90.835484 • Stay limit: 14 days • Total sites: Dispersed • RV sites: Undefined • Max RV Length: 16 • RV fee: Free • No water • No toilets • Elevation: 114

Utica

Natchez Trace NP - Rocky Springs • Agency: National Park Service • Tel: 800-305-7417 • Location: 13 miles W of Utica (limited services), 22 miles S of Vicksburg • GPS: Lat 32.086627 Lon -90.799167 • Open: All year • Total sites: 20 • RV sites: 20 • RV fee: Free • Central water • Flush toilets • Elevation: 207

Vancleave

Pascagoula River WMA - Cane/Fletcher • Agency: State • Tel: 228-588-3878 • Location: 8 miles N of Vancleave (limited services), 19 miles NW of Escatawpa • GPS: Lat 30.653852 Lon -88.634287 • Total sites: Dispersed • RV sites: Undefined • Max RV Length: 18 • RV fee: Free • No toilets • Activities: Hunting • Elevation: 14

Pascagoula River WMA - Graham Lake • Agency: State • Tel: 228-588-3878 • Location: 7 miles NE of Vancleave (limited services), 18 miles NW of Escatawpa • GPS: Lat 30.617234 Lon -88.635699 • Total sites: Dispersed • RV sites: Undefined • Max RV Length: 18 • RV fee: Free • No toilets • Activities: Hunting • Elevation: 12

Vicksburg

Phil Bryant WMA Dispersed 1 • Agency: State • Tel: 601-432-2199 • Location: 20 miles N of Vicksburg • GPS: Lat 32.549064 Lon -90.954654 • Total sites: Dispersed • RV sites: Undefined • RV fee: Free • No water • No toilets • Elevation: 99

Phil Bryant WMA Dispersed 2 • Agency: State • Tel: 601-432-2199 • Location: 22 miles N of Vicksburg • GPS: Lat 32.553439 Lon -90.955603 • Total sites: Dispersed • RV sites: Undefined • RV fee: Free • No water • No toilets • Elevation: 96

Phil Bryant WMA Dispersed 3 • Agency: State • Tel: 601-432-2199 • Location: 29 miles N of Vicksburg • GPS: Lat 32.533014 Lon -90.948339 • Total sites: Dispersed • RV sites: Undefined • RV fee: Free • No water • No toilets • Elevation: 95

Water Valley

Bynum Creek (Enid Lake) • Agency: Corps of Engineers • Tel: 662-563-4571 • Location: 13 miles NW of Water Valley • GPS: Lat 34.177727 Lon -89.735574 • Open: All year • Total sites: 5 • RV sites: 5 • Max RV Length: 20 • RV fee: Free • Central water • Vault toilets • Activities: Power boating • Elevation: 246

Point Pleasant (Enid Lake) • Agency: Corps of Engineers • Tel: 662-563-4571 • Location: 14 miles W of Water Valley • GPS: Lat 34.137198 Lon -89.838522 • Open: All year • Total sites: 3 • RV sites: 3 • Max RV Length: 20 • RV fee: Free • Central water • Vault toilets • Activities: Power boating, non-power boating • Elevation: 299

Prophet Bridge (Enid Lake) • Agency: Corps of Engineers • Tel: 662-563-4571 • Location: 3 miles NW of Water Valley • GPS: Lat 34.199789 Lon -89.669724 • Total sites: 2 • RV sites: 2 • RV fee: Free • No water • No toilets • Elevation: 280

Wiggins

Fairley Bridge Landing (Desoto NF) • Agency: US Forest Service • Tel: 601-965-1600 • Location: 12 miles NE of Wiggins • GPS: Lat 30.918153 Lon -88.966392 • Open: All year • Stay limit: 14 days • Total sites: 3 • RV sites: 3 • RV fee: Free • No water • Vault toilets • Activities: Hiking, non-power boating • Elevation: 108

Missouri

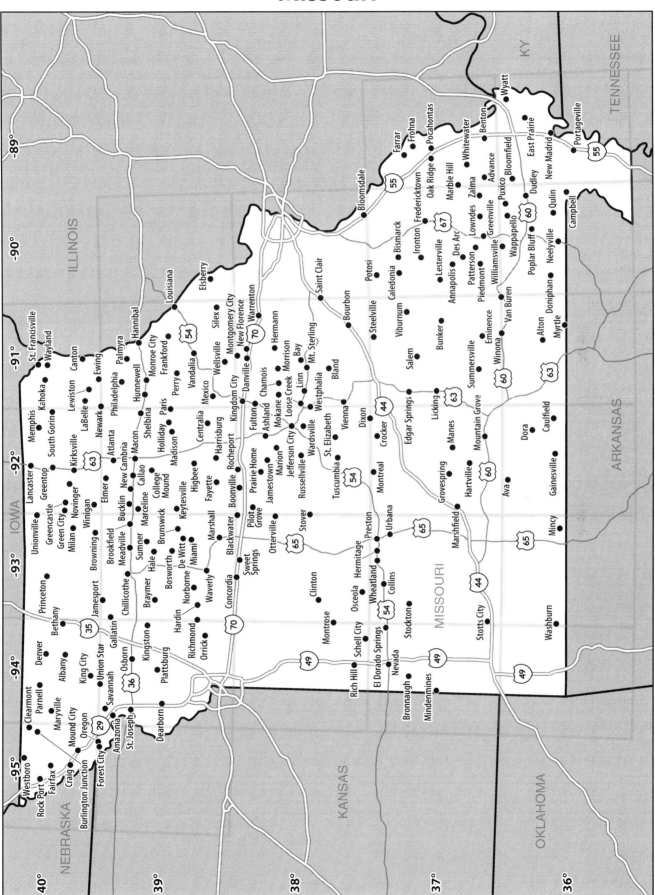

Missouri — Camping Areas

Abbreviation	Description
CA	Conservation Area
CG	Campground
MDC	Missouri Department of Conservation
NF	National Forest
RA	Recreation Area
WA	Wildlife Area

Advance

Duck Creek CA Greenbrier Unit - MDC • Agency: State • Tel: 573-290-5730 • Location: 7 miles W of Advance • GPS: Lat 37.103372 Lon -90.027847 • Open: All year • Total sites: Dispersed • RV sites: Undefined • RV fee: Free • No water • No toilets • Activities: Hiking, fishing, hunting • Elevation: 381

Albany

Andy Denton Access - North Lot - MDC • Agency: State • Tel: 816-271-3100 • Location: 13 miles S of Albany • GPS: Lat 40.097571 Lon -94.351107 • Open: All year • Total sites: Dispersed • RV sites: Undefined • RV fee: Free • No water • No toilets • Activities: Fishing, hunting, non-power boating • Elevation: 820

Andy Denton Access - South Lot - MDC • Agency: State • Tel: 816-271-3100 • Location: 14 miles S of Albany • GPS: Lat 40.093053 Lon -94.350605 • Open: All year • Total sites: Dispersed • RV sites: Undefined • RV fee: Free • No water • No toilets • Activities: Fishing, hunting, non-power boating • Elevation: 869

Elam Bend CA - Lot 1 - MDC • Agency: State • Tel: 660-646-6122 • Location: 14 miles SE of Albany • GPS: Lat 40.091288 Lon -94.267626 • Open: All year • Total sites: Dispersed • RV sites: Undefined • RV fee: Free • No water • Vault toilets • Activities: Fishing, hunting, non-power boating • Elevation: 814

Elam Bend CA - Lot 2 - MDC • Agency: State • Tel: 660-646-6122 • Location: 14 miles SE of Albany • GPS: Lat 40.090996 Lon -94.266847 • Open: All year • Total sites: Dispersed • RV sites: Undefined • RV fee: Free • No water • No toilets • Activities: Fishing, hunting, non-power boating • Elevation: 814

Elam Bend CA - Lot 3 - MDC • Agency: State • Tel: 660-646-6122 • Location: 14 miles SE of Albany • GPS: Lat 40.091411 Lon -94.257271 • Open: All year • Total sites: Dispersed • RV sites: Undefined • RV fee: Free • No water • No toilets • Activities: Fishing, hunting, non-power boating • Elevation: 810

Elam Bend CA - Lot 4 - MDC • Agency: State • Tel: 660-646-6122 • Location: 18 miles SE of Albany • GPS: Lat 40.076119 Lon -94.254605 • Open: All year • Total sites: Dispersed • RV sites: Undefined • RV fee: Free • No water • No toilets • Activities: Fishing, hunting, non-power boating • Elevation: 804

Emmett and Leah Seat Memorial CA - MDC • Agency: State • Tel: 660-646-6122 • Location: 16 miles NE of Albany • GPS: Lat 40.410294 Lon -94.247012 • Open: All year • Total sites: Dispersed • RV sites: Undefined • RV fee: Free • No water • No toilets • Activities: Fishing, hunting • Elevation: 1102

Emmett and Leah Seat Memorial CA - MDC • Agency: State • Tel: 660-646-6122 • Location: 16 miles NE of Albany • GPS: Lat 40.410891 Lon -94.257572 • Open: All year • Total sites: Dispersed • RV sites: Undefined • RV fee: Free • No water • No toilets • Activities: Fishing, hunting • Elevation: 1106

Alton

McCormack Lake RA (Mark Twain NF) • Agency: US Forest Service • Location: 16 miles NE of Alton • GPS: Lat 36.821904 Lon -91.352333 • Total sites: 8 • RV sites: 8 • RV fee: Free • Central water • Vault toilets • Activities: Fishing, non-power boating • Elevation: 607

Amazonia

Worthwine Island CA - MDC • Agency: State • Tel: 816-271-3100 • Location: 4 miles SW of Amazonia (limited services), 9 miles NW of St Joseph • GPS: Lat 39.854793 Lon -94.932481 • Open: All year • Total sites: Dispersed • RV sites: Undefined • RV fee: Free • No water • No toilets • Activities: Hiking, fishing, hunting, non-power boating • Elevation: 820

Annapolis

Funk Memorial State Forest - MDC • Agency: State • Tel: 573-223-4525 • Location: 10 miles S of Annapolis (limited services), 19 miles N of Piedmont • GPS: Lat 37.312074 Lon -90.722218 • Open: All year • Total sites: Dispersed • RV sites: Undefined • RV fee: Free • No water • No toilets • Activities: Hunting • Elevation: 1106

Ashland

Pine Ridge RA (Mark Twain NF) • Agency: US Forest Service • Location: 6 miles E of Ashland • GPS: Lat 38.7589 Lon -92.14439 • Total sites: 8 • RV sites: 8 • Max RV Length: 34 • RV fee: Free • Central water • Vault toilets • Activities: Hiking • Elevation: 787

Atlanta

Atlanta CA - Site 1 - MDC • Agency: State • Tel: 660-785-2420 • Location: 1 mile S of Atlanta (limited services), 11 miles N of Macon • GPS: Lat 39.889776 Lon -92.485611 • Open: All year • Total sites: Dispersed • RV sites: Undefined • RV fee: Free • No water • No toilets • Activities: Fishing, hunting • Elevation: 909

Atlanta CA - Site 10 - MDC • Agency: State • Tel: 660-785-2420 • Location: 4 miles SW of Atlanta (limited services), 10 miles NW of Macon • GPS: Lat 39.864899 Lon -92.508403 • Open: All year • Total sites: Dispersed • RV sites: Undefined • RV fee: Free • No water • No toilets • Activities: Fishing, hunting • Elevation: 919

Atlanta CA - Site 11 - MDC • Agency: State • Tel: 660-785-2420 • Location: 4 miles SW of Atlanta (limited services), 10 miles NW of Macon • GPS: Lat 39.861555 Lon -92.508677 • Open: All year • Total sites: Dispersed • RV sites: Undefined • RV fee: Free • No water • No toilets • Activities: Fishing, hunting • Elevation: 919

Atlanta CA - Site 12 - MDC • Agency: State • Tel: 660-785-2420 • Location: 3 miles S of Atlanta (limited services), 9 miles N of Macon • GPS: Lat 39.869735 Lon -92.482853 • Open: All year • Total sites: Dispersed • RV sites: Undefined • RV fee: Free • No water • No toilets • Activities: Fishing, hunting • Elevation: 889

Atlanta CA - Site 2 - MDC • Agency: State • Tel: 660-785-2420 • Location: 3 miles SW of Atlanta (limited services), 16 miles N of Macon • GPS: Lat 39.888208 Lon -92.495967 • Open: All year • Total sites: Dispersed • RV sites: Undefined • RV fee: Free • No water • No toilets • Activities: Fishing, hunting • Elevation: 853

Atlanta CA - Site 3 - MDC • Agency: State • Tel: 660-785-2420 • Location: 2 miles SW of Atlanta (limited services), 16 miles NW of Macon • GPS: Lat 39.886462 Lon -92.504562 • Open: All year • Total sites: Dispersed • RV sites: Undefined • RV fee: Free • No water • No toilets • Activities: Fishing, hunting • Elevation: 919

Atlanta CA - Site 4 - MDC • Agency: State • Tel: 660-785-2420 • Location: 3 miles SW of Atlanta (limited services), 16 miles NW of Macon • GPS: Lat 39.883963 Lon -92.514126 • Open: All year • Total sites: Dispersed • RV sites: Undefined • RV fee: Free • No water • No toilets • Activities: Fishing, hunting • Elevation: 909

Atlanta CA - Site 5 - MDC • Agency: State • Tel: 660-785-2420 • Location: 3 miles SW of Atlanta (limited services), 17 miles NW of Macon • GPS: Lat 39.877542 Lon -92.518109 • Open: All year • Total sites: Dispersed • RV sites: Undefined • RV fee: Free • No water • No toilets • Activities: Fishing, hunting • Elevation: 892

Atlanta CA - Site 6 - MDC • Agency: State • Tel: 660-785-2420 • Location: 3 miles SW of Atlanta (limited services), 10 miles NW of Macon • GPS: Lat 39.876384 Lon -92.506034 • Open: All year • Total sites: Dispersed • RV sites: Undefined • RV fee: Free • No water • No toilets • Activities: Fishing, hunting • Elevation: 912

Atlanta CA - Site 7 - MDC • Agency: State • Tel: 660-785-2420 • Location: 3 miles SW of Atlanta (limited services), 10 miles NW of Macon • GPS: Lat 39.874983 Lon -92.506065 • Open: All year • Total sites: Dispersed • RV sites: Undefined • RV fee: Free • No water • No toilets • Activities: Fishing, hunting • Elevation: 925

Atlanta CA - Site 8 (Shooting Range) - MDC • Agency: State • Tel: 660-785-2420 • Location: 3 miles SW of Atlanta (limited services), 10 miles NW of Macon • GPS: Lat 39.871209 Lon -92.506418 • Open: All year • Total sites: Dispersed • RV sites: Undefined • RV fee: Free • No water • Vault toilets • Activities: Fishing, hunting • Elevation: 915

Atlanta CA - Site 9 - MDC • Agency: State • Tel: 660-785-2420 • Location: 4 miles SW of Atlanta (limited services), 10 miles NW of Macon • GPS: Lat 39.870821 Lon -92.501399 • Open: All year • Total sites: Dispersed • RV sites: Undefined • RV fee: Frec • No water • No toilets • Activities: Fishing, hunting • Elevation: 925

Ava

Rippee CA - MDC • Agency: State • Tel: 417-256-7161 • Location: 14 miles SE of Ava • GPS: Lat 36.870406 Lon -92.470378 • Open: All year • Total sites: Dispersed • RV sites: Undefined • RV fee: Free • No water • Vault toilets • Activities: Fishing, hunting, non-power boating • Elevation: 807

Vera Cruz Access 1 - MDC • Agency: State • Tel: 417-256-7161 • Location: 12 miles SE of Ava • GPS: Lat 36.918608 Lon -92.496778 • Open: All year • Total sites: Dispersed • RV sites: Undefined • RV fee: Free • No water • Vault toilets • Activities: Fishing, hunting, non-power boating • Elevation: 837

Vera Cruz Access 2 - MDC • Agency: State • Tel: 417-256-7161 • Location: 12 miles SE of Ava • GPS: Lat 36.914465 Lon -92.495969 • Open: All year • Total sites: Dispersed • RV sites: Undefined • RV fee: Free • No water • Vault toilets • Activities: Fishing, hunting, non-power boating • Elevation: 827

Bay

Held's Island Access - MDC • Agency: State • Tel: 573-815-7900 • Location: 6 miles NW of Bay (limited services), 21 miles N of Owensville • GPS: Lat 38.552753 Lon -91.598095 • Open: All year • Total sites: Dispersed • RV sites: Undefined • RV fee: Free • No water • Vault toilets • Activities: Fishing, power boating, non-power boating • Elevation: 532

Benton

General Watkins CA - MDC • Agency: State • Tel: 573-290-5730 • Location: 4 miles SW of Benton • GPS: Lat 37.075822 Lon -89.609147 • Open: All year • Total sites: Dispersed • RV sites: Undefined • RV fee: Free • No water • No toilets • Activities: Hiking, fishing, hunting • Elevation: 486

Bethany

Grand Trace CA - MDC • Agency: State • Tel: 660-646-6122 • Location: 8 miles NW of Bethany • GPS: Lat 40.323928 Lon -94.123777 • Open: All year • Total sites: Dispersed • RV sites: Undefined • RV fee: Free • No water • No toilets • Activities: Fishing, hunting • Elevation: 1079

Wayne Helton Memorial Wildlife Area - Lot 1 - MDC • Agency: State • Tel: 660-646-6122 • Location: 13 miles E of Bethany • GPS: Lat 40.249438 Lon -93.806478 • Open: All year • Total sites: Dispersed • RV sites: Undefined • RV fee: Free • No water • No toilets • Activities: Fishing, hunting • Elevation: 968

Wayne Helton Memorial Wildlife Area - Lot 2 - MDC • Agency: State • Tel: 660-646-6122 • Location: 15 miles E of Bethany • GPS: Lat 40.235893 Lon -93.827741 • Open: All year • Total sites: Dispersed • RV sites: Undefined • RV fee: Free • No water • No toilets • Activities: Fishing, hunting • Elevation: 961

Bismarck

Bismarck CA - MDC • Agency: State • Tel: 573-290-5730 • Location: 4 miles SW of Bismarck • GPS: Lat 37.732251 Lon -90.638309 • Open: All year • Total sites: Dispersed • RV sites: Undefined • RV fee: Free • No water • Vault toilets • Activities: Fishing, hunting • Elevation: 1060

Blackwater

Harriman Hill Access - MDC • Agency: State • Tel: 573-815-7900 • Location: 6 miles SE of Blackwater (limited services), 10 miles SW of Booneville • GPS: Lat 38.935342 Lon -92.944169 • Open: All year • Total sites: Dispersed • RV sites: Undefined • RV fee: Free • No water • Vault toilets • Activities: Fishing, power boating, non-power boating • Elevation: 607

Bland

Canaan CA North - MDC • Agency: State • Tel: 573-815-7900 • Location: 4 miles NE of Bland (limited services), 9 miles NE of Belle • GPS: Lat 38.341964 Lon -91.596023 • Open: All year • Total sites: 8 • RV sites: 8 • RV fee: Free • No water • No toilets • Activities: Hiking, hunting, equestrian area • Elevation: 807

Canaan CA South - MDC • Agency: State • Tel: 573-815-7900 • Location: 2 miles NE of Bland (limited services), 7 miles NE of Belle • GPS: Lat 38.321774 Lon -91.609347 • Open: All year • Total sites: 6 • RV sites: 6 • RV fee: Free • No water • No toilets • Activities: Hiking, hunting, equestrian area • Elevation: 817

Bloomfield

Holly Ridge CA - MDC • Agency: State • Tel: 573-290-5730 • Location: 3 miles S of Bloomfield • GPS: Lat 36.850862 Lon -89.92226 • Open: All year • Total sites: Dispersed • RV sites: Undefined • RV fee: Free • No water • No toilets • Activities: Hiking, hunting, equestrian area • Elevation: 564

Bloomsdale

Magnolia Hollow CA - MDC • Agency: State • Tel: 573-290-5730 • Location: 7 miles NE of Bloomsdale (limited services), 15 miles NW of Ste Genevieve • GPS: Lat 38.038457 Lon -90.141426 • Open: All year • Total sites: 4 • RV sites: 4 • RV fee: Free • No water • No toilets • Activities: Hiking, mountain biking, hunting • Elevation: 627

Boonville

Franklin Island CA - MDC • Agency: State • Tel: 573-815-7900 • Location: 4 miles NE of Boonville • GPS: Lat 38.985991 Lon -92.719833 • Open: All year • Total sites: Dispersed • RV sites: Undefined • RV fee: Free • No water • No toilets • Activities: Hiking, fishing, power boating, hunting, non-power boating • Elevation: 600

Bosworth

Bosworth Access - MDC • Agency: State • Tel: 660-646-6122 • Location: 4 miles E of Bosworth (limited services), 13 miles NW of Brunswick • GPS: Lat 39.474969 Lon -93.265311 • Open: All year • Total sites: Dispersed • RV sites: Undefined • RV fee: Free • No water • No toilets • Activities: Fishing, non-power boating • Elevation: 656

Bourbon

Pea Ridge CA Camp 1 - MDC • Agency: State • Tel: 636-441-4554 • Location: 16 miles SE of Bourbon • GPS: Lat

38.087037 Lon -91.019329 • Open: All year • Total sites: Dispersed • RV sites: Undefined • RV fee: Free • No water • No toilets • Activities: Fishing, hunting • Elevation: 935

Braymer

Bunch Hollow CA - 1 - MDC • Agency: State • Tel: 660-646-6122 • Location: 10 miles E of Braymer (limited services), 17 miles S of Chillicothe • GPS: Lat 39.588143 Lon -93.626968 • Open: All year • Total sites: Dispersed • RV sites: Undefined • RV fee: Free • No water • No toilets • Activities: Hiking, fishing, hunting, equestrian area • Elevation: 853

Bunch Hollow CA - 2 - MDC • Agency: State • Tel: 660-646-6122 • Location: 12 miles E of Braymer (limited services), 18 miles SW of Chillicothe • GPS: Lat 39.579878 Lon -93.613868 • Open: All year • Total sites: Dispersed • RV sites: Undefined • RV fee: Free • No water • No toilets • Activities: Hiking, fishing, hunting, equestrian area • Elevation: 958

Bunch Hollow CA - 3 - MDC • Agency: State • Tel: 660-646-6122 • Location: 13 miles E of Braymer (limited services), 19 miles SW of Chillicothe • GPS: Lat 39.583848 Lon -93.612435 • Open: All year • Total sites: Dispersed • RV sites: Undefined • RV fee: Free • No water • No toilets • Activities: Hiking, fishing, hunting, equestrian area • Elevation: 932

Bunch Hollow CA - 4 - MDC • Agency: State • Tel: 660-646-6122 • Location: 12 miles E of Braymer (limited services), 19 miles SW of Chillicothe • GPS: Lat 39.568905 Lon -93.616526 • Open: All year • Total sites: Dispersed • RV sites: Undefined • RV fee: Free • No water • No toilets • Activities: Hiking, fishing, hunting, equestrian area • Elevation: 955

Bunch Hollow CA - 5 - MDC • Agency: State • Tel: 660-646-6122 • Location: 12 miles SE of Braymer (limited services), 17 miles SW of Chillicothe • GPS: Lat 39.569533 Lon -93.607497 • Open: All year • Total sites: Dispersed • RV sites: Undefined • RV fee: Free • No water • No toilets • Activities: Hiking, fishing, hunting, equestrian area • Elevation: 965

Bronnaugh

Bushwhacker Lake CA Southwest CG - MDC • Agency: State • Tel: 417-895-6880 • Location: 6 miles SE of Bronnaugh (limited services), 16 miles S of Nevada • GPS: Lat 37.659592 Lon -94.423081 • Open: All year • Total sites: Dispersed • RV sites: Undefined • RV fee: Free • No water • Vault toilets • Activities: Hiking, fishing, hunting, equestrian area • Elevation: 843

Bushwhacker Lake CA West CG - MDC • Agency: State • Tel: 417-895-6880 • Location: 5 miles SE of Bronnaugh (limited services), 16 miles S of Nevada • GPS: Lat 37.668092 Lon -94.415664 • Open: All year • Total sites: Dispersed • RV sites: Undefined • RV fee: Free • No water • Vault toilets • Activities: Hiking, fishing, hunting, equestrian area • Elevation: 843

Brookfield

Brookfield City Lake • Agency: Municipal • Tel: 660-258-5644 • Location: 3 miles W of Brookfield • GPS: Lat 39.800345 Lon -93.018929 • Total sites: Dispersed • RV sites: Undefined • RV fee: Free • No water • Vault toilets • Elevation: 816

Browning

Rocky Ford Access - MDC • Agency: State • Tel: 660-785-2420 • Location: 2 miles N of Browning (limited services), 10 miles S of Milan • GPS: Lat 40.065319 Lon -93.166864 • Open: All year • Total sites: Dispersed • RV sites: Undefined • RV fee: Free • No water • No toilets • Activities: Fishing, non-power boating • Elevation: 781

Brunswick

Herring Memorial Park • Agency: Municipal • Tel: 660-548-3028 • Location: In Brunswick • GPS: Lat 39.429419 Lon -93.133595 • Open: All year • Total sites: 6 • RV sites: 6 • RV fee: Free • Electric sites: 6 • Central water • Flush toilets • Elevation: 784

Lewis and Clark City Campsite • Agency: Municipal • Tel: 660-548-3028 • Location: In Brunswick • GPS: Lat 39.422236 Lon -93.131821 • Open: All year • Total sites: 3 • RV sites: 3 • RV fee: Free • Electric sites: 3 • No water • Vault toilets • Activities: Fishing, non-power boating • Elevation: 656

Bucklin

Mussel Fork CA Lot 1 - MDC • Agency: State • Tel: 660-646-6122 • Location: 3 miles SE of Bucklin (limited services), 6 miles NE of Marceline • GPS: Lat 39.758371 Lon -92.870208 • Open: All year • Total sites: Dispersed • RV sites: Undefined • RV fee: Free • No water • No toilets • Activities: Hiking, fishing, hunting, non-power boating • Elevation: 843

Mussel Fork CA Lot 10 - MDC • Agency: State • Tel: 660-646-6122 • Location: 3 miles S of Bucklin (limited services), 6 miles NE of Marceline • GPS: Lat 39.748322 Lon -92.884472 • Open: All year • Total sites: Dispersed • RV sites: Undefined • RV fee: Free • No water • No toilets • Activities: Hiking, fishing, hunting, non-power boating • Elevation: 830

Mussel Fork CA Lot 2 - MDC • Agency: State • Tel: 660-646-6122 • Location: 3 miles SE of Bucklin (limited services), 6 miles NE of Marceline • GPS: Lat 39.758569 Lon -92.860529 • Open: All year • Total sites: Dispersed • RV sites: Undefined • RV fee: Free • No water • No toilets • Activities: Hiking, fishing, hunting, non-power boating • Elevation: 768

Mussel Fork CA Lot 3 - MDC • Agency: State • Tel: 660-646-6122 • Location: 4 miles SE of Bucklin (limited services), 7 miles NE of Marceline • GPS: Lat 39.748187 Lon -92.870029 • Open: All year • Total sites: Dispersed • RV sites: Undefined • RV fee: Free • No water • No toilets • Activities: Hiking, fishing, hunting, non-power boating • Elevation: 863

Mussel Fork CA Lot 4 - MDC • Agency: State • Tel: 660-646-6122 • Location: 4 miles SE of Bucklin (limited services), 7 miles NE of Marceline • GPS: Lat 39.747042 Lon -92.864569 • Open: All year • Total sites: Dispersed • RV sites: Undefined • RV fee: Free • No water • No toilets • Activities: Hiking, fishing, hunting, non-power boating • Elevation: 827

Mussel Fork CA Lot 5 - MDC • Agency: State • Tel: 660-646-6122 • Location: 4 miles SE of Bucklin (limited services), 7 miles NE of Marceline • GPS: Lat 39.740447 Lon -92.873027 • Open: All year • Total sites: Dispersed • RV sites: Undefined • RV fee: Free • No water • No toilets • Activities: Hiking, fishing, hunting, non-power boating • Elevation: 853

Bunker

Little Scotia Pond (Mark Twain NF) • Agency: US Forest Service • Location: 10 miles NW of Bunker (limited services), 20 miles SE of Salem • GPS: Lat 37.529541 Lon -91.330078 • Total sites: 14 • RV sites: 14 • RV fee: Free • Central water • Vault toilets • Activities: Hiking, fishing • Elevation: 1371

Burlington Junction

Bilby Ranch Lake CA - Lot 2 - MDC • Agency: State • Tel: 816-271-3100 • Location: 12 miles SW of Burlington Junction (limited services), 18 miles W of Maryville • GPS: Lat 40.363527 Lon -95.177775 • Open: All year • Total sites: Dispersed • RV sites: Undefined • RV fee: Free • No water • No toilets • Activities: Hiking, fishing, hunting, non-power boating • Elevation: 1089

Bilby Ranch Lake CA - Lot 3 - MDC • Agency: State • Tel: 816-271-3100 • Location: 9 miles SW of Burlington Junction (limited services), 17 miles W of Maryville • GPS: Lat 40.376837 Lon -95.141284 • Open: All year • Total sites: Dispersed • RV sites: Undefined • RV fee: Free • No water • No toilets • Activities: Hiking, fishing, hunting, non-power boating • Elevation: 1060

Bilby Ranch Lake CA - Lot 4 - MDC • Agency: State • Tel: 816-271-3100 • Location: 10 miles SW of Burlington Junction (limited services), 15 miles W of Maryville • GPS: Lat 40.361708 Lon -95.126849 • Open: All year • Total sites: Dispersed • RV sites: Undefined • RV fee: Free • No water • No toilets • Activities: Hiking, fishing, hunting, non-power boating • Elevation: 1056

Caledonia

Bootleg Access - MDC • Agency: State • Tel: 636-441-4554 • Location: 3 miles N of Caledonia (limited services), 9 miles S of Potosi • GPS: Lat 37.814837 Lon -90.770853 • Open: All year • Total sites: Dispersed • RV sites: Undefined • RV fee: Free • No water • No toilets • Activities: Hiking, fishing, hunting, non-power boating • Elevation: 853

Callao

Dodd Access - MDC • Agency: State • Tel: 660-785-2420 • Location: 8 miles NW of Callao (limited services), 15 miles NW of Macon • GPS: Lat 39.835594 Lon -92.683755 • Open: All year • Total sites: Dispersed • RV sites: Undefined • RV fee: Free • No water • No toilets • Activities: Fishing, non-power boating • Elevation: 705

Campbell

Wilhelmina CA Lot 1 - MDC • Agency: State • Tel: 573-290-5730 • Location: 6 miles NW of Campbell • GPS: Lat 36.526814 Lon -90.175926 • Open: All year • Total sites: Dispersed • RV sites: Undefined • RV fee: Free • No water • No toilets • Activities: Fishing, hunting, non-power boating • Elevation: 312

Wilhelmina CA Lot 2 - MDC • Agency: State • Tel: 573-290-5730 • Location: 6 miles NW of Campbell • GPS: Lat 36.514147 Lon -90.193641 • Open: All year • Total sites: Dispersed • RV sites: Undefined • RV fee: Free • No water • No toilets • Activities: Fishing, hunting, non-power boating • Elevation: 308

Wilhelmina CA Lot 3 - MDC • Agency: State • Tel: 573-290-5730 • Location: 8 miles NW of Campbell • GPS: Lat 36.538041 Lon -90.199105 • Open: All year • Total sites: Dispersed • RV sites: Undefined • RV fee: Free • No water • No toilets • Activities: Fishing, hunting, non-power boating • Elevation: 318

Canton

Buck and Doe Run CA - MDC • Agency: State • Tel: 660-785-2420 • Location: 9 miles N of Canton • GPS: Lat 40.256623 Lon -91.529387 • Open: All year • Total sites: Dispersed • RV sites: Undefined • RV fee: Free • No water • No toilets • Activities: Hunting • Elevation: 502

Fenway Landing (Mississippi River) • Agency: Corps of Engineers • Tel: 217-228-0890 • Location: 9 miles N of Canton • GPS: Lat 40.233446 Lon -91.507224 • Open: All year • Total sites: 15 • RV sites: 15 • RV fee: Free • No water • Vault toilets • Activities: Power boating, non-power boating • Elevation: 505

Sunnyside School Access - MDC • Agency: State • Tel: 660-785-2420 • Location: 6 miles S of Canton • GPS: Lat 40.087084 Lon -91.543755 • Open: All year • Total sites: Dispersed • RV sites: Undefined • RV fee: Free • No water • No toilets • Activities: Fishing, hunting, non-power boating • Elevation: 538

Caulfield

Patrick Bridge Access - MDC • Agency: State • Tel: 417-256-7161 • Location: 9 miles NW of Caulfield (limited services), 25 miles SW of West Plains • GPS: Lat 36.643538 Lon -92.221901 • Open: All year • Total sites: Dispersed • RV sites: Undefined • RV fee: Free • No water • Vault toilets • Activities: Hiking, fishing, hunting, non-power boating • Elevation: 643

Centralia

Tri-City Community Lake - MDC • Agency: State • Tel: 573-815-7900 • Location: 4 miles SW of Centralia • GPS: Lat 39.192171 Lon -92.20551 • Open: All year • Total sites: Dispersed • RV sites: Undefined • RV fee: Free • No water • Vault toilets • Activities: Fishing, hunting • Elevation: 866

Chamois

Ben Branch Lake CA - MDC • Agency: State • Tel: 573-815-7900 • Location: 10 miles S of Chamois (limited services), 28 miles E of Jefferson City • GPS: Lat 38.570436 Lon -91.789545 • Open: All year • Total sites: Dispersed • RV sites: Undefined • RV fee: Free • No water • Vault toilets • Activities: Hiking, hunting, non-power boating • Elevation: 837

Chamois Access - MDC • Agency: State • Tel: 573-815-7900 • Location: 1 mile N of Chamois (limited services), 18 miles N of Linn • GPS: Lat 38.680751 Lon -91.773398 • Open: All year • Total sites: 4 • RV sites: 4 • RV fee: Free • Electric sites: 4 • Water at site • No toilets • Activities: Fishing, non-power boating • Elevation: 532

Chillicothe

Bunch Hollow CA - 10 - MDC • Agency: State • Tel: 660-646-6122 • Location: 14 miles S of Chillicothe • GPS: Lat 39.595355 Lon -93.585656 • Open: All year • Total sites: Dispersed • RV sites: Undefined • RV fee: Free • No water • No toilets • Activities: Hiking, fishing, hunting, equestrian area • Elevation: 958

Bunch Hollow CA - 11 - MDC • Agency: State • Tel: 660-646-6122 • Location: 14 miles S of Chillicothe • GPS: Lat 39.588322 Lon -93.571066 • Open: All year • Total sites: Dispersed • RV sites: Undefined • RV fee: Free • No water • No toilets • Activities: Hiking, fishing, hunting, equestrian area • Elevation: 876

Bunch Hollow CA - 12 - MDC • Agency: State • Tel: 660-646-6122 • Location: 14 miles S of Chillicothe • GPS: Lat 39.588136 Lon -93.557078 • Open: All year • Total sites: Dispersed • RV sites: Undefined • RV fee: Free • No water • No toilets • Activities: Hiking, fishing, hunting, equestrian area • Elevation: 899

Bunch Hollow CA - 13 - MDC • Agency: State • Tel: 660-646-6122 • Location: 13 miles S of Chillicothe • GPS: Lat 39.599119 Lon -93.561888 • Open: All year • Total sites: Dispersed • RV sites: Undefined • RV fee: Free • No water • No toilets • Activities: Hiking, fishing, hunting, equestrian area • Elevation: 932

Bunch Hollow CA - 6 - MDC • Agency: State • Tel: 660-646-6122 • Location: 16 miles S of Chillicothe • GPS: Lat 39.571363 Lon -93.589635 • Open: All year • Total sites: Dispersed • RV sites: Undefined • RV fee: Free • No water • No toilets • Activities: Hiking, fishing, hunting, equestrian area • Elevation: 965

Bunch Hollow CA - 7 - MDC • Agency: State • Tel: 660-646-6122 • Location: 16 miles S of Chillicothe • GPS: Lat 39.578376 Lon -93.589572 • Open: All year • Total sites: Dispersed • RV sites: Undefined • RV fee: Free • No water • No toilets • Activities: Hiking, fishing, hunting, equestrian area • Elevation: 974

Bunch Hollow CA - 8 - MDC • Agency: State • Tel: 660-646-6122 • Location: 15 miles S of Chillicothe • GPS: Lat 39.581092 Lon -93.585232 • Open: All year • Total sites: Dispersed • RV sites: Undefined • RV fee: Free • No water • No toilets • Activities: Hiking, fishing, hunting, equestrian area • Elevation: 961

Bunch Hollow CA - 9 - MDC • Agency: State • Tel: 660-646-6122 • Location: 15 miles S of Chillicothe • GPS: Lat 39.588314 Lon -93.580501 • Open: All year • Total sites: Dispersed • RV sites: Undefined • RV fee: Free • No water • No toilets • Activities: Hiking, fishing, hunting, equestrian area • Elevation: 951

Poosey CA #11 - MDC • Agency: State • Tel: 660-646-6122 • Location: 13 miles NW of Chillicothe • GPS: Lat 39.902098 Lon -93.689583 • Open: All year • Total sites: Dispersed • RV sites: Undefined • RV fee: Free • No water • Vault toilets • Activities: Hiking, mountain biking, fishing, hunting • Elevation: 902

Clearmont

Possum Walk Access - MDC • Agency: State • Tel: 816-271-3100 • Location: 2 miles W of Clearmont (limited services), 20 miles NW of Maryville • GPS: Lat 40.510518 Lon -95.068962 • Open: All year • Total sites: Dispersed • RV sites: Undefined • RV fee: Free • No water • No toilets • Activities: Fishing, non-power boating • Elevation: 935

Clinton

Haysler A. Poague CA Pool 1 - MDC • Agency: State • Tel: 816-862-6488 • Location: 5 miles NW of Clinton • GPS: Lat 38.423171 Lon -93.828668 • Open: All year • Total sites: Dispersed • RV sites: Undefined • RV fee: Free • No water • No toilets • Activities: Fishing, hunting • Elevation: 794

Haysler A. Poague CA Pool 10 - MDC • Agency: State • Tel: 816-862-6488 • Location: 6 miles NW of Clinton • GPS: Lat 38.409317 Lon -93.841724 • Open: All year • Total sites: Dispersed • RV sites: Undefined • RV fee: Free • No water • No toilets • Activities: Fishing, hunting • Elevation: 791

Haysler A. Poague CA Pool 11 - MDC • Agency: State • Tel: 816-862-6488 • Location: 6 miles NW of Clinton • GPS: Lat 38.411453 Lon -93.844382 • Open: All year • Total sites: Dispersed • RV sites: Undefined • RV fee: Free • No water • No toilets • Activities: Fishing, hunting • Elevation: 800

Haysler A. Poague CA Pool 13 - MDC • Agency: State • Tel: 816-862-6488 • Location: 6 miles NW of Clinton • GPS: Lat 38.417472 Lon -93.853977 • Open: All year • Total sites: Dispersed • RV sites: Undefined • RV fee: Free • No water • No toilets • Activities: Fishing, hunting • Elevation: 784

Haysler A. Poague CA Pool 14 - MDC • Agency: State • Tel: 816-862-6488 • Location: 6 miles NW of Clinton • GPS: Lat 38.421363 Lon -93.853877 • Open: All year • Total sites: Dispersed • RV sites: Undefined • RV fee: Free • No water • No toilets • Activities: Fishing, hunting • Elevation: 814

Haysler A. Poague CA Pool 5 - MDC • Agency: State • Tel: 816-862-6488 • Location: 5 miles NW of Clinton • GPS: Lat 38.415928 Lon -93.834334 • Open: All year • Total sites: Dispersed • RV sites: Undefined • RV fee: Free • No water • No toilets • Activities: Fishing, hunting • Elevation: 764

Haysler A. Poague CA Pool 7 - MDC • Agency: State • Tel: 816-862-6488 • Location: 5 miles NW of Clinton • GPS: Lat 38.412132 Lon -93.831625 • Open: All year • Total sites: Dispersed • RV sites: Undefined • RV fee: Free • No water • No toilets • Activities: Fishing, hunting • Elevation: 758

Haysler A. Poague CA Pool 8 - MDC • Agency: State • Tel: 816-862-6488 • Location: 5 miles NW of Clinton • GPS: Lat 38.414585 Lon -93.833652 • Open: All year • Total sites: Dispersed • RV sites: Undefined • RV fee: Free • No water • No toilets • Activities: Fishing, hunting • Elevation: 771

Haysler A. Poague CA Pool No # - MDC • Agency: State • Tel: 816-862-6488 • Location: 6 miles NW of Clinton • GPS: Lat 38.410071 Lon -93.832319 • Open: All year • Total sites: Dispersed • RV sites: Undefined • RV fee: Free • No water • No toilets • Activities: Fishing, hunting • Elevation: 784

College Mound

Thomas Hill Reservoir CA (Hwy T Campground) - MDC • Agency: State • Tel: 660-785-2420 • Location: 2 miles W of College Mound (limited services), 15 miles SW of Macon • GPS: Lat 39.623514 Lon -92.61693 • Open: All year • Total sites: 19 • RV sites: 19 • RV fee: Free • Flush toilets • Activities: Fishing, hunting, non-power boating • Elevation: 768

Collins

Birdsong CA Lot 1 - MDC • Agency: State • Tel: 660-885-6981 • Location: 7 miles W of Collins (limited services), 15 miles NE of Stockton • GPS: Lat 37.878477 Lon -93.718677 • Open: All year • Total sites: Dispersed • RV sites: Undefined • RV fee: Free • No water • No toilets • Activities: Fishing, hunting • Elevation: 751

Birdsong CA Lot 2 - MDC • Agency: State • Tel: 660-885-6981 • Location: 8 miles SW of Collins (limited services), 16 miles NE of Stockton • GPS: Lat 37.869713 Lon -93.709043 • Open: All year • Total sites: Dispersed • RV sites: Undefined • RV fee: Free • No water • No toilets • Activities: Fishing, hunting • Elevation: 768

Blackjack Access - MDC • Agency: State • Tel: 660-885-6981 • Location: 10 miles W of Collins (limited services), 16 miles N of Stockton • GPS: Lat 37.884764 Lon -93.743882 • Open: All year • Total sites: Dispersed • RV sites: Undefined • RV fee: Free • No water • Vault toilets • Activities: Fishing, hunting, non-power boating • Elevation: 751

Concordia

Ralph and Martha Perry Memorial CA Lot A - MDC • Agency: State • Tel: 660-530-5500 • Location: 6 miles S of Concordia • GPS: Lat 38.911956 Lon -93.54465 • Open: All year • Total sites: Dispersed • RV sites: Undefined • RV fee: Free • No water • No toilets • Activities: Hiking, fishing, hunting • Elevation: 679

Ralph and Martha Perry Memorial CA Lot C - MDC • Agency: State • Tel: 660-530-5500 • Location: 9 miles SE of Concordia • GPS: Lat 38.899761 Lon -93.506923 • Open: All year • Total sites: Dispersed • RV sites: Undefined • RV fee: Free • No water • No toilets • Activities: Hiking, fishing, hunting • Elevation: 755

Ralph and Martha Perry Memorial CA Lot D - MDC • Agency: State • Tel: 660-530-5500 • Location: 8 miles SE of Concordia • GPS: Lat 38.889245 Lon -93.533682 • Open: All year • Total sites: Dispersed • RV sites: Undefined • RV fee: Free • No water • No toilets • Activities: Hiking, fishing, hunting • Elevation: 712

Ralph and Martha Perry Memorial CA Lot E - MDC • Agency: State • Tel: 660-530-5500 • Location: 8 miles SE of Concordia • GPS: Lat 38.889282 Lon -93.538675 • Open: All year • Total sites: Dispersed • RV sites: Undefined • RV fee: Free • No water • No toilets • Activities: Hiking, fishing, hunting • Elevation: 745

Craig

H. F. Thurnau CA Lot 1 - MDC • Agency: State • Tel: 816-271-3100 • Location: 4 miles W of Craig (limited services), 17 miles NW of Mound City • GPS: Lat 40.182787 Lon -95.444219 • Open: All year • Total sites: Dispersed • RV sites: Undefined • RV fee: Free • No water • No toilets • Activities: Fishing, hunting • Elevation: 879

H. F. Thurnau CA Lot 2 - MDC • Agency: State • Tel: 816-271-3100 • Location: 5 miles W of Craig (limited services), 18 miles NW of Mound City • GPS: Lat 40.169354 Lon -95.457213 • Open: All year • Total sites: Dispersed • RV sites: Undefined • RV fee: Free • No water • No toilets • Activities: Fishing, hunting • Elevation: 912

Crocker

Schlicht Springs Access - MDC • Agency: State • Tel: 573-368-2225 • Location: 4 miles SW of Crocker (limited services), 10 miles NW of Waynesville • GPS: Lat 37.903378 Lon -92.285639 • Open: All year • Total sites: Dispersed • RV sites: Undefined • RV fee: Free • No water • Vault toilets • Activities: Fishing, non-power boating • Elevation: 810

Danville

Loutre Lick Access - MDC • Agency: State • Tel: 573-254-3990 • Location: 4 miles SW of Danville (limited services), 10 miles SW of Montgomery City • GPS: Lat 38.881222 Lon -91.580436 • Open: All year • Total sites: Dispersed • RV sites: Undefined • RV fee: Free • No wa-

ter • No toilets • Activities: Fishing, hunting, non-power boating • Elevation: 571

De Witt

McKinny CA - MDC • Agency: State • Tel: 660-646-6122 • Location: 2 miles SW of De Witt (limited services), 14 miles E of Carrollton • GPS: Lat 39.370801 Lon -93.242079 • Open: All year • Total sites: Dispersed • RV sites: Undefined • RV fee: Free • No water • No toilets • Activities: Hunting • Elevation: 679

Dearborn

Burton Bridge Access - MDC • Agency: State • Tel: 816-271-3100 • Location: 8 miles NE of Dearborn (limited services), 14 miles SE of St Joseph • GPS: Lat 39.581049 Lon -94.717561 • Open: All year • Total sites: Dispersed • RV sites: Undefined • RV fee: Free • No water • No toilets • Activities: Fishing, non-power boating • Elevation: 817

Denver

Sowards Ford Access - MDC • Agency: State • Tel: 660-646-6122 • Location: 1 mile S of Denver (limited services), 12 miles N of Albany • GPS: Lat 40.388828 Lon -94.321331 • Open: All year • Total sites: 10 • RV sites: 10 • RV fee: Free • No water • Vault toilets • Activities: Fishing, hunting • Elevation: 896

Des Arc

Graves Mountain CA - MDC • Agency: State • Tel: 573-223-4525 • Location: 9 miles E of Des Arc (limited services), 19 miles NE of Piedmont • GPS: Lat 37.296865 Lon -90.514477 • Open: All year • Total sites: Dispersed • RV sites: Undefined • RV fee: Free • No water • No toilets • Activities: Hiking, hunting • Elevation: 673

Dixon

Rinquelin Trail Lake CA - MDC • Agency: State • Tel: 573-815-7900 • Location: 9 miles NW of Dixon • GPS: Lat 38.085833 Lon -92.152157 • Open: All year • Total sites: Dispersed • RV sites: Undefined • RV fee: Free • No water • Vault toilets • Activities: Fishing, hunting • Elevation: 1017

Doniphan

Fourche Creek CA - MDC • Agency: State • Tel: 573-226-3616 • Location: 19 miles SW of Doniphan • GPS: Lat 36.505555 Lon -91.037662 • Open: All year • Total sites: Dispersed • RV sites: Undefined • RV fee: Free • No water • No toilets • Activities: Hunting • Elevation: 620

Fourche Lake RA (Mark Twain NF) • Agency: US Forest Service • Location: 7 miles SW of Doniphan • GPS: Lat 36.599501 Lon -90.930136 • Total sites: 6 • RV sites: 6 • RV fee: Free • Central water • Vault toilets • Activities: Fishing, non-power boating • Elevation: 568

Little Black CA - MDC • Agency: State • Tel: 573-226-3616 • Location: 11 miles N of Doniphan • GPS: Lat 36.763558 Lon -90.803942 • Open: All year • Total sites: Dispersed • RV sites: Undefined • RV fee: Free • No water • No toilets • Activities: Hiking, fishing, hunting • Elevation: 659

Mudpuppy CA - MDC • Agency: State • Tel: 573-226-3616 • Location: 13 miles NE of Doniphan • GPS: Lat 36.715514 Lon -90.716136 • Open: All year • Total sites: Dispersed • RV sites: Undefined • RV fee: Free • No water • No toilets • Activities: Fishing, hunting, non-power boating • Elevation: 371

Dora

Blair Bridge Access - MDC • Agency: State • Tel: 417-256-7161 • Location: 10 miles S of Dora (limited services), 23 miles W of West Plains • GPS: Lat 36.654427 Lon -92.229522 • Open: All year • Total sites: Dispersed • RV sites: Undefined • RV fee: Free • No toilets • Activities: Fishing, non-power boating • Elevation: 676

Hebron Access - MDC • Agency: State • Tel: 417-256-7161 • Location: 7 miles N of Dora (limited services), 20 miles SW of Willow Springs • GPS: Lat 36.850905 Lon -92.186674 • Open: All year • Total sites: 5 • RV sites: 5 • RV fee: Free • No water • No toilets • Activities: Fishing, non-power boating • Elevation: 778

Dudley

Oak Ridge CA - MDC • Agency: State • Tel: 573-290-5730 • Location: 1 mile W of Dudley (limited services), 7 miles W of Dexter • GPS: Lat 36.790307 Lon -90.107172 • Open: All year • Total sites: Dispersed • RV sites: Undefined • RV fee: Free • No water • No toilets • Activities: Hunting • Elevation: 331

Otter Slough CA Cul-de-Sac - MDC • Agency: State • Tel: 573-290-5730 • Location: 9 miles SW of Dudley (limited services), 17 miles SW of Dexter • GPS: Lat 36.699408 Lon -90.143595 • Open: All year • Total sites: Dispersed • RV sites: Undefined • RV fee: Free • No water • No toilets • Activities: Hiking, fishing, hunting • Elevation: 318

Otter Slough CA Pool 14 - MDC • Agency: State • Tel: 573-290-5730 • Location: 7 miles S of Dudley (limited services), 12 miles SW of Dexter • GPS: Lat 36.713228 Lon -90.101331 • Open: All year • Total sites: Dispersed • RV sites: Undefined • RV fee: Free • No water • No toilets • Activities: Hiking, fishing, hunting • Elevation: 312

Otter Slough CA St Francis Bridge - MDC • Agency: State • Tel: 573-290-5730 • Location: 9 miles SW of Dudley (limited services), 17 miles SW of Dexter • GPS: Lat 36.694386 Lon -90.139363 • Open: All year • Total sites: Dispersed • RV sites: Undefined • RV fee: Free • No water • No toilets • Activities: Hiking, fishing, hunting • Elevation: 312

East Prairie

Dorena Access - MDC • Agency: State • Tel: 573-290-5730 • Location: 18 miles SE of East Prairie • GPS: Lat 36.614968 Lon -89.20761 • Open: All year • Total sites: Dispersed • RV sites: Undefined • RV fee: Free • No water • No toilets • Activities: Fishing • Elevation: 285

Edgar Springs

Richard F. Clement Memorial Forest - MDC • Agency: State • Tel: 573-729-3182 • Location: 7 miles NE of Edgar Springs (limited services), 18 miles S of Rolla • GPS: Lat 37.749451 Lon -91.774333 • Open: All year • Total sites: Dispersed • RV sites: Undefined • RV fee: Free • No water • No toilets • Activities: Hiking, hunting • Elevation: 1165

El Dorado Springs

Taberville Access - MDC • Agency: State • Tel: 417-876-5226 • Location: 9 miles N of El Dorado Springs • GPS: Lat 38.003345 Lon -93.995294 • Open: All year • Total sites: Dispersed • RV sites: Undefined • RV fee: Free • No water • No toilets • Activities: Fishing, non-power boating • Elevation: 722

Elmer

Hidden Hollow CA - East Lot - MDC • Agency: State • Tel: 660-785-2420 • Location: 3 miles N of Elmer (limited services), 17 miles SW of Kirksville • GPS: Lat 39.992214 Lon -92.637768 • Open: All year • Total sites: Dispersed • RV sites: Undefined • RV fee: Free • No water • No toilets • Activities: Hunting • Elevation: 902

Hidden Hollow CA - MDC • Agency: State • Tel: 660-785-2420 • Location: 2 miles N of Elmer (limited services), 20 miles SW of Kirksville • GPS: Lat 39.981384 Lon -92.645899 • Open: All year • Total sites: Dispersed • RV sites: Undefined • RV fee: Free • No water • No toilets • Activities: Hunting • Elevation: 869

Hidden Hollow CA - North Lot - MDC • Agency: State • Tel: 660-785-2420 • Location: 4 miles N of Elmer (limited services), 17 miles SW of Kirksville • GPS: Lat 39.998633 Lon -92.638449 • Open: All year • Total sites: Dispersed • RV sites: Undefined • RV fee: Free • No water • No toilets • Activities: Hunting • Elevation: 902

Elsberry

Hamburg Ferry Access - MDC • Agency: State • Tel: 573-248-2530 • Location: 6 miles NE of Elsberry • GPS: Lat 39.228955 Lon -90.724583 • Open: All year • Total sites: Dispersed • RV sites: Undefined • RV fee: Free • No water • Vault toilets • Activities: Fishing, non-power boating • Elevation: 456

Eminence

Angeline CA - Pigeon Hollow - MDC • Agency: State • Tel: 573-226-3616 • Location: 3 miles N of Eminence • GPS: Lat 37.181911 Lon -91.347701 • Open: All year • Total sites: Dispersed • RV sites: Undefined • RV fee: Free • No water • No toilets • Activities: Hiking, fishing, hunting, non-power boating, equestrian area • Elevation: 906

Rocky Creek CA - MDC • Agency: State • Tel: 573-226-3616 • Location: 14 miles E of Eminence • GPS: Lat 37.165837 Lon -91.169279 • Open: All year • Total sites: Dispersed • RV sites: Undefined • RV fee: Free • No water • No toilets • Activities: Hiking, fishing, hunting • Elevation: 571

Sunklands CA East Lot - MDC • Agency: State • Tel: 573-226-3616 • Location: 13 miles N of Eminence • GPS: Lat 37.284182 Lon -91.421111 • Open: All year • Total sites: Dispersed • RV sites: Undefined • RV fee: Free • No water • No toilets • Activities: Hiking, fishing, hunting • Elevation: 1079

Sunklands CA South Lot - MDC • Agency: State • Tel: 573-226-3616 • Location: 16 miles NW of Eminence • GPS: Lat 37.270991 Lon -91.470934 • Open: All year • Total sites: Dispersed • RV sites: Undefined • RV fee: Free • No water • No toilets • Activities: Hiking, fishing, hunting • Elevation: 1079

Ewing

Tolona Access - MDC • Agency: State • Tel: 660-785-2420 • Location: 5 miles N of Ewing (limited services), 7 miles SE of Lewiston • GPS: Lat 40.055367 Lon -91.730679 • Open: All year • Total sites: Dispersed • RV sites: Undefined • RV fee: Free • No water • No toilets • Activities: Fishing, hunting, non-power boating • Elevation: 577

Fairfax

Bilby Ranch Lake CA - CG - MDC • Agency: State • Tel: 816-271-3100 • Location: 11 miles E of Fairfax (limited services), 15 miles W of Maryville • GPS: Lat 40.334594 Lon -95.176127 • Open: All year • Total sites: Dispersed • RV sites: Undefined • RV fee: Free • No water • Vault toi-

lets • Activities: Hiking, fishing, hunting, non-power boating • Elevation: 1129

Bilby Ranch Lake CA - Lot 1 - MDC • Agency: State • Tel: 816-271-3100 • Location: 11 miles E of Fairfax (limited services), 16 miles W of Maryville • GPS: Lat 40.339448 Lon -95.178314 • Open: All year • Total sites: Dispersed • RV sites: Undefined • RV fee: Free • No water • No toilets • Activities: Hiking, fishing, hunting, non-power boating • Elevation: 1145

Farrar

Red Rock Landing CA - MDC • Agency: State • Tel: 573-290-5730 • Location: 5 miles NE of Farrar (limited services), 13 miles E of Perryville • GPS: Lat 37.745496 Lon -89.660153 • Total sites: 3 • RV sites: 3 • RV fee: Free • No water • No toilets • Activities: Hiking, swimming, hunting • Elevation: 328

Fayette

Moniteau Creek CA #1 - MDC • Agency: State • Tel: 573-815-7900 • Location: 8 miles SE of Fayette • GPS: Lat 39.104883 Lon -92.57614 • Open: All year • Total sites: Dispersed • RV sites: Undefined • RV fee: Free • No water • No toilets • Activities: Fishing, hunting • Elevation: 620

Moniteau Creek CA #2 - MDC • Agency: State • Tel: 573-815-7900 • Location: 9 miles SE of Fayette • GPS: Lat 39.102006 Lon -92.570217 • Open: All year • Total sites: Dispersed • RV sites: Undefined • RV fee: Free • No water • No toilets • Activities: Fishing, hunting • Elevation: 682

Moniteau Creek CA #3 - MDC • Agency: State • Tel: 573-815-7900 • Location: 7 miles SE of Fayette • GPS: Lat 39.086217 Lon -92.602791 • Open: All year • Total sites: Dispersed • RV sites: Undefined • RV fee: Free • No water • No toilets • Activities: Fishing, hunting • Elevation: 630

Forest City

Bob Brown CA - MDC • Agency: State • Tel: 816-271-3100 • Location: 4 miles W of Forest City (limited services), 15 miles S of Mound City • GPS: Lat 39.978449 Lon -95.247997 • Open: All year • Total sites: Dispersed • RV sites: Undefined • RV fee: Free • No water • Vault toilets • Activities: Hiking, fishing, hunting • Elevation: 846

Frankford

Ranacker CA - Lot 1 - MDC • Agency: State • Tel: 573-248-2530 • Location: 3 miles SE of Frankford (limited services), 10 miles NW of Bowling Green • GPS: Lat

39.459054 Lon -91.289554 • Open: All year • Total sites: Dispersed • RV sites: Undefined • RV fee: Free • No water • Vault toilets • Activities: Fishing, hunting • Elevation: 663

Ranacker CA - Lot 2 - MDC • Agency: State • Tel: 573-248-2530 • Location: 4 miles SE of Frankford (limited services), 11 miles NW of Bowling Green • GPS: Lat 39.455773 Lon -91.296208 • Open: All year • Total sites: Dispersed • RV sites: Undefined • RV fee: Free • No water • No toilets • Activities: Fishing, hunting • Elevation: 692

Ranacker CA - Lot 3 - MDC • Agency: State • Tel: 573-248-2530 • Location: 4 miles SE of Frankford (limited services), 11 miles NW of Bowling Green • GPS: Lat 39.454484 Lon -91.300969 • Open: All year • Total sites: Dispersed • RV sites: Undefined • RV fee: Free • No water • Vault toilets • Activities: Fishing, hunting • Elevation: 630

Fredericktown

Amidon Memorial CA - MDC • Agency: State • Tel: 573-290-5730 • Location: 10 miles E of Fredericktown • GPS: Lat 37.544853 Lon -90.150925 • Open: All year • Total sites: Dispersed • RV sites: Undefined • RV fee: Free • No water • No toilets • Activities: Hiking, fishing, hunting • Elevation: 732

Frohna

Seventy-Six Conservation Area - MDC • Agency: State • Tel: 573-290-5730 • Location: 8 miles N of Frohna (limited services), 20 miles E of Perryville • GPS: Lat 37.719061 Lon -89.613289 • Open: All year • Total sites: Dispersed • RV sites: Undefined • RV fee: Free • No water • No toilets • Activities: Fishing, hunting • Elevation: 371

Fulton

Dry Fork (Mark Twain NF) • Agency: US Forest Service • Tel: 573-364-4621 • Location: 10 miles SW of Fulton • GPS: Lat 38.783924 Lon -92.125471 • Open: Apr-Nov • Total sites: 8 • RV sites: 8 • Max RV Length: 30 • RV fee: Free (donation appreciated) • Central water • Vault toilets • Activities: Hiking • Elevation: 781

Gainesville

Caney Mountain CA Camp 1 - MDC • Agency: State • Tel: 417-256-7161 • Location: 8 miles NE of Gainesville (limited services), 36 miles SW of West Plains • GPS: Lat 36.677177 Lon -92.394173 • Open: All year • Total sites: Dispersed • RV sites: Undefined • RV fee: Free • No wa-

ter • Vault toilets • Activities: Hiking, mountain biking, hunting • Elevation: 892

Caney Mountain CA Camp 2 - MDC • Agency: State • Tel: 417-256-7161 • Location: 5 miles N of Gainesville (limited services), 31 miles SE of Ava • GPS: Lat 36.666471 Lon -92.425899 • Open: All year • Total sites: Dispersed • RV sites: Undefined • RV fee: Free • No water • Vault toilets • Activities: Hiking, mountain biking, hunting • Elevation: 1007

Caney Mountain CA Camp 3 - MDC • Agency: State • Tel: 417-256-7161 • Location: 13 miles N of Gainesville (limited services), 22 miles SE of Ava • GPS: Lat 36.715586 Lon -92.468065 • Open: All year • Total sites: Dispersed • RV sites: Undefined • RV fee: Free • No water • No toilets • Activities: Hiking, mountain biking, hunting • Elevation: 1168

Gallatin

Gallatin CA - MDC • Agency: State • Tel: 660-646-6122 • Location: 7 miles SE of Gallatin • GPS: Lat 39.843029 Lon -93.919658 • Open: All year • Total sites: Dispersed • RV sites: Undefined • RV fee: Free • No water • No toilets • Activities: Hiking, hunting • Elevation: 873

Holmes Bend Access - MDC • Agency: State • Tel: 660-646-6122 • Location: 3 miles SE of Gallatin • GPS: Lat 39.892764 Lon -93.931851 • Open: All year • Total sites: Dispersed • RV sites: Undefined • RV fee: Free • No water • No toilets • Activities: Fishing, hunting, non-power boating • Elevation: 843

Green City

Dark Hollow Natural Area - MDC • Agency: State • Tel: 660-785-2420 • Location: 4 miles N of Green City (limited services), 14 miles NE of Milan • GPS: Lat 40.320777 Lon -92.937959 • Total sites: Dispersed • RV sites: Undefined (camp in/near parking lot) • RV fee: Free • No water • No toilets • Activities: Hunting • Elevation: 1039

Union Ridge CA - Lot A - MDC • Agency: State • Tel: 660-785-2420 • Location: 10 miles NE of Green City (limited services), 20 miles NE of Milan • GPS: Lat 40.347894 Lon -92.886227 • Open: All year • Total sites: Dispersed • RV sites: Undefined • RV fee: Free • No water • No toilets • Activities: Hiking, fishing, hunting • Elevation: 1040

Union Ridge CA - Lot R - MDC • Agency: State • Tel: 660-785-2420 • Location: 4 miles NE of Green City (limited services), 14 miles NE of Milan • GPS: Lat 40.311562 Lon -92.912643 • Open: All year • Total sites: Dispersed • RV sites: Undefined • RV fee: Free • No water • No toilets • Activities: Hiking, fishing, hunting • Elevation: 1004

Greencastle

Union Ridge CA - Lot B - MDC • Agency: State • Tel: 660-785-2420 • Location: 9 miles N of Greencastle (limited services), 21 miles NW of Kirksville • GPS: Lat 40.343337 Lon -92.856592 • Open: All year • Total sites: Dispersed • RV sites: Undefined • RV fee: Free • No water • No toilets • Activities: Hiking, fishing, hunting • Elevation: 1030

Union Ridge CA - Lot C - MDC • Agency: State • Tel: 660-785-2420 • Location: 8 miles N of Greencastle (limited services), 20 miles NW of Kirksville • GPS: Lat 40.335953 Lon -92.850009 • Open: All year • Total sites: Dispersed • RV sites: Undefined • RV fee: Free • No water • No toilets • Activities: Hiking, fishing, hunting • Elevation: 1037

Union Ridge CA - Lot D - MDC • Agency: State • Tel: 660-785-2420 • Location: 7 miles NE of Greencastle (limited services), 19 miles NW of Kirksville • GPS: Lat 40.330995 Lon -92.840195 • Open: All year • Total sites: Dispersed • RV sites: Undefined • RV fee: Free • No water • No toilets • Activities: Hiking, fishing, hunting • Elevation: 1024

Union Ridge CA - Lot E - MDC • Agency: State • Tel: 660-785-2420 • Location: 5 miles NE of Greencastle (limited services), 20 miles NW of Kirksville • GPS: Lat 40.321559 Lon -92.850929 • Open: All year • Total sites: Dispersed • RV sites: Undefined • RV fee: Free • No water • No toilets • Activities: Hiking, fishing, hunting • Elevation: 942

Union Ridge CA - Lot F - MDC • Agency: State • Tel: 660-785-2420 • Location: 3 miles NE of Greencastle (limited services), 20 miles NW of Kirksville • GPS: Lat 40.285821 Lon -92.849017 • Open: All year • Total sites: Dispersed • RV sites: Undefined • RV fee: Free • No water • No toilets • Activities: Hiking, fishing, hunting • Elevation: 997

Union Ridge CA - Lot G - MDC • Agency: State • Tel: 660-785-2420 • Location: 4 miles NE of Greencastle (limited services), 16 miles NW of Kirksville • GPS: Lat 40.291412 Lon -92.831062 • Open: All year • Total sites: Dispersed • RV sites: Undefined • RV fee: Free • No water • No toilets • Activities: Hiking, fishing, hunting • Elevation: 951

Greencastle

Union Ridge CA - Lot H - MDC • Agency: State • Tel: 660-785-2420 • Location: 5 miles NE of Greencastle (limited services), 16 miles NW of Kirksville • GPS: Lat 40.283852 Lon -92.826181 • Open: All year • Total sites: Dispersed • RV sites: Undefined • RV fee: Free • No water • No toilets • Activities: Hiking, fishing, hunting • Elevation: 846

Union Ridge CA - Lot J - MDC • Agency: State • Tel: 660-785-2420 • Location: 3 miles N of Greencastle (limited services), 20 miles NW of Kirksville • GPS: Lat 40.298049 Lon -92.871742 • Open: All year • Total sites: Dispersed • RV sites: Undefined • RV fee: Free • No water • No toilets • Activities: Hiking, fishing, hunting • Elevation: 1001

Union Ridge CA - Lot K - MDC • Agency: State • Tel: 660-785-2420 • Location: 3 miles N of Greencastle (limited services), 20 miles NW of Kirksville • GPS: Lat 40.304644 Lon -92.866673 • Open: All year • Total sites: Dispersed • RV sites: Undefined • RV fee: Free • No water • No toilets • Activities: Hiking, fishing, hunting • Elevation: 958

Union Ridge CA - Lot L - MDC • Agency: State • Tel: 660-785-2420 • Location: 4 miles N of Greencastle (limited services), 21 miles NW of Kirksville • GPS: Lat 40.316949 Lon -92.865036 • Open: All year • Total sites: Dispersed • RV sites: Undefined • RV fee: Free • No water • No toilets • Activities: Hiking, fishing, hunting • Elevation: 853

Union Ridge CA - Lot M - MDC • Agency: State • Tel: 660-785-2420 • Location: 6 miles NE of Greencastle (limited services), 20 miles NW of Kirksville • GPS: Lat 40.314278 Lon -92.843568 • Open: All year • Total sites: Dispersed • RV sites: Undefined • RV fee: Free • No water • No toilets • Activities: Hiking, fishing, hunting • Elevation: 873

Union Ridge CA - Lot N - MDC • Agency: State • Tel: 660-785-2420 • Location: 5 miles N of Greencastle (limited services), 20 miles NW of Kirksville • GPS: Lat 40.321343 Lon -92.863053 • Open: All year • Total sites: Dispersed • RV sites: Undefined • RV fee: Free • No water • No toilets • Activities: Hiking, fishing, hunting • Elevation: 863

Union Ridge CA - Lot P - MDC • Agency: State • Tel: 660-785-2420 • Location: 2 miles N of Greencastle (limited services), 19 miles NW of Kirksville • GPS: Lat 40.287011 Lon -92.881087 • Open: All year • Total sites: Dispersed • RV sites: Undefined • RV fee: Free • No water • No toilets • Activities: Hiking, fishing, hunting • Elevation: 1050

Greencastle

Union Ridge CA - Lot S - MDC • Agency: State • Tel: 660-785-2420 • Location: 4 miles NW of Greencastle (limited services), 18 miles NE of Milan • GPS: Lat 40.311388 Lon -92.898307 • Open: All year • Total sites: Dispersed • RV sites: Undefined • RV fee: Free • No water • No toilets • Activities: Hiking, fishing, hunting • Elevation: 1014

Union Ridge CA - Lot T - MDC • Agency: State • Tel: 660-785-2420 • Location: 4 miles NW of Greencastle (limited services), 17 miles NE of Milan • GPS: Lat 40.303897 Lon -92.897169 • Open: All year • Total sites: Dispersed • RV sites: Undefined • RV fee: Free • No water • No toilets • Activities: Hiking, fishing, hunting • Elevation: 1010

Union Ridge CA - Lot U - MDC • Agency: State • Tel: 660-785-2420 • Location: 5 miles NW of Greencastle (limited services), 19 miles NE of Milan • GPS: Lat 40.313867 Lon -92.893357 • Open: All year • Total sites: Dispersed • RV sites: Undefined • RV fee: Free • No water • No toilets • Activities: Hiking, fishing, hunting • Elevation: 961

Greentop

Mullanix Ford Access - MDC • Agency: State • Tel: 660-785-2424 • Location: 7 miles W of Greentop (limited services), 16 miles NW of Kirksville • GPS: Lat 40.342205 Lon -92.684063 • Open: All year • Total sites: Dispersed • RV sites: Undefined • RV fee: Free • No water • No toilets • Activities: Fishing, non-power boating • Elevation: 787

Greenville

Blue Springs (Wappapello Lake) • Agency: Corps of Engineers • Tel: 573-222-8562 • Location: 8 miles S of Greenville (limited services), 28 miles SE of Piedmont • GPS: Lat 37.028829 Lon -90.416247 • Open: All year • Total sites: 2 • RV sites: 2 • RV fee: Free • No water • No toilets • Activities: Power boating, non-power boating • Elevation: 387

Coldwater CA Lot 1 - MDC • Agency: State • Tel: 573-223-4525 • Location: 12 miles N of Greenville (limited services), 22 miles NE of Piedmont • GPS: Lat 37.276454 Lon -90.420773 • Open: All year • Total sites: Dispersed • RV sites: Undefined • RV fee: Free • No water • No toilets • Activities: Hiking, hunting • Elevation: 735

Coldwater CA Lot 2 - MDC • Agency: State • Tel: 573-223-4525 • Location: 20 miles NE of Greenville (limited services), 28 miles NE of Piedmont • GPS: Lat 37.288742 Lon -90.324004 • Open: All year • Total sites: Dispersed • RV sites: Undefined • RV fee: Free • No water • No toilets • Activities: Hiking, hunting • Elevation: 833

Coldwater CA Lot 5 - MDC • Agency: State • Tel: 573-223-4525 • Location: 14 miles NE of Greenville (limited services), 21 miles SW of Marble Hill • GPS: Lat 37.221997 Lon -90.306043 • Open: All year • Total sites: Dispersed • RV sites: Undefined • RV fee: Free • No water • No toilets • Activities: Hiking, hunting • Elevation: 732

Lost Creek Landing (Wappapello Lake) • Agency: Corps of Engineers • Tel: 573-222-8562 • Location: 14 miles SE of Greenville (limited services), • GPS: Lat 37.017312 Lon -90.299396 • Open: All year • Total sites: 3 • RV sites: 3 (in parking lot) • RV fee: Free • No water • No toilets • Activities: Power boating, non-power boating • Elevation: 364

Sulphur Springs (Wappapello Lake) • Agency: Corps of Engineers • Tel: 573-222-8562 • Location: 6 miles S of Greenville (limited services), 26 miles SE of Piedmont • GPS: Lat 37.069825 Lon -90.426586 • Open: All year • Total sites: 4 • RV sites: 4 • RV fee: Free • No water • Vault toilets • Activities: Power boating, non-power boating • Elevation: 486

Grovespring

John Alva Fuson, MD CA Lowell - MDC • Agency: State • Tel: 417-256-7161 • Location: 5 miles NW of Grovespring (limited services), 17 miles S of Lebanon • GPS: Lat 37.451435 Lon -92.620434 • Open: All year • Total sites: Dispersed • RV sites: Undefined • RV fee: Free • No water • No toilets • Activities: Hiking, hunting • Elevation: 1237

John Alva Fuson, MD CA Smittle - MDC • Agency: State • Tel: 417-256-7161 • Location: 6 miles NW of Grovespring (limited services), 17 miles S of Lebanon • GPS: Lat 37.457202 Lon -92.626374 • Open: All year • Total sites: Dispersed • RV sites: Undefined • RV fee: Free • No water • No toilets • Activities: Hiking, hunting • Elevation: 1191

Hale

Little Compton Lake CA 1 - MDC • Agency: State • Tel: 660-646-6122 • Location: 7 miles SE of Hale (limited services), 27 miles SW of Brookfield • GPS: Lat 39.544319 Lon -93.281161 • Open: All year • Total sites: Dispersed • RV sites: Undefined • RV fee: Free • No water • Vault toilets • Activities: Fishing, hunting, non-power boating • Elevation: 669

Little Compton Lake CA 2 - MDC • Agency: State • Tel: 660-646-6122 • Location: 7 miles SE of Hale (limited services), 27 miles SW of Brookfield • GPS: Lat 39.545708 Lon -93.282532 • Open: All year • Total sites: Dispersed • RV sites: Undefined • RV fee: Free • No water • No toilets • Activities: Fishing, hunting, non-power boating • Elevation: 671

Little Compton Lake CA 3-4 - MDC • Agency: State • Tel: 660-646-6122 • Location: 7 miles SE of Hale (limited services), 27 miles SW of Brookfield • GPS: Lat 39.541388 Lon -93.279762 • Open: All year • Total sites: Dispersed • RV sites: Undefined • RV fee: Free • No water • No toilets • Notes: Another spot 400' south at end of road • Activities: Fishing, hunting, non-power boating • Elevation: 674

Hannibal

Edward Anderson CA - MDC • Agency: State • Tel: 573-248-2530 • Location: 13 miles SE of Hannibal • GPS: Lat 39.593871 Lon -91.210316 • Open: All year • Total sites: Dispersed • RV sites: Undefined • RV fee: Free • No water • No toilets • Activities: Fishing, hunting • Elevation: 663

Hardin

Hardin CA - MDC • Agency: State • Tel: 660-646-6122 • Location: 1 mile S of Hardin (limited services), 9 miles SE of Richmond • GPS: Lat 39.254193 Lon -93.834097 • Open: All year • Total sites: Dispersed • RV sites: Undefined • RV fee: Free • No water • No toilets • Activities: Fishing, hunting • Elevation: 689

Harrisburg

Lick Creek CA - MDC • Agency: State • Tel: 573-815-7900 • Location: 7 miles E of Harrisburg (limited services), 16 miles N of Columbia • GPS: Lat 39.150019 Lon -92.384991 • Open: All year • Total sites: Dispersed • RV sites: Undefined • RV fee: Free • No water • No toilets • Activities: Hiking, fishing, hunting, non-power boating • Elevation: 768

Hartville

Buzzard Bluff Access - MDC • Agency: State • Tel: 417-256-7161 • Location: 10 miles NE of Hartville • GPS: Lat 37.330952 Lon -92.389869 • Open: All year • Total sites: Dispersed • RV sites: Undefined • RV fee: Free • No water • No toilets • Activities: Fishing, hunting, non-power boating • Elevation: 1116

Hermann

Daniel Boone CA Camp 1 - MDC • Agency: State • Tel: 636-441-4554 • Location: 9 miles NE of Hermann • GPS: Lat 38.786958 Lon -91.372391 • Open: All year • Total sites: Dispersed • RV sites: Undefined • RV fee: Free • No water • No toilets • Activities: Hiking, mountain biking, fishing, hunting, equestrian area • Elevation: 889

Daniel Boone CA Camp 10 - MDC • Agency: State • Tel: 636-441-4554 • Location: 7 miles NE of Hermann • GPS: Lat 38.764242 Lon -91.393405 • Open: All year • Total sites: Dispersed • RV sites: Undefined • RV fee: Free • No water • No toilets • Activities: Hiking, mountain biking, fishing, hunting, equestrian area • Elevation: 915

Daniel Boone CA Camp 2 - MDC • Agency: State • Tel: 636-441-4554 • Location: 9 miles NE of Hermann • GPS: Lat 38.785832 Lon -91.375295 • Open: All year • Total sites: Dispersed • RV sites: Undefined • RV fee: Free • No water • No toilets • Activities: Hiking, mountain biking, fishing, hunting, equestrian area • Elevation: 873

Daniel Boone CA Camp 3 - MDC • Agency: State • Tel: 636-441-4554 • Location: 9 miles NE of Hermann • GPS: Lat 38.782268 Lon -91.381084 • Open: All year • Total sites: Dispersed • RV sites: Undefined • RV fee: Free • No water • No toilets • Activities: Hiking, mountain biking, fishing, hunting, equestrian area • Elevation: 899

Daniel Boone CA Camp 5 - MDC • Agency: State • Tel: 636-441-4554 • Location: 8 miles NE of Hermann • GPS: Lat 38.778615 Lon -91.392765 • Open: All year • Total sites: Dispersed • RV sites: Undefined • RV fee: Free • No water • No toilets • Activities: Hiking, mountain biking, fishing, hunting, equestrian area • Elevation: 928

Daniel Boone CA Camp 6 - MDC • Agency: State • Tel: 636-441-4554 • Location: 8 miles NE of Hermann • GPS: Lat 38.772405 Lon -91.400526 • Open: All year • Total sites: Dispersed • RV sites: Undefined • RV fee: Free • No water • No toilets • Activities: Hiking, mountain biking, fishing, hunting, equestrian area • Elevation: 925

Daniel Boone CA Camp 7 - MDC • Agency: State • Tel: 636-441-4554 • Location: 8 miles NE of Hermann • GPS: Lat 38.771941 Lon -91.405108 • Open: All year • Total sites: 14 • RV sites: 14 • RV fee: Free • No water • No toilets • Activities: Hiking, mountain biking, fishing, hunting, equestrian area • Elevation: 922

Daniel Boone CA Camp 9 - MDC • Agency: State • Tel: 636-441-4554 • Location: 7 miles NE of Hermann • GPS: Lat 38.767192 Lon -91.392005 • Open: All year • Total sites: Dispersed • RV sites: Undefined • RV fee: Free • No water • No toilets • Activities: Hiking, mountain biking, fishing, hunting, equestrian area • Elevation: 876

Hermitage

Cross Timbers Access - MDC • Agency: State • Tel: 417-532-7612 • Location: 5 miles N of Hermitage (limited services), 24 miles S of Warsaw • GPS: Lat 37.981979 Lon -93.312645 • Open: All year • Total sites: Dispersed • RV sites: Undefined • RV fee: Free • No water • Vault toilets • Activities: Fishing, hunting, non-power boating • Elevation: 745

Higbee

Rudolf Bennitt CA - Sites 1-5 - MDC • Agency: State • Tel: 573-815-7900 • Location: 8 miles SE of Higbee (limited services), 12 miles S of Moberly • GPS: Lat 39.264297 Lon -92.439575 • Open: All year • Total sites: Dispersed • RV sites: Undefined • RV fee: Free • No water • No toilets • Activities: Hiking, mountain biking, fishing, power boating, hunting, non-power boating, equestrian area • Elevation: 873

Rudolf Bennitt CA - Sites 17-18 - MDC • Agency: State • Tel: 573-815-7900 • Location: 6 miles SE of Higbee (limited services), 14 miles S of Moberly • GPS: Lat 39.260532 Lon -92.460805 • Open: All year • Total sites: Dispersed • RV sites: Undefined • RV fee: Free • No water • No toilets • Activities: Hiking, mountain biking, fishing, power boating, hunting, non-power boating, equestrian area • Elevation: 896

Rudolf Bennitt CA - Sites 19-21 - MDC • Agency: State • Tel: 573-815-7900 • Location: 6 miles SE of Higbee (limited services), 15 miles S of Moberly • GPS: Lat 39.249489 Lon -92.463779 • Open: All year • Total sites: Dispersed • RV sites: Undefined • RV fee: Free • No water • No toilets • Activities: Hiking, mountain biking, fishing, power boating, hunting, non-power boating, equestrian area • Elevation: 896

Rudolf Bennitt CA - Sites 22-24 - MDC • Agency: State • Tel: 573-815-7900 • Location: 8 miles SE of Higbee (limited services), 14 miles S of Moberly • GPS: Lat 39.244946 Lon -92.444436 • Open: All year • Total sites: Dispersed • RV sites: Undefined • RV fee: Free • No water • No toilets • Activities: Hiking, mountain biking, fishing, power boating, hunting, non-power boating, equestrian area • Elevation: 882

Rudolf Bennitt CA - Sites 6-16 - MDC • Agency: State • Tel: 573-815-7900 • Location: 7 miles SE of Higbee (limited services), 14 miles S of Moberly • GPS: Lat 39.263832 Lon -92.469656 • Open: All year • Total sites: Dispersed • RV sites: Undefined • RV fee: Free • No water • No toilets • Activities: Hiking, mountain biking, fishing, power boating, hunting, non-power boating, equestrian area • Elevation: 886

Holliday

Ruby Clark Willingham WA - MDC • Agency: State • Tel: 573-248-2530 • Location: 3 miles E of Holliday (limited services), 7 miles W of Paris • GPS: Lat 39.495716 Lon -92.090796 • Open: All year • Total sites: Dispersed • RV sites: Undefined • RV fee: Free • No water • No toilets • Activities: Hunting • Elevation: 764

Hunnewell

Hunnewell Access - MDC • Agency: State • Tel: 573-983-2201 • Location: 4 miles W of Hunnewell (limited services), 11 miles W of Monroe City • GPS: Lat 39.667945 Lon -91.901864 • Open: All year • Total sites: Dispersed • RV sites: Undefined • RV fee: Free • No water • No toilets • Activities: Fishing, non-power boating • Elevation: 653

Ironton

Buford Mountain CA - MDC • Agency: State • Tel: 573-223-4525 • Location: 8 miles NW of Ironton • GPS: Lat 37.686391 Lon -90.691799 • Open: All year • Total sites: Dispersed • RV sites: Undefined • RV fee: Free • No water • No toilets • Activities: Hiking, hunting • Elevation: 1214

Ketcherside Mountain CA - MDC • Agency: State • Tel: 573-223-4525 • Location: 6 miles SW of Ironton • GPS: Lat 37.555069 Lon -90.687667 • Open: All year • Total sites: Dispersed • RV sites: Undefined • RV fee: Free • No water • Vault toilets • Activities: Hiking, hunting • Elevation: 1309

Jamesport

Poosey CA #20 - MDC • Agency: State • Tel: 660-646-6122 • Location: 9 miles SE of Jamesport (limited services), 14 miles NW of Chillicothe • GPS: Lat 39.923281 Lon -93.697505 • Open: All year • Total sites: Dispersed • RV sites: Undefined • RV fee: Free • No water • Vault toilets • Activities: Hiking, mountain biking, fishing, hunting • Elevation: 942

Poosey CA #6 - MDC • Agency: State • Tel: 660-646-6122 • Location: 9 miles SE of Jamesport (limited services), 16 miles NW of Chillicothe • GPS: Lat 39.9522 Lon -93.674618 • Open: All year • Total sites: Dispersed • RV sites: Undefined • RV fee: Free • No water • Vault toilets • Activities: Hiking, mountain biking, fishing, hunting • Elevation: 827

Jamestown

Plowboy Bend CA - MDC • Agency: State • Tel: 573-815-7900 • Location: 6 miles NE of Jamestown (limited services), 26 miles NW of Jefferson City • GPS: Lat 38.805148 Lon -92.410399 • Open: All year • Total sites: Dispersed • RV sites: Undefined • RV fee: Free • No water • No toilets • Activities: Fishing, power boating, hunting, non-power boating • Elevation: 568

Plowboy Bend CA - Riverbottom Road - MDC • Agency: State • Tel: 573-815-7900 • Location: 6 miles NE of Jamestown (limited services), 26 miles NW of Jefferson City • GPS: Lat 38.812018 Lon -92.414521 • Open: All year • Total sites: Dispersed • RV sites: Undefined • RV fee: Free • No water • No toilets • Activities: Fishing, power boating, hunting, non-power boating • Elevation: 578

Jefferson City

Honey Creek Access - MDC • Agency: State • Tel: 573-815-7900 • Location: 8 miles S of Jefferson City • GPS: Lat 38.491354 Lon -92.234912 • Open: All year • Total sites:

Dispersed • RV sites: Undefined • RV fee: Free • No water • No toilets • Activities: Fishing, hunting, non-power boating • Elevation: 597

Mari-Osa Access - MDC • Agency: State • Tel: 573-815-7900 • Location: 9 miles SE of Jefferson City • GPS: Lat 38.492264 Lon -92.010882 • Open: All year • Total sites: Dispersed • RV sites: Undefined • RV fee: Free • No water • Vault toilets • Activities: Fishing, non-power boating • Elevation: 512

Kahoka

Charlie Heath Memorial CA - North Lot - MDC • Agency: State • Tel: 660-785-2420 • Location: 19 miles NW of Kahoka • GPS: Lat 40.590623 Lon -91.873947 • Open: All year • Total sites: Dispersed • RV sites: Undefined • RV fee: Free • No water • No toilets • Activities: Hiking, mountain biking, fishing, non-power boating, equestrian area • Elevation: 686

Charlie Heath Memorial CA - Northwest Lot - MDC • Agency: State • Tel: 660-785-2420 • Location: 21 miles NW of Kahoka • GPS: Lat 40.591056 Lon -91.905868 • Open: All year • Total sites: Dispersed • RV sites: Undefined • RV fee: Free • No water • No toilets • Activities: Hiking, mountain biking, fishing, non-power boating, equestrian area • Elevation: 705

Charlie Heath Memorial CA - South Lot - MDC • Agency: State • Tel: 660-785-2420 • Location: 17 miles NW of Kahoka • GPS: Lat 40.562082 Lon -91.853565 • Open: All year • Total sites: Dispersed • RV sites: Undefined • RV fee: Free • No water • No toilets • Activities: Hiking, mountain biking, fishing, non-power boating, equestrian area • Elevation: 636

Charlie Heath Memorial CA - West Lot - MDC • Agency: State • Tel: 660-785-2420 • Location: 19 miles NW of Kahoka • GPS: Lat 40.579232 Lon -91.900032 • Open: All year • Total sites: Dispersed • RV sites: Undefined • RV fee: Free • No water • No toilets • Activities: Hiking, mountain biking, fishing, non-power boating, equestrian area • Elevation: 728

Clark CA - Nixon Tract - MDC • Agency: State • Tel: 660-785-2420 • Location: 12 miles NW of Kahoka • GPS: Lat 40.561041 Lon -91.799447 • Open: All year • Total sites: Dispersed • RV sites: Undefined • RV fee: Free • No water • No toilets • Activities: Fishing, hunting • Elevation: 718

Fox Valley Lake CA - Site 1 - MDC • Agency: State • Tel: 660-785-2420 • Location: 10 miles NW of Kahoka • GPS: Lat 40.498929 Lon -91.765483 • Open: All year • Total sites: Dispersed • RV sites: Undefined • RV fee: Free • Central water • Vault toilets • Elevation: 637

Fox Valley Lake CA - Site 2 - MDC • Agency: State • Tel: 660-785-2420 • Location: 9 miles NW of Kahoka • GPS: Lat 40.50293 Lon -91.767359 • Open: All year • Total sites: 5 • RV sites: 5 • RV fee: Free • Central water • Vault toilets • Activities: Fishing, hunting, non-power boating • Elevation: 663

Fox Valley Lake CA - Site 3 - MDC • Agency: State • Tel: 660-785-2420 • Location: 9 miles NW of Kahoka • GPS: Lat 40.503451 Lon -91.771011 • Open: All year • Total sites: Dispersed • RV sites: Undefined • RV fee: Free • Central water • Vault toilets • Elevation: 637

Fox Valley Lake CA - Site 4 - MDC • Agency: State • Tel: 660-785-2420 • Location: 9 miles NW of Kahoka • GPS: Lat 40.502393 Lon -91.775755 • Open: All year • Total sites: Dispersed • RV sites: Undefined • RV fee: Free • Central water • Vault toilets • Elevation: 644

Fox Valley Lake CA - Site 5 - MDC • Agency: State • Tel: 660-785-2420 • Location: 6 miles NW of Kahoka • GPS: Lat 40.488555 Lon -91.770581 • Open: All year • Total sites: Dispersed • RV sites: Undefined • RV fee: Free • Central water • Vault toilets • Elevation: 715

Fox Valley Lake CA - Site 6 - MDC • Agency: State • Tel: 660-785-2420 • Location: 7 miles NW of Kahoka • GPS: Lat 40.482448 Lon -91.784978 • Open: All year • Total sites: Dispersed • RV sites: Undefined • RV fee: Free • Central water • No toilets • Elevation: 707

Fox Valley Lake CA - Site 7 - MDC • Agency: State • Tel: 660-785-2420 • Location: 7 miles NW of Kahoka • GPS: Lat 40.478206 Lon -91.785328 • Open: All year • Total sites: Dispersed • RV sites: Undefined • RV fee: Free • Central water • No toilets • Elevation: 740

Fox Valley Lake CA - Site 8 - MDC • Agency: State • Tel: 660-785-2420 • Location: 6 miles NW of Kahoka • GPS: Lat 40.451366 Lon -91.823524 • Open: All year • Total sites: Dispersed • RV sites: Undefined • RV fee: Free • Central water • Vault toilets • Elevation: 715

Neeper CA - MDC • Agency: State • Tel: 660-785-2420 • Location: 8 miles S of Kahoka • GPS: Lat 40.323915 Lon -91.748292 • Open: All year • Total sites: Dispersed • RV sites: Undefined • RV fee: Free • No water • No toilets • Activities: Hunting • Elevation: 709

Keytesville

Maxwell Taylor City Park • Agency: Municipal • Tel: 660-288-3745 • Location: In Keytesville (limited services), 8 miles W of Sailbury • GPS: Lat 39.43783 Lon -92.93866 • Total sites: 3 • RV sites: 3 • RV fee: Free (donation appreciated) • Electric sites: 1 • Elevation: 709

King City

King Lake CA - Berlin Road - MDC • Agency: State • Tel: 660-646-6122 • Location: 5 miles E of King City (limited services), 16 miles SE of Stanberry • GPS: Lat 40.038823 Lon -94.441406 • Open: All year • Total sites: Dispersed • RV sites: Undefined • RV fee: Free • No water • No toilets • Activities: Fishing, hunting • Elevation: 1007

King Lake CA - King Lake - MDC • Agency: State • Tel: 660-646-6122 • Location: 10 miles SE of King City (limited services), 22 miles SE of Stanberry • GPS: Lat 40.021939 Lon -94.433418 • Open: All year • Total sites: Dispersed • RV sites: Undefined • RV fee: Free • No water • No toilets • Activities: Fishing, power boating, hunting, non-power boating • Elevation: 988

Kingdom City

Moores Mills Access - MDC • Agency: State • Tel: 573-815-7900 • Location: 11 miles SE of Kingdom City (limited services), 13 miles NE of Fulton • GPS: Lat 38.912183 Lon -91.809025 • Open: All year • Total sites: Dispersed • RV sites: Undefined • RV fee: Free • No water • No toilets • Activities: Fishing, non-power boating • Elevation: 673

Kingston

Bonanza CA - Lot 1 - MDC • Agency: State • Tel: 660-646-6122 • Location: 5 miles SE of Kingston (limited services), 12 miles S of Hamilton • GPS: Lat 39.619685 Lon -93.988766 • Open: All year • Total sites: Dispersed • RV sites: Undefined • RV fee: Free • No water • No toilets • Activities: Mountain biking, fishing, hunting, equestrian area • Elevation: 873

Bonanza CA - Lot 2 - MDC • Agency: State • Tel: 660-646-6122 • Location: 6 miles SE of Kingston (limited services), 13 miles S of Hamilton • GPS: Lat 39.619514 Lon -93.970659 • Open: All year • Total sites: Dispersed • RV sites: Undefined • RV fee: Free • No water • No toilets • Activities: Mountain biking, fishing, hunting, equestrian area • Elevation: 906

Bonanza CA - Lot 3 - MDC • Agency: State • Tel: 660-646-6122 • Location: 6 miles SE of Kingston (limited services), 13 miles S of Hamilton • GPS: Lat 39.620052 Lon -93.964451 • Open: All year • Total sites: Dispersed • RV sites: Undefined • RV fee: Free • No water • No toilets • Activities: Mountain biking, fishing, hunting, equestrian area • Elevation: 889

Bonanza CA - Lot 4 - MDC • Agency: State • Tel: 660-646-6122 • Location: 7 miles SE of Kingston (limited services), 14 miles S of Hamilton • GPS: Lat 39.612641 Lon -93.963603 • Open: All year • Total sites: Dispersed • RV sites: Undefined • RV fee: Free • No water • No toilets • Activities: Mountain biking, fishing, hunting, equestrian area • Elevation: 935

Bonanza CA - Lot 5 - MDC • Agency: State • Tel: 660-646-6122 • Location: 7 miles SE of Kingston (limited services), 14 miles S of Hamilton • GPS: Lat 39.626537 Lon -93.957412 • Open: All year • Total sites: Dispersed • RV sites: Undefined • RV fee: Free • No water • No toilets • Activities: Mountain biking, fishing, hunting, equestrian area • Elevation: 935

Bonanza CA - Lot 6 - MDC • Agency: State • Tel: 660-646-6122 • Location: 7 miles SE of Kingston (limited services), 15 miles S of Hamilton • GPS: Lat 39.626003 Lon -93.951794 • Open: All year • Total sites: Dispersed • RV sites: Undefined • RV fee: Free • No water • No toilets • Activities: Mountain biking, fishing, hunting, equestrian area • Elevation: 955

Bonanza CA - Lot 7 - MDC • Agency: State • Tel: 660-646-6122 • Location: 8 miles SE of Kingston (limited services), 15 miles S of Hamilton • GPS: Lat 39.626778 Lon -93.949067 • Open: All year • Total sites: Dispersed • RV sites: Undefined • RV fee: Free • No water • No toilets • Activities: Mountain biking, fishing, hunting, equestrian area • Elevation: 961

Bonanza CA - Lot 8 - MDC • Agency: State • Tel: 660-646-6122 • Location: 8 miles SE of Kingston (limited services), 15 miles S of Hamilton • GPS: Lat 39.626351 Lon -93.942409 • Open: All year • Total sites: Dispersed • RV sites: Undefined • RV fee: Free • No water • No toilets • Activities: Mountain biking, fishing, hunting, equestrian area • Elevation: 935

Bonanza CA - Lot 9 - MDC • Agency: State • Tel: 660-646-6122 • Location: 8 miles SE of Kingston (limited services), 15 miles SE of Hamilton • GPS: Lat 39.626798 Lon -93.931475 • Open: All year • Total sites: Dispersed • RV sites: Undefined • RV fee: Free • No water • No toilets • Activities: Mountain biking, fishing, hunting, equestrian area • Elevation: 853

Bonanza CA - Lot 10 - MDC • Agency: State • Tel: 660-646-6122 • Location: 8 miles SE of Kingston (limited services), 15 miles S of Hamilton • GPS: Lat 39.621951 Lon -93.946942 • Open: All year • Total sites: Dispersed • RV sites: Undefined • RV fee: Free • No water • No toilets • Activities: Mountain biking, fishing, hunting, equestrian area • Elevation: 922

Bonanza CA - Lot 11 - MDC • Agency: State • Tel: 660-646-6122 • Location: 8 miles SE of Kingston (limited services), 15 miles S of Hamilton • GPS: Lat 39.620522 Lon -93.945823 • Open: All year • Total sites: Dispersed • RV sites: Undefined • RV fee: Free • No water • No toilets • Activities: Mountain biking, fishing, hunting, equestrian area • Elevation: 896

Bonanza CA - Lot 12 - MDC • Agency: State • Tel: 660-646-6122 • Location: 10 miles SE of Kingston (limited services), 21 miles SE of Hamilton • GPS: Lat 39.612855 Lon -93.926288 • Open: All year • Total sites: Dispersed • RV sites: Undefined • RV fee: Free • No water • No toilets • Activities: Mountain biking, fishing, hunting, equestrian area • Elevation: 866

Kirksville

Big Creek CA - Forest Lake - MDC • Agency: State • Tel: 660-785-2420 • Location: 2 miles W of Kirksville • GPS: Lat 40.184028 Lon -92.623324 • Open: All year • Total sites: Dispersed • RV sites: Undefined • RV fee: Free • No water • No toilets • Activities: Hiking, mountain biking, fishing, hunting • Elevation: 853

Big Creek CA - Royal Oaks - MDC • Agency: State • Tel: 660-785-2420 • Location: 5 miles W of Kirksville • GPS: Lat 40.155491 Lon -92.622337 • Open: All year • Total sites: Dispersed • RV sites: Undefined • RV fee: Free • No water • No toilets • Activities: Hiking, mountain biking, fishing, hunting • Elevation: 932

Big Creek CA - Thousand Hills Trail - MDC • Agency: State • Tel: 660-785-2420 • Location: 2 miles W of Kirksville • GPS: Lat 40.170228 Lon -92.617679 • Open: All year • Total sites: Dispersed • RV sites: Undefined • RV fee: Free • No water • No toilets • Activities: Hiking, mountain biking, fishing, hunting • Elevation: 948

Elmer A. Cook Memorial Access - MDC • Agency: State • Tel: 660-785-2424 • Location: 10 miles SW of Kirksville • GPS: Lat 40.124418 Lon -92.693254 • Open: All year • Total sites: Dispersed • RV sites: Undefined • RV fee: Free • No water • No toilets • Activities: Fishing, non-power boating • Elevation: 758

Sugar Creek CA - Lot A Horse Camp - MDC • Agency: State • Tel: 660-785-2420 • Location: 6 miles SW of Kirksville • GPS: Lat 40.118995 Lon -92.639669 • Open: All year • Total sites: Dispersed • RV sites: Undefined • RV fee: Free • No water • Vault toilets • Activities: Hiking, mountain biking, fishing, hunting • Elevation: 971

Sugar Creek CA - Lot B - MDC • Agency: State • Tel: 660-785-2420 • Location: 8 miles SW of Kirksville • GPS: Lat 40.109808 Lon -92.650519 • Open: All year • Total sites: Dispersed • RV sites: Undefined • RV fee: Free • No water • No toilets • Activities: Hiking, mountain biking, fishing, hunting • Elevation: 951

Sugar Creek CA - Lot C - MDC • Agency: State • Tel: 660-785-2420 • Location: 8 miles SW of Kirksville • GPS: Lat 40.113818 Lon -92.651069 • Open: All year • Total sites: Dispersed • RV sites: Undefined • RV fee: Free • No water • No toilets • Activities: Hiking, mountain biking, fishing, hunting • Elevation: 896

Sugar Creek CA - Lot D - MDC • Agency: State • Tel: 660-785-2420 • Location: 7 miles SW of Kirksville • GPS: Lat 40.111078 Lon -92.636173 • Open: All year • Total sites: Dispersed • RV sites: Undefined • RV fee: Free • No water • No toilets • Activities: Hiking, mountain biking, fishing, hunting • Elevation: 978

Sugar Creek CA - Lot E - MDC • Agency: State • Tel: 660-785-2420 • Location: 8 miles SW of Kirksville • GPS: Lat 40.101015 Lon -92.632543 • Open: All year • Total sites: Dispersed • RV sites: Undefined • RV fee: Free • No water • No toilets • Activities: Hiking, mountain biking, fishing, hunting • Elevation: 965

Sugar Creek CA - Lot F - MDC • Agency: State • Tel: 660-785-2420 • Location: 8 miles SW of Kirksville • GPS: Lat 40.092651 Lon -92.618824 • Open: All year • Total sites: Dispersed • RV sites: Undefined • RV fee: Free • No water • No toilets • Notes: No generators • Activities: Hiking, mountain biking, fishing, hunting • Elevation: 814

Sugar Creek CA - Lot G - MDC • Agency: State • Tel: 660-785-2420 • Location: 7 miles SW of Kirksville • GPS: Lat 40.106029 Lon -92.605307 • Open: All year • Total sites: Dispersed • RV sites: Undefined • RV fee: Free • No water • Vault toilets • Notes: No generators • Activities: Hiking, mountain biking, fishing, hunting • Elevation: 978

Sugar Creek CA - Lot H - MDC • Agency: State • Tel: 660-785-2420 • Location: 7 miles SW of Kirksville • GPS: Lat 40.103089 Lon -92.607805 • Open: All year • Total sites: Dispersed • RV sites: Undefined • RV fee: Free • No water • No toilets • Activities: Hiking, mountain biking, fishing, hunting • Elevation: 974

Sugar Creek CA - Lot I - MDC • Agency: State • Tel: 660-785-2420 • Location: 7 miles SW of Kirksville • GPS: Lat 40.102294 Lon -92.615113 • Open: All year • Total sites: Dispersed • RV sites: Undefined • RV fee: Free • No water • No toilets • Activities: Hiking, mountain biking, fishing, hunting • Elevation: 886

LaBelle

LaBelle Lake CA - MDC • Agency: State • Tel: 660-785-2420 • Location: 2 miles S of LaBelle (limited services), 22 miles W of Canton • GPS: Lat 40.091773 Lon -91.902123 • Open: All year • Total sites: 6 • RV sites: 6 • RV fee: Free • No water • Vault toilets • Activities: Fishing, hunting • Elevation: 705

Lancaster

Archangel Access - MDC • Agency: State • Tel: 660-785-2420 • Location: 10 miles SW of Lancaster • GPS: Lat 40.484803 Lon -92.685135 • Open: All year • Total sites: Dispersed • RV sites: Undefined • RV fee: Free • No water • No toilets • Activities: Fishing, non-power boating • Elevation: 794

Rebel's Cove CA - Lot A - MDC • Agency: State • Tel: 660-785-2420 • Location: 19 miles NW of Lancaster • GPS: Lat 40.569916 Lon -92.710761 • Open: All year • Total sites: Dispersed • RV sites: Undefined • RV fee: Free • No water • No toilets • Activities: Fishing, hunting, non-power boating • Elevation: 794

Rebel's Cove CA - Lot B - MDC • Agency: State • Tel: 660-785-2420 • Location: 18 miles NW of Lancaster • GPS: Lat 40.564908 Lon -92.725089 • Open: All year • Total sites: Dispersed • RV sites: Undefined • RV fee: Free • No water • No toilets • Activities: Fishing, hunting, non-power boating • Elevation: 860

Rebel's Cove CA - Lot C - MDC • Agency: State • Tel: 660-785-2420 • Location: 16 miles NW of Lancaster • GPS: Lat 40.552318 Lon -92.725092 • Open: All year • Total sites: Dispersed • RV sites: Undefined • RV fee: Free • No water • No toilets • Activities: Fishing, hunting, non-power boating • Elevation: 919

Rebel's Cove CA - Lot D - MDC • Agency: State • Tel: 660-785-2420 • Location: 17 miles NW of Lancaster • GPS: Lat 40.553665 Lon -92.711774 • Open: All year • Total sites: Dispersed • RV sites: Undefined • RV fee: Free • No water • No toilets • Activities: Fishing, hunting, non-power boating • Elevation: 912

Rebel's Cove CA - Lot E - MDC • Agency: State • Tel: 660-785-2420 • Location: 17 miles NW of Lancaster • GPS: Lat 40.554924 Lon -92.703955 • Open: All year • Total sites: Dispersed • RV sites: Undefined • RV fee: Free • No water • Vault toilets • Activities: Fishing, hunting, non-power boating • Elevation: 850

Rebel's Cove CA - Lot F - MDC • Agency: State • Tel: 660-785-2420 • Location: 12 miles NW of Lancaster • GPS: Lat 40.558727 Lon -92.701985 • Open: All year • Total sites: Dispersed • RV sites: Undefined • RV fee: Free • No water • Activities: Fishing, hunting, non-power boating • Elevation: 817

Rebel's Cove CA - Lot G - MDC • Agency: State • Tel: 660-785-2420 • Location: 11 miles NW of Lancaster • GPS: Lat 40.564293 Lon -92.689217 • Open: All year • Total sites: Dispersed • RV sites: Undefined • RV fee: Free • No water • Activities: Fishing, hunting, non-power boating • Elevation: 824

Rebel's Cove CA - Lot H - MDC • Agency: State • Tel: 660-785-2420 • Location: 15 miles W of Lancaster • GPS: Lat 40.539286 Lon -92.722815 • Open: All year • Total sites: Dispersed • RV sites: Undefined • RV fee: Free • No water • Activities: Fishing, hunting, non-power boating • Elevation: 938

Rebel's Cove CA - Lot I - MDC • Agency: State • Tel: 660-785-2420 • Location: 16 miles W of Lancaster • GPS: Lat 40.538285 Lon -92.704048 • Open: All year • Total sites: Dispersed • RV sites: Undefined • RV fee: Free • No water • Activities: Fishing, hunting, non-power boating • Elevation: 830

Rebel's Cove CA - Lot J - MDC • Agency: State • Tel: 660-785-2420 • Location: 11 miles NW of Lancaster • GPS: Lat 40.565073 Lon -92.688951 • Open: All year • Total sites: Dispersed • RV sites: Undefined • RV fee: Free • No water • Activities: Fishing, hunting, non-power boating • Elevation: 886

Rebel's Cove CA - Lot K - MDC • Agency: State • Tel: 660-785-2420 • Location: 9 miles NW of Lancaster • GPS: Lat 40.566676 Lon -92.669139 • Open: All year • Total sites: Dispersed • RV sites: Undefined • RV fee: Free • No water • Activities: Fishing, hunting, non-power boating • Elevation: 978

Rebel's Cove CA - Lot L - MDC • Agency: State • Tel: 660-785-2420 • Location: 9 miles NW of Lancaster • GPS: Lat 40.553852 Lon -92.674326 • Open: All year • Total sites: Dispersed • RV sites: Undefined • RV fee: Free • No water • Activities: Fishing, hunting, non-power boating • Elevation: 886

Rebel's Cove CA - Lot M - MDC • Agency: State • Tel: 660-785-2420 • Location: 11 miles NW of Lancaster • GPS: Lat 40.563303 Lon -92.697908 • Open: All year • Total sites: Dispersed • RV sites: Undefined • RV fee: Free • No water • Activities: Fishing, hunting, non-power boating • Elevation: 840

Lesterville

Lower Taum Sauk Lake - Union Electric • Agency: Utility Company • Tel: 573-290-5858 • Location: 8 miles N of Lesterville (limited services), 17 miles SW of Ironton • GPS: Lat 37.504031 Lon -90.828273 • Total sites: 20 • RV sites: 20 • RV fee: Free • Vault toilets • Activities: Hiking, fishing, non-power boating • Elevation: 807

Lewistown

Deer Ridge CA - Bluestem - MDC • Agency: State • Tel: 573-248-2530 • Location: 12 miles N of Lewistown (limited services), 24 miles NW of Canton • GPS: Lat 40.214604 Lon -91.854563 • Open: All year • Total sites: Dispersed • RV sites: Undefined • RV fee: Free • No toilets • Activities: Hiking, mountain biking, fishing, hunting, equestrian area • Elevation: 686

Deer Ridge CA - Collie Dog - MDC • Agency: State • Tel: 573-248-2530 • Location: 12 miles N of Lewistown (limited services), 24 miles NW of Canton • GPS: Lat 40.218407 Lon -91.850043 • Open: All year • Total sites: Dispersed • RV sites: Undefined • RV fee: Free • No toilets • Activities: Hiking, mountain biking, fishing, hunting, equestrian area • Elevation: 663

Deer Ridge CA - Fox - MDC • Agency: State • Tel: 573-248-2530 • Location: 7 miles N of Lewistown (limited services), 21 miles NW of Canton • GPS: Lat 40.177233 Lon -91.814775 • Open: All year • Total sites: Dispersed • RV sites: Undefined • RV fee: Free • No water • Vault toilets • Activities: Hiking, mountain biking, fishing, hunting, equestrian area • Elevation: 735

Deer Ridge CA - Horse - MDC • Agency: State • Tel: 573-248-2530 • Location: 9 miles N of Lewistown (limited services), 22 miles NW of Canton • GPS: Lat 40.170195 Lon -91.797353 • Open: All year • Total sites: Dispersed • RV sites: Undefined • RV fee: Free • No toilets • Activities: Hiking, mountain biking, fishing, hunting, equestrian area • Elevation: 692

Deer Ridge CA - Lake - MDC • Agency: State • Tel: 573-248-2530 • Location: 9 miles N of Lewistown (limited services), 23 miles NW of Canton • GPS: Lat 40.182254 Lon -91.828868 • Open: All year • Total sites: Dispersed • RV sites: Undefined • RV fee: Free • No water • Vault toilets • Activities: Hiking, mountain biking, fishing, hunting, equestrian area • Elevation: 709

Deer Ridge CA - Levengood - MDC • Agency: State • Tel: 573-248-2530 • Location: 9 miles N of Lewistown (limited services), 23 miles NW of Canton • GPS: Lat 40.194366 Lon -91.820959 • Open: All year • Total sites: Dispersed • RV sites: Undefined • RV fee: Free • No toilets • Activities: Hiking, mountain biking, fishing, hunting, equestrian area • Elevation: 715

Deer Ridge CA - Lone Oak - MDC • Agency: State • Tel: 573-248-2530 • Location: 10 miles N of Lewistown (limited services), 21 miles NW of Canton • GPS: Lat 40.207444 Lon -91.837352 • Open: All year • Total sites: Dispersed • RV sites: Undefined • RV fee: Free • No toilets • Activities: Hiking, mountain biking, fishing, hunting, equestrian area • Elevation: 620

Deer Ridge CA - Savanna - MDC • Agency: State • Tel: 573-248-2530 • Location: 10 miles N of Lewistown (limited services), 24 miles NW of Canton • GPS: Lat 40.207492 Lon -91.863494 • Open: All year • Total sites: Dispersed • RV sites: Undefined • RV fee: Free • No toilets • Activities: Hiking, mountain biking, fishing, hunting, equestrian area • Elevation: 696

Licking

Big Piney Trail Camp (Mark Twain NF) • Agency: US Forest Service • Location: 10 miles NW of Licking • GPS: Lat 37.560908 Lon -92.012028 • Total sites: 2 • RV sites:

2 • RV fee: Free • No water • Vault toilets • Activities: equestrian area • Elevation: 1130

Paddy Creek (Mark Twain NF) • Agency: US Forest Service • Location: 17 miles NW of Licking • GPS: Lat 37.555656 Lon -92.042308 • Total sites: 23 • RV sites: 23 • Max RV Length: 34 • RV fee: Free (donation appreciated) • No water • Vault toilets • Activities: Hiking, swimming • Elevation: 890

Linn

Rollins Ferry Access - MDC • Agency: State • Tel: 573-815-7900 • Location: 7 miles S of Linn • GPS: Lat 38.393402 Lon -91.820808 • Open: All year • Total sites: Dispersed • RV sites: Undefined • RV fee: Free • No water • Vault toilets • Activities: Fishing, non-power boating • Elevation: 591

Loose Creek

Bonnots Mill Access - MDC (Osage River) • Agency: State • Tel: 573-815-7900 • Location: 7 miles N of Loose Creek (limited services), 18 miles E of Jefferson City • GPS: Lat 38.573781 Lon -91.972295 • Open: All year • Total sites: Dispersed • RV sites: Undefined • RV fee: Free • No water • Vault toilets • Activities: Fishing, power boating, non-power boating • Elevation: 548

Louisiana

Calumet Creek Access - MDC • Agency: State • Tel: 573-248-2530 • Location: 5 miles SE of Louisiana • GPS: Lat 39.399586 Lon -90.967194 • Open: All year • Total sites: Dispersed • RV sites: Undefined • RV fee: Free • No water • Vault toilets • Activities: Fishing, non-power boating • Elevation: 482

Dupont Reservation CA - MDC • Agency: State • Tel: 573-248-2530 • Location: 16 miles NW of Louisiana • GPS: Lat 39.550641 Lon -91.161152 • Open: All year • Total sites: 20 • RV sites: 20 • RV fee: Free • No water • Vault toilets • Activities: Fishing, hunting • Elevation: 446

Ted Shanks CA - MDC • Agency: State • Tel: 573-248-2530 • Location: 15 miles NW of Louisiana • GPS: Lat 39.544231 Lon -91.165735 • Open: All year • Total sites: Dispersed • RV sites: Undefined • RV fee: Free • No water • Vault toilets • Activities: Fishing, hunting, non-power boating • Elevation: 456

Lowndes

Iron Bridge Access - MDC • Agency: State • Tel: 573-223-4525 • Location: 1 mile NW of Lowndes (limited services), 24 miles NW of Advance • GPS: Lat 37.155141 Lon -90.272484 • Open: All year • Total sites: Dispersed • RV sites: Undefined • RV fee: Free • No water • No toilets • Activities: Fishing, hunting, non-power boating • Elevation: 453

Macon

Bee Hollow CA - MDC • Agency: State • Tel: 660-785-2420 • Location: 9 miles S of Macon • GPS: Lat 39.622401 Lon -92.510124 • Open: All year • Total sites: Dispersed • RV sites: Undefined • RV fee: Free • No water • No toilets • Activities: Fishing, hunting • Elevation: 810

Redman CA - MDC • Agency: State • Tel: 660-785-2420 • Location: 15 miles NE of Macon • GPS: Lat 39.858282 Lon -92.337185 • Open: All year • Total sites: Dispersed • RV sites: Undefined • RV fee: Free • No water • No toilets • Activities: Hunting • Elevation: 840

Madison

Woodlawn Access - MDC • Agency: State • Tel: 573-248-2530 • Location: 5 miles N of Madison (limited services), 17 miles NE of Moberly • GPS: Lat 39.541286 Lon -92.212478 • Open: All year • Total sites: Dispersed • RV sites: Undefined • RV fee: Free • No water • No toilets • Activities: Fishing, hunting, non-power boating • Elevation: 705

Manes

Wilbur Allen CA - MDC • Agency: State • Tel: 417-256-7161 • Location: 3 miles NW of Manes (limited services), 34 miles SE of Lebanon • GPS: Lat 37.396666 Lon -92.398459 • Open: All year • Total sites: Dispersed • RV sites: Undefined • RV fee: Free • No water • No toilets • Activities: Hiking, fishing, hunting, non-power boating • Elevation: 1060

Marble Hill

Castor River CA Trace Creek - MDC • Agency: State • Tel: 573-290-5730 • Location: 14 miles W of Marble Hill • GPS: Lat 37.296553 Lon -90.181525 • Open: All year • Total sites: Dispersed • RV sites: Undefined • RV fee: Free • No water • No toilets • Activities: Hiking, fishing, hunting • Elevation: 571

Coldwater CA Lot 3 - MDC • Agency: State • Tel: 573-223-4525 • Location: 20 miles W of Marble Hill • GPS: Lat 37.274309 Lon -90.255938 • Open: All year • Total sites: Dispersed • RV sites: Undefined • RV fee: Free • No water • No toilets • Activities: Hiking, hunting • Elevation: 640

Coldwater CA Lot 4 - MDC • Agency: State • Tel: 573-223-4525 • Location: 19 miles SW of Marble Hill • GPS: Lat 37.239945 Lon -90.271289 • Open: All year • Total

sites: Dispersed • RV sites: Undefined • RV fee: Free • No water • No toilets • Activities: Hiking, hunting • Elevation: 587

Grassy Towersite - MDC • Agency: State • Tel: 573-290-5730 • Location: 9 miles W of Marble Hill • GPS: Lat 37.282315 Lon -90.065435 • Open: All year • Total sites: Dispersed • RV sites: Undefined • RV fee: Free • No water • No toilets • Notes: Permit required • Activities: Hunting • Elevation: 794

Marceline

Mussel Fork CA Lot 6 - MDC • Agency: State • Tel: 660-646-6122 • Location: 5 miles NE of Marceline • GPS: Lat 39.731463 Lon -92.865702 • Open: All year • Total sites: Dispersed • RV sites: Undefined • RV fee: Free • No water • No toilets • Activities: Hiking, fishing, hunting, non-power boating • Elevation: 807

Mussel Fork CA Lot 7 - MDC • Agency: State • Tel: 660-646-6122 • Location: 8 miles NE of Marceline • GPS: Lat 39.729006 Lon -92.853658 • Open: All year • Total sites: Dispersed • RV sites: Undefined • RV fee: Free • No water • No toilets • Activities: Hiking, fishing, hunting, non-power boating • Elevation: 814

Mussel Fork CA Lot 8 - MDC • Agency: State • Tel: 660-646-6122 • Location: 6 miles NE of Marceline • GPS: Lat 39.725914 Lon -92.839944 • Open: All year • Total sites: Dispersed • RV sites: Undefined • RV fee: Free • No water • No toilets • Activities: Hiking, fishing, hunting, non-power boating • Elevation: 830

Mussel Fork CA Lot 9 - MDC • Agency: State • Tel: 660-646-6122 • Location: 4 miles E of Marceline • GPS: Lat 39.715781 Lon -92.857629 • Open: All year • Total sites: Dispersed • RV sites: Undefined • RV fee: Free • No water • No toilets • Activities: Hiking, fishing, hunting, non-power boating • Elevation: 820

Marion

Marion Access - MDC • Agency: State • Tel: 573-815-7900 • Location: In Marion (limited services), 12 miles NW of Jefferson City • GPS: Lat 38.690562 Lon -92.364957 • Open: All year • Total sites: Dispersed • RV sites: Undefined • RV fee: Free • No water • Vault toilets • Activities: Fishing, non-power boating • Elevation: 564

Marion Bottoms CA - MDC • Agency: State • Tel: 573-815-7900 • Location: 3 miles NW of Marion (limited services), 15 miles NW of Jefferson City • GPS: Lat 38.724165 Lon -92.395138 • Open: All year • Total sites: Dispersed • RV sites: Undefined • RV fee: Free • No water • No toilets • Activities: Fishing, hunting, non-power boating • Elevation: 568

Marshall

Grand Pass CA - Lot 1 - MDC • Agency: State • Tel: 660-646-6122 • Location: 13 miles NW of Marshall • GPS: Lat 39.270623 Lon -93.313191 • Open: All year • Total sites: Dispersed • RV sites: Undefined • RV fee: Free • No water • Vault toilets • Activities: Hiking, fishing, hunting • Elevation: 656

Grand Pass CA - Lot 2 - MDC • Agency: State • Tel: 660-646-6122 • Location: 14 miles NW of Marshall • GPS: Lat 39.271497 Lon -93.328509 • Open: All year • Total sites: Dispersed • RV sites: Undefined • RV fee: Free • No water • No toilets • Activities: Hiking, fishing, hunting • Elevation: 656

Grand Pass CA - Lot 3 - MDC • Agency: State • Tel: 660-646-6122 • Location: 15 miles NW of Marshall • GPS: Lat 39.280144 Lon -93.281655 • Open: All year • Total sites: Dispersed • RV sites: Undefined • RV fee: Free • No water • No toilets • Activities: Hiking, fishing, hunting • Elevation: 640

Marshfield

Compton Hollow CA Lot 1 - MDC • Agency: State • Tel: 417-895-6880 • Location: 10 miles SW of Marshfield • GPS: Lat 37.239748 Lon -93.012744 • Open: All year • Total sites: Dispersed • RV sites: Undefined • RV fee: Free • No water • No toilets • Activities: Hiking, mountain biking, hunting, equestrian area • Elevation: 1394

Compton Hollow CA Lot 2 - MDC • Agency: State • Tel: 417-895-6881 • Location: 12 miles SW of Marshfield • GPS: Lat 37.226768 Lon -93.008637 • Open: All year • Total sites: Dispersed • RV sites: Undefined • RV fee: Free • No water • No toilets • Activities: Hiking, mountain biking, hunting • Elevation: 1466

Compton Hollow CA Lot 3 - MDC • Agency: State • Tel: 417-895-6882 • Location: 11 miles SW of Marshfield • GPS: Lat 37.226603 Lon -92.994837 • Open: All year • Total sites: Dispersed • RV sites: Undefined • RV fee: Free • No water • No toilets • Activities: Hiking, mountain biking, hunting • Elevation: 1483

Maryville

Bridgewater Access - MDC • Agency: State • Tel: 816-271-3100 • Location: 7 miles S of Maryville • GPS: Lat 40.242271 Lon -94.836312 • Open: All year • Total sites: Dispersed • RV sites: Undefined • RV fee: Free • No water • No toilets • Activities: Fishing, non-power boating • Elevation: 991

Nodaway County Community Lake - MDC • Agency: State • Tel: 816-271-3100 • Location: 6 miles N of Maryville • GPS: Lat 40.432132 Lon -94.854063 • Open: All year • Total sites: Dispersed • RV sites: Undefined • RV fee: Free • No water • Vault toilets • Activities: Hiking, fishing, hunting, non-power boating • Elevation: 1155

Meadville

Fountain Grove CA - Lot 1 - MDC • Agency: State • Tel: 660-646-6122 • Location: 6 miles S of Meadville (limited services), 19 miles SE of Chillicothe • GPS: Lat 39.715064 Lon -93.319717 • Open: All year • Total sites: Dispersed • RV sites: Undefined • RV fee: Free • Central water • Vault toilets • Activities: Hiking, fishing, hunting, non-power boating • Elevation: 712

Fountain Grove CA - Lot 10 - MDC • Agency: State • Tel: 660-646-6122 • Location: 6 miles S of Meadville (limited services), 19 miles SE of Chillicothe • GPS: Lat 39.699276 Lon -93.302333 • Open: All year • Total sites: Dispersed • RV sites: Undefined • RV fee: Free • No water • No toilets • Activities: Hiking, fishing, hunting, non-power boating • Elevation: 679

Fountain Grove CA - Lot 2 - MDC • Agency: State • Tel: 660-646-6122 • Location: 6 miles S of Meadville (limited services), 19 miles SE of Chillicothe • GPS: Lat 39.718654 Lon -93.323018 • Open: All year • Total sites: Dispersed • RV sites: Undefined • RV fee: Free • No water • Vault toilets • Activities: Hiking, fishing, hunting, non-power boating • Elevation: 712

Fountain Grove CA - Lot 3 - MDC • Agency: State • Tel: 660-646-6122 • Location: 6 miles SW of Meadville (limited services), 18 miles SE of Chillicothe • GPS: Lat 39.72264 Lon -93.32353 • Open: All year • Total sites: Dispersed • RV sites: Undefined • RV fee: Free • No water • No toilets • Activities: Hiking, fishing, hunting, non-power boating • Elevation: 732

Fountain Grove CA - Lot 4 - MDC • Agency: State • Tel: 660-646-6122 • Location: 7 miles SW of Meadville (limited services), 16 miles SE of Chillicothe • GPS: Lat 39.725461 Lon -93.351121 • Open: All year • Total sites: Dispersed • RV sites: Undefined • RV fee: Free • No water • No toilets • Activities: Hiking, fishing, hunting, non-power boating • Elevation: 673

Fountain Grove CA - Lot 5 - MDC • Agency: State • Tel: 660-646-6122 • Location: 6 miles SW of Meadville (limited services), 15 miles SE of Chillicothe • GPS: Lat 39.735997 Lon -93.344781 • Open: All year • Total sites: Dispersed • RV sites: Undefined • RV fee: Free • No water • Vault toilets • Activities: Hiking, fishing, hunting, non-power boating • Elevation: 696

Fountain Grove CA - Lot 6 - MDC • Agency: State • Tel: 660-646-6122 • Location: 5 miles SW of Meadville (limited services), 13 miles SE of Chillicothe • GPS: Lat 39.746667 Lon -93.344187 • Open: All year • Total sites: Dispersed • RV sites: Undefined • RV fee: Free • No water • No toilets • Activities: Hiking, fishing, hunting, non-power boating • Elevation: 689

Fountain Grove CA - Lot 7 - MDC • Agency: State • Tel: 660-646-6122 • Location: 5 miles SW of Meadville (limited services), 14 miles SE of Chillicothe • GPS: Lat 39.739232 Lon -93.340245 • Open: All year • Total sites: Dispersed • RV sites: Undefined • RV fee: Free • No water • No toilets • Activities: Hiking, fishing, hunting, non-power boating • Elevation: 702

Fountain Grove CA - Lot 8 - MDC • Agency: State • Tel: 660-646-6122 • Location: 6 miles S of Meadville (limited services), 19 miles SE of Chillicothe • GPS: Lat 39.710279 Lon -93.322477 • Open: All year • Total sites: Dispersed • RV sites: Undefined • RV fee: Free • No water • No toilets • Activities: Hiking, fishing, hunting, non-power boating • Elevation: 751

Fountain Grove CA - Lot 9 - MDC • Agency: State • Tel: 660-646-6122 • Location: 6 miles S of Meadville (limited services), 19 miles SE of Chillicothe • GPS: Lat 39.700728 Lon -93.303604 • Open: All year • Total sites: Dispersed • RV sites: Undefined • RV fee: Free • No water • Vault toilets • Activities: Hiking, fishing, hunting, non-power boating • Elevation: 689

Memphis

Indian Hills CA - Lot 1 - MDC • Agency: State • Tel: 660-785-2420 • Location: 16 miles SW of Memphis • GPS: Lat 40.323232 Lon -92.302751 • Open: All year • Total sites: Dispersed • RV sites: Undefined • RV fee: Free • No water • No toilets • Activities: Fishing, hunting • Elevation: 820

Indian Hills CA - Lot 2 - MDC • Agency: State • Tel: 660-785-2420 • Location: 13 miles SW of Memphis • GPS: Lat 40.335972 Lon -92.279788 • Open: All year • Total sites: Dispersed • RV sites: Undefined • RV fee: Free • No water • No toilets • Activities: Fishing, hunting • Elevation: 774

Indian Hills CA - Lot 3 - MDC • Agency: State • Tel: 660-785-2420 • Location: 12 miles SW of Memphis • GPS: Lat 40.353231 Lon -92.267874 • Open: All year • Total sites: Dispersed • RV sites: Undefined • RV fee: Free • No water • No toilets • Activities: Fishing, hunting • Elevation: 827

Indian Hills CA - Lot 4 - MDC • Agency: State • Tel: 660-785-2420 • Location: 14 miles SW of Memphis • GPS: Lat 40.339894 Lon -92.265892 • Open: All year • Total sites: Dispersed • RV sites: Undefined • RV fee: Free • No water • No toilets • Activities: Fishing, hunting • Elevation: 804

Indian Hills CA - Lot 5 - MDC • Agency: State • Tel: 660-785-2420 • Location: 15 miles SW of Memphis • GPS: Lat 40.327901 Lon -92.269203 • Open: All year • Total sites: Dispersed • RV sites: Undefined • RV fee: Free • No water • No toilets • Activities: Fishing, hunting • Elevation: 718

Indian Hills CA - Lot 6 - MDC • Agency: State • Tel: 660-785-2420 • Location: 15 miles SW of Memphis • GPS: Lat 40.320804 Lon -92.243455 • Open: All year • Total sites: Dispersed • RV sites: Undefined • RV fee: Free • No water • No toilets • Activities: Fishing, hunting • Elevation: 807

Indian Hills CA - Lot 7 - MDC • Agency: State • Tel: 660-785-2420 • Location: 11 miles SW of Memphis • GPS: Lat 40.333691 Lon -92.240292 • Open: All year • Total sites: Dispersed • RV sites: Undefined • RV fee: Free • No water • No toilets • Activities: Fishing, hunting • Elevation: 758

Indian Hills CA - Lot 8 - MDC • Agency: State • Tel: 660-785-2420 • Location: 10 miles SW of Memphis • GPS: Lat 40.347254 Lon -92.238668 • Open: All year • Total sites: Dispersed • RV sites: Undefined • RV fee: Free • No water • No toilets • Activities: Fishing, hunting • Elevation: 787

Indian Hills CA - Lot 9 - MDC • Agency: State • Tel: 660-785-2420 • Location: 11 miles S of Memphis • GPS: Lat 40.322759 Lon -92.217036 • Open: All year • Total sites: Dispersed • RV sites: Undefined • RV fee: Free • No water • No toilets • Activities: Fishing, hunting • Elevation: 712

Mexico

White (Robert M. II) CA #1 - MDC • Agency: State • Tel: 573-815-7900 • Location: 14 miles N of Mexico • GPS: Lat 39.330583 Lon -91.847624 • Open: All year • Total sites: Dispersed • RV sites: Undefined • RV fee: Free • No water • No toilets • Activities: Fishing, hunting • Elevation: 722

White (Robert M. II) CA #2 - MDC • Agency: State • Tel: 573-815-7900 • Location: 13 miles N of Mexico • GPS: Lat 39.323405 Lon -91.873403 • Open: All year • Total sites: Dispersed • RV sites: Undefined • RV fee: Free • No water • No toilets • Activities: Fishing, hunting • Elevation: 742

White (Robert M. II) CA #3 - MDC • Agency: State • Tel: 573-815-7900 • Location: 14 miles N of Mexico • GPS: Lat 39.337587 Lon -91.87063 • Open: All year • Total sites: Dispersed • RV sites: Undefined • RV fee: Free • No water • No toilets • Activities: Fishing, hunting • Elevation: 745

Miami

Miami Access - MDC • Agency: State • Tel: 573-815-7900 • Location: In Miami (limited services), 18 miles N of Marshall • GPS: Lat 39.325662 Lon -93.228729 • Open: All year • Total sites: Dispersed • RV sites: Undefined • RV fee: Free • No water • Vault toilets • Activities: Fishing, non-power boating • Elevation: 679

Milan

Locust Creek CA - Lot A - MDC • Agency: State • Tel: 660-785-2420 • Location: 3 miles SW of Milan • GPS: Lat 40.188616 Lon -93.165666 • Open: All year • Total sites: Dispersed • RV sites: Undefined • RV fee: Free • No water • No toilets • Activities: Fishing, hunting, non-power boating • Elevation: 915

Locust Creek CA - Lot B - MDC • Agency: State • Tel: 660-785-2420 • Location: 3 miles SW of Milan • GPS: Lat 40.184463 Lon -93.174185 • Open: All year • Total sites: Dispersed • RV sites: Undefined • RV fee: Free • No water • No toilets • Activities: Fishing, hunting, non-power boating • Elevation: 800

Locust Creek CA - Lot C - MDC • Agency: State • Tel: 660-785-2420 • Location: 4 miles SW of Milan • GPS: Lat 40.178912 Lon -93.175119 • Open: All year • Total sites: Dispersed • RV sites: Undefined • RV fee: Free • No water • No toilets • Activities: Fishing, hunting, non-power boating • Elevation: 794

Locust Creek CA - Lot D - MDC • Agency: State • Tel: 660-785-2420 • Location: 4 miles SW of Milan • GPS: Lat 40.183903 Lon -93.179126 • Open: All year • Total sites: Dispersed • RV sites: Undefined • RV fee: Free • No water • Flush toilets • Activities: Fishing, hunting, non-power boating • Elevation: 840

Locust Creek CA - Lot E - MDC • Agency: State • Tel: 660-785-2420 • Location: 4 miles SW of Milan • GPS: Lat 40.185549 Lon -93.186231 • Open: All year • Total sites: Dispersed • RV sites: Undefined • RV fee: Free • No water • No toilets • Activities: Fishing, hunting, non-power boating • Elevation: 909

Locust Creek CA - Lot F - MDC • Agency: State • Tel: 660-785-2420 • Location: 6 miles SW of Milan • GPS: Lat 40.182888 Lon -93.194365 • Open: All year • Total sites: Dispersed • RV sites: Undefined • RV fee: Free • No water • No toilets • Activities: Fishing, hunting, non-power boating • Elevation: 955

Locust Creek CA - Lot G - MDC • Agency: State • Tel: 660-785-2420 • Location: 8 miles SW of Milan • GPS: Lat 40.163852 Lon -93.200024 • Open: All year • Total sites: Dispersed • RV sites: Undefined • RV fee: Free • No water • No toilets • Activities: Fishing, hunting, non-power boating • Elevation: 922

Locust Creek CA - Lot H - MDC • Agency: State • Tel: 660-785-2420 • Location: 8 miles SW of Milan • GPS: Lat 40.163399 Lon -93.196519 • Open: All year • Total sites: Dispersed • RV sites: Undefined • RV fee: Free • No water • No toilets • Activities: Fishing, hunting, non-power boating • Elevation: 925

Locust Creek CA - Lot I - MDC • Agency: State • Tel: 660-785-2420 • Location: 9 miles SW of Milan • GPS: Lat 40.166312 Lon -93.196152 • Open: All year • Total sites: Dispersed • RV sites: Undefined • RV fee: Free • No water • No toilets • Activities: Fishing, hunting, non-power boating • Elevation: 902

Locust Creek CA - Lot K - MDC • Agency: State • Tel: 660-785-2420 • Location: 3 miles SW of Milan • GPS: Lat 40.177945 Lon -93.156344 • Open: All year • Total sites: Dispersed • RV sites: Undefined • RV fee: Free • No water • No toilets • Activities: Fishing, hunting, non-power boating • Elevation: 938

Locust Creek CA - Lot L - MDC • Agency: State • Tel: 660-785-2420 • Location: 4 miles SW of Milan • GPS: Lat 40.168946 Lon -93.166615 • Open: All year • Total sites: Dispersed • RV sites: Undefined • RV fee: Free • No water • No toilets • Activities: Fishing, hunting, non-power boating • Elevation: 906

Locust Creek CA - Lot M - MDC • Agency: State • Tel: 660-785-2420 • Location: 4 miles SW of Milan • GPS: Lat 40.168167 Lon -93.172952 • Open: All year • Total sites: Dispersed • RV sites: Undefined • RV fee: Free • No water • No toilets • Activities: Fishing, hunting, non-power boating • Elevation: 850

Locust Creek CA - Lot N - MDC • Agency: State • Tel: 660-785-2420 • Location: 4 miles SW of Milan • GPS: Lat 40.167533 Lon -93.164307 • Open: All year • Total sites: Dispersed • RV sites: Undefined • RV fee: Free • No water • No toilets • Activities: Fishing, hunting, non-power boating • Elevation: 889

Locust Creek CA - Lot O - MDC • Agency: State • Tel: 660-785-2420 • Location: 9 miles SW of Milan • GPS: Lat 40.154299 Lon -93.176308 • Open: All year • Total sites: Dispersed • RV sites: Undefined • RV fee: Free • No water • No toilets • Activities: Fishing, hunting, non-power boating • Elevation: 807

Sears Community Lake - MDC • Agency: State • Tel: 660-785-2420 • Location: 6 miles NE of Milan • GPS: Lat 40.262118 Lon -93.075709 • Open: All year • Total sites: Dispersed • RV sites: Undefined • RV fee: Free • No water • No toilets • Activities: Fishing, hunting • Elevation: 942

Mincy

Drury-Mincy CA - MDC • Agency: State • Tel: 417-256-7161 • Location: 1 mile S of Mincy (limited services), 11 miles SE of Branson • GPS: Lat 36.553376 Lon -93.108017 • Open: All year • Total sites: 10 • RV sites: 10 • RV fee: Free • No water • Vault toilets • Activities: Hiking, fishing, hunting • Elevation: 945

Mindenmines

Shawnee Trail CA - MDC • Agency: State • Tel: 417-629-3423 • Location: 4 miles SE of Mindenmines (limited services), 19 miles SW of Lamar • GPS: Lat 37.437102 Lon -94.568921 • Open: All year • Total sites: Dispersed • RV sites: Undefined • RV fee: Free • No water • Vault toilets • Activities: Fishing, hunting • Elevation: 945

Mokane

Mokane Access - MDC • Agency: State • Tel: 573-815-7900 • Location: 2 miles SW of Mokane (limited services), 20 miles NE of Jefferson City • GPS: Lat 38.653623 Lon -91.884617 • Open: All year • Total sites: Dispersed • RV sites: Undefined • RV fee: Free • No water • No toilets • Activities: Fishing, power boating, non-power boating • Elevation: 528

Monroe City

Elmslie Memorial CA - MDC • Agency: State • Tel: 573-248-2530 • Location: 9 miles N of Monroe City • GPS: Lat 39.749008 Lon -91.739849 • Open: All year • Total sites: Dispersed • RV sites: Undefined • RV fee: Free • No water • No toilets • Activities: Fishing, hunting, non-power boating • Elevation: 646

Hunnewell Lake RA - MDC • Agency: State • Tel: 573-983-2201 • Location: 10 miles NW of Monroe City • GPS: Lat 39.712105 Lon -91.862734 • Open: All year • Total sites: 20 • RV sites: 20 • RV fee: Free • No water • Vault toilets • Activities: Fishing, hunting • Elevation: 718

Montgomery City

Whetstone Creek CA - Big Lake - MDC • Agency: State • Tel: 573-815-7900 • Location: 20 miles SW of Montgomery City • GPS: Lat 38.966942 Lon -91.731479 • Open: All year • Total sites: Dispersed • RV sites: Undefined • RV fee: Free • No water • Vault toilets • Activities: Fishing, hunting, non-power boating • Elevation: 791

Whetstone Creek CA - Shooting Range - MDC • Agency: State • Tel: 573-815-7900 • Location: 16 miles SW of Montgomery City • GPS: Lat 38.950293 Lon -91.690146 • Open: All year • Total sites: Dispersed • RV sites: Undefined • RV fee: Free • No water • No toilets • Activities: Fishing, hunting, non-power boating • Elevation: 663

Montreal

Toronto Springs CA - MDC • Agency: State • Tel: 573-346-2210 • Location: 6 miles NE of Montreal (limited services), 15 miles E of Camdenton • GPS: Lat 37.998319 Lon -92.513968 • Open: All year • Total sites: Dispersed • RV sites: Undefined • RV fee: Free • No water • No toilets • Activities: Fishing, hunting, non-power boating • Elevation: 748

Montrose

Montrose CA North Side - MDC • Agency: State • Tel: 660-693-4666 • Location: 4 miles N of Montrose (limited services), 15 miles SW of Clinton • GPS: Lat 38.309604 Lon -93.971851 • Open: All year • Total sites: Dispersed • RV sites: Undefined • RV fee: Free • No water • Vault toilets • Activities: Fishing, non-power boating • Elevation: 774

Montrose CA South Ramp - MDC • Agency: State • Tel: 660-693-4666 • Location: 4 miles N of Montrose (limited services), 16 miles SW of Clinton • GPS: Lat 38.300057 Lon -93.960161 • Open: All year • Total sites: Dispersed • RV sites: Undefined • RV fee: Free • No water • Vault toilets • Activities: Fishing, non-power boating • Elevation: 745

Morrison

Fredericksburg Ferry Access - MDC • Agency: State • Tel: 573-815-7900 • Location: 10 miles S of Morrison (limited services), 21 miles SW of Hermann • GPS: Lat 38.603137 Lon -91.633237 • Open: All year • Total sites: 10 • RV sites: 10 • RV fee: Free • No water • Vault toilets • Activities: Fishing, non-power boating • Elevation: 522

Mound City

Jamerson C. McCormack CA - MDC • Agency: State • Tel: 816-271-3100 • Location: 9 miles S of Mound City • GPS: Lat 40.052064 Lon -95.244276 • Open: All year • Total sites: Dispersed • RV sites: Undefined • RV fee: Free • No water • No toilets • Activities: Hiking, hunting • Elevation: 965

Nodaway Valley CA Lot 1 - MDC • Agency: State • Tel: 816-271-3100 • Location: 12 miles E of Mound City • GPS: Lat 40.108061 Lon -95.022904 • Open: All year • Total sites: Dispersed • RV sites: Undefined • RV fee: Free • No water • No toilets • Activities: Fishing, hunting, non-power boating • Elevation: 906

Nodaway Valley CA Lot 2 - MDC • Agency: State • Tel: 816-271-3100 • Location: 13 miles E of Mound City • GPS: Lat 40.101266 Lon -95.022634 • Open: All year • Total sites: Dispersed • RV sites: Undefined • RV fee: Free • No water • No toilets • Activities: Fishing, hunting, non-power boating • Elevation: 899

Nodaway Valley CA Lot 3 - MDC • Agency: State • Tel: 816-271-3100 • Location: 11 miles SE of Mound City • GPS: Lat 40.092485 Lon -95.078759 • Open: All year • Total sites: Dispersed • RV sites: Undefined • RV fee: Free • No water • No toilets • Activities: Fishing, hunting, non-power boating • Elevation: 932

Nodaway Valley CA Lot 4 - MDC • Agency: State • Tel: 816-271-3100 • Location: 14 miles SE of Mound City • GPS: Lat 40.078115 Lon -95.076426 • Open: All year • Total sites: Dispersed • RV sites: Undefined • RV fee: Free • No water • No toilets • Activities: Fishing, hunting, non-power boating • Elevation: 863

Rush Bottoms CA - MDC • Agency: State • Tel: 816-271-3100 • Location: 15 miles SW of Mound City • GPS: Lat 40.055937 Lon -95.416574 • Open: All year • Total sites: Dispersed • RV sites: Undefined • RV fee: Free • No water • No toilets • Notes: Near RR tracks • Activities: Fishing, hunting • Elevation: 873

Mountain Grove

Shannon Ranch CA - MDC • Agency: State • Tel: 417-256-7161 • Location: 14 miles S of Mountain Grove • GPS: Lat 36.943756 Lon -92.326423 • Open: All year • Total sites: 2 • RV sites: 2 • RV fee: Free • No water • No toilets • Activities: Hiking, hunting • Elevation: 1214

Mt. Sterling

Cooper Hill CA - MDC • Agency: State • Tel: 573-815-7900 • Location: 4 miles SW of Mt. Sterling (limited services), 14 miles NE of Belle • GPS: Lat 38.431811 Lon -91.666483 • Open: All year • Total sites: Dispersed • RV sites: Undefined • RV fee: Free • No water • No toilets • Activities: Fishing, hunting, non-power boating • Elevation: 574

Myrtle

Myrtle Access - MDC • Agency: State • Tel: 573-226-3616 • Location: 5 miles E of Myrtle (limited services), 22 miles E of Thayer • GPS: Lat 36.51164 Lon -91.170577 • Open: All year • Total sites: Dispersed • RV sites: Undefined • RV fee: Free • No water • No toilets • Activities: Fishing, non-power boating • Elevation: 384

Neelyville

Corkwood CA - MDC • Agency: State • Tel: 573-290-5730 • Location: 1 mile W of Neelyville (limited services), 15 miles SW of Poplar Bluff • GPS: Lat 36.557273 Lon -90.531298 • Open: All year • Total sites: Dispersed • RV sites: Undefined • RV fee: Free • No water • No toilets • Activities: Hiking, hunting • Elevation: 295

Nevada

Cephas Ford Access - MDC • Agency: State • Tel: 417-395-2341 • Location: 8 miles N of Nevada • GPS: Lat 37.949391 Lon -94.355815 • Open: All year • Total sites: Dispersed • RV sites: Undefined • RV fee: Free • No water • Vault toilets • Activities: Fishing, hunting, non-power boating • Elevation: 761

New Cambria

Griffiths Memorial CA - MDC • Agency: State • Tel: 660-785-2420 • Location: 3 miles N of New Cambria (limited services), 18 miles NW of Macon • GPS: Lat 39.811994 Lon -92.746627 • Open: All year • Total sites: Dispersed • RV sites: Undefined • RV fee: Free • No water • No toilets • Activities: Fishing, hunting • Elevation: 869

New Florence

Danville CA - Glade - MDC • Agency: State • Tel: 573-815-7900 • Location: 7 miles SW of New Florence (limited services), 12 miles S of Montgomery City • GPS: Lat 38.865311 Lon -91.504796 • Open: All year • Total sites: Dispersed • RV sites: Undefined • RV fee: Free • No toilets • Activities: Hiking, hunting • Elevation: 653

Danville CA - Post Oak - MDC • Agency: State • Tel: 573-815-7900 • Location: 6 miles SW of New Florence (limited services), 11 miles S of Montgomery City • GPS: Lat 38.872197 Lon -91.510689 • Open: All year • Total sites: Dispersed • RV sites: Undefined • RV fee: Free • No water • No toilets • Activities: Hiking, hunting • Elevation: 846

Danville CA - Site 4 - MDC • Agency: State • Tel: 573-815-7900 • Location: 6 miles SW of New Florence (limited services), 11 miles S of Montgomery City • GPS: Lat 38.867402 Lon -91.514178 • Open: All year • Total sites: Dispersed • RV sites: Undefined • RV fee: Free • No toilets • Activities: Hiking, hunting • Elevation: 817

Danville CA - Turkey Ridge - MDC • Agency: State • Tel: 573-815-7900 • Location: 6 miles SW of New Florence (limited services), 11 miles S of Montgomery City • GPS: Lat 38.873432 Lon -91.535064 • Open: All year • Total sites: Dispersed • RV sites: Undefined • RV fee: Free • No toilets • Activities: Hiking, hunting • Elevation: 827

New Madrid

Donaldson Point CA - MDC • Agency: State • Tel: 573-290-5730 • Location: 11 miles SE of New Madrid • GPS: Lat 36.554553 Lon -89.410955 • Open: All year • Total sites: Dispersed • RV sites: Undefined • RV fee: Free • No water • No toilets • Activities: Hiking, fishing, hunting, non-power boating • Elevation: 302

Newark

Sever (Henry) Lake CA - Horse Camp - MDC • Agency: State • Tel: 660-785-2420 • Location: 3 miles N of Newark (limited services), 19 miles SE of Edina • GPS: Lat 40.014877 Lon -91.985334 • Open: All year • Total sites: 6 • RV sites: 6 • RV fee: Free • Central water • Vault toilets • Activities: Fishing, power boating, hunting, non-power boating, equestrian area • Elevation: 715

Sever (Henry) Lake CA - Main CG - MDC • Agency: State • Tel: 660-785-2420 • Location: 1 mile N of Newark (limited services), 22 miles SE of Edina • GPS: Lat 40.008021 Lon -91.972649 • Open: All year • Total sites: 84 • RV sites: 84 • RV fee: Free • Central water • Vault toilets • Activities: Fishing, power boating, hunting, non-power boating • Elevation: 728

Norborne

W. L. Schifferdecker CA Lot 1 - MDC • Agency: State • Tel: 660-646-6122 • Location: 5 miles N of Norborne (limited services), 11 miles W of Carrollton • GPS: Lat 39.372707 Lon -93.682185 • Open: All year • Total sites: Dispersed • RV sites: Undefined • RV fee: Free • No water • No toilets • Activities: Fishing, hunting • Elevation: 751

W. L. Schifferdecker CA Lot 2 - MDC • Agency: State • Tel: 660-646-6122 • Location: 5 miles N of Norborne (limited services), 11 miles W of Carrollton • GPS: Lat 39.372757 Lon -93.674798 • Open: All year • Total sites: Dispersed • RV sites: Undefined • RV fee: Free • No water • No toilets • Activities: Fishing, hunting • Elevation: 742

W. L. Schifferdecker CA Lot 3 - MDC • Agency: State • Tel: 660-646-6122 • Location: 5 miles N of Norborne (limited services), 11 miles W of Carrollton • GPS: Lat 39.372039 Lon -93.673952 • Open: All year • Total sites: Dispersed • RV sites: Undefined • RV fee: Free • No water • No toilets • Activities: Fishing, hunting • Elevation: 718

Novinger

Henry Truitt Access - MDC • Agency: State • Tel: 660-785-2424 • Location: 1 mile E of Novinger (limited services), 6 miles NW of Kirksville • GPS: Lat 40.234951 Lon -92.685393 • Open: All year • Total sites: Dispersed • RV sites: Undefined • RV fee: Free • No water • No toilets • Activities: Fishing, non-power boating • Elevation: 758

Shoemaker CA - Spring Creek - MDC • Agency: State • Tel: 660-785-2420 • Location: 7 miles NW of Novinger (limited services), 14 miles NW of Kirksville • GPS: Lat 40.294072 Lon -92.799133 • Open: All year • Total sites: Dispersed • RV sites: Undefined • RV fee: Free • No water • No toilets • Activities: Hunting • Elevation: 800

Shoemaker CA - Stahl Road - MDC • Agency: State • Tel: 660-785-2420 • Location: 7 miles NW of Novinger (limited services), 15 miles NW of Kirksville • GPS: Lat 40.284347 Lon -92.800866 • Open: All year • Total sites: Dispersed • RV sites: Undefined • RV fee: Free • No water • No toilets • Activities: Hunting • Elevation: 948

Oak Ridge

Maintz Wildlife Preserve - MDC • Agency: State • Tel: 573-290-5730 • Location: 5 miles W of Oak Ridge (limited services), 10 miles NW of Jackson • GPS: Lat 37.487524 Lon -89.797563 • Open: All year • Total sites: Dispersed • RV sites: Undefined • RV fee: Free • No water • No toilets • Activities: Hiking, fishing, hunting • Elevation: 541

Oregon

Payne Landing Access - MDC • Agency: State • Tel: 816-271-3100 • Location: 6 miles S of Oregon • GPS: Lat 39.907911 Lon -95.161627 • Open: All year • Total sites: Dispersed • RV sites: Undefined • RV fee: Free • No water • No toilets • Activities: Fishing • Elevation: 846

Riverbreaks CA Lot A - MDC • Agency: State • Tel: 816-271-3100 • Location: 6 miles S of Oregon • GPS: Lat 39.919409 Lon -95.091458 • Open: All year • Total sites: Dispersed • RV sites: Undefined • RV fee: Free • No toilets • Activities: Hiking, fishing, hunting, equestrian area • Elevation: 988

Riverbreaks CA Lot C - MDC • Agency: State • Tel: 816-271-3100 • Location: 5 miles S of Oregon • GPS: Lat 39.924953 Lon -95.115471 • Open: All year • Total sites: Dispersed • RV sites: Undefined • RV fee: Free • No toilets • Activities: Hiking, fishing, hunting, equestrian area • Elevation: 1070

Riverbreaks CA Lot D - MDC • Agency: State • Tel: 816-271-3100 • Location: 5 miles S of Oregon • GPS: Lat 39.930516 Lon -95.115548 • Open: All year • Total sites: Dispersed • RV sites: Undefined • RV fee: Free • No toilets • Activities: Hiking, fishing, hunting, equestrian area • Elevation: 1092

Riverbreaks CA Lot E - MDC • Agency: State • Tel: 816-271-3100 • Location: 3 miles S of Oregon • GPS: Lat 39.939737 Lon -95.124864 • Open: All year • Total sites: Dispersed • RV sites: Undefined • RV fee: Free • No toilets • Activities: Hiking, fishing, hunting, equestrian area • Elevation: 1099

Riverbreaks CA Lot G - MDC • Agency: State • Tel: 816-271-3100 • Location: 5 miles S of Oregon • GPS: Lat 39.934913 Lon -95.147983 • Open: All year • Total sites: Dispersed • RV sites: Undefined • RV fee: Free • No toilets • Activities: Hiking, fishing, hunting, equestrian area • Elevation: 919

Wolf Creek Bend CA- MDC • Agency: State • Tel: 816-271-3100 • Location: 6 miles SW of Oregon • GPS: Lat 39.931577 Lon -95.198282 • Open: All year • Total sites: Dispersed • RV sites: Undefined • RV fee: Free • No water • No toilets • Activities: Fishing, hunting • Elevation: 856

Orrick

Cooley Lake CA - MDC • Agency: State • Tel: 816-858-5718 • Location: 7 miles W of Orrick (limited services), 11 miles E of Liberty • GPS: Lat 39.228248 Lon -94.234699 • Open: All year • Total sites: Dispersed • RV sites: Undefined • RV fee: Free • No water • Vault toilets • Activities: Hiking, fishing, hunting • Elevation: 722

Osborn

Pony Express Lake CA East Camp - MDC • Agency: State • Tel: 660-646-6122 • Location: 5 miles N of Osborn (limited services), 10 miles NW of Cameron • GPS: Lat 39.800296 Lon -94.379184 • Open: All year • Total sites: 6 • RV sites: 6 • RV fee: Free • No water • Vault toilets • Activities: Hiking, fishing, hunting • Elevation: 991

Pony Express Lake CA West Camp - MDC • Agency: State • Tel: 660-646-6122 • Location: 5 miles NW of Osborn (limited services), 10 miles NW of Cameron • GPS: Lat 39.797424 Lon -94.396918 • Open: All year • Total sites: Dispersed • RV sites: Undefined • RV fee: Free • No water • Vault toilets • Activities: Hiking, fishing, hunting • Elevation: 1020

Osceola

Kings Prairie Access - MDC • Agency: State • Tel: 660-885-6981 • Location: 8 miles SE of Osceola • GPS: Lat 37.994957 Lon -93.611864 • Open: All year • Total sites: Dispersed • RV sites: Undefined • RV fee: Free • No water • No toilets • Activities: Fishing, hunting, non-power boating • Elevation: 764

Otterville

Lamine River CA Camp 1 - MDC • Agency: State • Tel: 660-530-5500 • Location: 1 mile E of Otterville (limited services), 12 miles E of Sedalia • GPS: Lat 38.705376 Lon -92.978926 • Open: All year • Total sites: Dispersed • RV sites: Undefined • RV fee: Free • No water • No toilets • Activities: Fishing, hunting, non-power boating • Elevation: 689

Lamine River CA Camp 2 - MDC • Agency: State • Tel: 660-530-5500 • Location: 2 miles N of Otterville (limited services), 13 miles E of Sedalia • GPS: Lat 38.730528 Lon -92.992076 • Open: All year • Total sites: Dispersed • RV sites: Undefined • RV fee: Free • No water • No toilets • Activities: Fishing, hunting, non-power boating • Elevation: 702

Lamine River CA Camp 3 Potter Ford - MDC • Agency: State • Tel: 660-530-5500 • Location: 5 miles SE of Otterville (limited services), 15 miles E of Sedalia • GPS: Lat 38.665474 Lon -92.949692 • Open: All year • Total sites: Dispersed • RV sites: Undefined • RV fee: Free • No water • No toilets • Activities: Fishing, hunting, non-power boating • Elevation: 699

Lamine River CA Camp 4 - MDC • Agency: State • Tel: 660-530-5500 • Location: 8 miles SE of Otterville (limited services), 17 miles E of Sedalia • GPS: Lat 38.663551 Lon -92.933451 • Open: All year • Total sites: Dispersed • RV sites: Undefined • RV fee: Free • No water • No toilets • Activities: Fishing, hunting, non-power boating • Elevation: 751

Palmyra

Black Hawk Access - MDC • Agency: State • Tel: 573-248-2530 • Location: 10 miles NW of Palmyra • GPS: Lat 39.859445 Lon -91.673863 • Open: All year • Total sites: Dispersed • RV sites: Undefined • RV fee: Free • No water • No toilets • Activities: Fishing, hunting, non-power boating • Elevation: 584

Fabius Chute Access - MDC • Agency: State • Tel: 573-248-2530 • Location: 8 miles NE of Palmyra • GPS: Lat 39.860368 Lon -91.453483 • Open: All year • Total sites: Dispersed • RV sites: Undefined • RV fee: Free • No water • No toilets • Activities: Fishing, non-power boating • Elevation: 522

McPike Access - MDC • Agency: State • Tel: 573-248-2530 • Location: 16 miles NW of Palmyra • GPS: Lat 39.908092 Lon -91.678844 • Open: All year • Total sites: Dispersed • RV sites: Undefined • RV fee: Free • No water • No toilets • Activities: Fishing, hunting, non-power boating • Elevation: 587

Soulard Access - MDC • Agency: State • Tel: 573-248-2530 • Location: 8 miles NE of Palmyra • GPS: Lat 39.888983 Lon -91.488338 • Open: All year • Total sites: Dispersed • RV sites: Undefined • RV fee: Free • No water • No toilets • Activities: Fishing, hunting, non-power boating • Elevation: 508

Paris

Cedar Bluff Access - MDC • Agency: State • Tel: 573-248-2530 • Location: 5 miles SW of Paris • GPS: Lat 39.436545 Lon -92.050488 • Open: All year • Total sites: Dispersed • RV sites: Undefined • RV fee: Free • No water • No toilets • Activities: Fishing, hunting, non-power boating • Elevation: 702

Paris Access - MDC • Agency: State • Tel: 573-248-2530 • Location: In Paris • GPS: Lat 39.487994 Lon -92.000846 • Open: All year • Total sites: Dispersed • RV sites: Undefined • RV fee: Free • No water • Vault toilets • Activities: Fishing, non-power boating • Elevation: 636

Parnell

Keever Bridge Access - MDC • Agency: State • Tel: 816-271-3100 • Location: 1 mile SW of Parnell (limited services), 18 miles NE of Maryville • GPS: Lat 40.430017 Lon -94.634585 • Open: All year • Total sites: Dispersed • RV sites: Undefined • RV fee: Free • No water • No toilets • Activities: Fishing, non-power boating • Elevation: 1034

Patterson

Wappapello Lake Lot 1 - MDC • Agency: State • Tel: 573-223-4525 • Location: 3 miles NE of Patterson (limited services), 11 miles NE of Piedmont • GPS: Lat 37.197269 Lon -90.499204 • Open: All year • Total sites: Dispersed • RV sites: Undefined • RV fee: Free • No water • No toilets • Activities: Hiking, mountain biking, fishing, hunting, non-power boating, equestrian area • Elevation: 436

Wappapello Lake Lot 2 - MDC • Agency: State • Tel: 573-223-4525 • Location: 5 miles NE of Patterson (limited services), 14 miles NE of Piedmont • GPS: Lat 37.211171 Lon -90.497191 • Open: All year • Total sites: Dispersed • RV sites: Undefined • RV fee: Free • No water • No toilets • Activities: Hiking, mountain biking, fishing, hunting, non-power boating, equestrian area • Elevation: 495

Wappapello Lake Lot 3 - MDC • Agency: State • Tel: 573-223-4525 • Location: 6 miles NE of Patterson (limited services), 14 miles NE of Piedmont • GPS: Lat 37.216334 Lon -90.505856 • Open: All year • Total sites: Dispersed • RV sites: Undefined • RV fee: Free • No water • No toilets • Activities: Hiking, mountain biking, fishing, hunting, non-power boating, equestrian area • Elevation: 466

Wappapello Lake Lot 4 - MDC • Agency: State • Tel: 573-223-4525 • Location: 7 miles NE of Patterson (limited services), 15 miles NE of Piedmont • GPS: Lat 37.229035 Lon -90.505108 • Open: All year • Total sites: Dispersed • RV sites: Undefined • RV fee: Free • No water • No toilets • Activities: Hiking, mountain biking, fishing, hunting, non-power boating, equestrian area • Elevation: 466

Wappapello Lake Lot 5 - MDC • Agency: State • Tel: 573-223-4525 • Location: 4 miles N of Patterson (limited services), 13 miles NE of Piedmont • GPS: Lat 37.230275 Lon -90.516306 • Open: All year • Total sites: Dispersed • RV sites: Undefined • RV fee: Free • No water • No toilets • Activities: Hiking, mountain biking, fishing, hunting, non-power boating, equestrian area • Elevation: 407

Wappapello Lake Lot 6 - MDC • Agency: State • Tel: 573-223-4525 • Location: 4 miles N of Patterson (limited services), 13 miles NE of Piedmont • GPS: Lat 37.216285 Lon -90.526477 • Open: All year • Total sites: Dispersed • RV sites: Undefined • RV fee: Free • No water • No toilets • Activities: Hiking, mountain biking, fishing, hunting, non-power boating, equestrian area • Elevation: 423

Perry

Santa Fe Access - MDC • Agency: State • Tel: 573-248-2530 • Location: 10 miles SW of Perry (limited services), 19 miles NE of Mexico • GPS: Lat 39.374226 Lon -91.806137 • Open: All year • Total sites: Dispersed • RV sites: Undefined • RV fee: Free • No water • No toilets • Activities: Fishing, non-power boating • Elevation: 653

Philadelphia

Callahan Mounds Access - North Site - MDC • Agency: State • Tel: 573-248-2530 • Location: 3 miles W of Philadelphia (limited services), 15 miles NW of Palmyra • GPS: Lat 39.830422 Lon -91.785413 • Open: All year • Total sites: Dispersed • RV sites: Undefined • RV fee: Free • No water • No toilets • Activities: Fishing, hunting • Elevation: 594

Callahan Mounds Access - South Site - MDC • Agency: State • Tel: 573-248-2530 • Location: 4 miles SW of Philadelphia (limited services), 16 miles NW of Palmyra • GPS: Lat 39.822434 Lon -91.788946 • Open: All year • Total sites: Dispersed • RV sites: Undefined • RV fee: Free • No water • No toilets • Activities: Fishing, hunting • Elevation: 653

Dunn Ford Access - MDC • Agency: State • Tel: 573-248-2530 • Location: 4 miles N of Philadelphia (limited services), 17 miles NW of Palmyra • GPS: Lat 39.889211 Lon -91.760423 • Open: All year • Total sites: Dispersed • RV sites: Undefined • RV fee: Free • No water • No toilets • Activities: Fishing, hunting, non-power boating • Elevation: 646

Piedmont

Flatwoods CA - MDC • Agency: State • Tel: 573-223-4525 • Location: 5 miles E of Piedmont • GPS: Lat 37.139914 Lon -90.612157 • Open: All year • Total sites: Dispersed • RV sites: Undefined • RV fee: Free • No water • No toilets • Activities: Hiking, hunting • Elevation: 827

Pilot Grove

Roberts Bluff Access - MDC • Agency: State • Tel: 573-815-7900 • Location: 7 miles NW of Pilot Grove (limited services), 15 miles SW of Boonville • GPS: Lat 38.922092 Lon -92.980743 • Open: All year • Total sites: Dispersed • RV sites: Undefined • RV fee: Free • No toilets • Activities: Fishing, non-power boating • Elevation: 614

Plattsburg

McGee Family CA - MDC • Agency: State • Tel: 816-271-3100 • Location: 2 miles SE of Plattsburg • GPS: Lat 39.54391 Lon -94.42304 • Open: All year • Total sites: Dispersed • RV sites: Undefined • RV fee: Free • No water • No toilets • Activities: Fishing, hunting • Elevation: 965

Pocahontas

Apple Creek CA Lot 1 - MDC • Agency: State • Tel: 573-290-5730 • Location: 5 miles NE of Pocahontas (limited services), 13 miles NE of Jackson • GPS: Lat 37.544119 Lon -89.580376 • Open: All year • Total sites: Dispersed • RV sites: Undefined • RV fee: Free • No water • No toilets • Activities: Hiking, fishing, hunting, non-power boating • Elevation: 581

Apple Creek CA Lot 2 - MDC • Agency: State • Tel: 573-290-5730 • Location: 9 miles NE of Pocahontas (limited services), 17 miles NE of Jackson • GPS: Lat 37.563384 Lon -89.541409 • Open: All year • Total sites: 3 • RV sites: 3 • RV fee: Free • No water • No toilets • Activities: Hiking, fishing, hunting, non-power boating • Elevation: 463

Poplar Bluff

Dan River Access - MDC • Agency: State • Tel: 573-290-5730 • Location: 5 miles SE of Poplar Bluff • GPS: Lat 36.703116 Lon -90.334724 • Open: All year • Total sites: Dispersed • RV sites: Undefined • RV fee: Free • No water • No toilets • Activities: Hiking, fishing, hunting • Elevation: 331

Stephen J. Sun CA - MDC • Agency: State • Tel: 573-290-5730 • Location: 6 miles N of Poplar Bluff • GPS: Lat 36.816513 Lon -90.376146 • Open: All year • Total

sites: Dispersed • RV sites: Undefined • RV fee: Free • No water • No toilets • Activities: Hiking, fishing, hunting, non-power boating • Elevation: 361

Portageville

Girvin CA - MDC • Agency: State • Tel: 573-290-5730 • Location: 13 miles SE of Portageville • GPS: Lat 36.355812 Lon -89.555267 • Open: All year • Total sites: Dispersed • RV sites: Undefined • RV fee: Free • No water • No toilets • Activities: Hiking, fishing, hunting • Elevation: 292

Potosi

Berryman (Mark Twain NF) • Agency: US Forest Service • Location: 17 miles W of Potosi • GPS: Lat 37.929903 Lon -91.062986 • Total sites: 8 • RV sites: 8 • Max RV Length: 34 • RV fee: Free • No water • Vault toilets • Activities: Hiking, mountain biking • Elevation: 1053

Pea Ridge CA Camp 2 - MDC • Agency: State • Tel: 636-441-4554 • Location: 16 miles NW of Potosi • GPS: Lat 38.070511 Lon -91.000934 • Open: All year • Total sites: Dispersed • RV sites: Undefined • RV fee: Free • No water • No toilets • Activities: Fishing, hunting • Elevation: 827

Pea Ridge CA Camp 3 - MDC • Agency: State • Tel: 636-441-4554 • Location: 15 miles NW of Potosi • GPS: Lat 38.064763 Lon -90.980338 • Open: All year • Total sites: Dispersed • RV sites: Undefined • RV fee: Free • No water • No toilets • Activities: Fishing, hunting • Elevation: 892

Pea Ridge CA Camp 4 - MDC • Agency: State • Tel: 636-441-4554 • Location: 14 miles NW of Potosi • GPS: Lat 38.079293 Lon -90.959126 • Open: All year • Total sites: Dispersed • RV sites: Undefined • RV fee: Free • No water • No toilets • Activities: Fishing, hunting • Elevation: 994

Pea Ridge CA Camp 5 - MDC • Agency: State • Tel: 636-441-4554 • Location: 14 miles NW of Potosi • GPS: Lat 38.085508 Lon -90.882523 • Open: All year • Total sites: Dispersed • RV sites: Undefined • RV fee: Free • No water • No toilets • Activities: Fishing, hunting • Elevation: 1148

Prairie Home

Prairie Home CA #2 - MDC • Agency: State • Tel: 660-530-5500 • Location: 3 miles S of Prairie Home (limited services), 12 miles N of California • GPS: Lat 38.782416 Lon -92.595211 • Open: All year • Total sites: Dispersed • RV sites: Undefined • RV fee: Free • No toilets • Activities: Hiking, fishing, hunting, equestrian area • Elevation: 879

Prairie Home CA #4 - MDC • Agency: State • Tel: 660-530-5500 • Location: 4 miles S of Prairie Home (limited services), 11 miles N of California • GPS: Lat 38.777933 Lon -92.59427 • Open: All year • Total sites: Dispersed • RV sites: Undefined • RV fee: Free • No toilets • Activities: Hiking, fishing, hunting, equestrian area • Elevation: 876

Prairie Home CA #5 - MDC • Agency: State • Tel: 660-530-5500 • Location: 5 miles S of Prairie Home (limited services), 13 miles N of California • GPS: Lat 38.778117 Lon -92.581199 • Open: All year • Total sites: Dispersed • RV sites: Undefined • RV fee: Free • No toilets • Activities: Hiking, fishing, hunting, equestrian area • Elevation: 853

Prairie Home CA #6 - MDC • Agency: State • Tel: 660-530-5500 • Location: 5 miles S of Prairie Home (limited services), 13 miles N of California • GPS: Lat 38.774404 Lon -92.573879 • Open: All year • Total sites: Dispersed • RV sites: Undefined • RV fee: Free • No toilets • Activities: Hiking, fishing, hunting, equestrian area • Elevation: 709

Prairie Home CA #9 - MDC • Agency: State • Tel: 660-530-5500 • Location: 6 miles S of Prairie Home (limited services), 10 miles N of California • GPS: Lat 38.759689 Lon -92.585254 • Open: All year • Total sites: Dispersed • RV sites: Undefined • RV fee: Free • No toilets • Activities: Hiking, fishing, hunting, equestrian area • Elevation: 676

Preston

Mule Shoe CA - MDC • Agency: State • Tel: 417-532-7612 • Location: 9 miles NE of Preston (limited services), 28 miles SE of Warsaw • GPS: Lat 37.991369 Lon -93.094509 • Open: All year • Total sites: Dispersed • RV sites: Undefined • RV fee: Free • No water • No toilets • Activities: Hiking, fishing, swimming, hunting, non-power boating • Elevation: 804

Princeton

Lake Paho CA Site B - MDC • Agency: State • Tel: 660-646-6122 • Location: 4 miles W of Princeton • GPS: Lat 40.407685 Lon -93.657199 • Open: All year • Total sites: 14 • RV sites: 14 • RV fee: Free • No water • No toilets • Activities: Hiking, fishing, power boating, hunting, non-power boating • Elevation: 994

Lake Paho CA Site C - MDC • Agency: State • Tel: 660-646-6122 • Location: 5 miles NW of Princeton • GPS: Lat 40.417125 Lon -93.665927 • Open: All year • Total sites: 10 • RV sites: 10 • RV fee: Free • No water • No toilets • Activities: Hiking, fishing, power boating, hunting, non-power boating • Elevation: 958

Lake Paho CA Site D - MDC • Agency: State • Tel: 660-646-6122 • Location: 6 miles NW of Princeton • GPS: Lat 40.414564 Lon -93.665957 • Open: All year • Total sites: 11 • RV sites: 11 • RV fee: Free • No water • No toi-

lets • Activities: Hiking, fishing, power boating, hunting, non-power boating • Elevation: 968

Puxico

Crowleys Ridge CA - MDC • Agency: State • Tel: 573-290-5730 • Location: 11 miles E of Puxico • GPS: Lat 36.945224 Lon -89.993163 • Open: All year • Total sites: Dispersed • RV sites: Undefined • RV fee: Free • No water • No toilets • Activities: Hiking, fishing, hunting • Elevation: 456

Duck Creek CA Headquarters CG - MDC • Agency: State • Tel: 573-290-5730 • Location: 9 miles NE of Puxico • GPS: Lat 37.04614 Lon -90.07358 • Open: All year • Total sites: Dispersed • RV sites: Undefined • RV fee: Free • No water • Vault toilets • Activities: Hiking, fishing, hunting • Elevation: 341

Duck Creek CA Pool 1 - MDC • Agency: State • Tel: 573-290-5730 • Location: 7 miles NE of Puxico • GPS: Lat 37.022536 Lon -90.104314 • Open: All year • Total sites: 7 • RV sites: 7 • RV fee: Free • No water • Vault toilets • Activities: Hiking, fishing, hunting • Elevation: 351

Qulin

Coon Island CA - MDC • Agency: State • Tel: 573-290-5730 • Location: 10 miles SW of Qulin (limited services), 23 miles S of Poplar Bluff • GPS: Lat 36.514925 Lon -90.363134 • Open: All year • Total sites: Dispersed • RV sites: Undefined • RV fee: Free • No water • Vault toilets • Activities: Hiking, fishing, hunting • Elevation: 315

Rich Hill

Four Rivers CA - Busch Wetlands - MDC • Agency: State • Tel: 417-395-2341 • Location: 10 miles SE of Rich Hill • GPS: Lat 38.041369 Lon -94.271774 • Open: All year • Total sites: Dispersed • RV sites: Undefined • RV fee: Free • No water • Vault toilets • Activities: Hiking, fishing, hunting • Elevation: 774

Harmony Mission Lake CA - MDC • Agency: State • Tel: 417-395-2341 • Location: 4 miles SW of Rich Hill • GPS: Lat 38.085155 Lon -94.429897 • Open: All year • Total sites: Dispersed • RV sites: Undefined • RV fee: Free • No water • No toilets • Activities: Hiking, fishing, hunting • Elevation: 879

Old Town Access - MDC • Agency: State • Tel: 417-395-2341 • Location: 4 miles N of Rich Hill • GPS: Lat 38.140992 Lon -94.364772 • Open: All year • Total sites: Dispersed • RV sites: Undefined • RV fee: Free • No water • No toilets • Activities: Fishing, hunting, non-power boating • Elevation: 761

Peabody CA Lot 1 - MDC • Agency: State • Tel: 417-395-2341 • Location: 4 miles W of Rich Hill • GPS: Lat 38.098745 Lon -94.449579 • Open: All year • Total sites: Dispersed • RV sites: Undefined • RV fee: Free • No water • No toilets • Activities: Hiking, fishing, hunting • Elevation: 932

Peabody CA Lot 2 - MDC • Agency: State • Tel: 417-395-2341 • Location: 5 miles W of Rich Hill • GPS: Lat 38.091138 Lon -94.446844 • Open: All year • Total sites: Dispersed • RV sites: Undefined • RV fee: Free • No water • No toilets • Activities: Hiking, fishing, hunting • Elevation: 922

Richmond

Crooked River CA - Lot 1 - MDC • Agency: State • Tel: 660-646-6122 • Location: 13 miles NW of Richmond • GPS: Lat 39.409365 Lon -94.062645 • Open: All year • Total sites: Dispersed • RV sites: Undefined • RV fee: Free • No water • No toilets • Activities: Fishing, hunting, non-power boating • Elevation: 771

Crooked River CA - Lot 2 - MDC • Agency: State • Tel: 660-646-6122 • Location: 13 miles NW of Richmond • GPS: Lat 39.405068 Lon -94.059888 • Open: All year • Total sites: Dispersed • RV sites: Undefined • RV fee: Free • No water • No toilets • Activities: Fishing, hunting, non-power boating • Elevation: 787

Crooked River CA - Lot 3 - MDC • Agency: State • Tel: 660-646-6122 • Location: 10 miles NW of Richmond • GPS: Lat 39.386189 Lon -94.039507 • Open: All year • Total sites: Dispersed • RV sites: Undefined • RV fee: Free • No water • No toilets • Activities: Fishing, hunting, non-power boating • Elevation: 774

Crooked River CA - Lot 4 - MDC • Agency: State • Tel: 660-646-6122 • Location: 12 miles NW of Richmond • GPS: Lat 39.392142 Lon -94.030478 • Open: All year • Total sites: Dispersed • RV sites: Undefined • RV fee: Free • No water • No toilets • Activities: Fishing, hunting, non-power boating • Elevation: 912

Crooked River CA - Lot 5 - MDC • Agency: State • Tel: 660-646-6122 • Location: 11 miles NW of Richmond • GPS: Lat 39.399791 Lon -94.042079 • Open: All year • Total sites: Dispersed • RV sites: Undefined • RV fee: Free • No water • No toilets • Activities: Fishing, hunting, non-power boating • Elevation: 814

Crooked River CA - Lot 6 - MDC • Agency: State • Tel: 660-646-6122 • Location: 11 miles NW of Richmond • GPS: Lat 39.408777 Lon -94.044581 • Open: All year • Total sites: Dispersed • RV sites: Undefined • RV fee: Free • No water • No toilets • Activities: Fishing, hunting, non-power boating • Elevation: 837

Crooked River CA - Lot 7 - MDC • Agency: State • Tel: 660-646-6122 • Location: 12 miles NW of Richmond • GPS: Lat 39.413799 Lon -94.053859 • Open: All year • Total sites: Dispersed • RV sites: Undefined • RV fee: Free • No water • No toilets • Activities: Fishing, hunting, non-power boating • Elevation: 784

Wagner (Frank E.) CA Lot 1 - MDC • Agency: State • Tel: 660-646-6122 • Location: 12 miles NE of Richmond • GPS: Lat 39.39229 Lon -93.894459 • Open: All year • Total sites: Dispersed • RV sites: Undefined • RV fee: Free • No water • No toilets • Activities: Hunting • Elevation: 879

Wagner (Frank E.) CA Lot 2 - MDC • Agency: State • Tel: 660-646-6122 • Location: 11 miles NE of Richmond • GPS: Lat 39.385511 Lon -93.895436 • Open: All year • Total sites: Dispersed • RV sites: Undefined • RV fee: Free • No water • No toilets • Activities: Hunting • Elevation: 850

Rocheport

Davisdale CA Camp 3 - MDC • Agency: State • Tel: 573-815-7900 • Location: 4 miles NW of Rocheport (limited services), 11 miles NE of Booneville • GPS: Lat 39.004494 Lon -92.615736 • Open: All year • Total sites: Dispersed • RV sites: Undefined • RV fee: Free • No water • No toilets • Activities: Hiking, fishing, hunting • Elevation: 630

Davisdale CA Camp 4 - MDC • Agency: State • Tel: 573-815-7900 • Location: 5 miles NW of Rocheport (limited services), 9 miles NE of Booneville • GPS: Lat 39.015323 Lon -92.636427 • Open: All year • Total sites: Dispersed • RV sites: Undefined • RV fee: Free • No water • No toilets • Activities: Hiking, fishing, hunting • Elevation: 781

Davisdale CA Camp 5 - MDC • Agency: State • Tel: 573-815-7900 • Location: 5 miles NW of Rocheport (limited services), 8 miles NE of Booneville • GPS: Lat 38.994298 Lon -92.628497 • Open: All year • Total sites: Dispersed • RV sites: Undefined • RV fee: Free • No water • No toilets • Activities: Hiking, fishing, hunting • Elevation: 594

Davisdale CA Camp 6 - MDC • Agency: State • Tel: 573-815-7900 • Location: 6 miles NW of Rocheport (limited services), 14 miles NE of Booneville • GPS: Lat 39.029735 Lon -92.610426 • Open: All year • Total sites: Dispersed • RV sites: Undefined • RV fee: Free • No water • No toilets • Activities: Hiking, fishing, hunting • Elevation: 659

Davisdale CA Camp 7 - MDC • Agency: State • Tel: 573-815-7900 • Location: 7 miles NW of Rocheport (limited services), 12 miles NE of Booneville • GPS: Lat 39.036005 Lon -92.629203 • Open: All year • Total sites: Dispersed • RV sites: Undefined • RV fee: Free • No water • No toilets • Activities: Hiking, fishing, hunting • Elevation: 771

Rock Port

Aspinwall Bend - MDC • Agency: State • Tel: 816-271-3100 • Location: 17 miles SW of Rock Port • GPS: Lat 40.316766 Lon -95.626126 • Open: All year • Total sites: Dispersed • RV sites: Undefined • RV fee: Free • No water • No toilets • Activities: Fishing, hunting • Elevation: 889

Brickyard Hill CA - Charity Lake CG - MDC • Agency: State • Tel: 816-271-3100 • Location: 8 miles NW of Rock Port • GPS: Lat 40.474679 Lon -95.583734 • Open: All year • Total sites: Dispersed • RV sites: Undefined • RV fee: Free • No water • Vault toilets • Activities: Hiking, fishing, hunting • Elevation: 1056

Brickyard Hill CA - East CG - MDC • Agency: State • Tel: 816-271-3100 • Location: 5 miles NW of Rock Port • GPS: Lat 40.460632 Lon -95.555209 • Open: All year • Total sites: 7 • RV sites: 7 • RV fee: Free • No water • No toilets • Activities: Hiking, fishing, hunting • Elevation: 1138

Deroin Bend CA - MDC • Agency: State • Tel: 816-271-3100 • Location: 12 miles S of Rock Port • GPS: Lat 40.279553 Lon -95.549568 • Open: All year • Total sites: Dispersed • RV sites: Undefined • RV fee: Free • No water • No toilets • Activities: Fishing, hunting • Elevation: 882

Hoot Owl Bend Access - MDC • Agency: State • Tel: 816-271-3100 • Location: 14 miles SW of Rock Port • GPS: Lat 40.315636 Lon -95.616902 • Open: All year • Total sites: 3 • RV sites: 3 • RV fee: Free • No water • Vault toilets • Activities: Fishing, non-power boating • Elevation: 879

Langdon Bend Access - MDC • Agency: State • Tel: 816-271-3100 • Location: 15 miles SW of Rock Port • GPS: Lat 40.338951 Lon -95.621374 • Open: All year • Total sites: Dispersed • RV sites: Undefined • RV fee: Free • No water • Vault toilets • Activities: Fishing • Elevation: 912

Lower Hamburg Bend CA - MDC • Agency: State • Tel: 816-271-3100 • Location: 25 miles NW of Rock Port (limited services), 8 miles SW of Hamburg, IA • GPS: Lat 40.550043 Lon -95.758227 • Open: All year • Total sites: Dispersed • RV sites: Undefined • RV fee: Free • No water • No toilets • Activities: Fishing, hunting • Elevation: 909

Nishnabotna CA - MDC • Agency: State • Tel: 816-271-3100 • Location: 13 miles NW of Rock Port • GPS: Lat 40.459813 Lon -95.665848 • Open: All year • Total sites: Dispersed • RV sites: Undefined • RV fee: Free • No toilets • Activities: Hiking, fishing, hunting • Elevation: 889

Star School Hill Prairie CA North - MDC • Agency: State • Tel: 816-271-3100 • Location: 15 miles NW of Rockport • GPS: Lat 40.560507 Lon -95.634198 • Open: All year • Total sites: Dispersed • RV sites: Undefined • RV fee: Free • No water • No toilets • Activities: Hunting • Elevation: 991

Star School Hill Prairie CA South - MDC • Agency: State • Tel: 816-271-3100 • Location: 14 miles NW of Rockport • GPS: Lat 40.549355 Lon -95.624721 • Open: All year • Total sites: Dispersed • RV sites: Undefined • RV fee: Free • No water • No toilets • Activities: Hunting • Elevation: 997

Watson Access - MDC • Agency: State • Tel: 816-271-3100 • Location: 14 miles NW of Rock Port • GPS: Lat 40.498951 Lon -95.677039 • Open: All year • Total sites: Dispersed • RV sites: Undefined • RV fee: Free • No water • No toilets • Activities: Fishing • Elevation: 899

Russellville

Scrivner Road CA - MDC • Agency: State • Tel: 573-815-7900 • Location: 4 miles SE of Russellville (limited services), 14 miles SW of Jefferson City • GPS: Lat 38.490067 Lon -92.398443 • Open: All year • Total sites: Dispersed • RV sites: Undefined • RV fee: Free • No water • Vault toilets • Activities: Fishing, hunting, non-power boating • Elevation: 800

Saint Clair

Little Indian Creek CA - MDC • Agency: State • Tel: 636-441-4554 • Location: 11 miles S of Saint Clair • GPS: Lat 38.214381 Lon -90.930831 • Open: All year • Total sites: 12 • RV sites: 12 • RV fee: Free • No water • Vault toilets • Activities: Hiking, mountain biking, fishing, hunting • Elevation: 623

Salem

Indian Trail CA Camp 2 - MDC • Agency: State • Tel: 573-729-3182 • Location: 14 miles NE of Salem • GPS: Lat 37.744557 Lon -91.376911 • Open: All year • Total sites: Dispersed • RV sites: Undefined • RV fee: Free • No water • No toilets • Activities: Hiking, fishing, hunting, equestrian area • Elevation: 1266

Indian Trail CA Camp 3 - MDC • Agency: State • Tel: 573-729-3182 • Location: 16 miles NE of Salem • GPS: Lat 37.722876 Lon -91.359684 • Open: All year • Total sites: Dispersed • RV sites: Undefined • RV fee: Free • No water • No toilets • Activities: Hiking, fishing, hunting, equestrian area • Elevation: 1316

Indian Trail CA Camp 4 - MDC • Agency: State • Tel: 573-729-3182 • Location: 12 miles SE of Salem • GPS: Lat 37.683744 Lon -91.369053 • Open: All year • Total sites: Dispersed • RV sites: Undefined • RV fee: Free • No water • No toilets • Activities: Hiking, fishing, hunting, equestrian area • Elevation: 1293

Indian Trail CA Camp 5 - MDC • Agency: State • Tel: 573-729-3182 • Location: 16 miles NE of Salem • GPS: Lat 37.693175 Lon -91.340395 • Open: All year • Total sites: Dispersed • RV sites: Undefined • RV fee: Free • No water • No toilets • Activities: Hiking, fishing, hunting, equestrian area • Elevation: 1355

Shawnee Mac Lakes CA - MDC • Agency: State • Tel: 573-729-3182 • Location: 2 miles E of Salem • GPS: Lat 37.649087 Lon -91.512968 • Open: All year • Total sites: Dispersed • RV sites: Undefined • RV fee: Free • No water • Vault toilets • Activities: Hiking, fishing, non-power boating • Elevation: 1217

White River Trace CA - MDC • Agency: State • Tel: 573-368-2225 • Location: 11 miles W of Salem • GPS: Lat 37.624257 Lon -91.726967 • Open: All year • Total sites: Dispersed • RV sites: Undefined • RV fee: Free • No water • Vault toilets • Activities: Hiking, fishing, hunting • Elevation: 1207

Savannah

Hadorn Bridge Access - MDC • Agency: State • Tel: 816-271-3100 • Location: 6 miles N of Savannah • GPS: Lat 40.012701 Lon -94.796853 • Open: All year • Total sites: Dispersed • RV sites: Undefined • RV fee: Free • No water • No toilets • Activities: Fishing, hunting, non-power boating • Elevation: 925

Happy Holler Lake CA - Lot 1 - MDC • Agency: State • Tel: 816-271-3100 • Location: 9 miles NE of Savannah • GPS: Lat 39.966914 Lon -94.792199 • Open: All year • Total sites: Dispersed • RV sites: Undefined • RV fee: Free • No water • No toilets • Activities: Hiking, fishing, hunting • Elevation: 925

Happy Holler Lake CA - Lot 2 - MDC • Agency: State • Tel: 816-271-3100 • Location: 3 miles NE of Savannah • GPS: Lat 39.960719 Lon -94.785175 • Open: All year • Total sites: Dispersed • RV sites: Undefined • RV fee: Free • No water • No toilets • Activities: Hiking, fishing, hunting • Elevation: 1001

Happy Holler Lake CA - Lot 3 - MDC • Agency: State • Tel: 816-271-3100 • Location: 5 miles NE of Savannah • GPS: Lat 39.959513 Lon -94.765832 • Open: All year • Total sites: Dispersed • RV sites: Undefined • RV fee: Free • No water • No toilets • Activities: Hiking, fishing, hunting • Elevation: 1014

Happy Holler Lake CA - Lot 4 - MDC • Agency: State • Tel: 816-271-3100 • Location: 6 miles NE of Savannah • GPS: Lat 39.964056 Lon -94.769678 • Open: All

year • Total sites: Dispersed • RV sites: Undefined • RV fee: Free • No water • No toilets • Activities: Hiking, fishing, hunting • Elevation: 892

Happy Holler Lake CA - Lot 5 - MDC • Agency: State • Tel: 816-271-3100 • Location: 7 miles NE of Savannah • GPS: Lat 39.973716 Lon -94.760365 • Open: All year • Total sites: Dispersed • RV sites: Undefined • RV fee: Free • No water • No toilets • Activities: Hiking, fishing, hunting • Elevation: 1047

Happy Holler Lake CA - Lot 6 - MDC • Agency: State • Tel: 816-271-3100 • Location: 8 miles NE of Savannah • GPS: Lat 39.974745 Lon -94.775056 • Open: All year • Total sites: Dispersed • RV sites: Undefined • RV fee: Free • No water • No toilets • Activities: Hiking, fishing, hunting • Elevation: 928

Happy Holler Lake CA - Lot 7 - MDC • Agency: State • Tel: 816-271-3100 • Location: 9 miles NE of Savannah • GPS: Lat 40.003216 Lon -94.735149 • Open: All year • Total sites: Dispersed • RV sites: Undefined • RV fee: Free • No water • No toilets • Activities: Hiking, fishing, hunting • Elevation: 1060

Happy Holler Lake CA - Lot 8 - MDC • Agency: State • Tel: 816-271-3100 • Location: 10 miles NE of Savannah • GPS: Lat 40.013322 Lon -94.729588 • Open: All year • Total sites: Dispersed • RV sites: Undefined • RV fee: Free • No water • No toilets • Activities: Hiking, fishing, hunting • Elevation: 1056

Happy Holler Lake CA - Lot 9 - MDC • Agency: State • Tel: 816-271-3100 • Location: 11 miles NE of Savannah • GPS: Lat 40.029605 Lon -94.737965 • Open: All year • Total sites: Dispersed • RV sites: Undefined • RV fee: Free • No water • No toilets • Activities: Hiking, fishing, hunting • Elevation: 965

Honey Creek CA Site 1 - MDC • Agency: State • Tel: 816-271-3100 • Location: 10 miles W of Savannah • GPS: Lat 39.946773 Lon -94.964959 • Open: All year • Total sites: Dispersed • RV sites: Undefined • RV fee: Free • No water • No toilets • Activities: Hiking, mountain biking, fishing, hunting, non-power boating, equestrian area • Elevation: 1056

Honey Creek CA Site 2 - MDC • Agency: State • Tel: 816-271-3100 • Location: 11 miles W of Savannah • GPS: Lat 39.939263 Lon -94.983041 • Open: All year • Total sites: Dispersed • RV sites: Undefined • RV fee: Free • No water • No toilets • Activities: Hiking, mountain biking, fishing, hunting, non-power boating, equestrian area • Elevation: 942

Honey Creek CA Site 3 - MDC • Agency: State • Tel: 816-271-3100 • Location: 10 miles W of Savannah • GPS: Lat 39.957054 Lon -94.974029 • Open: All year • Total sites: Dispersed • RV sites: Undefined • RV fee: Free • No water • No toilets • Activities: Hiking, mountain biking, fishing, hunting, non-power boating, equestrian area • Elevation: 1056

Honey Creek CA Site 4 - MDC • Agency: State • Tel: 816-271-3100 • Location: 11 miles W of Savannah • GPS: Lat 39.951839 Lon -94.990758 • Open: All year • Total sites: Dispersed • RV sites: Undefined • RV fee: Free • No water • No toilets • Activities: Hiking, mountain biking, fishing, hunting, non-power boating, equestrian area • Elevation: 882

Honey Creek CA Site 5 - MDC • Agency: State • Tel: 816-271-3100 • Location: 11 miles W of Savannah • GPS: Lat 39.948963 Lon -94.986597 • Open: All year • Total sites: Dispersed • RV sites: Undefined • RV fee: Free • No water • No toilets • Activities: Hiking, mountain biking, fishing, hunting, non-power boating, equestrian area • Elevation: 919

Honey Creek CA Site 6 - MDC • Agency: State • Tel: 816-271-3100 • Location: 11 miles W of Savannah • GPS: Lat 39.945197 Lon -94.986589 • Open: All year • Total sites: Dispersed • RV sites: Undefined • RV fee: Free • No water • No toilets • Activities: Hiking, mountain biking, fishing, hunting, non-power boating, equestrian area • Elevation: 909

Honey Creek CA Site 7 - MDC • Agency: State • Tel: 816-271-3100 • Location: 11 miles W of Savannah • GPS: Lat 39.941827 Lon -94.988748 • Open: All year • Total sites: Dispersed • RV sites: Undefined • RV fee: Free • No water • No toilets • Activities: Hiking, mountain biking, fishing, hunting, non-power boating, equestrian area • Elevation: 942

Monkey Mountain CA #1 - MDC • Agency: State • Tel: 816-271-3100 • Location: 13 miles W of Savannah • GPS: Lat 39.936994 Lon -95.008425 • Open: All year • Total sites: Dispersed • RV sites: Undefined • RV fee: Free • No water • No toilets • Activities: Hiking, fishing, hunting, non-power boating • Elevation: 860

Monkey Mountain CA #2 - MDC • Agency: State • Tel: 816-271-3100 • Location: 17 miles W of Savannah • GPS: Lat 39.931341 Lon -95.020568 • Open: All year • Total sites: Dispersed • RV sites: Undefined • RV fee: Free • No water • No toilets • Elevation: 1053

Monkey Mountain CA #3 - MDC • Agency: State • Tel: 816-271-3100 • Location: 12 miles SW of Savannah • GPS: Lat 39.909791 Lon -95.010877 • Open: All year • Total sites: Dispersed • RV sites: Undefined • RV fee: Free • No water • No toilets • Elevation: 932

Rochester Falls Access - MDC • Agency: State • Tel: 816-271-3100 • Location: 10 miles SE of Savannah • GPS: Lat 39.908437 Lon -94.691661 • Open: All year • Total sites: 11 • RV sites: 11 • RV fee: Free • No water • Vault toi-

lets • Activities: Fishing, non-power boating • Elevation: 896

Schell City

Schell-Osage CA North CG - MDC • Agency: State • Tel: 417-432-3414 • Location: 4 miles E of Schell City (limited services), 13 miles N of El Dorado Springs • GPS: Lat 38.013743 Lon -94.060481 • Open: All year • Total sites: Dispersed • RV sites: Undefined • RV fee: Free • No water • Vault toilets • Activities: Hiking, fishing, hunting • Elevation: 748

Schell-Osage CA South CG - MDC • Agency: State • Tel: 417-432-3414 • Location: 4 miles E of Schell City (limited services), 13 miles N of El Dorado Springs • GPS: Lat 38.004533 Lon -94.0600083 • Open: All year • Total sites: Dispersed • RV sites: Undefined • RV fee: Free • No water • Vault toilets • Activities: Hiking, fishing, hunting • Elevation: 745

Shelbina

Arrow-Wood CA - MDC • Agency: State • Tel: 573-248-2530 • Location: 3 miles N of Shelbina • GPS: Lat 39.742561 Lon -92.040012 • Open: All year • Total sites: Dispersed • RV sites: Undefined • RV fee: Free • No water • No toilets • Activities: Fishing, hunting, non-power boating • Elevation: 712

Pin Oak CA - MDC • Agency: State • Tel: 660-785-2420 • Location: 10 miles NW of Shelbina • GPS: Lat 39.778007 Lon -92.145844 • Open: All year • Total sites: Dispersed • RV sites: Undefined • RV fee: Free • No water • No toilets • Activities: Hunting • Elevation: 732

Silex

William R. Logan CA Lot 1 - MDC • Agency: State • Tel: 636-441-4554 • Location: 3 miles W of Silex (limited services), 17 miles NW of Troy • GPS: Lat 39.151544 Lon -91.050849 • Open: All year • Total sites: Dispersed • RV sites: Undefined • RV fee: Free • No water • Vault toilets • Activities: Hiking, mountain biking, fishing, hunting • Elevation: 699

William R. Logan CA Lot 2 - MDC • Agency: State • Tel: 636-441-4554 • Location: 5 miles NE of Silex (limited services), 16 miles NW of Troy • GPS: Lat 39.162491 Lon -91.042979 • Open: All year • Total sites: Dispersed • RV sites: Undefined • RV fee: Free • No water • No toilets • Activities: Hiking, mountain biking, fishing, hunting • Elevation: 712

William R. Logan CA Lot 3 - MDC • Agency: State • Tel: 636-441-4554 • Location: 7 miles NE of Silex (limited services), 15 miles N of Troy • GPS: Lat 39.143098 Lon -91.020731 • Open: All year • Total sites: Dispersed • RV sites: Undefined • RV fee: Free • No water • Vault toilets • Activities: Hiking, mountain biking, fishing, hunting • Elevation: 682

South Gorin

Ella Ewing Lake CA - MDC • Agency: State • Tel: 660-785-2420 • Location: 2 miles NE of South Gorin (limited services), 17 miles SE of Memphis • GPS: Lat 40.342445 Lon -92.007915 • Open: All year • Total sites: Dispersed • RV sites: Undefined • RV fee: Free • No water • Vault toilets • Activities: Fishing, hunting • Elevation: 742

St. Elizabeth

Osage-Tavern Access - MDC • Agency: State • Tel: 573-346-2210 • Location: 5 miles N of St. Elizabeth (limited services), 28 miles S of Jefferson City • GPS: Lat 38.317236 Lon -92.287587 • Open: All year • Total sites: 23 • RV sites: 23 • RV fee: Free • No water • Vault toilets • Activities: Fishing, non-power boating • Elevation: 656

St. Francisville

Fort Pike Access - MDC • Agency: State • Tel: 573-248-2530 • Location: In St. Francisville (limited services), 14 miles NE of Kahoka • GPS: Lat 40.460793 Lon -91.566712 • Open: All year • Total sites: Dispersed • RV sites: Undefined • RV fee: Free • No water • No toilets • Activities: Fishing, non-power boating • Elevation: 505

Frost Island CA - North Lot - MDC • Agency: State • Tel: 660-785-2420 • Location: 1 mile E of St. Francisville (limited services), 15 miles NE of Kahoka • GPS: Lat 40.456866 Lon -91.548215 • Open: All year • Total sites: Dispersed • RV sites: Undefined • RV fee: Free • No water • No toilets • Activities: Fishing, hunting, non-power boating • Elevation: 502

Frost Island CA - South Lot - MDC • Agency: State • Tel: 660-785-2420 • Location: 2 miles SE of St. Francisville (limited services), 13 miles E of Kahoka • GPS: Lat 40.436244 Lon -91.535086 • Open: All year • Total sites: Dispersed • RV sites: Undefined • RV fee: Free • No water • No toilets • Activities: Fishing, hunting, non-power boating • Elevation: 499

Frost Island CA - West Lot - MDC • Agency: State • Tel: 660-785-2420 • Location: 1 mile E of St. Francisville (limited services), 12 miles E of Kahoka • GPS: Lat 40.448132 Lon -91.555797 • Open: All year • Total sites: Dispersed • RV sites: Undefined • RV fee: Free • No water • No toilets • Activities: Fishing, hunting, non-power boating • Elevation: 512

St. Joseph

Agency CA - MDC • Agency: State • Tel: 816-271-3100 • Location: 9 miles SE of St. Joseph • GPS: Lat 39.627244 Lon -94.731238 • Open: All year • Total sites: Dispersed • RV sites: Undefined • RV fee: Free • No water • No toilets • Activities: Hiking, fishing, hunting, non-power boating • Elevation: 853

Arthur DuPree CA - MDC • Agency: State • Tel: 816-271-3100 • Location: In St. Joseph • GPS: Lat 39.786021 Lon -94.883088 • Open: All year • Total sites: Dispersed • RV sites: Undefined • RV fee: Free • No water • No toilets • Activities: Hiking, fishing, hunting, non-power boating • Elevation: 824

Bluffwoods CA - Camp 1 - MDC • Agency: State • Tel: 816-271-3100 • Location: 8 miles SW of St. Joseph • GPS: Lat 39.620455 Lon -94.942655 • Open: All year • Total sites: Dispersed • RV sites: Undefined • RV fee: Free • No water • Vault toilets • Activities: Hiking, hunting • Elevation: 1020

Bluffwoods CA - Camp 2 - MDC • Agency: State • Tel: 816-271-3100 • Location: 8 miles SW of St. Joseph • GPS: Lat 39.643928 Lon -94.933094 • Open: All year • Total sites: Dispersed • RV sites: Undefined • RV fee: Free • No water • No toilets • Notes: Permit required • Activities: Hiking, hunting • Elevation: 1027

Steelville

Huzzah CA - MDC • Agency: State • Tel: 636-441-4554 • Location: 12 miles NE of Steelville • GPS: Lat 38.022688 Lon -91.20112 • Open: Sep-May • Total sites: 18 • RV sites: 18 • RV fee: Free • No water • No toilets • Activities: Hiking, fishing, hunting, non-power boating • Elevation: 699

Stockton

Bluff Springs CA - MDC • Agency: State • Tel: 417-895-6880 • Location: 8 miles NE of Stockton • GPS: Lat 37.785901 Lon -93.761345 • Open: All year • Total sites: Dispersed • RV sites: Undefined • RV fee: Free • No water • No toilets • Activities: Hunting • Elevation: 951

Stotts City

Talbot (Robert E.) CA - MDC • Agency: State • Tel: 417-895-6880 • Location: 5 miles N of Stotts City (limited services), 13 miles NW of Mt Vernon • GPS: Lat 37.171334 Lon -93.947312 • Open: All year • Total sites: 6 • RV sites: Undefined • RV fee: Free • No water • No toilets • Activities: Hiking, mountain biking, fishing, hunting, non-power boating, equestrian area • Elevation: 1217

Stover

Big Buffalo Creek CA - MDC • Agency: State • Tel: 660-530-5500 • Location: 11 miles SW of Stover (limited services), 19 miles SW of Versailles • GPS: Lat 38.333683 Lon -93.089095 • Open: All year • Total sites: 20 • RV sites: 10 • RV fee: Free • No water • No toilets • Activities: Hiking, mountain biking, fishing, hunting • Elevation: 774

Summersville

Gist Ranch CA Lot 1 - MDC • Agency: State • Tel: 417-256-7161 • Location: 7 miles NW of Summersville (limited services), 18 miles SE of Houston • GPS: Lat 37.210503 Lon -91.764006 • Open: All year • Total sites: Dispersed • RV sites: Undefined • RV fee: Free • No water • No toilets • Activities: Hiking, fishing, hunting • Elevation: 1457

Gist Ranch CA Lot 2 - MDC • Agency: State • Tel: 417-256-7161 • Location: 11 miles W of Summersville (limited services), 21 miles NW of Mountain View • GPS: Lat 37.169625 Lon -91.768491 • Open: All year • Total sites: Dispersed • RV sites: Undefined • RV fee: Free • No water • No toilets • Activities: Hiking, fishing, hunting • Elevation: 1411

Gist Ranch CA Lot 3 - MDC • Agency: State • Tel: 417-256-7161 • Location: 13 miles W of Summersville (limited services), 19 miles SE of Houston • GPS: Lat 37.169565 Lon -91.803591 • Open: All year • Total sites: Dispersed • RV sites: Undefined • RV fee: Free • No water • No toilets • Activities: Hiking, fishing, hunting • Elevation: 1312

Sunklands CA West Lot - MDC • Agency: State • Tel: 573-226-3616 • Location: 11 miles N of Summersville (limited services), 24 miles N of Mountain View • GPS: Lat 37.303975 Lon -91.614552 • Open: All year • Total sites: Dispersed • RV sites: Undefined • RV fee: Free • No water • No toilets • Activities: Hiking, fishing, hunting • Elevation: 1247

Sumner

Yellow Creek CA Lot 1 - MDC • Agency: State • Tel: 660-646-6122 • Location: 5 miles S of Sumner (limited services), 22 miles SW of Brookfield • GPS: Lat 39.578742 Lon -93.235796 • Open: All year • Total sites: Dispersed • RV sites: Undefined • RV fee: Free • No water • No toilets • Activities: Hiking, fishing, hunting • Elevation: 676

Yellow Creek CA Lot 1 - MDC • Agency: State • Tel: 660-646-6122 • Location: 5 miles S of Sumner (limited services), 22 miles SW of Brookfield • GPS: Lat 39.585641 Lon -93.235552 • Open: All year • Total sites: Dispersed • RV sites: Undefined • RV fee: Free • No water • No toilets • Activities: Hiking, fishing, hunting • Elevation: 682

Sweet Springs

Ralph and Martha Perry Memorial CA Lot B - MDC • Agency: State • Tel: 660-530-5500 • Location: 3 miles W of Sweet Springs • GPS: Lat 38.948904 Lon -93.467695 • Open: All year • Total sites: Dispersed • RV sites: Undefined • RV fee: Free • No water • No toilets • Activities: Hiking, fishing, hunting • Elevation: 663

Tuscumbia

Saline Valley CA - MDC • Agency: State • Tel: 573-346-2210 • Location: 5 miles N of Tuscumbia (limited services), 9 miles SE of Eldon • GPS: Lat 38.282611 Lon -92.440358 • Open: All year • Total sites: 7 • RV sites: 7 • RV fee: Free • No water • Vault toilets • Activities: Hiking, fishing, hunting • Elevation: 581

Union Star

Elrod Mill Access - MDC • Agency: State • Tel: 816-271-3100 • Location: 6 miles NW of Union Star (limited services), 12 miles SW of King City • GPS: Lat 39.999312 Lon -94.693187 • Open: All year • Total sites: Dispersed • RV sites: Undefined • RV fee: Free • No water • Vault toilets • Activities: Fishing, hunting, non-power boating • Elevation: 971

Unionville

Mineral Hills CA - Lot A - MDC • Agency: State • Tel: 660-785-2420 • Location: 6 miles S of Unionville • GPS: Lat 40.421794 Lon -92.987337 • Open: All year • Total sites: Dispersed • RV sites: Undefined • RV fee: Free • No water • No toilets • Activities: Fishing, hunting • Elevation: 1053

Mineral Hills CA - Lot B - MDC • Agency: State • Tel: 660-785-2420 • Location: 6 miles S of Unionville • GPS: Lat 40.426633 Lon -92.973559 • Open: All year • Total sites: Dispersed • RV sites: Undefined • RV fee: Free • No water • No toilets • Activities: Fishing, hunting • Elevation: 1037

Mineral Hills CA - Lot C - MDC • Agency: State • Tel: 660-785-2420 • Location: 8 miles SE of Unionville • GPS: Lat 40.413976 Lon -92.959709 • Open: All year • Total sites: Dispersed • RV sites: Undefined • RV fee: Free • No water • No toilets • Activities: Fishing, hunting • Elevation: 1027

Mineral Hills CA - Lot D - MDC • Agency: State • Tel: 660-785-2420 • Location: 9 miles SE of Unionville • GPS: Lat 40.402803 Lon -92.945863 • Open: All year • Total sites: Dispersed • RV sites: Undefined • RV fee: Free • No water • No toilets • Activities: Fishing, hunting • Elevation: 1043

Mineral Hills CA - Lot E - MDC • Agency: State • Tel: 660-785-2420 • Location: 6 miles SE of Unionville • GPS: Lat 40.423561 Lon -92.943751 • Open: All year • Total sites: Dispersed • RV sites: Undefined • RV fee: Free • No water • No toilets • Activities: Fishing, hunting • Elevation: 997

Morris Prairie CA - MDC • Agency: State • Tel: 660-785-2420 • Location: 11 miles SE of Unionville • GPS: Lat 40.389605 Lon -92.938381 • Open: All year • Total sites: Dispersed • RV sites: Undefined • RV fee: Free • No water • No toilets • Activities: Fishing, hunting • Elevation: 1017

Urbana

Lead Mine CA - Boat Ramp - MDC • Agency: State • Tel: 417-532-7612 • Location: 16 miles E of Urbana (limited services), 24 miles NE of Buffalo • GPS: Lat 37.863238 Lon -92.897609 • Open: All year • Total sites: Dispersed • RV sites: Undefined • RV fee: Free • No water • No toilets • Activities: Hiking, mountain biking, fishing, hunting, non-power boating, equestrian area • Elevation: 764

Lead Mine CA Lot 1 - MDC • Agency: State • Tel: 417-532-7612 • Location: 14 miles E of Urbana (limited services), 21 miles NE of Buffalo • GPS: Lat 37.849355 Lon -92.93194 • Open: All year • Total sites: Dispersed • RV sites: Undefined • RV fee: Free • No water • Vault toilets • Activities: Hiking, mountain biking, fishing, hunting, non-power boating, equestrian area • Elevation: 1089

Lead Mine CA Lot 2 - MDC • Agency: State • Tel: 417-532-7612 • Location: 15 miles E of Urbana (limited services), 22 miles NE of Buffalo • GPS: Lat 37.861237 Lon -92.914098 • Open: All year • Total sites: Dispersed • RV sites: Undefined • RV fee: Free • No water • No toilets • Activities: Hiking, mountain biking, fishing, hunting, non-power boating, equestrian area • Elevation: 768

Van Buren

Clearwater CA - MDC • Agency: State • Tel: 573-663-7130 • Location: 14 miles NE of Van Buren • GPS: Lat 37.084057 Lon -90.879963 • Open: All year • Total sites: 10 • RV sites: 10 • RV fee: Free • No water • No toilets • Activities: Hiking, mountain biking, hunting • Elevation: 794

Vandalia

Vandalia Community Lake - MDC • Agency: State • Tel: 573-815-7900 • Location: 6 miles SW of Vandalia • GPS: Lat 39.238899 Lon -91.538948 • Open: All year • Total sites: Dispersed • RV sites: Undefined • RV fee: Free • No water • Vault toilets • Activities: Fishing, hunting, non-power boating • Elevation: 755

Vandalia Community Lake Main CG - MDC • Agency: State • Tel: 573-815-7900 • Location: 6 miles SW of Vandalia • GPS: Lat 39.235354 Lon -91.535594 • Open: All year • Total sites: 10 • RV sites: 10 • RV fee: Free • No water • Vault toilets • Activities: Fishing, hunting, non-power boating • Elevation: 758

Viburnum

Indian Trail CA Camp 1 - MDC • Agency: State • Tel: 573-729-3182 • Location: 13 miles W of Viburnum (limited services), 19 miles NE of Salem • GPS: Lat 37.726294 Lon -91.314423 • Open: All year • Total sites: Dispersed • RV sites: Undefined • RV fee: Free • No water • No toilets • Activities: Hiking, fishing, hunting, equestrian area • Elevation: 1243

Vienna

Paydown Access - MDC • Agency: State • Tel: 573-815-7900 • Location: 13 miles NE of Vienna • GPS: Lat 38.229561 Lon -91.815763 • Open: All year • Total sites: 6 • RV sites: 6 • RV fee: Free • No water • Vault toilets • Activities: Fishing, non-power boating • Elevation: 617

Spring Creek Gap CA #1 - MDC • Agency: State • Tel: 573-815-7900 • Location: 10 miles E of Vienna • GPS: Lat 38.16599 Lon -91.788355 • Open: All year • Total sites: Dispersed • RV sites: Undefined • RV fee: Free • No water • No toilets • Activities: Hiking, hunting • Elevation: 1047

Spring Creek Gap CA #2 - MDC • Agency: State • Tel: 573-815-7900 • Location: 12 miles SE of Vienna • GPS: Lat 38.140378 Lon -91.808704 • Open: All year • Total sites: Dispersed • RV sites: Undefined • RV fee: Free • No water • No toilets • Activities: Hiking, hunting • Elevation: 1083

Wappapello

Poplar Bluff CA - MDC • Agency: State • Tel: 573-290-5730 • Location: 7 miles N of Wappapello (limited services), 24 miles N of Poplar Bluff • GPS: Lat 36.818271 Lon -90.339931 • Open: All year • Total sites: Dispersed • RV sites: Undefined • RV fee: Free • No water • No toilets • Activities: Hiking, fishing, hunting • Elevation: 456

Possum Creek (Wappapello Lake) • Agency: Corps of Engineers • Tel: 573-222-8562 • Location: 3 miles NW of Wappapello (limited services), 20 miles N of Poplar Bluff • GPS: Lat 36.963968 Lon -90.302329 • Open: All year • Total sites: 2 • RV sites: 2 • RV fee: Free • No water • Vault toilets • Activities: Power boating, non-power boating • Elevation: 440

Yokum School CA - MDC • Agency: State • Tel: 573-290-5730 • Location: 5 miles N of Wappapello (limited services), 22 miles N of Poplar Bluff • GPS: Lat 37.010618 Lon -90.277967 • Open: All year • Total sites: Dispersed • RV sites: Undefined • RV fee: Free • No water • No toilets • Activities: Hiking, hunting • Elevation: 581

Wardsville

Pikes Camp Access - MDC • Agency: State • Tel: 573-815-7900 • Location: 2 miles S of Wardsville (limited services), 8 miles S of Jefferson City • GPS: Lat 38.463816 Lon -92.169043 • Open: All year • Total sites: Dispersed • RV sites: Undefined • RV fee: Free • No water • Vault toilets • Activities: Fishing, hunting, non-power boating • Elevation: 548

Warrenton

Little Lost Creek CA Lot 1 MDC • Agency: State • Tel: 636-441-4554 • Location: 11 miles SW of Warrenton • GPS: Lat 38.779117 Lon -91.289512 • Open: All year • Total sites: Dispersed • RV sites: Undefined • RV fee: Free • No water • No toilets • Activities: Hiking, mountain biking, hunting • Elevation: 843

Little Lost Creek CA Lot 2 MDC • Agency: State • Tel: 636-441-4554 • Location: 9 miles SW of Warrenton • GPS: Lat 38.797062 Lon -91.281371 • Open: All year • Total sites: Dispersed • RV sites: Undefined • RV fee: Free • No water • No toilets • Activities: Hiking, mountain biking, hunting • Elevation: 892

Little Lost Creek CA Lot 3 MDC • Agency: State • Tel: 636-441-4554 • Location: 11 miles SW of Warrenton • GPS: Lat 38.758277 Lon -91.263652 • Open: All year • Total sites: Dispersed • RV sites: Undefined • RV fee: Free • No water • No toilets • Activities: Hiking, mountain biking, hunting • Elevation: 876

Little Lost Creek CA Lot 4 MDC • Agency: State • Tel: 636-441-4554 • Location: 9 miles SW of Warrenton • GPS: Lat 38.779085 Lon -91.253354 • Open: All year • Total sites: Dispersed • RV sites: Undefined • RV fee: Free • No water • No toilets • Activities: Hiking, mountain biking, hunting • Elevation: 866

Washburn

Flag Spring CA Lot 1 - MDC • Agency: State • Tel: 417-895-6880 • Location: 8 miles NW of Washburn (limited services), 16 miles SW of Cassville • GPS: Lat 36.628345 Lon -94.065083 • Open: All year • Total sites: Dispersed • RV sites: Undefined • RV fee: Free • No water • No toilets • Activities: Hiking, hunting, equestrian area • Elevation: 1401

Flag Spring CA Lot 2 - MDC • Agency: State • Tel: 417-895-6880 • Location: 7 miles NW of Washburn (limited services), 16 miles SW of Cassville • GPS: Lat 36.619587

Lon -94.062478 • Open: All year • Total sites: Dispersed • RV sites: Undefined • RV fee: Free • No water • No toilets • Activities: Hiking, hunting, equestrian area • Elevation: 1388

Flag Spring CA Lot 3 - MDC • Agency: State • Tel: 417-895-6880 • Location: 7 miles NW of Washburn (limited services), 16 miles SW of Cassville • GPS: Lat 36.611742 Lon -94.064284 • Open: All year • Total sites: Dispersed • RV sites: Undefined • RV fee: Free • No water • No toilets • Activities: Hiking, hunting, equestrian area • Elevation: 1398

Flag Spring CA Lot 4 - MDC • Agency: State • Tel: 417-895-6880 • Location: 7 miles NW of Washburn (limited services), 15 miles SW of Cassville • GPS: Lat 36.608174 Lon -94.059257 • Open: All year • Total sites: Dispersed • RV sites: Undefined • RV fee: Free • No water • No toilets • Activities: Hiking, hunting, equestrian area • Elevation: 1358

Flag Spring CA Lot 5 - MDC • Agency: State • Tel: 417-895-6880 • Location: 6 miles NW of Washburn (limited services), 14 miles SW of Cassville • GPS: Lat 36.603677 Lon -94.049547 • Open: All year • Total sites: Dispersed • RV sites: Undefined • RV fee: Free • No water • No toilets • Activities: Hiking, hunting, equestrian area • Elevation: 1434

Flag Spring CA Lot 6 - MDC • Agency: State • Tel: 417-895-6880 • Location: 5 miles NW of Washburn (limited services), 13 miles SW of Cassville • GPS: Lat 36.607265 Lon -94.036138 • Open: All year • Total sites: Dispersed • RV sites: Undefined • RV fee: Free • No water • No toilets • Activities: Hiking, hunting, equestrian area • Elevation: 1430

Flag Spring CA Lot 7 - MDC • Agency: State • Tel: 417-895-6880 • Location: 5 miles NW of Washburn (limited services), 13 miles SW of Cassville • GPS: Lat 36.614218 Lon -94.028739 • Open: All year • Total sites: Dispersed • RV sites: Undefined • RV fee: Free • No water • No toilets • Activities: Hiking, hunting, equestrian area • Elevation: 1490

Waverly

Baltimore Bend CA Lot 1 - MDC • Agency: State • Tel: 816-228-3766 • Location: 6 miles W of Waverly (limited services), 18 miles SW of Carrollton • GPS: Lat 39.219161 Lon -93.610387 • Open: All year • Total sites: Dispersed • RV sites: Undefined • RV fee: Free • No water • No toilets • Activities: Hiking, fishing, hunting • Elevation: 876

Baltimore Bend CA Lot 2 - MDC • Agency: State • Tel: 816-228-3766 • Location: 6 miles W of Waverly (limited services), 18 miles SW of Carrollton • GPS: Lat 39.217064

Lon -93.599755 • Open: All year • Total sites: Dispersed • RV sites: Undefined • RV fee: Free • No water • No toilets • Activities: Hiking, fishing, hunting • Elevation: 902

Baltimore Bend CA Lot 3 - MDC • Agency: State • Tel: 816-228-3766 • Location: 5 miles NW of Waverly (limited services), 17 miles SW of Carrollton • GPS: Lat 39.221996 Lon -93.587073 • Open: All year • Total sites: Dispersed • RV sites: Undefined • RV fee: Free • No water • No toilets • Notes: Near RR tracks • Activities: Hiking, fishing, hunting • Elevation: 686

Baltimore Bend CA Lot 4 - MDC • Agency: State • Tel: 816-228-3766 • Location: 5 miles NW of Waverly (limited services), 16 miles SW of Carrollton • GPS: Lat 39.216541 Lon -93.584874 • Open: All year • Total sites: Dispersed • RV sites: Undefined • RV fee: Free • No water • No toilets • Activities: Hiking, fishing, hunting • Elevation: 837

Baltimore Bend CA Lot 5 - MDC • Agency: State • Tel: 816-228-3766 • Location: 5 miles NW of Waverly (limited services), 16 miles SW of Carrollton • GPS: Lat 39.215036 Lon -93.575846 • Open: All year • Total sites: Dispersed • RV sites: Undefined • RV fee: Free • No water • No toilets • Activities: Hiking, fishing, hunting • Elevation: 853

Wayland

Geode Access - MDC • Agency: State • Tel: 573-248-2530 • Location: 1 mile W of Wayland (limited services), 8 miles SE of Kahoka • GPS: Lat 40.392607 Lon -91.597173 • Open: All year • Total sites: Dispersed • RV sites: Undefined • RV fee: Free • No water • No toilets • Activities: Fishing, non-power boating • Elevation: 525

Rose Pond CA - MDC • Agency: State • Tel: 660-785-2420 • Location: 9 miles SE of Wayland (limited services), 17 miles SE of Kahoka • GPS: Lat 40.335923 Lon -91.517632 • Open: All year • Total sites: Dispersed • RV sites: Undefined • RV fee: Free • No water • No toilets • Activities: Fishing, hunting • Elevation: 502

Wellsville

Marshall I. Diggs CA - MDC • Agency: State • Tel: 573-815-7900 • Location: 6 miles W of Wellsville (limited services), 13 miles NW of Montgomery City • GPS: Lat 39.068251 Lon -91.629988 • Open: All year • Total sites: Dispersed • RV sites: Undefined • RV fee: Free • No water • Vault toilets • Activities: Fishing, hunting, non-power boating • Elevation: 778

Wellsville Lake CA - MDC • Agency: State • Tel: 573-815-7900 • Location: 3 miles S of Wellsville (limited services), 7 miles NW of Montgomery City • GPS: Lat

39.035066 Lon -91.580593 • Open: All year • Total sites: Dispersed • RV sites: Undefined • RV fee: Free • No water • Vault toilets • Activities: Fishing, hunting, non-power boating • Elevation: 735

Westboro

Tarkio Prairie CA Lot 1 - MDC • Agency: State • Tel: 816-271-3100 • Location: 8 miles SE of Westboro (limited services), 22 miles NW of Rock Port • GPS: Lat 40.50764 Lon -95.217073 • Open: All year • Total sites: Dispersed • RV sites: Undefined • RV fee: Free • No water • No toilets • Activities: Fishing, hunting • Elevation: 1119

Tarkio Prairie CA Lot 2 - MDC • Agency: State • Tel: 816-271-3100 • Location: 9 miles SE of Westboro (limited services), 23 miles NW of Rock Port • GPS: Lat 40.506244 Lon -95.202318 • Open: All year • Total sites: Dispersed • RV sites: Undefined • RV fee: Free • No water • No toilets • Activities: Fishing, hunting • Elevation: 1060

Westphalia

Dr Bernard Bruns Access - MDC • Agency: State • Tel: 573-815-7900 • Location: 4 miles E of Westphalia (limited services), 14 miles SE of Jefferson City • GPS: Lat 38.451305 Lon -91.965902 • Open: All year • Total sites: Dispersed • RV sites: Undefined • RV fee: Free • No water • No toilets • Activities: Fishing, non-power boating • Elevation: 571

Painted Rock CA - Clubhouse Lake - MDC • Agency: State • Tel: 573-815-7900 • Location: 8 miles SW of Westphalia (limited services), 20 miles SE of Jefferson City • GPS: Lat 38.398645 Lon -92.112351 • Open: All year • Total sites: Dispersed • RV sites: Undefined • RV fee: Free • No water • No toilets • Activities: Fishing, hunting, non-power boating • Elevation: 587

Painted Rock CA - Osage Bluff - MDC • Agency: State • Tel: 573-815-7900 • Location: 7 miles SW of Westphalia (limited services), 19 miles SE of Jefferson City • GPS: Lat 38.412213 Lon -92.109203 • Open: All year • Total sites: Dispersed • RV sites: Undefined • RV fee: Free • No water • No toilets • Activities: Hiking, fishing, hunting, non-power boating • Elevation: 745

Wheatland

John F Murphy Memorial State Forest - MDC • Agency: State • Tel: 417-532-7612 • Location: 1 mile E of Wheatland (limited services), 24 miles S of Warsaw • GPS: Lat 37.946303 Lon -93.389624 • Total sites: 10 • RV sites: 10 • RV fee: Free • No water • Vault toilets • Activities: Hiking, hunting • Elevation: 1089

Whitewater

Lake Girardeau CA - MDC • Agency: State • Tel: 573-290-5730 • Location: 6 miles NW of Whitewater (limited services), 16 miles SW of Jackson • GPS: Lat 37.281916 Lon -89.846502 • Open: All year • Total sites: Dispersed • RV sites: Undefined • RV fee: Free • No water • Vault toilets • Activities: Hiking, fishing, non-power boating • Elevation: 433

Williamsville

Bradley A. Hammer Memorial CA Lot 1 - MDC • Agency: State • Tel: 573-290-5730 • Location: 1 mile S of Williamsville (limited services), 20 miles NW of Poplar Bluff • GPS: Lat 36.963221 Lon -90.554536 • Open: All year • Total sites: Dispersed • RV sites: Undefined • RV fee: Free • No water • No toilets • Activities: Fishing, hunting, non-power boating • Elevation: 404

Bradley A. Hammer Memorial CA Lot 2 - MDC • Agency: State • Tel: 573-290-5730 • Location: 3 miles SE of Williamsville (limited services), 17 miles NW of Poplar Bluff • GPS: Lat 36.963729 Lon -90.563945 • Open: All year • Total sites: Dispersed • RV sites: Undefined • RV fee: Free • No water • No toilets • Activities: Fishing, hunting, non-power boating • Elevation: 404

Winigan

Montgomery Woods CA - MDC • Agency: State • Tel: 660-785-2420 • Location: 8 miles W of Winigan (limited services), 20 miles SW of Kirksville • GPS: Lat 40.040617 Lon -92.832592 • Open: All year • Total sites: Dispersed • RV sites: Undefined • RV fee: Free • No water • No toilets • Activities: Hunting • Elevation: 994

Winona

Peck Ranch CA Headquarters Area - MDC • Agency: State • Tel: 417-256-7161 • Location: 12 miles SE of Winona • GPS: Lat 37.041995 Lon -91.186606 • Open: All year • Total sites: Dispersed • RV sites: Undefined • RV fee: Free • No water • No toilets • Activities: Hiking, hunting • Elevation: 791

Peck Ranch CA Mill Creek - MDC • Agency: State • Tel: 417-256-7161 • Location: 13 miles SE of Winona • GPS: Lat 37.042178 Lon -91.207712 • Open: All year • Total sites: Dispersed • RV sites: Undefined • RV fee: Free • No water • No toilets • Activities: Hiking, hunting • Elevation: 837

Wyatt

Bird's Blue Hole - MDC • Agency: State • Tel: 573-290-5730 • Location: 8 miles NE of Wyatt (limited services), 13 miles NE of Charleston • GPS: Lat 36.964031 Lon -89.126808 • Open: All year • Total sites: Dispersed • RV sites: Undefined • RV fee: Free • No water • No toilets • Activities: Fishing, non-power boating • Elevation: 308

Joseph Hunter Moore Access - MDC • Agency: State • Tel: 573-290-5730 • Location: 9 miles NE of Wyatt (limited services), 13 miles E of Charleston • GPS: Lat 36.912188 Lon -89.122404 • Open: All year • Total sites: Dispersed • RV sites: Undefined • RV fee: Free • No water • No toilets • Activities: Fishing • Elevation: 285

Zalma

Castor River CA Horse Camp - MDC • Agency: State • Tel: 573-290-5730 • Location: 7 miles NW of Zalma (limited services), 19 miles NW of Advance • GPS: Lat 37.183211 Lon -90.155068 • Open: All year • Total sites: 8 • RV sites: 8 • RV fee: Free • No water • No toilets • Activities: Hiking, fishing, hunting, equestrian area • Elevation: 505

Castor River CA Lot 2 - MDC • Agency: State • Tel: 573-290-5730 • Location: 7 miles NW of Zalma (limited services), 19 miles NW of Advance • GPS: Lat 37.183388 Lon -90.153533 • Open: All year • Total sites: 4 • RV sites: 4 • RV fee: Free • No water • No toilets • Activities: Hiking, fishing, hunting, equestrian area • Elevation: 476

Nebraska

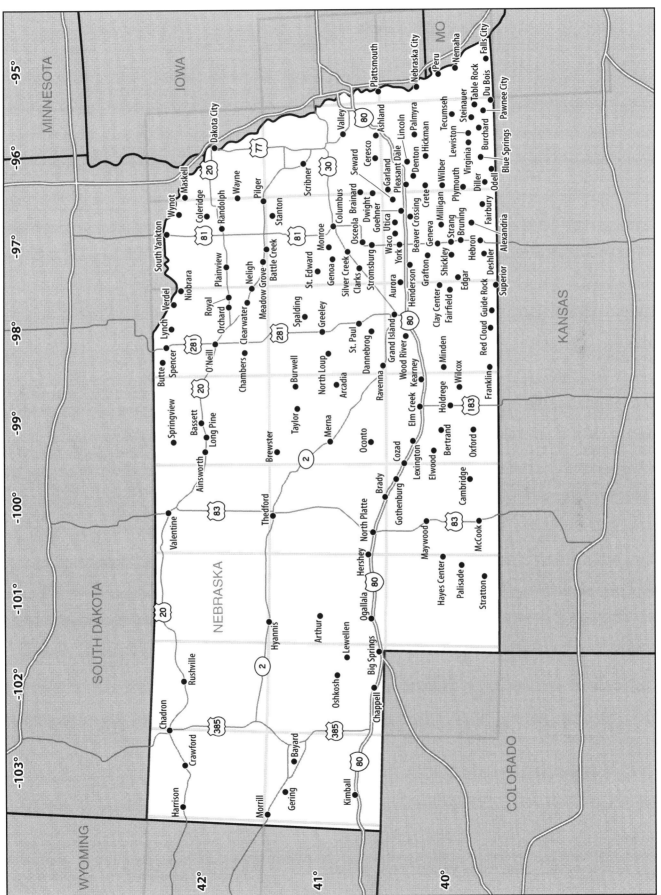

Nebraska — Camping Areas

Abbreviation	Description
GPC	Game & Parks Commission
LBBNRD	Lower Big Blue Natural Resources District
LLNRD	Lower Loup Natural Resources District
LPD	Loup Power District
LPSNRD	Lower Platte South Natural Resources District
MNNRD	Middle Niobrara Natural Resources District
NNRD	Nemaha Natural Resources District
RA	Recreation Area
SRA	State Recreation Area
WMA	Wildlife Management Area

Ainsworth

Keller Park WMA • Agency: State • Location: 12 miles NE of Ainsworth • GPS: Lat 42.665069 Lon -99.783088 • Total sites: Dispersed • RV sites: Undefined • RV fee: Free • No water • No toilets • Elevation: 2336

Willow Lake B.C. WMA • Agency: State • Location: 32 miles SW of Ainsworth • GPS: Lat 42.232758 Lon -100.087406 • Open: All year • Total sites: Dispersed • RV sites: Undefined (camping allowed throughout unless posted) • RV fee: Free • No water • No toilets • Activities: Hiking, fishing, hunting • Elevation: 2700

Alexandria

Alexandria WMA • Agency: State • Location: 2 miles SE of Alexandria (limited services), 18 miles NW of Fairbury • GPS: Lat 40.230555 Lon -97.368838 • Total sites: Dispersed • RV sites: Undefined • RV fee: Free • No water • No toilets • Elevation: 1453

Arcadia

Arcadia Diversion Dam WMA • Agency: State • Location: 14 miles NW of Arcadia (limited services), 26 miles SW of Ord • GPS: Lat 41.498587 Lon -99.244445 • Open: All year • Total sites: Dispersed • RV sites: Undefined (camping allowed throughout unless posted) • RV fee: Free • No water • No toilets • Activities: Hiking, fishing, hunting • Elevation: 2218

Arthur

Arthur Park • Agency: Municipal • Location: In Arthur (limited services), 36 miles N of Ogallala • GPS: Lat 41.570649 Lon -101.690549 • Total sites: 8 • RV sites: 8 • RV fee: Free • Central water • Vault toilets • Elevation: 3648

Ashland

Catfish Run WMA • Agency: State • Location: 2 miles NE of Ashland • GPS: Lat 41.054067 Lon -96.336359 • Open: All year • Total sites: Dispersed • RV sites: Undefined (camping allowed throughout unless posted) • RV fee: Free • No water • No toilets • Activities: Hiking, fishing, hunting • Elevation: 1063

Aurora

Gadwall WMA • Agency: State • Location: 6 miles NW of Aurora • GPS: Lat 40.937963 Lon -98.037814 • Total sites: Dispersed • RV sites: Undefined • RV fee: Free • No water • No toilets • Elevation: 1819

Pintail WMA • Agency: State • Location: 8 miles SE of Aurora • GPS: Lat 40.785466 Lon -97.940456 • Total sites: Dispersed • RV sites: Undefined • RV fee: Free • No water • No toilets • Elevation: 1770

Streeter Municipal Park • Agency: Municipal • Tel: 402-694-6992 • Location: In Aurora • GPS: Lat 40.873634 Lon -98.003056 • Open: May-Oct • Stay limit: 3 days • Total sites: 20 • RV sites: 18 • Max RV Length: 27 • RV fee: Free (donation appreciated) • Electric sites: 18 • Central water • No toilets • Activities: Swimming • Elevation: 1775

Bassett

Bassett RA • Agency: Municipal • Tel: 402-684-3338 • Location: In Bassett (limited services), 17 miles E of Ainsworth • GPS: Lat 42.575873 Lon -99.546716 • Total sites: Dispersed • RV sites: Undefined • RV fee: Free • No water • Elevation: 2330

Fred Thomas WMA • Agency: State • Location: 11 miles N of Bassett (limited services), 28 miles NE of Ainsworth • GPS: Lat 42.721008 Lon -99.588803 • Total sites: Dispersed • RV sites: Undefined • RV fee: Free • No water • No toilets • Activities: Fishing • Elevation: 1923

Twin Lakes Rock County WMA • Agency: State • Tel: 402-359-5165 • Location: 21 miles S of Bassett (limited services), 37 miles SE of Ainsworth • GPS: Lat 42.313618 Lon -99.48681 • Open: All year • Total sites: Dispersed • RV sites: Undefined (camping allowed throughout unless posted) • RV fee: Free • No water • No toilets • Activities: Hiking, fishing, hunting • Elevation: 2484

Battle Creek

Oak Valley WMA • Agency: State • Location: 5 miles SW of Battle Creek (limited services), 15 miles SW of Norfolk • GPS: Lat 41.952795 Lon -97.639228 • Total sites: Dispersed • RV sites: Undefined • RV fee: Free • No water • No toilets • Elevation: 1745

Bayard

Arnold Trupp WMA • Agency: State • Location: 6 miles N of Bayard • GPS: Lat 41.841038 Lon -103.342206 • Total sites: Dispersed • RV sites: Undefined • RV fee: Free • No water • No toilets • Elevation: 4020

Chet and Jane Fleisbach WMA • Agency: State • Location: 6 miles SE of Bayard • GPS: Lat 41.692117 Lon -103.260256 • Total sites: Dispersed • RV sites: Undefined • RV fee: Free • No water • No toilets • Elevation: 3739

Beaver Crossing

Beaver Crossing Municipal • Agency: Municipal • Tel: 402-532-3925 • Location: In Beaver Crossing (limited services), 10 miles N of Friend • GPS: Lat 40.77726 Lon -97.27661 • Open: Apr-Nov • Total sites: 6 • RV sites: 6 • RV fee: Free (donation appreciated) • Electric sites: 6 • Water at site • Flush toilets • Activities: Swimming • Elevation: 1476

Bertrand

High Basin WMA • Agency: State • Location: 4 miles N of Bertrand (limited services), 18 miles NW of Holdrege • GPS: Lat 40.568125 Lon -99.636553 • Total sites: Dispersed • RV sites: Undefined • RV fee: Free • No water • No toilets • Elevation: 2478

Big Springs

Goldeneye WMA • Agency: State • Location: 5 miles SW of Big Springs (limited services), 24 miles SW of Ogallala • GPS: Lat 41.040072 Lon -102.128293 • Open: All year • Total sites: Dispersed • RV sites: Undefined (camping allowed throughout unless posted) • RV fee: Free • No water • No toilets • Activities: Hiking, fishing, hunting • Elevation: 3396

Feits Memorial Park • Agency: Municipal • Tel: 402-645-3539 • Location: In Blue Springs (limited services), 13 miles SE of Beatrice • GPS: Lat 40.139704 Lon -96.655062 • Open: All year • Stay limit: 3 days • Total sites: 15 • RV sites: 5 • RV fee: Free • Central water • Vault toilets • Activities: Fishing, swimming, power boating, non-power boating • Elevation: 1220

Brady

Brady WMA • Agency: State • Location: 3 miles S of Brady (limited services), 15 miles NW of Gothenburg • GPS: Lat 40.998418 Lon -100.375837 • Total sites: Dispersed • RV sites: Undefined • RV fee: Free • No water • No toilets • Elevation: 2647

Brady WMA • Agency: State • Location: 1 mile S of Brady (limited services), 14 miles NW of Gothenburg • GPS: Lat 41.017703 Lon -100.375451 • Total sites: Dispersed • RV sites: Undefined • RV fee: Free • No water • No toilets • Activities: Fishing • Elevation: 2664

Chester Island WMA • Agency: State • Location: 4 miles SW of Brady (limited services), 17 miles NW of Gothenburg • GPS: Lat 40.989684 Lon -100.395903 • Total sites: Dispersed • RV sites: Undefined • RV fee: Free • No water • No toilets • Activities: Fishing • Elevation: 2652

Jeffrey Canyon/Reservoir WMA • Agency: State • Location: 8 miles SW of Brady (limited services), 20 miles NW of Gothenburg • GPS: Lat 40.952132 Lon -100.403422 • Open: All year • Total sites: Dispersed • RV sites: Undefined (camping allowed throughout unless posted) • RV fee: Free • No water • No toilets • Activities: Hiking, fishing, hunting • Elevation: 2789

Jeffrey Lake WMA • Agency: State • Location: 7 miles SW of Brady (limited services), 19 miles NW of Gothenburg • GPS: Lat 40.954602 Lon -100.397643 • Total sites: Dispersed • RV sites: Undefined • RV fee: Free • No water • No toilets • Elevation: 2785

West Brady WMA • Agency: State • Location: 4 miles SW of Brady (limited services), 16 miles NW of Gothenburg • GPS: Lat 41.016168 Lon -100.417457 • Total sites: Dispersed • RV sites: Undefined • RV fee: Free • No water • No toilets • Elevation: 2663

Brainard

Timber Point RA - LPSNRD • Agency: State • Tel: 402-476-2729 • Location: 3 miles SE of Brainard (limited services), 23 miles W of Wahoo • GPS: Lat 41.162184 Lon -96.965988 • Open: All year • Total sites: 3 • RV sites: 3 • RV fee: Free • No water • Vault toilets • Activities: Hiking, fishing, power boating, hunting • Elevation: 1503

Brewster

Milburn Dam WMA • Agency: State • Location: 17 miles SE of Brewster (limited services), 30 miles NW of Broken Bow • GPS: Lat 41.751073 Lon -99.771737 • Open: All year • Total sites: 10 • RV sites: 10 • RV fee: Free • Central water • Vault toilets • Activities: Hiking, fishing, hunting • Elevation: 2487

Bruning

Dry Sandy WMA • Agency: State • Location: 4 miles NE of Bruning (limited services), 15 miles SE of Geneva • GPS: Lat 40.350497 Lon -97.516985 • Total sites: Dispersed • RV sites: Undefined • RV fee: Free • No water • No toilets • Elevation: 1573

Prairie Marsh WMA • Agency: State • Location: 5 miles W of Bruning (limited services), 16 miles SW of Geneva • GPS: Lat 40.346914 Lon -97.650911 • Total sites: Dispersed • RV sites: Undefined • RV fee: Free • No water • No toilets • Elevation: 1614

Burchard

Burchard Lake WMA • Agency: State • Location: 9 miles NE of Burchard (limited services), 13 miles NW of Pawnee City • GPS: Lat 40.168223 Lon -96.303532 • Total sites: Dispersed • RV sites: Undefined • RV fee: Free • No water • No toilets • Activities: Fishing • Elevation: 1328

Pawnee Prairie 1 • Agency: State • Location: 9 miles SE of Burchard (limited services), 13 miles SW of Pawnee City • GPS: Lat 40.043318 Lon -96.312985 • Total sites: Dispersed • RV sites: Undefined • RV fee: Free • No water • No toilets • Elevation: 1405

Pawnee Prairie 2 • Agency: State • Location: 10 miles SE of Burchard (limited services), 14 miles SW of Pawnee City • GPS: Lat 40.029985 Lon -96.313354 • Total sites: Dispersed • RV sites: Undefined • RV fee: Free • No water • No toilets • Elevation: 1413

Pawnee Prairie 3 • Agency: State • Location: 11 miles SE of Burchard (limited services), 18 miles SW of Pawnee City • GPS: Lat 40.023619 Lon -96.331424 • Total sites: Dispersed • RV sites: Undefined • RV fee: Free • No water • No toilets • Elevation: 1483

Burwell

Calamus Reservoir WMA • Agency: State • Location: 6 miles NW of Burwell • GPS: Lat 41.830148 Lon -99.207757 • Total sites: Dispersed • RV sites: Undefined • RV fee: Free • No water • No toilets • Elevation: 2188

Gracie Creek Pond • Agency: State • Location: 15 miles NW of Burwell • GPS: Lat 41.926249 Lon -99.320598 • Total sites: Dispersed • RV sites: Undefined • RV fee: Free • Vault toilets • Elevation: 2261

Kent Diversion Dam WMA • Agency: State • Location: 8 miles W of Burwell • GPS: Lat 41.762128 Lon -99.267448 • Open: All year • Total sites: Dispersed • RV sites: Undefined (camping allowed throughout unless posted) • RV fee: Free • No water • No toilets • Activities: Hiking, fishing, hunting • Elevation: 2224

Butte

Hull Lake WMA • Agency: State • Location: 5 miles SW of Butte (limited services), 33 miles NE of Atkinson • GPS: Lat 42.8666281 Lon -98.88109 • Total sites: Dispersed • RV sites: Undefined • RV fee: Free • No water • No toilets • Elevation: 1808

Cambridge

Cambridge City RV Park • Agency: Municipal • Tel: 308-697-3711 • Location: In Cambridge • GPS: Lat 40.282721 Lon -100.159779 • Total sites: 11 • RV sites: 11 • RV fee: Free (donation appreciated) • Electric sites: 11 • Water at site • Flush toilets • Notes: Near RR tracks • Activities: Fishing, swimming • Elevation: 2293

Cambridge Diversion Dam WMA • Agency: State • Location: 2 miles E of Cambridge • GPS: Lat 40.285162 Lon -100.121066 • Open: All year • Total sites: Dispersed • RV sites: Undefined (camping allowed throughout unless posted) • RV fee: Free • No water • No toilets • Activities: Hiking, fishing, hunting • Elevation: 2254

Ceresco

Jack Sinn Memorial WMA • Agency: State • Location: 1 mile SE of Ceresco (limited services), 13 miles N of Lincoln • GPS: Lat 41.045397 Lon -96.635377 • Total sites: Dispersed • RV sites: Undefined • RV fee: Free • No water • No toilets • Elevation: 1173

Chadron

Bordeaux WMA • Agency: State • Location: 6 miles E of Chadron • GPS: Lat 42.800611 Lon -102.890573 • Total sites: Dispersed • RV sites: Undefined • RV fee: Free • No water • No toilets • Elevation: 3596

Chadron Creek Ranch WMA • Agency: State • Location: 10 miles S of Chadron • GPS: Lat 42.678562 Lon -102.990382 • Total sites: Dispersed • RV sites: Undefined • RV fee: Free • No water • No toilets • Elevation: 4150

Chambers

Goose Lake WMA • Agency: State • Location: 19 miles SE of Chambers (limited services), 31 miles S of O'Neill • GPS: Lat 42.113681 Lon -98.570826 • Open: All year • Total sites: 10 • RV sites: 10 • RV fee: Free • No water • No toilets • Activities: Hiking, fishing, swimming, power boating, non-power boating • Elevation: 2060

Swan Lake WMA • Agency: State • Location: 15 miles W of Chambers (limited services), 26 miles S of Atkinson • GPS: Lat 42.169248 Lon -99.022485 • Open: All year • Total sites: Dispersed • RV sites: Undefined (camping allowed throughout unless posted) • RV fee: Free • No water • No toilets • Activities: Hiking, fishing, hunting • Elevation: 2313

Chappell

Goldenrod WMA • Agency: State • Location: 4 miles SE of Chappell (limited services), 31 miles SE of Sidney • GPS: Lat 41.061125 Lon -102.420838 • Total sites: Dispersed • RV sites: Undefined • RV fee: Free • No water • No toilets • Notes: Near RR tracks • Elevation: 3634

Clarks

Mormon Trail State Wayside Park • Agency: State • Location: 2 miles SW of Clarks (limited services), 8 miles NE of Central City • GPS: Lat 41.191765 Lon -97.873345 • Open: All year • Stay limit: 2 days • Total sites: Dispersed • RV sites: Undefined • RV fee: Free • Central water • Vault toilets • Activities: Fishing • Elevation: 1644

Clay Center

White Front WMA • Agency: State • Location: 3 miles NW of Clay Center (limited services), 17 miles E of Hastings • GPS: Lat 40.549454 Lon -98.089348 • Total sites: Dispersed • RV sites: Undefined • RV fee: Free • No water • No toilets • Activities: Fishing • Elevation: 1795

Clearwater

Hackberry Creek WMA • Agency: State • Location: 2 miles NE of Clearwater (limited services), 7 miles NW of Neligh • GPS: Lat 42.182299 Lon -98.155349 • Total sites: Dispersed • RV sites: Undefined • RV fee: Free • No water • No toilets • Elevation: 1780

Coleridge

Coleridge Village Park • Agency: Municipal • Tel: 402-283-4464 • Location: In Coleridge (limited services), 9 miles SE of Hartington • GPS: Lat 42.509454 Lon -97.203997 • Open: All year • Total sites: 4 • RV sites: 4 • RV fee: Free (donation appreciated) • Electric sites: 4 • Water at site • No toilets • Elevation: 1544

Columbus

Flat Water Landing WMA • Agency: State • Location: 2 miles S of Columbus • GPS: Lat 41.399707 Lon -97.367808 • Total sites: Dispersed • RV sites: Undefined • RV fee: Free • No water • No toilets • Elevation: 1443

Lake North - LPD • Agency: Utility Company • Tel: 402-564-3171 • Location: 3 miles N of Columbus • GPS: Lat 41.496078 Lon -97.352518 • Open: May-Oct • Total sites: 125 • RV sites: 25 • RV fee: Free • Electric sites: 12 • Central water • Vault toilets • Activities: Hiking, fishing, swimming, power boating, non-power boating • Elevation: 1532

Loup Park - LPD (Lake Babcock) • Agency: Utility Company • Tel: 402-564-3171 • Location: 3 miles N of Columbus • GPS: Lat 41.496188 Lon -97.382091 • Open: May-Oct • Total sites: 170 • RV sites: 50 • RV fee: Free • Electric sites: 28 • Central water • Vault toilets • Activities: Hiking, mountain biking • Elevation: 1562

Powerhouse Park - LPD • Agency: Utility Company • Tel: 402-564-3171 • Location: 1 mile NE of Columbus • GPS: Lat 41.462427 Lon -97.329004 • Open: Summer weekends only • Total sites: 26 • RV sites: 6 • RV fee: Free • Central water • Vault toilets • Activities: Fishing • Elevation: 1437

Tailrace Park - LPD • Agency: Utility Company • Tel: 402-562-5709 • Location: 5 miles SE of Columbus • GPS: Lat 41.400906 Lon -97.281201 • Total sites: 36 • RV sites: 6 • RV fee: Free • No water • No toilets • Elevation: 1424

Wilkinson WMA • Agency: State • Location: 5 miles NW of Columbus • GPS: Lat 41.500619 Lon -97.465544 • Total sites: Dispersed • RV sites: Undefined • RV fee: Free • No water • No toilets • Elevation: 1515

Cozad

Cozad WMA • Agency: State • Location: 1 mile S of Cozad • GPS: Lat 40.840673 Lon -99.985082 • Open: All year • Total sites: Dispersed • RV sites: Undefined (camping allowed throughout unless posted) • RV fee: Free • No water • No toilets • Activities: Hiking, fishing, hunting • Elevation: 2493

East Willow Island WMA • Agency: State • Location: 2 miles W of Cozad • GPS: Lat 40.864123 Lon -100.033735 • Total sites: Dispersed • RV sites: Undefined • RV fee: Free • No water • No toilets • Activities: Fishing • Elevation: 2507

West Cozad WMA • Agency: State • Location: 2 miles SW of Cozad • GPS: Lat 40.853288 Lon -100.007401 • Total sites: Dispersed • RV sites: Undefined • RV fee: Free • No water • No toilets • Elevation: 2495

Willow Island WMA • Agency: State • Location: 6 miles NW of Cozad • GPS: Lat 40.878121 Lon -100.071094 • Total sites: Dispersed • RV sites: Undefined • RV fee: Free • No water • No toilets • Activities: Fishing • Elevation: 2523

Crawford

Fort Robinson WMA • Agency: State • Location: 6 miles NW of Crawford • GPS: Lat 42.712265 Lon -103.480424 • Total sites: Dispersed • RV sites: Undefined • RV fee: Free • No water • No toilets • Elevation: 4044

Petersen WMA • Agency: State • Tel: 308-762-5605 • Location: 9 miles W of Crawford • GPS: Lat 42.661449 Lon -103.574454 • Total sites: Dispersed • RV sites: Undefined • RV fee: Free • No water • No toilets • Elevation: 4628

Ponderosa WMA • Agency: State • Location: 7 miles SE of Crawford • GPS: Lat 42.645369 Lon -103.317408 • Total sites: Dispersed • RV sites: Undefined • RV fee: Free • No water • No toilets • Elevation: 4248

Whitney Inlet WMA • Agency: State • Location: 10 miles NE of Crawford • GPS: Lat 42.785726 Lon -103.322621 • Total sites: Dispersed • RV sites: Undefined • RV fee: Free • No water • No toilets • Activities: Fishing • Elevation: 3488

Crete

Teal Reservoir WMA • Agency: State • Location: 8 miles SE of Crete • GPS: Lat 40.559004 Lon -96.875331 • Open: All year • Total sites: Dispersed • RV sites: Undefined (camping allowed throughout unless posted) • RV fee: Free • No water • No toilets • Activities: Hiking, fishing, hunting • Elevation: 1417

Dakota City

Omadi Bend WMA • Agency: State • Location: 7 miles S of Dakota City (limited services), 10 miles S of South Sioux City • GPS: Lat 42.34968 Lon -96.43229 • Open: All year • Total sites: Dispersed • RV sites: Undefined (camping allowed throughout unless posted) • RV fee: Free • No water • No toilets • Activities: Hiking, fishing, hunting • Elevation: 1076

Dannebrog

Harold W. Anderson WMA • Agency: State • Location: 4 miles NE of Dannebrog (limited services), 7 miles SW of St Paul • GPS: Lat 41.143354 Lon -98.505627 • Total sites: Dispersed • RV sites: Undefined • RV fee: Free • No water • No toilets • Elevation: 1854

Denton

Yankee Hill WMA • Agency: State • Location: 4 miles SE of Denton (limited services), 8 miles SW of Lincoln • GPS: Lat 40.726647 Lon -96.794537 • Open: All year • Total sites: Dispersed • RV sites: Undefined • RV fee: Free • No water • No toilets • Notes: 3 day limit • Activities: Hiking, fishing, hunting • Elevation: 1263

Deshler

Washington Park • Agency: Municipal • Tel: 402-365-4260 • Location: In Deshler (limited services), 10 miles SW of Hebron • GPS: Lat 40.136195 Lon -97.721259 • Open: All year • Total sites: 10 • RV sites: 10 • RV fee: Free (donation appreciated) • Electric sites: 10 • Water at site • Flush toilets • Activities: Swimming • Elevation: 1549

Diller

Arrowhead WMA • Agency: State • Location: 6 miles E of Diller (limited services), 17 miles SW of Beatrice • GPS: Lat 40.097927 Lon -96.866878 • Open: All year • Total sites: Dispersed • RV sites: Undefined (camping allowed throughout unless posted) • RV fee: Free • No water • No toilets • Activities: Hiking, fishing, hunting • Elevation: 1339

Du Bois

Four-Mile Creek WMA • Agency: State • Location: 8 miles E of Du Bois (limited services), 16 miles SE of Pawnee City • GPS: Lat 40.044099 Lon -95.935701 • Total sites: Dispersed • RV sites: Undefined • RV fee: Free • No water • No toilets • Elevation: 1144

Kinter's Ford WMA • Agency: State • Location: 5 miles NE of Du Bois (limited services), 13 miles SE of Pawnee City • GPS: Lat 40.059002 Lon -95.994188 • Total sites: Dispersed • RV sites: Undefined • RV fee: Free • No water • No toilets • Elevation: 1046

Lores Branch WMA • Agency: State • Location: 3 miles NW of Du Bois (limited services), 8 miles SE of Pawnee City • GPS: Lat 40.043939 Lon -96.089049 • Total sites: Dispersed • RV sites: Undefined • RV fee: Free • No water • No toilets • Elevation: 1085

Prairie Knoll WMA • Agency: State • Location: 3 miles NW of Du Bois (limited services), 8 miles SE of Pawnee City • GPS: Lat 40.058894 Lon -96.070355 • Total sites: Dispersed • RV sites: Undefined • RV fee: Free • No water • No toilets • Elevation: 1191

Dwight

Redtail WMA • Agency: State • Location: 1 mile E of Dwight (limited services), 16 miles NE of Seward • GPS: Lat 41.082998 Lon -96.995717 • Total sites: Dispersed • RV sites: Undefined • RV fee: Free • No water • No toilets • Elevation: 1477

Edgar

Bluewing WMA • Agency: State • Location: 4 miles W of Edgar (limited services), 31 miles SE of Hastings • GPS: Lat 40.368789 Lon -98.051702 • Total sites: Dispersed • RV sites: Undefined • RV fee: Free • No water • No toilets • Elevation: 1739

Greenhead WMA • Agency: State • Location: 6 miles NE of Edgar (limited services), 35 miles SE of Hastings • GPS: Lat 40.441256 Lon -97.938314 • Total sites: Dispersed • RV sites: Undefined • RV fee: Free • No water • No toilets • Elevation: 1732

Smartweed Marsh West • Agency: State • Location: 5 miles SW of Edgar (limited services), 34 miles SE of Hastings • GPS: Lat 40.343707 Lon -98.029954 • Total sites: Dispersed • RV sites: Undefined • RV fee: Free • No water • No toilets • Elevation: 1734

Smartweed Marsh WMA • Agency: State • Location: 5 miles SW of Edgar (limited services), 37 miles SE of Hastings • GPS: Lat 40.336361 Lon -98.014811 • Total sites: Dispersed • RV sites: Undefined • RV fee: Free • No water • No toilets • Elevation: 1718

Elm Creek

Blue Hole East WMA • Agency: State • Location: 3 miles S of Elm Creek (limited services), 17 miles W of Kearney • GPS: Lat 40.689259 Lon -99.366529 • Open: All year • Total sites: Dispersed • RV sites: Undefined (camping allowed throughout unless posted) • RV fee: Free • No water • No toilets • Activities: Hiking, fishing, hunting • Elevation: 2254

Blue Hole WMA • Agency: State • Location: 3 miles S of Elm Creek (limited services), 16 miles W of Kearney • GPS: Lat 40.687412 Lon -99.38288 • Open: All year • Total sites: Dispersed • RV sites: Undefined (camping allowed throughout unless posted) • RV fee: Free • No water • No toilets • Activities: Hiking, fishing, hunting • Elevation: 2257

Coot Shallows WMA • Agency: State • Location: 6 miles SE of Elm Creek (limited services), 12 miles W of Kearney • GPS: Lat 40.684224 Lon -99.288267 • Total sites: Dispersed • RV sites: Undefined • RV fee: Free • No water • No toilets • Activities: Fishing • Elevation: 2220

Elwood

Elwood Reservoir WMA • Agency: State • Location: 4 miles NE of Elwood (limited services), 14 miles SW of Lexington • GPS: Lat 40.628657 Lon -99.847557 • Open: All year • Total sites: Dispersed • RV sites: Undefined (camping allowed throughout unless posted) • RV fee: Free • No water • No toilets • Activities: Hiking, fishing, hunting • Elevation: 2629

Fairbury

Flathead WMA • Agency: State • Location: 1 mile S of Fairbury • GPS: Lat 40.124879 Lon -97.189623 • Total sites: Dispersed • RV sites: Undefined • RV fee: Free • No water • No toilets • Elevation: 1310

Rose Creek WMA - East • Agency: State • Location: 6 miles SW of Fairbury • GPS: Lat 40.082255 Lon -97.227178 • Total sites: Dispersed • RV sites: Undefined • RV fee: Free • No water • No toilets • Elevation: 1372

Rose Creek WMA - West • Agency: State • Location: 9 miles SW of Fairbury • GPS: Lat 40.067188 Lon -97.248827 • Total sites: Dispersed • RV sites: Undefined • RV fee: Free • No water • No toilets • Elevation: 1356

Fairfield

Bulrush WMA • Agency: State • Location: 3 miles SE of Fairfield (limited services), 28 miles SE of Hastings • GPS: Lat 40.393948 Lon -98.082716 • Total sites: Dispersed • RV sites: Undefined • RV fee: Free • No water • No toilets • Elevation: 1757

Kissinger Basin WMA • Agency: State • Location: 1 mile N of Fairfield (limited services), 23 miles SE of Hastings • GPS: Lat 40.450645 Lon -98.108192 • Total sites: Dispersed • RV sites: Undefined • RV fee: Free • No water • No toilets • Elevation: 1780

Falls City

Margrave WMA • Agency: State • Location: 9 miles SE of Falls City • GPS: Lat 40.014688 Lon -95.473025 • Total sites: Dispersed • RV sites: Undefined • RV fee: Free • No water • No toilets • Elevation: 890

Franklin

Ash Grove WMA • Agency: State • Location: 5 miles S of Franklin (limited services), 28 miles SE of Alma • GPS: Lat 40.031405 Lon -98.971087 • Open: All year • Total sites: Dispersed • RV sites: Undefined (camping allowed throughout unless posted) • RV fee: Free • No water • No toilets • Activities: Hiking, fishing, hunting • Elevation: 1982

Limestone Bluffs WMA • Agency: State • Location: 9 miles SE of Franklin (limited services), 32 miles SE of Alma • GPS: Lat 40.002444 Lon -98.880291 • Total sites:

Dispersed • RV sites: Undefined • RV fee: Free • No water • No toilets • Activities: Fishing • Elevation: 2100

Garland

Oak Glen WMA • Agency: State • Location: 2 miles N of Garland (limited services), 11 miles NE of Seward • GPS: Lat 40.977106 Lon -96.981865 • Total sites: Dispersed • RV sites: Undefined • RV fee: Free • No water • No toilets • Elevation: 1534

Geneva

Sandpiper WMA • Agency: State • Location: 7 miles SW of Geneva • GPS: Lat 40.495836 Lon -97.710117 • Total sites: Dispersed • RV sites: Undefined • RV fee: Free • No water • No toilets • Elevation: 1667

Genoa

Don Dworak WMA • Agency: State • Location: 2 miles S of Genoa • GPS: Lat 41.420384 Lon -97.734319 • Total sites: Dispersed • RV sites: Undefined • RV fee: Free • No water • No toilets • Elevation: 1549

Sunny Hollow WMA • Agency: State • Location: 6 miles S of Genoa • GPS: Lat 41.378413 Lon -97.733747 • Total sites: Dispersed • RV sites: Undefined • RV fee: Free • No water • No toilets • Elevation: 1591

Gering

Buffalo Creek WMA • Agency: State • Location: 13 miles SE of Gering • GPS: Lat 41.702797 Lon -103.574847 • Total sites: Dispersed • RV sites: Undefined • RV fee: Free • No water • No toilets • Elevation: 4114

Goehner

Straight Water WMA • Agency: State • Location: 3 miles N of Goehner (limited services), 9 miles SW of Seward • GPS: Lat 40.865672 Lon -97.234609 • Total sites: Dispersed • RV sites: Undefined • RV fee: Free • No water • No toilets • Elevation: 1570

Gothenburg

Blue Heron WMA • Agency: State • Location: 1 mile S of Gothenburg • GPS: Lat 40.914206 Lon -100.170504 • Total sites: Dispersed • RV sites: Undefined • RV fee: Free • No water • No toilets • Elevation: 2562

East Gothenburg WMA • Agency: State • Location: 5 miles SE of Gothenburg • GPS: Lat 40.888087 Lon -100.106478 • Total sites: Dispersed • RV sites: Undefined • RV fee: Free • No water • No toilets • Activities: Fishing • Elevation: 2543

West Gothenburg WMA • Agency: State • Location: 8 miles NW of Gothenburg • GPS: Lat 40.986229 Lon -100.300552 • Total sites: Dispersed • RV sites: Undefined • RV fee: Free • No water • No toilets • Activities: Fishing • Elevation: 2641

Grafton

Bluebill WMA • Agency: State • Location: 1 mile NE of Grafton (limited services), 13 miles NW of Geneva • GPS: Lat 40.640235 Lon -97.705258 • Total sites: Dispersed • RV sites: Undefined • RV fee: Free • No water • No toilets • Elevation: 1680

Grand Island

Cornhusker WMA • Agency: State • Location: 5 miles W of Grand Island • GPS: Lat 40.902219 Lon -98.455172 • Total sites: Dispersed • RV sites: Undefined • RV fee: Free • No water • No toilets • Elevation: 1903

Deep Well WMA • Agency: State • Location: 9 miles SE of Grand Island • GPS: Lat 40.843169 Lon -98.222526 • Open: All year • Total sites: Dispersed • RV sites: Undefined (camping allowed throughout unless posted) • RV fee: Free • No water • No toilets • Activities: Hiking, fishing, hunting • Elevation: 1873

Greeley

Greeley City Park • Agency: Municipal • Tel: 308-428-4010 • Location: In Greeley (limited services), 25 miles N of St Paul • GPS: Lat 41.551247 Lon -98.537541 • Open: May-Sep • Stay limit: 3 days • Total sites: 10 • RV sites: 10 • RV fee: Free • Electric sites: 10 • Water at site • No toilets • Activities: Swimming • Elevation: 2014

Guide Rock

Guide Rock Diversion Dam WMA • Agency: State • Location: 3 miles W of Guide Rock (limited services), 9 miles SE of Red Cloud • GPS: Lat 40.067292 Lon -98.377507 • Total sites: Dispersed • RV sites: Undefined • RV fee: Free • No water • No toilets • Activities: Fishing • Elevation: 1652

Harrison

Gilbert-Baker WMA • Agency: State • Tel: 308-668-2211 • Location: 7 miles NW of Harrison (limited services), 32 miles NW of Crawford • GPS: Lat 42.767085 Lon -103.926027 • Total sites: Dispersed • RV sites: Undefined • RV fee: Free • Central water • Vault toilets • Activities: Fishing, hunting • Elevation: 4442

Harrison City Park • Agency: Municipal • Location: In Harrison (limited services), 26 miles W of Crawford • GPS: Lat 42.689752 Lon -103.885327 • Total sites:

2 • RV sites: 2 • Max RV Length: 40 • RV fee: Free (donation appreciated) • Electric sites: 2 • Central water • Flush toilets • Elevation: 4884

Hayes Center

Hayes Center WMA • Agency: State • Location: 12 miles NE of Hayes Center (limited services), 40 miles NW of McCook • GPS: Lat 40.590546 Lon -100.931122 • Open: All year • Total sites: 10 • RV sites: 10 • RV fee: Free • No water • No toilets • Activities: Hiking, fishing, swimming, hunting, non-power boating • Elevation: 2835

Hebron

Little Blue East WMA • Agency: State • Location: 5 miles E of Hebron • GPS: Lat 40.165096 Lon -97.498091 • Total sites: Dispersed • RV sites: Undefined • RV fee: Free • No water • No toilets • Elevation: 1428

Little Blue WMA • Agency: State • Location: 5 miles E of Hebron • GPS: Lat 40.157006 Lon -97.517199 • Total sites: Dispersed • RV sites: Undefined • RV fee: Free • No water • No toilets • Elevation: 1456

Henderson

Kirkpatrick Basin South WMA • Agency: State • Location: 6 miles NE of Henderson (limited services), 11 miles SW of York • GPS: Lat 40.800259 Lon -97.722758 • Total sites: Dispersed • RV sites: Undefined • RV fee: Free • No water • No toilets • Elevation: 1683

Hershey

East Sutherland WMA • Agency: State • Location: 5 miles SW of Hershey (limited services), 17 miles W of North Platte • GPS: Lat 41.141235 Lon -101.059594 • Total sites: Dispersed • RV sites: Undefined • RV fee: Free • No water • No toilets • Activities: Fishing • Elevation: 2926

Kelly Avery WMA • Agency: State • Location: 2 miles S of Hershey (limited services), 14 miles W of North Platte • GPS: Lat 41.134706 Lon -100.998256 • Stay limit: 3-6 days • Total sites: Dispersed • RV sites: Undefined • RV fee: Free • No water • No toilets • Activities: Fishing • Elevation: 2907

Hickman

Hedgefield WMA • Agency: State • Location: 5 miles SE of Hickman (limited services), 19 miles SE of Lincoln • GPS: Lat 40.604425 Lon -96.57075 • Open: All year • Total sites: Dispersed • RV sites: Undefined (camping allowed throughout unless posted) • RV fee: Free • No water • No toilets • Activities: Hiking, fishing, hunting • Elevation: 1296

Holdrege

West Sacramento WMA • Agency: State • Location: 8 miles SE of Holdrege • GPS: Lat 40.358094 Lon -99.303788 • Total sites: Dispersed • RV sites: Undefined • RV fee: Free • No water • No toilets • Elevation: 2282

Hyannis

Avocet WMA • Agency: State • Location: 2 miles E of Hyannis (limited services), 60 miles E of Alliance • GPS: Lat 41.995116 Lon -101.729513 • Open: All year • Total sites: Dispersed • RV sites: Undefined (camping allowed throughout unless posted) • RV fee: Free • No water • No toilets • Activities: Hiking, fishing, hunting • Elevation: 3694

Cottonwood/Steverson WMA • Agency: State • Location: 31 miles N of Hyannis (limited services), 70 miles SE of Gordon • GPS: Lat 42.401285 Lon -101.694967 • Open: All year • Total sites: Dispersed • RV sites: Undefined (camping allowed throughout unless posted) • RV fee: Free • No water • No toilets • Activities: Hiking, fishing, hunting • Elevation: 3596

DeFair Lake WMA • Agency: State • Location: 4 miles SE of Hyannis (limited services), 62 miles E of Alliance • GPS: Lat 41.962692 Lon -101.719437 • Open: All year • Total sites: Dispersed • RV sites: Undefined (camping allowed throughout unless posted) • RV fee: Free • No water • No toilets • Activities: Hiking, fishing, hunting • Elevation: 3694

Frye Lake WMA • Agency: State • Location: 2 miles NE of Hyannis (limited services), 59 miles E of Alliance • GPS: Lat 42.016287 Lon -101.753191 • Open: All year • Total sites: Dispersed • RV sites: Undefined (camping allowed throughout unless posted) • RV fee: Free • No water • No toilets • Activities: Hiking, fishing, hunting • Elevation: 3727

Kearney

Bassway Strip WMA • Agency: State • Location: 9 miles E of Kearney • GPS: Lat 40.686463 Lon -98.948598 • Total sites: Dispersed • RV sites: Undefined • RV fee: Free • No water • No toilets • Activities: Fishing • Elevation: 2100

Bufflehead WMA • Agency: State • Location: 4 miles SE of Kearney • GPS: Lat 40.670531 Lon -99.017921 • Total sites: Dispersed • RV sites: Undefined • RV fee: Free • No water • No toilets • Activities: Fishing • Elevation: 2123

East Odessa WMA • Agency: State • Location: 5 miles SW of Kearney • GPS: Lat 40.670743 Lon -99.164945 • Total sites: Dispersed • RV sites: Undefined • RV fee: Free • No water • No toilets • Elevation: 2172

East Odessa WMA • Agency: State • Location: 6 miles SW of Kearney • GPS: Lat 40.659749 Lon -99.159879 • Total sites: Dispersed • RV sites: Undefined • RV fee: Free • No water • No toilets • Elevation: 2192

Kimball

Oliver Reservoir SRA • Agency: State • Tel: 308-254-2377 • Location: 8 miles W of Kimball • GPS: Lat 41.231185 Lon -103.830738 • Open: All year • Stay limit: 14 days • Total sites: 175 • RV sites: 50 • RV fee: Free (donation appreciated) • Central water • Vault toilets • Activities: Fishing, swimming, power boating, non-power boating • Elevation: 4833

Lewellen

Clear Creek WMA 1 • Agency: State • Location: 5 miles SE of Lewellen (limited services), 32 miles NW of Ogallala • GPS: Lat 41.297167 Lon -102.063182 • Open: All year • Total sites: Dispersed • RV sites: Undefined (camping allowed throughout unless posted) • RV fee: Free • No water • No toilets • Activities: Hiking, fishing, hunting • Elevation: 3274

Clear Creek WMA 2 • Agency: State • Location: 5 miles SE of Lewellen (limited services), 31 miles NW of Ogallala • GPS: Lat 41.299737 Lon -102.076929 • Open: All year • Total sites: Dispersed • RV sites: Undefined (camping allowed throughout unless posted) • RV fee: Free • No water • No toilets • Activities: Hiking, fishing, hunting • Elevation: 3279

Lewiston

Mayberry WMA/Rock Creek Reservoir • Agency: State • Location: 6 miles SE of Lewiston (limited services), 19 miles NW of Pawnee City • GPS: Lat 40.219008 Lon -96.324162 • Open: All year • Total sites: Dispersed • RV sites: Undefined (camping allowed throughout unless posted) • RV fee: Free • No water • No toilets • Activities: Hiking, fishing, hunting • Elevation: 1319

Lexington

Darr WMA • Agency: State • Location: 8 miles W of Lexington • GPS: Lat 40.783646 Lon -99.849601 • Total sites: Dispersed • RV sites: Undefined • RV fee: Free • No water • No toilets • Activities: Fishing • Elevation: 2438

Dogwood WMA • Agency: State • Location: 10 miles SE of Lexington • GPS: Lat 40.697989 Lon -99.612839 • Total sites: Dispersed • RV sites: Undefined • RV fee: Free • No water • No toilets • Activities: Fishing • Elevation: 2346

East Phillips Canyon WMA • Agency: State • Location: 10 miles SW of Lexington • GPS: Lat 40.685728 Lon -99.777187 • Total sites: Dispersed • RV sites: Undefined • RV fee: Free • No water • No toilets • Elevation: 2522

Plum Creek WMA • Agency: State • Location: 12 miles SW of Lexington • GPS: Lat 40.700929 Lon -99.917836 • Total sites: Dispersed • RV sites: Undefined • RV fee: Free • No water • No toilets • Activities: Fishing • Elevation: 2677

Lincoln

Helmuth Public Acess Area • Agency: State • Location: 6 miles N of Lincoln • GPS: Lat 40.943612 Lon -96.709953 • Total sites: Dispersed • RV sites: Undefined • RV fee: Free • No water • No toilets • Elevation: 1174

Killdeer WMA/Salt Creek Resevoir • Agency: State • Location: 10 miles SW of Lincoln • GPS: Lat 40.677867 Lon -96.76577 • Open: All year • Total sites: Dispersed • RV sites: Undefined • RV fee: Free • No water • No toilets • Notes: 3 day limit • Activities: Hiking, fishing, hunting • Elevation: 1339

Little Salt Creek West WMA • Agency: State • Location: 9 miles N of Lincoln • GPS: Lat 40.973046 Lon -96.721004 • Total sites: Dispersed • RV sites: Undefined • RV fee: Free • No water • No toilets • Elevation: 1235

Little Salt Creek WMA • Agency: State • Location: 6 miles N of Lincoln • GPS: Lat 40.944469 Lon -96.711445 • Total sites: Dispersed • RV sites: Undefined • RV fee: Free • No water • No toilets • Elevation: 1180

Long Pine

Long Pine WMA • Agency: State • Location: 2 miles N of Long Pine (limited services), 9 miles E of Ainsworth • GPS: Lat 42.556031 Lon -99.700515 • Total sites: Dispersed • RV sites: Undefined • RV fee: Free • No water • No toilets • Elevation: 2290

Pine Glen WMA • Agency: State • Location: 11 miles N of Long Pine (limited services), 18 miles NE of Ainsworth • GPS: Lat 42.671583 Lon -99.700624 • Total sites: Dispersed • RV sites: Undefined • RV fee: Free • No water • No toilets • Elevation: 2211

Lynch

Niobrara River • Agency: County • Location: 5 miles S of Lynch (limited services), 32 miles NE of O'Neill • GPS: Lat 42.772405 Lon -98.441827 • Total sites: Dispersed • RV sites: Undefined • RV fee: Free • No water • No toilets • Elevation: 1408

Sunshine Bottoms WMA • Agency: State • Location: 9 miles NE of Lynch (limited services), 45 miles NE of O'Neill • GPS: Lat 42.921136 Lon -98.407813 • Total sites: Dispersed • RV sites: Undefined • RV fee: Free • No water • No toilets • Activities: Fishing, power boating • Elevation: 1230

Maskell

Mulberry Bend WMA • Agency: State • Location: 5 miles NE of Maskell (limited services), 26 miles NE of Hartington • GPS: Lat 42.714249 Lon -96.943782 • Open: All year • Total sites: Dispersed • RV sites: Undefined (camping allowed throughout unless posted) • RV fee: Free • No water • Vault toilets • Activities: Hiking, fishing, hunting • Elevation: 1116

Maywood

Cedar Valley WMA • Agency: State • Location: 10 miles NW of Maywood (limited services), 27 miles S of North Platte • GPS: Lat 40.740349 Lon -100.703176 • Total sites: Dispersed • RV sites: Undefined • RV fee: Free • No water • No toilets • Activities: Fishing • Elevation: 2759

Wellfleet WMA • Agency: State • Location: 10 miles NW of Maywood (limited services), 27 miles S of North Platte • GPS: Lat 40.754842 Lon -100.740355 • Total sites: Dispersed • RV sites: Undefined • RV fee: Free • No water • Vault toilets • Activities: Fishing • Elevation: 2812

Wellfleet WMA • Agency: State • Location: 10 miles NW of Maywood (limited services), 27 miles S of North Platte • GPS: Lat 40.758716 Lon -100.748952 • Total sites: Dispersed • RV sites: Undefined • RV fee: Free • No water • No toilets • Elevation: 2813

McCook

Karrer Park • Agency: Municipal • Tel: 308-345-2022 • Location: In McCook • GPS: Lat 40.197507 Lon -100.602895 • Open: All year • Stay limit: 3 days • Total sites: 7 • RV sites: 7 • Max RV Length: 30 • RV fee: Free (donation appreciated) • Electric sites: 7 • Central water • Flush toilets • Elevation: 2520

Meadow Grove

Mill Stone Wayside Park • Agency: Municipal • Tel: 402-634-2225 • Location: In Meadow Grove (limited services), 14 miles W of Norfolk • GPS: Lat 42.032185 Lon -97.728496 • Open: All year • Total sites: 4 • RV sites: 4 • RV fee: Free (donation appreciated) • Electric sites: 4 (15-amp only) • Central water • Vault toilets • Elevation: 1618

Yellowbanks WMA • Agency: State • Location: 5 miles NE of Meadow Grove (limited services), 14 miles W of Norfolk • GPS: Lat 42.04684 Lon -97.669969 • Open: All year • Total sites: Dispersed • RV sites: Undefined (camping allowed throughout unless posted) • RV fee: Free • No water • No toilets • Activities: Hiking, fishing, hunting • Elevation: 1680

Merna

Berggren-Young WMA • Agency: State • Location: 3 miles E of Merna (limited services), 8 miles NW of Broken Bow • GPS: Lat 41.481635 Lon -99.713064 • Total sites: Dispersed • RV sites: Undefined • RV fee: Free • No water • No toilets • Elevation: 2793

Milligan

Swan Creek WMA • Agency: State • Location: 8 miles E of Milligan (limited services), 19 miles E of Geneva • GPS: Lat 40.511429 Lon -97.251464 • Open: All year • Total sites: Dispersed • RV sites: Undefined (camping allowed throughout unless posted) • RV fee: Free • No water • No toilets • Activities: Hiking, fishing, hunting • Elevation: 1490

Minden

Northeast Sacramento WMA • Agency: State • Location: 7 miles SW of Minden • GPS: Lat 40.423178 Lon -98.993918 • Total sites: Dispersed • RV sites: Undefined • RV fee: Free • No water • No toilets • Elevation: 2179

Monroe

Lookingglass Creek WMA • Agency: State • Location: 1 mile S of Monroe (limited services), 13 miles NW of Columbus • GPS: Lat 41.467787 Lon -97.603349 • Open: All year • Total sites: Dispersed • RV sites: Undefined (camping allowed throughout unless posted) • RV fee: Free • No water • No toilets • Activities: Hiking, fishing, hunting • Elevation: 1509

Morrill

Kiowa WMA • Agency: State • Location: 3 miles S of Morrill (limited services), 9 miles W of Mitchell • GPS: Lat 41.924577 Lon -103.929511 • Total sites: Dispersed • RV sites: Undefined • RV fee: Free • No water • No toilets • Elevation: 4017

Nebraska City

Hamburg Bend WMA • Agency: State • Location: 8 miles SE of Nebraska City • GPS: Lat 40.598952 Lon

-95.770876 • Total sites: Dispersed • RV sites: Undefined • RV fee: Free • No water • No toilets • Elevation: 913

Wilson Creek WMA • Agency: State • Location: 12 miles NW of Nebraska City • GPS: Lat 40.704371 Lon -96.059103 • Open: All year • Total sites: Dispersed • RV sites: Undefined (camping allowed throughout unless posted) • RV fee: Free • No water • No toilets • Activities: Hiking, fishing, hunting • Elevation: 1109

Neligh

Red Wing WMA • Agency: State • Location: 4 miles NW of Neligh • GPS: Lat 42.157972 Lon -98.106663 • Total sites: Dispersed • RV sites: Undefined • RV fee: Free • No water • No toilets • Elevation: 1759

Nemaha

Aspinwall Bend WMA • Agency: State • Location: 1 mile S of Nemaha (limited services), 13 miles SE of Auburn • GPS: Lat 40.325261 Lon -95.675554 • Open: All year • Total sites: Dispersed • RV sites: Undefined (camping allowed throughout unless posted) • RV fee: Free • No water • No toilets • Activities: Hiking, fishing, hunting • Elevation: 888

Langdon Bend WMA • Agency: State • Location: 3 miles SE of Nemaha (limited services), 15 miles SE of Auburn • GPS: Lat 40.328694 Lon -95.641144 • Total sites: Dispersed • RV sites: Undefined • RV fee: Free • No water • No toilets • Elevation: 893

Niobrara

Bazile Creek WMA • Agency: State • Location: 4 miles E of Niobrara (limited services), 23 miles N of Creighton • GPS: Lat 42.757557 Lon -97.952896 • Open: All year • Total sites: Dispersed • RV sites: Undefined (camping allowed throughout unless posted) • RV fee: Free • No water • No toilets • Activities: Hiking, fishing, hunting • Elevation: 1230

Ferry Landing WMA • Agency: State • Location: 3 miles NE of Niobrara (limited services), 30 miles N of Creighton • GPS: Lat 42.763769 Lon -97.991995 • Open: All year • Total sites: Dispersed • RV sites: Undefined (camping allowed throughout unless posted) • RV fee: Free • No water • No toilets • Activities: Hiking, fishing, hunting • Elevation: 1211

North Loup

Davis Creek RA - LLNRD • Agency: State • Location: 7 miles S of North Loup (limited services), 18 miles SE of Ord • GPS: Lat 41.419311 Lon -98.765885 • Open: All year • Total sites: 67 • RV sites: 42 • RV fee: Free • Electric sites: 42 • Central water • Flush toilets • Activities: Hiking, fishing, hunting • Elevation: 2111

North Platte

Birdwood Lake WMA • Agency: State • Location: 5 miles W of North Platte • GPS: Lat 41.116398 Lon -100.830265 • Total sites: Dispersed • RV sites: Undefined • RV fee: Free • No water • No toilets • Elevation: 2841

Box Elder Canyon WMA • Agency: State • Location: 15 miles SE of North Platte • GPS: Lat 41.027447 Lon -100.572804 • Open: All year • Total sites: Dispersed • RV sites: Undefined (camping allowed throughout unless posted) • RV fee: Free • No water • No toilets • Activities: Hiking, fishing, hunting • Elevation: 2772

Crystal Lake WMA • Agency: State • Location: 10 miles SE of North Platte • GPS: Lat 41.082778 Lon -100.615703 • Total sites: Dispersed • RV sites: Undefined • RV fee: Free • No water • No toilets • Activities: Fishing • Elevation: 2749

East Hershey WMA • Agency: State • Location: 7 miles W of North Platte • GPS: Lat 41.125608 Lon -100.902508 • Open: All year • Total sites: Dispersed • RV sites: Undefined (camping allowed throughout unless posted) • RV fee: Free • No water • No toilets • Activities: Hiking, fishing, hunting • Elevation: 2858

East Hershey WMA • Agency: State • Location: 8 miles W of North Platte • GPS: Lat 41.130375 Lon -100.907125 • Total sites: Dispersed • RV sites: Undefined • RV fee: Free • No water • No toilets • Elevation: 2864

Fremont Slough WMA • Agency: State • Location: 6 miles SE of North Platte • GPS: Lat 41.096569 Lon -100.668982 • Open: All year • Total sites: Dispersed • RV sites: Undefined (camping allowed throughout unless posted) • RV fee: Free • No water • No toilets • Activities: Hiking, fishing, hunting • Elevation: 2762

Pawnee Slough WMA • Agency: State • Location: 11 miles SE of North Platte • GPS: Lat 41.082735 Lon -100.542741 • Total sites: Dispersed • RV sites: Undefined • RV fee: Free • No water • No toilets • Activities: Fishing • Elevation: 2730

West Maxwell WMA • Agency: State • Location: 14 miles SE of North Platte • GPS: Lat 41.057134 Lon -100.542543 • Total sites: Dispersed • RV sites: Undefined • RV fee: Free • No water • No toilets • Activities: Fishing • Elevation: 2713

O'Neill

Carney City Park • Agency: Municipal • Tel: 402-336-3640 • Location: In O'Neill • GPS: Lat 42.451001 Lon -98.644819 • Open: Apr-Sep • Total sites: 22 • RV sites: 18 • RV fee: Free (donation appreciated) • Electric sites: 18 (15-amp only) • Water at site • Flush toilets • Activities: Fishing • Elevation: 1972

Dry Creek WMA • Agency: State • Location: 2 miles SE of O'Neill • GPS: Lat 42.440021 Lon -98.613441 • Total sites: Dispersed • RV sites: Undefined • RV fee: Free • No water • No toilets • Activities: Fishing • Elevation: 1956

Oconto

Pressey WMA-North Access • Agency: State • Location: 5 miles NE of Oconto (limited services), 15 miles S of Broken Bow • GPS: Lat 41.19338 Lon -99.709144 • Open: All year • Total sites: Dispersed • RV sites: Undefined (camping allowed throughout unless posted) • RV fee: Free • No water • No toilets • Activities: Hiking, fishing, hunting • Elevation: 2431

Pressey WMA-South Access • Agency: State • Location: 5 miles NE of Oconto (limited services), 16 miles S of Broken Bow • GPS: Lat 41.18321 Lon -99.702681 • Open: All year • Total sites: Dispersed • RV sites: Undefined (camping allowed throughout unless posted) • RV fee: Free • No water • No toilets • Activities: Hiking, fishing, hunting • Elevation: 2424

Odell

Diamond Lake WMA - Big Indian Creek Reservoir 5-F • Agency: State • Location: 4 miles W of Odell (limited services), 19 miles SE of Fairbury • GPS: Lat 40.041459 Lon -96.869047 • Open: All year • Total sites: Dispersed • RV sites: Undefined (camping allowed throughout unless posted) • RV fee: Free • No water • No toilets • Activities: Hiking, fishing, hunting • Elevation: 1368

Donald Whitney Memorial WMA • Agency: State • Location: 4 miles W of Odell (limited services), 19 miles SE of Fairbury • GPS: Lat 40.045366 Lon -96.864109 • Total sites: Dispersed • RV sites: Undefined • RV fee: Free • No water • No toilets • Elevation: 1363

Ogallala

Ogallala Strip WMA • Agency: State • Location: 2 miles SW of Ogallala • GPS: Lat 41.111829 Lon -101.754181 • Total sites: Dispersed • RV sites: Undefined • RV fee: Free • No water • No toilets • Elevation: 3228

Orchard

Orchard City Park • Agency: Municipal • Location: In Orchard (limited services), 21 m NW of Neligh • GPS: Lat 42.335059 Lon -98.244935 • Total sites: 4 • RV sites: 2 • RV fee: Free (donation appreciated) • Electric sites: 2 • Water at site • Flush toilets • Notes: 5 nights free • Elevation: 1952

Osceola

Flatsedge WMA • Agency: State • Location: 6 miles NE of Osceola (limited services), 24 miles SW of Columbus • GPS: Lat 41.224731 Lon -97.483176 • Total sites: Dispersed • RV sites: Undefined • RV fee: Free • No water • No toilets • Elevation: 1657

Oshkosh

Crescent Lake WMA • Agency: State • Location: 22 miles N of Oshkosh (limited services), 55 miles SE of Alliance • GPS: Lat 41.709187 Lon -102.406367 • Total sites: Dispersed • RV sites: Undefined • RV fee: Free • No water • Vault toilets • Activities: Fishing, power boating • Elevation: 3803

Oxford

Oxford WMA 1 • Agency: State • Location: 5 miles NW of Oxford (limited services), 12 miles SE of Arapahoe • GPS: Lat 40.257615 Lon -99.723739 • Total sites: Dispersed • RV sites: Undefined • RV fee: Free • No water • No toilets • Elevation: 2089

Oxford WMA 2 • Agency: State • Location: 6 miles W of Oxford (limited services), 12 miles SE of Arapahoe • GPS: Lat 40.248969 Lon -99.721881 • Total sites: Dispersed • RV sites: Undefined • RV fee: Free • No water • No toilets • Activities: Fishing • Elevation: 2116

Palisade

Frenchman WMA • Agency: State • Location: 1 mile NE of Palisade (limited services), 29 miles NW of McCook • GPS: Lat 40.357837 Lon -101.098157 • Open: All year • Total sites: Dispersed • RV sites: Undefined (camping allowed throughout unless posted) • RV fee: Free • No water • No toilets • Notes: 5 ton weight limit on bridge • Activities: Hiking, fishing, hunting • Elevation: 2746

Palmyra

Triple Creek WMA • Agency: State • Location: 4 miles SW of Palmyra (limited services), 23 miles SE of Lincoln • GPS: Lat 40.661914 Lon -96.40617 • Open: All year • Total sites: Dispersed • RV sites: Undefined (camping allowed throughout unless posted) • RV fee: Free • No water • No toilets • Activities: Hiking, fishing, hunting • Elevation: 1191

Pawnee City

Taylor's Branch WMA • Agency: State • Location: 4 miles NE of Pawnee City • GPS: Lat 40.142181 Lon -96.119056 • Total sites: Dispersed • RV sites: Undefined • RV fee: Free • No water • No toilets • Elevation: 1231

Peru

Kansas Bend WMA • Agency: State • Location: 2 miles E of Peru (limited services), 13 miles NE of Auburn • GPS: Lat 40.483383 Lon -95.698465 • Open: All year • Total sites: Dispersed • RV sites: Undefined (camping allowed throughout unless posted) • RV fee: Free • No water • No toilets • Activities: Hiking, fishing, hunting • Elevation: 915

Peru Bottoms WMA • Agency: State • Location: 3 miles NE of Peru (limited services), 14 miles NE of Auburn • GPS: Lat 40.508308 Lon -95.716115 • Total sites: Dispersed • RV sites: Undefined • RV fee: Free • No water • No toilets • Elevation: 906

Pilger

Black Island WMA • Agency: State • Location: 3 miles E of Pilger (limited services), 5 miles W of Wisner • GPS: Lat 42.000882 Lon -97.008801 • Open: All year • Total sites: Dispersed • RV sites: Undefined (camping allowed throughout unless posted) • RV fee: Free • No water • No toilets • Activities: Hiking, fishing, hunting • Elevation: 1398

Red Fox WMA • Agency: State • Location: 2 miles S of Pilger (limited services), 10 miles W of Wisner • GPS: Lat 41.986328 Lon -97.057152 • Open: All year • Total sites: Dispersed • RV sites: Undefined (camping allowed throughout unless posted) • RV fee: Free • No water • No toilets • Activities: Hiking, fishing, hunting • Elevation: 1414

Plainview

Chilvers Park • Agency: Municipal • Tel: 402-582-4928 • Location: In Plainview • GPS: Lat 42.351628 Lon -97.790696 • Open: All year • Stay limit: 3 days • Total sites: 4 • RV sites: 4 • RV fee: Free (donation appreciated) • Electric sites: 4 • Water at site • No toilets • Activities: Swimming • Elevation: 1700

Plattsmouth

Randall W. Schilling • Agency: State • Location: 3 miles N of Plattsmouth • GPS: Lat 41.040717 Lon -95.882252 • Total sites: Dispersed • RV sites: Undefined • RV fee: Free • No water • No toilets • Elevation: 956

William Gilmour WMA • Agency: State • Location: 5 miles SE of Plattsmouth • GPS: Lat 40.958722 Lon -95.845487 • Total sites: Dispersed • RV sites: Undefined • RV fee: Free • No water • No toilets • Elevation: 951

Pleasant Dale

Twin Lakes WMA - North • Agency: State • Location: 5 miles N of Pleasant Dale (limited services), 12 miles W of Lincoln • GPS: Lat 40.836414 Lon -96.948657 • Total sites: Dispersed • RV sites: Undefined • RV fee: Free • No water • No toilets • Elevation: 1354

Twin Lakes WMA - South • Agency: State • Location: 3 miles N of Pleasant Dale (limited services), 13 miles W of Lincoln • GPS: Lat 40.828735 Lon -96.944064 • Total sites: Dispersed • RV sites: Undefined • RV fee: Free • No water • No toilets • Elevation: 1355

Plymouth

Cub Creek RA (Southern) - LBBNRD • Agency: County • Tel: 402-228-3402 • Location: 8 miles SW of Plymouth (limited services), 11 miles NE of Fairbury • GPS: Lat 40.238756 Lon -97.048692 • Total sites: 6 • RV sites: 6 • RV fee: Free • Central water • Vault toilets • Activities: Hiking, mountain biking, fishing, swimming, power boating, non-power boating • Elevation: 1384

Randolph

Veterans Memorial City Park • Agency: Municipal • Tel: 402-337-0567 • Location: In Randolph (limited services), 26 miles N of Norfolk • GPS: Lat 42.376904 Lon -97.355061 • Open: All year • Total sites: 6 • RV sites: 6 • RV fee: Free (donation appreciated) • Electric sites: 6 • Water at site • Flush toilets • Activities: Swimming • Elevation: 1667

Ravenna

Buffalo County Lake • Agency: County • Tel: 308-452-3344 • Location: 2 miles SE of Ravenna • GPS: Lat 41.019679 Lon -98.890011 • Open: All year • Total sites: Dispersed • RV sites: Undefined • RV fee: Free • No water • Vault toilets • Notes: Near RR tracks • Activities: Fishing, swimming • Elevation: 2001

Red Cloud

Elm Creek WMA • Agency: State • Location: 6 miles NE of Red Cloud • GPS: Lat 40.118856 Lon -98.442773 • Total sites: Dispersed • RV sites: Undefined • RV fee: Free • No water • No toilets • Activities: Fishing • Elevation: 1732

Indian Creek WMA • Agency: State • Location: 1 mile S of Red Cloud • GPS: Lat 40.062342 Lon -98.519181 • Open: All year • Total sites: Dispersed • RV sites: Undefined (camping allowed throughout unless posted) • RV fee: Free • No water • No toilets • Activities: Hiking, fishing, hunting • Elevation: 1696

Narrows WMA • Agency: State • Location: 4 miles W of Red Cloud • GPS: Lat 40.088768 Lon -98.594416 • Total sites: Dispersed • RV sites: Undefined • RV fee: Free • No water • No toilets • Activities: Fishing • Elevation: 1777

Royal

Grove Lake WMA • Agency: State • Location: 3 miles N of Royal (limited services), 19 miles SW of Creighton • GPS: Lat 42.368327 Lon -98.115288 • Open: All year • Total sites: 15 • RV sites: 15 • RV fee: Free • Central water • Vault toilets • Activities: Fishing, swimming, hunting • Elevation: 1695

Rushville

Smith Lake WMA • Agency: State • Location: 22 miles S of Rushville (limited services), 37 miles SW of Gordon • GPS: Lat 42.408569 Lon -102.443695 • Open: All year • Total sites: Dispersed • RV sites: Undefined • RV fee: Free • No water • Vault toilets • Activities: Hiking, fishing, hunting • Elevation: 3829

Scribner

Powder Horn WMA • Agency: State • Location: 4 miles NW of Scribner (limited services), 8 miles S of West Point • GPS: Lat 41.715115 Lon -96.707868 • Total sites: Dispersed • RV sites: Undefined • RV fee: Free • No water • No toilets • Elevation: 1272

Seward

Bur Oak WMA • Agency: State • Location: 5 miles E of Seward • GPS: Lat 40.901141 Lon -97.002344 • Total sites: Dispersed • RV sites: Undefined • RV fee: Free • No water • No toilets • Elevation: 1533

Shickley

Green Wing WMA • Agency: State • Location: 6 miles NW of Shickley (limited services), 20 miles SW of Geneva • GPS: Lat 40.442033 Lon -97.824444 • Total sites: Dispersed • RV sites: Undefined • RV fee: Free • No water • No toilets • Elevation: 1697

Redhead WMA • Agency: State • Location: 6 miles W of Shickley (limited services), 20 miles SW of Geneva • GPS: Lat 40.431399 Lon -97.824011 • Total sites: Dispersed • RV sites: Undefined • RV fee: Free • No water • No toilets • Elevation: 1694

Sora WMA • Agency: State • Location: 7 miles SE of Shickley (limited services), 15 miles SW of Geneva • GPS: Lat 40.379991 Lon -97.658993 • Total sites: Dispersed • RV sites: Undefined • RV fee: Free • No water • No toilets • Elevation: 1618

Silver Creek

Bruce Cowgill WMA • Agency: State • Location: 2 miles NE of Silver Creek (limited services), 16 miles SW of Columbus • GPS: Lat 41.329641 Lon -97.626949 • Total sites: Dispersed • RV sites: Undefined • RV fee: Free • No water • No toilets • Elevation: 1532

South Yankton

Chalkrock WMA • Agency: State • Location: 5 miles S of South Yankton (limited services), 7 miles S of Yankton, SD • GPS: Lat 42.7989 Lon -97.373844 • Open: All year • Total sites: Dispersed • RV sites: Undefined (camping allowed throughout unless posted) • RV fee: Free • No water • No toilets • Activities: Hiking, fishing, hunting • Elevation: 1283

Spalding

Spalding City Park • Agency: Municipal • Tel: 308-497-2416 • Location: In Spalding (limited services), 19 miles W of Albion • GPS: Lat 41.684929 Lon -98.361488 • Open: All year • Total sites: 4 • RV sites: 4 • RV fee: Free (donation appreciated) • Electric sites: 4 • Water at site • No toilets • Elevation: 1893

Spalding Dam Site • Agency: Municipal • Tel: 308-497-2416 • Location: 1 mile S of Spalding (limited services), 20 miles W of Albion • GPS: Lat 41.680877 Lon -98.366062 • Open: All year • Total sites: 19 • RV sites: 4 • RV fee: Free (donation appreciated) • Electric sites: 4 • Water at site • Vault toilets • Notes: 2-day limit • Elevation: 1883

Spencer

Spencer Dam WMA • Agency: State • Location: 6 miles SE of Spencer (limited services), 24 miles N of O'Neill • GPS: Lat 42.807631 Lon -98.655662 • Total sites: Dispersed • RV sites: Undefined • RV fee: Free • No water • No toilets • Elevation: 1493

Springview

Cub Creek RA (Northern) - MNNRD • Agency: State • Tel: 402-376-3241 • Location: 8 miles W of Springview (limited services), 32 miles N of Ainsworth • GPS: Lat 42.824523 Lon -99.912506 • Open: All year • Total sites: Dispersed • RV sites: Undefined • RV fee: Free • Central water • Vault toilets • Activities: Hiking, fishing, power boating • Elevation: 2405

Holt Creek WMA • Agency: State • Location: 12 miles NE of Springview (limited services), 36 miles NE of Ainsworth • GPS: Lat 42.964158 Lon -99.705373 • Total sites: Dispersed • RV sites: Undefined • RV fee: Free • No water • No toilets • Elevation: 2124

Thomas Creek WMA • Agency: State • Location: 6 miles SE of Springview (limited services), 26 miles NE of Ainsworth • GPS: Lat 42.764929 Lon -99.701214 • Total sites: Dispersed • RV sites: Undefined • RV fee: Free • No water • No toilets • Elevation: 2360

St Paul

Leonard A Koziol WMA • Agency: State • Location: 5 miles NE of St Paul • GPS: Lat 41.267492 Lon -98.412878 • Total sites: Dispersed • RV sites: Undefined • RV fee: Free • No water • No toilets • Elevation: 1763

St. Edward

Beaver Bend WMA • Agency: State • Location: 1 mile NW of St. Edward (limited services), 11 miles SE of Albion • GPS: Lat 41.58304 Lon -97.88107 • Open: All year • Total sites: Dispersed • RV sites: Undefined (camping allowed throughout unless posted) • RV fee: Free • No water • No toilets • Activities: Hiking, fishing, hunting • Elevation: 1667

Stanton

Wood Duck WMA • Agency: State • Location: 7 miles SW of Stanton • GPS: Lat 41.929284 Lon -97.310519 • Total sites: Dispersed • RV sites: Undefined • RV fee: Free • No water • No toilets • Activities: Fishing • Elevation: 1473

Steinauer

Bowwood WMA • Agency: State • Location: 3 miles S of Steinauer (limited services), 11 miles NW of Pawnee City • GPS: Lat 40.171629 Lon -96.236972 • Total sites: Dispersed • RV sites: Undefined • RV fee: Free • No water • No toilets • Elevation: 1239

Strang

Strang City Park • Agency: Municipal • Tel: 402-759-4910 • Location: In Strang (limited services), 8 miles S of Geneva • GPS: Lat 40.413065 Lon -97.586818 • Total sites: 3 • RV sites: 3 • RV fee: Free • Electric sites: 3 • Central water • No toilets • Elevation: 1637

Stratton

Swanson Reservoir WMA • Agency: State • Location: 7 miles NE of Stratton (limited services), 28 miles W of McCook • GPS: Lat 40.167586 Lon -101.127344 • Total sites: Dispersed • RV sites: Undefined • RV fee: Free • No water • No toilets • Elevation: 2787

Stromsburg

Buckley City Park • Agency: Municipal • Tel: 402-764-2561 • Location: 1 mile S of Stromsburg • GPS: Lat 41.106456 Lon -97.600863 • Open: All year • Total sites: 12 • RV sites: 12 • RV fee: Free (donation appreciated) • Electric sites: 12 • Central water • Flush toilets • Activities: Swimming • Elevation: 1634

Superior

Lincoln Park West • Agency: Municipal • Tel: 402-879-4713 • Location: In Superior • GPS: Lat 40.020599 Lon -98.083205 • Open: All year • Total sites: 20 • RV sites: 20 • RV fee: Free (donation appreciated) • Electric sites: 20 • Water at site • No toilets • Notes: $5/day after 2 weeks • Activities: Fishing • Elevation: 1594

Table Rock

Table Rock WMA • Agency: State • Location: 2 miles NE of Table Rock (limited services), 9 miles NE of Pawnee City • GPS: Lat 40.187374 Lon -96.061358 • Total sites: Dispersed • RV sites: Undefined • RV fee: Free • No water • No toilets • Elevation: 1118

Taylor

Myrtle E Hall WMA • Agency: State • Location: 9 miles W of Taylor (limited services), 23 miles W of Burwell • GPS: Lat 41.754607 Lon -99.539589 • Total sites: Dispersed • RV sites: Undefined • RV fee: Free • No water • No toilets • Elevation: 2715

Tecumseh

Hickory Ridge WMA 1 • Agency: State • Location: 11 miles SW of Tecumseh • GPS: Lat 40.314791 Lon -96.351228 • Total sites: Dispersed • RV sites: Undefined • RV fee: Free • No water • No toilets • Elevation: 1400

Hickory Ridge WMA 2 • Agency: State • Location: 13 miles SW of Tecumseh • GPS: Lat 40.306232 Lon -96.364776 • Total sites: Dispersed • RV sites: Undefined • RV fee: Free • No water • No toilets • Elevation: 1392

Hickory Ridge WMA 3 • Agency: State • Location: 14 miles SW of Tecumseh • GPS: Lat 40.306218 Lon -96.377571 • Total sites: Dispersed • RV sites: Undefined • RV fee: Free • No water • No toilets • Elevation: 1348

Osage WMA - Central Unit • Agency: State • Location: 3 miles NW of Tecumseh • GPS: Lat 40.407088 Lon -96.222614 • Total sites: Dispersed • RV sites: Undefined • RV fee: Free • No water • No toilets • Elevation: 1222

Osage WMA - North Unit • Agency: State • Location: 5 miles NW of Tecumseh • GPS: Lat 40.426655 Lon -96.218239 • Total sites: Dispersed • RV sites: Undefined • RV fee: Free • No water • No toilets • Elevation: 1305

Osage WMA - South Unit • Agency: State • Location: 3 miles NW of Tecumseh • GPS: Lat 40.400616 Lon -96.217606 • Total sites: Dispersed • RV sites: Undefined • RV fee: Free • No water • No toilets • Elevation: 1234

Twin Oaks WMA 1 • Agency: State • Location: 4 miles SE of Tecumseh • GPS: Lat 40.342067 Lon -96.141124 • Total sites: Dispersed • RV sites: Undefined • RV fee: Free • No water • No toilets • Elevation: 1220

Twin Oaks WMA 2 • Agency: State • Location: 5 miles SE of Tecumseh • GPS: Lat 40.331401 Lon -96.141297 • Total sites: Dispersed • RV sites: Undefined • RV fee: Free • No water • No toilets • Elevation: 1248

Twin Oaks WMA 3 • Agency: State • Location: 6 miles SE of Tecumseh • GPS: Lat 40.314986 Lon -96.141361 • Total sites: Dispersed • RV sites: Undefined • RV fee: Free • No water • No toilets • Elevation: 1172

Twin Oaks WMA 4 • Agency: State • Location: 6 miles SE of Tecumseh • GPS: Lat 40.320358 Lon -96.132628 • Total sites: Dispersed • RV sites: Undefined • RV fee: Free • No water • No toilets • Elevation: 1230

Thedford

Thedford City Park • Agency: Municipal • Location: In Thedford (limited services), 65 miles N of North Platte • GPS: Lat 41.977775 Lon -100.582104 • Open: All year • Total sites: 4 • RV sites: 4 • RV fee: Free (donation appreciated) • Electric sites: 4 • Central water • No toilets • Notes: Near RR tracks • Elevation: 2877

Utica

Marsh Duck WMA • Agency: State • Location: 5 miles SW of Utica (limited services), 13 miles SE of York • GPS: Lat 40.858055 Lon -97.401635 • Total sites: Dispersed • RV sites: Undefined • RV fee: Free • No water • No toilets • Elevation: 1606

North Lake Basin WMA • Agency: State • Location: 1 mile N of Utica (limited services), 14 miles W of York • GPS: Lat 40.909573 Lon -97.349322 • Open: All year • Total sites: Dispersed • RV sites: Undefined (camping allowed throughout unless posted) • RV fee: Free • No water • No toilets • Activities: Hiking, fishing, hunting • Elevation: 1585

Shypoke WMA • Agency: State • Location: 2 miles SE of Utica (limited services), 16 miles W of York • GPS: Lat 40.880142 Lon -97.330722 • Total sites: Dispersed • RV sites: Undefined • RV fee: Free • No water • No toilets • Elevation: 1581

Valentine

Ballards Marsh WMA • Agency: State • Tel: 402-471-0641 • Location: 20 miles S of Valentine • GPS: Lat 42.595653 Lon -100.539434 • Open: All year • Total sites: 10 • RV sites: 10 • RV fee: Free • No water • Vault toilets • Activities: Hiking, fishing, hunting • Elevation: 2881

Big Alkali Lake WMA • Agency: State • Location: 22 miles S of Valentine • GPS: Lat 42.637942 Lon -100.606678 • Open: All year • Total sites: 10 • RV sites: 10 • RV fee: Free • No water • Vault toilets • Activities: Fishing, swimming, power boating, non-power boating • Elevation: 2877

Borman Bridge WMA • Agency: State • Location: 2 miles SE of Valentine • GPS: Lat 42.852308 Lon -100.511496 • Open: All year • Total sites: Dispersed • RV sites: Undefined (camping allowed throughout unless posted) • RV fee: Free • No water • No toilets • Activities: Hiking, fishing, hunting • Elevation: 2408

Valley

Elkhorn Crossing RA - NNRD • Agency: State • Tel: 402-444-6222 • Location: 5 miles NE of Valley • GPS: Lat 41.362201 Lon -96.301965 • Open: Apr-Oct • Total sites: 17 • RV sites: 8 • RV fee: Free • Water available • Vault toilets • Activities: Hiking, fishing, power boating • Elevation: 1131

Verdel

Verdel - GPC • Agency: State • Location: 3 miles NE of Verdel (limited services), 20 miles NW of Verdigre • GPS: Lat 42.830096 Lon -98.151804 • Total sites: Dispersed • RV sites: Undefined • RV fee: Free • No water • Vault toilets • Activities: Fishing, power boating • Elevation: 1227

Virginia

Wolf-Wildcat WMA - LBBNRD • Agency: County • Location: 6 miles S of Virginia (limited services), 18 miles SE of Beatrice • GPS: Lat 40.157369 Lon -96.498622 • Open: All year • Total sites: Dispersed • RV sites: Undefined • RV fee: Free • No toilets • Activities: Hiking, fishing, hunting, non-power boating • Elevation: 1339

Waco

Spikerush WMA • Agency: State • Location: 3 miles NW of Waco (limited services), 7 miles E of York • GPS: Lat 40.915438 Lon -97.487159 • Total sites: Dispersed • RV sites: Undefined • RV fee: Free • No water • No toilets • Elevation: 1628

Wayne

Thompson-Barnes WMA • Agency: State • Location: 6 miles N of Wayne • GPS: Lat 42.307771 Lon -97.042275 • Total sites: Dispersed • RV sites: Undefined • RV fee: Free • No water • No toilets • Elevation: 1585

Wilber

Divorky Acres WMA • Agency: State • Location: 13 miles NW of Wilber (limited services), 18 miles SW of Crete • GPS: Lat 40.524014 Lon -97.148682 • Total sites: Dispersed • RV sites: Undefined • RV fee: Free • No water • No toilets • Elevation: 1562

Wilcox

Sacramento-Wilcox WMA • Agency: State • Location: 5 miles NW of Wilcox (limited services), 8 miles SE of Holdrege • GPS: Lat 40.379863 Lon -99.245237 • Total sites: Dispersed • RV sites: Undefined • RV fee: Free • No water • No toilets • Elevation: 2247

South Sacramento WMA • Agency: State • Location: 6 miles SW of Wilcox (limited services), 13 miles SE of Holdrege • GPS: Lat 40.321721 Lon -99.236553 • Total sites: Dispersed • RV sites: Undefined • RV fee: Free • No water • No toilets • Elevation: 2253

Southeast Sacramento WMA • Agency: State • Location: 4 miles SW of Wilcox (limited services), 14 miles SE of Holdrege • GPS: Lat 40.337637 Lon -99.217287 • Total sites: Dispersed • RV sites: Undefined • RV fee: Free • No water • No toilets • Elevation: 2242

Wood River

Martin's Reach WMA • Agency: State • Location: 8 miles SW of Wood River • GPS: Lat 40.737817 Lon -98.635959 • Total sites: Dispersed • RV sites: Undefined • RV fee: Free • No water • No toilets • Activities: Fishing • Elevation: 1978

Wood River West WMA • Agency: State • Location: 7 miles S of Wood River (limited services), 18 miles SW of Grand Island • GPS: Lat 40.756945 Lon -98.610594 • Total sites: Dispersed • RV sites: Undefined • RV fee: Free • No water • No toilets • Elevation: 1971

Wynot

Wiseman WMA • Agency: State • Location: 7 miles W of Wynot (limited services), 20 miles NE of Hartington • GPS: Lat 42.758732 Lon -97.089729 • Total sites: Dispersed • RV sites: Undefined • RV fee: Free • No water • No toilets • Elevation: 1158

York

Kirkpatrick Basin North WMA • Agency: State • Location: 5 miles SW of York • GPS: Lat 40.832676 Lon -97.673893 • Total sites: Dispersed • RV sites: Undefined • RV fee: Free • No water • No toilets • Elevation: 1673

North Dakota

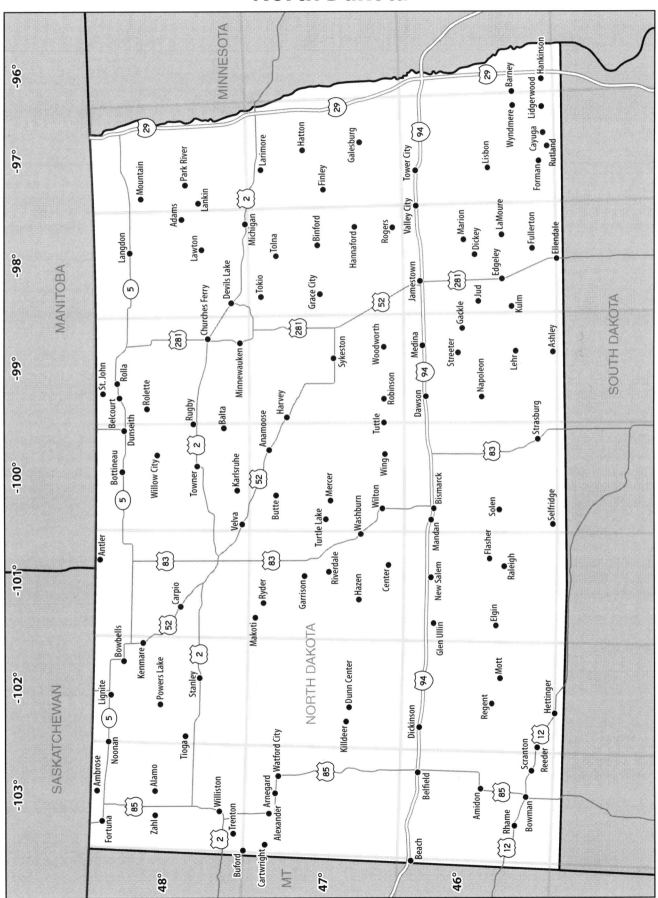

North Dakota — Camping Areas

Abbreviation	Description
CG	Campground
ND GFD	North Dakota Game and Fish Department
ND PRD	North Dakota Parks and Recreation Department
NG	National Grassland
OHV	Off-Highway Vehicle
RA	Recreation Area
SGMA	State Game Management Area
SHS	State Historic Site
SRA	State Recreation Area
WMA	Wildlife Management Area

Adams

Bylin Dam - ND GFD • Agency: State • Location: 6 miles SE of Adams (limited services), 14 miles W of Park River • GPS: Lat 48.367304 Lon -98.010936 • Total sites: Dispersed • RV sites: Undefined • RV fee: Free • No water • No toilets • Elevation: 1473

Alamo

Blue Ridge WMA • Agency: State • Tel: 701-328-6300 • Location: 8 miles NW of Alamo (limited services), 32 miles SW of Crosby • GPS: Lat 48.641816 Lon -103.554488 • Total sites: Dispersed • RV sites: Undefined • RV fee: Free • No water • No toilets • Elevation: 1998

Cottonwood Lake-Alamo - ND GFD • Agency: State • Location: 1 mile E of Alamo (limited services), 30 miles SW of Crosby • GPS: Lat 48.583307 Lon -103.450299 • Total sites: Dispersed • RV sites: Undefined • RV fee: Free • No water • No toilets • Elevation: 2087

Alexander

Leland Dam - ND GFD • Agency: State • Tel: 701-328-6300 • Location: 32 miles SW of Alexander (limited services), 46 miles SW of Watford City • GPS: Lat 47.559101 Lon -103.79869 • Open: All year • Total sites: Dispersed • RV sites: Undefined • RV fee: Free • No water • No toilets • Activities: Fishing, power boating, non-power boating • Elevation: 2192

Ambrose

Rud Anderson City Park • Agency: Municipal • Tel: 701-965-5500 • Location: In Ambrose (limited services), 12 miles NW of Crosby • GPS: Lat 48.952638 Lon -103.482282 • Total sites: 4 • RV sites: 4 • RV fee: Free • Electric sites: 2 (1 shared elec box) • No water • No toilets • Elevation: 2070

Amidon

Burning Coal Vein (Dakota Prairie NG) • Agency: US Forest Service • Tel: 701-227-7800 • Location: 14 miles NW of Amidon (limited services), 33 miles SW of Belfield • GPS: Lat 46.597091 Lon -103.443322 • Total sites: 5 • RV sites: 5 • RV fee: Free • Central water • Vault toilets • Activities: Hiking • Elevation: 2526

Davis Dam - ND GFD • Agency: State • Location: 21 miles NW of Amidon (limited services), 38 miles NW of Bowman • GPS: Lat 46.544753 Lon -103.660803 • Total sites: Dispersed • RV sites: Undefined • RV fee: Free • No water • No toilets • Elevation: 2749

Anamoose

Antelope Lake - ND GFD • Agency: State • Location: 12 miles NW of Anamoose (limited services), 20 miles NW of Harvey • GPS: Lat 47.944375 Lon -100.066184 • Total sites: Dispersed • RV sites: Undefined • RV fee: Free • No water • No toilets • Activities: Fishing • Elevation: 1522

Antler

Antler Memorial Park • Agency: Municipal • Tel: 701-267-3370 • Location: 2 miles N of Antler (limited services), 50 miles N of Minot • GPS: Lat 48.99172 Lon -101.278158 • Open: May-Nov • Total sites: Dispersed • RV sites: Undefined • RV fee: Free • Vault toilets • Elevation: 1526

Arnegard

Arnegard Dam - ND GFD • Agency: State • Location: 4 miles NW of Arnegard (limited services), 11 miles NW of Watford City • GPS: Lat 47.835315 Lon -103.485576 • Total sites: Dispersed • RV sites: Undefined • RV fee: Free • No water • No toilets • Elevation: 2172

Ashley

Blumhardt Dam - ND GFD • Agency: State • Tel: 701-328-6300 • Location: 18 miles NE of Ashley • GPS: Lat 46.129563 Lon -99.134071 • Total sites: Dispersed • RV sites: Undefined • RV fee: Free • No water • No toilets • Elevation: 2008

Dry Lake - ND GFD • Agency: State • Tel: 701-328-6300 • Location: 7 miles NW of Ashley • GPS: Lat 46.081779 Lon -99.438156 • Total sites: Dispersed • RV sites: Undefined • RV fee: Free • No water • No toilets • Elevation: 1975

Balta

Balta Dam WMA • Agency: State • Tel: 701-328-6300 • Location: 1 mile S of Balta (limited services), 15 miles S of Rugby • GPS: Lat 48.159425 Lon -100.039201 • Total sites: 8 • RV sites: 8 • RV fee: Free • Central water • Vault toilets • Elevation: 1526

Davis Dam - ND GFD • Agency: State • Location: 4 miles SW of Balta (limited services), 19 miles SW of Rugby • GPS: Lat 48.146971 Lon -100.093907 • Total sites: Dispersed • RV sites: Undefined • RV fee: Free • No water • No toilets • Elevation: 1496

Barney

Barney City Park • Agency: Municipal • Location: In Barney (limited services), 19 miles W of Wahpeton • GPS: Lat 46.268355 Lon -96.999039 • Open: All year • Total sites: 2 • RV sites: 2 • RV fee: Free • Electric sites: 2 • Central water • No toilets • Elevation: 1017

Beach

Camel's Hump Lake - ND GFD • Agency: State • Tel: 701-872-3121 • Location: 10 miles E of Beach • GPS: Lat 46.945899 Lon -103.816797 • Open: All year (closed to camping Tue-Wed) • Total sites: Dispersed • RV sites: Undefined • RV fee: Free • No water • No toilets • Activities: Fishing, non-power boating • Elevation: 2703

Odland Dam - ND GFD • Agency: State • Tel: 701-872-3121 • Location: 8 miles N of Beach • GPS: Lat 47.041345 Lon -104.015209 • Total sites: Dispersed • RV sites: Undefined • RV fee: Free • No water • Vault toilets • Activities: Fishing, power boating • Elevation: 2654

Belcourt

Belcourt Lake - ND GFD • Agency: State • Tel: 701-328-6300 • Location: 4 miles NW of Belcourt (limited services), 9 miles W of Rolla • GPS: Lat 48.87387 Lon -99.768149 • Total sites: Dispersed • RV sites: Undefined • RV fee: Free • No water • No toilets • Elevation: 2014

Jarvis Lake - ND GFD • Agency: State • Tel: 701-328-6300 • Location: 10 miles NW of Belcourt (limited services), 14 miles NW of Rolla • GPS: Lat 48.915715 Lon -99.85713 • Open: All year • Total sites: Dispersed • RV sites: Undefined • RV fee: Free • No water • Vault toilets • Activities: Fishing • Elevation: 2136

Belfield

Belfield Dam - ND GFD • Agency: State • Tel: 701-328-6300 • Location: In Belfield • GPS: Lat 46.878719 Lon -103.20579 • Total sites: Dispersed • RV sites: Undefined • RV fee: Free • No water • No toilets • Elevation: 2618

Binford

Lake Addie - ND GFD • Agency: State • Tel: 701-328-6300 • Location: 6 miles SW of Binford (limited services), 15 miles NW of Cooperstown • GPS: Lat 47.540222 Lon -98.286719 • Total sites: Dispersed • RV sites: Undefined • RV fee: Free • No water • No toilets • Elevation: 1437

Bismarck

Kimball Bottom • Agency: County • Tel: 701-255-0015 • Location: 8 miles S of Bismarck • GPS: Lat 46.679282 Lon -100.733354 • Total sites: Dispersed • RV sites: Undefined • RV fee: Free • No water • Vault toilets • Activities: Swimming, power boating • Elevation: 1631

Kimball Bottom OHV - ND PRD (Lake Oahe) • Agency: State • Tel: 701-328-5357 • Location: 9 miles S of Bismarck • GPS: Lat 46.667844 Lon -100.732906 • Total sites: Dispersed • RV sites: Undefined • RV fee: Free • Vault toilets • Activities: Motor sports • Elevation: 1627

Kniefel Landing • Agency: County • Tel: 701-222-6455 • Location: 5 miles NW of Bismarck • GPS: Lat 46.867106 Lon -100.870541 • Total sites: Dispersed • RV sites: Undefined • RV fee: Free • No water • Vault toilets • Activities: Power boating • Elevation: 1640

McDowell Dam - ND GFD • Agency: State • Tel: 701-328-6300 • Location: 7 miles E of Bismarck • GPS: Lat 46.827246 Lon -100.640312 • Open: All year • Total sites: Dispersed • RV sites: Undefined • RV fee: Free • No water • Vault toilets • Activities: Fishing, power boating, non-power boating • Elevation: 1749

Bottineau

Homen State Forest - Long Lake Access • Agency: State • Tel: 701-228-3700 • Location: 18 miles NE of Bottineau • GPS: Lat 48.928733 Lon -100.264221 • Total sites: Dispersed • RV sites: Undefined • RV fee: Free • Central water • Vault toilets • Elevation: 2175

Bowbells

Bowbells RV Park • Agency: Municipal • Tel: 701-377-2608 • Location: In Bowbells (limited services), 16 miles NW of Kenmare • GPS: Lat 48.803898 Lon -102.249979 • Open: May-Sep • Total sites: 3 • RV sites: 3 • RV fee: Free (donation appreciated) • Electric sites: 3 • Water at site • Flush toilets • Activities: Swimming • Elevation: 1965

Bowman

Bowman Lions Park Campground • Agency: Municipal • Tel: 701-523-3251 • Location: In Bowman • GPS: Lat 46.17684 Lon -103.39011 • Total sites: 6 • RV sites: 6 • RV fee: Free (donation appreciated) • Flush toilets • Elevation: 2940

Spring Creek WMA • Agency: State • Location: 19 miles SE of Bowman • GPS: Lat 46.007131 Lon -103.279221 • Open: All year (closed to camping Tue-Wed) • Total sites: Dispersed • RV sites: Undefined • RV fee: Free • No water • No toilets • Elevation: 2789

Buford

Fort Buford SHS • Agency: Municipal • Tel: 701-575-9034 • Location: 2 miles SW of Buford (limited services), 21 miles SW of Williston • GPS: Lat 47.985812 Lon -104.001493 • Stay limit: 4 days • Total sites: Dispersed • RV sites: Undefined • RV fee: Free • Central water • Elevation: 1903

Butte

Cottonwood Lake-Butte - ND GFD • Agency: State • Location: 4 miles N of Butte (limited services), 22 miles SE of Velva • GPS: Lat 47.879929 Lon -100.681211 • Total sites: Dispersed • RV sites: Undefined • RV fee: Free • No water • No toilets • Activities: Fishing • Elevation: 1604

Carpio

Lake Darling Landing #1 - ND GFD • Agency: State • Tel: 701-328-6300 • Location: 7 miles E of Carpio (limited services), 23 miles NW of Minot • GPS: Lat 48.460033 Lon -101.590275 • Total sites: Dispersed • RV sites: Undefined • RV fee: Free • No water • No toilets • Elevation: 1591

Lake Darling Landing #2 - ND GFD • Agency: State • Tel: 701-328-6300 • Location: 9 miles NE of Carpio (limited services), 24 miles NW of Minot • GPS: Lat 48.471221 Lon -101.581384 • Total sites: Dispersed • RV sites: Undefined • RV fee: Free • No water • No toilets • Elevation: 1601

Lake Darling Landing #3 - ND GFD • Agency: State • Tel: 701-328-6300 • Location: 9 miles NE of Carpio (limited services), 25 miles NW of Minot • GPS: Lat 48.477026 Lon -101.566206 • Total sites: Dispersed • RV sites: Undefined • RV fee: Free • No water • No toilets • Elevation: 1594

Lake Darling Spillway Ramp - ND GFD • Agency: State • Tel: 701-328-6300 • Location: 8 miles W of Carpio (limited services), 24 miles NW of Minot • GPS: Lat 48.459079 Lon -101.576739 • Total sites: Dispersed • RV sites: Undefined • RV fee: Free • No water • No toilets • Elevation: 1621

Cartwright

Sundheim Park • Agency: Municipal • Tel: 701-444-5440 • Location: 2 miles E of Cartwright (limited services), 4 miles E of Fairview, MT • GPS: Lat 47.860659 Lon -103.969352 • Total sites: Dispersed • RV sites: Undefined • RV fee: Free • No toilets • Activities: Disc golf • Elevation: 1857

Cayuga

Alkali Lake (Sargent Cty) - North Ramp - ND GFD • Agency: State • Location: 3 miles S of Cayuga (limited services), 15 miles SW of Lidgerwood • GPS: Lat 46.028157 Lon -97.385835 • Total sites: Dispersed • RV sites: Undefined • RV fee: Free • No water • No toilets • Elevation: 1142

Lake Tewaukan - ND GFD • Agency: State • Location: 5 miles SE of Cayuga (limited services), 17 miles SW of Lidgerwood • GPS: Lat 46.009663 Lon -97.360944 • Open: All year • Total sites: Dispersed • RV sites: Undefined • RV fee: Free • No water • Vault toilets • Activities: Fishing, power boating, non-power boating • Elevation: 1145

Center

Nelson Lake Park (East side) - ND GFD • Agency: State • Location: 9 miles SE of Center (limited services), 23 miles SW of Washburn • GPS: Lat 47.074912 Lon -101.205603 • Total sites: Dispersed • RV sites: Undefined • RV fee: Free • No water • No toilets • Elevation: 1916

Nelson Lake Park (West side) - ND GFD • Agency: State • Location: 5 miles SE of Center (limited services), 26 miles SW of Washburn • GPS: Lat 47.084993 Lon -101.235588 • Total sites: Dispersed • RV sites: Undefined • RV fee: Free • No water • No toilets • Elevation: 1932

Churches Ferry

Lake Irvine - ND GFD • Agency: State • Tel: 701-328-6300 • Location: 2 miles E of Churches Ferry (limited services), 18 miles NW of Devils Lake • GPS: Lat 48.265948 Lon -99.182953 • Open: All year • Total sites: Dispersed • RV sites: Undefined • RV fee: Free • No water • Vault toilets • Activities: Fishing • Elevation: 1440

Dawson

Lake Isabel - ND GFD • Agency: State • Tel: 701-328-6300 • Location: 3 miles S of Dawson (limited services),

24 miles N of Napoleon • GPS: Lat 46.825537 Lon -99.736599 • Open: All year • Total sites: Dispersed • RV sites: Undefined • RV fee: Free • No water • Vault toilets • Activities: Fishing • Elevation: 1732

Devils Lake

Cavanaugh Lake - ND GFD • Agency: State • Location: 9 miles N of Devils Lake • GPS: Lat 48.242831 Lon -98.897793 • Total sites: Dispersed • RV sites: Undefined • RV fee: Free • No water • No toilets • Elevation: 1466

Devils Lake - Creel Bay Landing • Agency: County • Location: 5 miles SW of Devils Lake • GPS: Lat 48.068362 Lon -98.932949 • Total sites: Dispersed • RV sites: Undefined • RV fee: Free • Central water • Vault toilets • Elevation: 1464

Devils Lake - Henegar Landing • Agency: County • Location: 2 miles W of Devils Lake • GPS: Lat 48.097963 Lon -98.901424 • Total sites: 33 • RV sites: 33 • RV fee: Free • Vault toilets • Elevation: 1417

Dickey

Heinrich-Martin Dam • Agency: State • Location: 8 miles NW of Dickey (limited services), 28 miles SE of Jamestown • GPS: Lat 46.594511 Lon -98.536592 • Open: All year • Total sites: Dispersed • RV sites: Undefined • RV fee: Free • No water • Vault toilets • Activities: Fishing • Elevation: 1421

Limesand - Seefeldt Dam - ND GFD • Agency: State • Tel: 701-328-6300 • Location: 9 miles SE of Dickey (limited services), 13 miles NW of LaMoure • GPS: Lat 46.486844 Lon -98.382748 • Open: All year • Total sites: Dispersed • RV sites: Undefined • RV fee: Free • No water • No toilets • Activities: Fishing, power boating, non-power boating • Elevation: 1414

Dickinson

Dickenson Dike - ND GFD • Agency: State • Location: In Dickinson • GPS: Lat 46.87203 Lon -102.82125 • Total sites: Dispersed • RV sites: Undefined • RV fee: Free • No water • No toilets • Elevation: 2408

Patterson Lake - ND GFD • Agency: State • Location: 4 miles SW of Dickinson • GPS: Lat 46.862709 Lon -102.845367 • Open: All year • Total sites: Dispersed • RV sites: Undefined • RV fee: Free • No water • Vault toilets • Activities: Fishing, power boating, non-power boating • Elevation: 2424

Dunn Center

Lake Ilo - ND GFD • Agency: State • Tel: 701-328-6300 • Location: 3 miles W of Dunn Center (limited services), 6 miles E of Killdeer • GPS: Lat 47.350336 Lon -102.65991 • Open: All year • Total sites: Dispersed • RV sites: Undefined • RV fee: Free • No water • Vault toilets • Activities: Fishing • Elevation: 2188

Dunseith

Carpenter Lake - ND GFD • Agency: State • Location: 13 miles NE of Dunseith (limited services), 20 miles NW of Rolla • GPS: Lat 48.952849 Lon -99.9752 • Total sites: Dispersed • RV sites: Undefined • RV fee: Free • No water • No toilets • Elevation: 2185

School Section Lake - ND GFD • Agency: State • Tel: 701-328-6300 • Location: 12 miles NE of Dunseith (limited services), 29 miles NE of Bottineau • GPS: Lat 48.950373 Lon -100.001726 • Open: All year • Total sites: Dispersed • RV sites: Undefined • RV fee: Free • No water • Vault toilets • Activities: Fishing, power boating, non-power boating • Elevation: 2198

Edgeley

Kulm-Edgeley Dam - ND GFD • Agency: State • Tel: 701-493-2208 • Location: 7 miles SE of Edgeley (limited services), 33 miles NW of Ellendale • GPS: Lat 46.328708 Lon -98.819122 • Open: All year • Total sites: Dispersed • RV sites: Undefined • RV fee: Free • No water • No toilets • Activities: Fishing, power boating, hunting, non-power boating • Elevation: 1739

Schlecht - Thom Dam - ND GFD • Agency: State • Tel: 701-328-6300 • Location: 6 miles W of Edgeley (limited services), 32 miles NW of Ellendale • GPS: Lat 46.363703 Lon -98.82994 • Open: All year • Total sites: Dispersed • RV sites: Undefined • RV fee: Free • No water • No toilets • Activities: Fishing, power boating, non-power boating • Elevation: 1749

Elgin

Heart Butte Res State Game Mgt. Area - ND GFD • Agency: State • Location: 16 miles N of Elgin • GPS: Lat 46.594826 Lon -101.82785 • Total sites: Dispersed • RV sites: Undefined • RV fee: Free • No water • Vault toilets • Activities: Fishing • Elevation: 2057

Lions and Elgin Parkboard City CG • Agency: Municipal • Tel: 701-584-3045 • Location: In Elgin • GPS: Lat 46.40214 Lon -101.837068 • Open: All year • Total sites: 14 • RV sites: 7 • RV fee: Free • Electric sites: 7 • No toilets • Elevation: 2336

Sheep Creek Dam SRA • Agency: State • Tel: 701-584-2354 • Location: 5 miles S of Elgin • GPS: Lat 46.33805 Lon -101.84881 • Total sites: 10 • RV sites: 5 • RV fee: Free • Electric sites: 5 • Central water • Vault toilets • Notes: 5-day limit • Elevation: 2224

Ellendale

Johnson's Gulch WMA • Agency: State • Location: 22 miles W of Ellendale • GPS: Lat 45.994207 Lon -98.880047 • Total sites: Dispersed • RV sites: Undefined • RV fee: Free • No water • No toilets • Activities: Hiking • Elevation: 1995

Wilson Dam - ND GFD • Agency: State • Tel: 701-328-6300 • Location: 20 miles NW of Ellendale • GPS: Lat 46.174785 Lon -98.752338 • Open: All year • Total sites: Dispersed • RV sites: Undefined • RV fee: Free • No water • Vault toilets • Activities: Fishing, power boating, non-power boating • Elevation: 1618

Finley

South Golden Lake-South Ramp - ND GFD • Agency: State • Tel: 701-328-6300 • Location: 12 miles NE of Finley (limited services), 19 miles NW of Mayville • GPS: Lat 47.562906 Lon -97.64106 • Total sites: Dispersed • RV sites: Undefined • RV fee: Free • No water • No toilets • Elevation: 1122

Flasher

Nygren Dam • Agency: County • Tel: 701-667-3363 • Location: 10 miles N of Flasher (limited services), 32 miles SW of Mandan • GPS: Lat 46.587266 Lon -101.207381 • Total sites: Dispersed • RV sites: Undefined • RV fee: Free • No water • Vault toilets • Activities: Fishing, power boating, non-power boating • Elevation: 2021

Forman

Forman Lions Campground • Agency: Municipal • Tel: 701-724-3338 • Location: In Forman (limited services), 25 miles W of Lidgerwood • GPS: Lat 46.105682 Lon -97.633121 • Total sites: 4 • RV sites: 4 • RV fee: Free • Electric sites: 4 • Water at site • No toilets • Elevation: 1237

Fortuna

Skjermo Lake - ND GFD • Agency: State • Tel: 701-965-6351 • Location: 7 miles NW of Fortuna (limited services), 29 miles W of Crosby • GPS: Lat 48.950458 Lon -103.881521 • Total sites: Dispersed • RV sites: Undefined • RV fee: Free • No water • No toilets • Activities: Power boating, non-power boating • Elevation: 2083

Fullerton

Fullerton City Park • Agency: Municipal • Tel: 701-375-7261 • Location: In Fullerton (limited services), 16 miles NE of Ellendale • GPS: Lat 46.162271 Lon -98.422516 • Total sites: 4 • RV sites: 4 • RV fee: Free • Electric sites: 4 • Central water • Flush toilets • Elevation: 1421

Gackle

Gackle RV Park • Agency: Municipal • Tel: 701-485-3243 • Location: In Gackle (limited services), 39 miles SW of Jamestown • GPS: Lat 46.626316 Lon -99.146876 • Total sites: 6 • RV sites: 6 • RV fee: Free • Electric sites: 6 • Water at site • Flush toilets • Elevation: 1936

Hehn - Schaffer Lake - ND GFD • Agency: State • Tel: 701-328-6300 • Location: 4 miles N of Gackle (limited services), 33 miles SW of Jamestown • GPS: Lat 46.68539 Lon -99.134411 • Open: All year • Total sites: Dispersed • RV sites: Undefined • RV fee: Free • No water • Vault toilets • Activities: Fishing, power boating • Elevation: 1890

Schlenker (Lehr) Dam - ND GFD • Agency: State • Tel: 701-328-6300 • Location: 10 miles E of Gackle (limited services), 29 miles SW of Jamestown • GPS: Lat 46.624474 Lon -98.930704 • Open: All year • Total sites: Dispersed • RV sites: Undefined • RV fee: Free • No water • No toilets • Activities: Fishing, power boating, non-power boating • Elevation: 1745

Galesburg

Galesburg City Campground • Agency: Municipal • Tel: 701-488-2220 • Location: In Galesburg (limited services), 21 miles SW of Mayville • GPS: Lat 47.269041 Lon -97.412571 • Total sites: 5 • RV sites: 2 • RV fee: Free • Electric sites: 2 • Central water • Elevation: 1083

Garrison

Audubon WMA • Agency: State • Location: 16 miles E of Garrison • GPS: Lat 47.625694 Lon -101.186324 • Open: All year (closed to camping Tue-Wed) • Total sites: Dispersed • RV sites: Undefined • RV fee: Free • Activities: Fishing • Elevation: 1854

Custer Mine Lake SGMA • Agency: State • Location: 7 miles SE of Garrison • GPS: Lat 47.623325 Lon -101.304876 • Open: All year (closed to camping Tue-Wed) • Total sites: Dispersed • RV sites: Undefined • RV fee: Free • No water • No toilets • Elevation: 1883

Douglas Creek (Sakakawea Lake) • Agency: Corps of Engineers • Tel: 701-654-7411, x247 • Location: 20 miles SW of Garrison • GPS: Lat 47.578241 Lon -101.574642 • Total sites: 17 • RV sites: 17 • RV fee: Free • Central water • Vault toilets • Activities: Fishing, power boating, hunting • Elevation: 1864

Douglas Creek WMA • Agency: State • Location: 20 miles SW of Garrison • GPS: Lat 47.567446 Lon -101.582227 • Open: All year (closed to camping Tue-Wed) • Total sites: Dispersed • RV sites: Undefined • RV fee: Free • Elevation: 1877

Glen Ullin

Heart Butte Reservoir - Koehlers Point (Lake Tschida) • Agency: State • Location: 16 miles S of Glen Ullin (limited services), 61 miles SE of Dickinson • GPS: Lat 46.612284 Lon -101.907565 • Open: Mar-Nov • Total sites: Dispersed • RV sites: Undefined • RV fee: Free • No water • Vault toilets • Activities: Fishing • Elevation: 2074

Heart Butte Reservoir - Schelle's Point (Lake Tschida) • Agency: State • Location: 17 miles S of Glen Ullin (limited services), 61 miles SE of Dickinson • GPS: Lat 46.619046 Lon -101.927771 • Open: Mar-Nov • Total sites: Dispersed • RV sites: Undefined • RV fee: Free • No water • Vault toilets • Activities: Fishing • Elevation: 2077

Grace City

Juanita Lake - ND GFD • Agency: State • Tel: 701-328-6300 • Location: 2 miles E of Grace City (limited services), 23 miles NE of Carrington • GPS: Lat 47.54075 Lon -98.755137 • Open: All year • Total sites: Dispersed • RV sites: Undefined • RV fee: Free • No water • Vault toilets • Activities: Fishing • Elevation: 1466

Hankinson

Lake Elsie North Ramp - ND GFD • Agency: State • Tel: 701-328-6300 • Location: 2 miles SW of Hankinson • GPS: Lat 46.052184 Lon -96.936045 • Total sites: Dispersed • RV sites: Undefined • RV fee: Free • No water • No toilets • Elevation: 1073

Hannaford

Lake Ashtabula-Karnack Landing - ND GFD • Agency: State • Tel: 701-328-6300 • Location: 11 miles SE of Hannaford (limited services), 17 miles SE of Cooperstown • GPS: Lat 47.269158 Lon -98.011541 • Total sites: Dispersed • RV sites: Undefined • RV fee: Free • No water • No toilets • Elevation: 1283

Harvey

Coal Mine Lake - ND GFD • Agency: State • Location: 18 miles SW of Harvey • GPS: Lat 47.67881 Lon -100.140227 • Total sites: Dispersed • RV sites: Unde-

fined • RV fee: Free • No water • No toilets • Elevation: 1618

Hatton

North Golden Lake-North Ramp - ND GFD • Agency: State • Tel: 701-328-6300 • Location: 10 miles W of Hatton (limited services), 22 miles NW of Mayville • GPS: Lat 47.608034 Lon -97.633587 • Total sites: Dispersed • RV sites: Undefined • RV fee: Free • No water • No toilets • Elevation: 1112

North Golden Lake-South Ramp - ND GFD • Agency: State • Tel: 701-328-6300 • Location: 12 miles SW of Hatton (limited services), 19 miles NW of Mayville • GPS: Lat 47.585486 Lon -97.627919 • Total sites: Dispersed • RV sites: Undefined • RV fee: Free • No water • No toilets • Elevation: 1106

South Golden Lake-North Ramp - ND GFD • Agency: State • Tel: 701-328-6300 • Location: 13 miles SW of Hatton (limited services), 18 miles NW of Mayville • GPS: Lat 47.572111 Lon -97.633313 • Total sites: Dispersed • RV sites: Undefined • RV fee: Free • No water • No toilets • Elevation: 1129

Hazen

John Moses Memorial Park • Agency: Municipal • Tel: 701-748-6948 • Location: In Hazen • GPS: Lat 47.298827 Lon -101.619068 • Open: May-Sep • Total sites: 2 • RV sites: 2 • RV fee: Free • Electric sites: 2 • Central water • Flush toilets • Elevation: 1732

Hettinger

North Lemmon Lake - SGMA • Agency: State • Tel: 701-328-6300 • Location: 32 miles E of Hettinger (limited services), 5 miles N of Lemmon, SD • GPS: Lat 46.011529 Lon -102.16656 • Open: All year • Total sites: Dispersed • RV sites: Undefined • RV fee: Free • No water • Vault toilets • Activities: Fishing, power boating, non-power boating • Elevation: 2507

Jamestown

Jamestown Reservoir - Boat Club Bay • Agency: County • Location: 5 miles N of Jamestown • GPS: Lat 46.985279 Lon -98.705408 • Open: All year • Total sites: Dispersed • RV sites: Undefined • RV fee: Free • No water • Vault toilets • Activities: Fishing • Elevation: 1470

Jamestown Reservoir - West Landing • Agency: County • Location: 5 miles N of Jamestown • GPS: Lat 46.96448 Lon -98.710563 • Open: All year • Total sites: Dispersed • RV sites: Undefined • RV fee: Free • Activities: Fishing • Elevation: 1424

Sandy Beach County Park • Agency: County • Tel: 701-252-6002 • Location: 15 miles NE of Jamestown • GPS: Lat 47.072648 Lon -98.595579 • Total sites: Dispersed • RV sites: Undefined • RV fee: Free • No water • Vault toilets • Activities: Fishing, swimming, power boating, non-power boating • Elevation: 1496

Jud

Kalmbach Lake - ND GFD • Agency: State • Tel: 701-328-6300 • Location: 6 miles SW of Jud (limited services), 40 miles SW of Jamestown • GPS: Lat 46.509076 Lon -98.989852 • Open: All year • Total sites: Dispersed • RV sites: Undefined • RV fee: Free • No water • Vault toilets • Activities: Fishing • Elevation: 1896

Schlecht - Weixel Dam - ND GFD • Agency: State • Tel: 701-328-6300 • Location: 5 miles S of Jud (limited services), 39 miles SW of Jamestown • GPS: Lat 46.458063 Lon -98.899827 • Open: All year • Total sites: Dispersed • RV sites: Undefined • RV fee: Free • No water • No toilets • Activities: Fishing, power boating, non-power boating • Elevation: 1821

Karlsruhe

George Lake - ND GFD • Agency: State • Tel: 701-328-6300 • Location: 12 miles NE of Karlsruhe (limited services), 40 miles SW of Rugby • GPS: Lat 48.126029 Lon -100.422749 • Total sites: Dispersed • RV sites: Undefined • RV fee: Free • No water • No toilets • Elevation: 1526

Kenmare

Nelson - Landers Pond - ND GFD • Agency: State • Tel: 701-328-6300 • Location: 6 miles S of Kenmare • GPS: Lat 48.61335 Lon -102.115869 • Total sites: Dispersed • RV sites: Undefined • RV fee: Free • No water • No toilets • Elevation: 2044

Killdeer

Killdeer City Park • Agency: Municipal • Tel: 701-764-5295 • Location: In Killdeer • GPS: Lat 47.364511 Lon -102.753525 • Total sites: 12 • RV sites: 12 • RV fee: Free (donation appreciated) • Electric sites: 12 • Central water • Flush toilets • Elevation: 2241

Kulm

Diamond Lake - ND GFD • Agency: State • Location: 6 miles N of Kulm (limited services), 40 miles NW of Ellendale • GPS: Lat 46.384111 Lon -98.955428 • Total sites: Dispersed • RV sites: Undefined • RV fee: Free • No water • No toilets • Elevation: 1929

Flood Lake-South Basin - ND GFD • Agency: State • Tel: 701-328-6300 • Location: 3 miles N of Kulm (limited services), 38 miles NW of Ellendale • GPS: Lat 46.35124 Lon -98.954669 • Total sites: Dispersed • RV sites: Undefined • RV fee: Free • No water • No toilets • Elevation: 1949

LaMoure

Twin Lake - ND GFD • Agency: State • Tel: 701-328-6300 • Location: 7 miles N of LaMoure • GPS: Lat 46.421116 Lon -98.285178 • Open: All year • Total sites: Dispersed • RV sites: Undefined • RV fee: Free • No water • No toilets • Activities: Fishing, power boating, non-power boating • Elevation: 1384

Langdon

Langdon Pond - ND GFD • Agency: State • Tel: 701-328-6300 • Location: In Langdon • GPS: Lat 48.753904 Lon -98.372826 • Open: All year • Total sites: Dispersed • RV sites: Undefined • RV fee: Free • No water • No toilets • Activities: Fishing, power boating, non-power boating • Elevation: 1594

Lankin

Majejcek Dam - West End - ND GFD • Agency: State • Tel: 701-328-6300 • Location: 9 miles S of Lankin (limited services), 23 miles SW of Park River • GPS: Lat 48.222117 Lon -97.953487 • Open: All year • Total sites: Dispersed • RV sites: Undefined • RV fee: Free • No water • No toilets • Activities: Fishing, power boating, non-power boating • Elevation: 1375

Larimore

Kolding Dam/Upper Turtle Reservoir - ND GFD • Agency: State • Location: 10 miles SW of Larimore • GPS: Lat 47.964824 Lon -97.775811 • Total sites: Dispersed • RV sites: Undefined • RV fee: Free • No water • No toilets • Activities: Fishing • Elevation: 1263

Lawton

Lawton Centennial Park Campground • Agency: Municipal • Tel: 701-655-3641 • Location: In Lawton (limited services), 36 miles NE of Devils Lake • GPS: Lat 48.302397 Lon -98.367417 • Total sites: 5 • RV sites: 1 • RV fee: Free • Electric sites: 1 • Elevation: 1519

Lehr

Lehr WMA • Agency: State • Tel: 701-328-6300 • Location: 4 miles E of Lehr (limited services), 22 miles N of Ashley • GPS: Lat 46.272564 Lon -99.294885 • Open: All year • Total sites: Dispersed • RV sites: Undefined • RV fee: Free • No water • No toilets • Activities: Fishing, power boating, non-power boating • Elevation: 1988

Mundt Dam - ND GFD • Agency: State • Tel: 701-328-6300 • Location: 9 miles NE of Lehr (limited services), 27 miles N of Ashley • GPS: Lat 46.328826 Lon -99.266516 • Open: All year • Total sites: Dispersed • RV sites: Undefined • RV fee: Free • No water • No toilets • Activities: Fishing, power boating, non-power boating • Elevation: 2041

Lidgerwood

Bisek Slough - ND GFD • Agency: State • Tel: 701-328-6300 • Location: 3 miles N of Lidgerwood • GPS: Lat 46.109981 Lon -97.167581 • Total sites: Dispersed • RV sites: Undefined • RV fee: Free • No water • No toilets • Elevation: 1086

Grass Lake - ND GFD • Agency: State • Location: 7 miles NW of Lidgerwood • GPS: Lat 46.108367 Lon -97.24905 • Total sites: Dispersed • RV sites: Undefined • RV fee: Free • No water • No toilets • Elevation: 1086

Lignite

Lignite City Park Campground • Agency: Municipal • Tel: 701-933-2850 • Location: In Lignite (limited services), 35 miles E of Crosby • GPS: Lat 48.876298 Lon -102.563542 • Total sites: 2 • RV sites: 2 • RV fee: Free • Electric sites: 2 • Central water • Flush toilets • Elevation: 1982

Lisbon

Dead Colt Creek South Ramp - ND GFD • Agency: State • Location: 9 miles SE of Lisbon • GPS: Lat 46.367546 Lon -97.614589 • Total sites: Dispersed • RV sites: Undefined • RV fee: Free • No water • No toilets • Elevation: 1132

Makoti

Hiddenwood Lake - ND GFD • Agency: State • Location: 8 miles S of Makoti (limited services), 25 miles SE of Parshall • GPS: Lat 47.846641 Lon -101.802024 • Open: All year • Total sites: Dispersed • RV sites: Undefined • RV fee: Free • No water • Vault toilets • Activities: Fishing • Elevation: 2119

Mandan

Crown Butte Dam • Agency: County • Tel: 701-667-3363 • Location: 9 miles NW of Mandan • GPS: Lat 46.868106 Lon -101.091063 • Total sites: Dispersed • RV

sites: Undefined • RV fee: Free • Central water • Vault toilets • Activities: Fishing • Elevation: 1952

Little Heart Bottoms • Agency: County • Tel: 701-667-3363 • Location: 14 miles SE of Mandan • GPS: Lat 46.687736 Lon -100.762536 • Total sites: 15 • RV sites: 15 • RV fee: Free • Vault toilets • Activities: Power boating • Elevation: 1634

Marion

Boom Lake (Marion Lake) - ND GFD • Agency: State • Tel: 701-328-6300 • Location: 1 mile W of Marion (limited services), 20 miles N of LaMoure • GPS: Lat 46.610952 Lon -98.342998 • Total sites: Dispersed • RV sites: Undefined • RV fee: Free • No water • No toilets • Elevation: 1447

Medina

Bader Lake - ND GFD • Agency: State • Location: 6 miles S of Medina (limited services), 32 miles W of Jamestown • GPS: Lat 46.820188 Lon -99.278696 • Total sites: Dispersed • RV sites: Undefined • RV fee: Free • No water • No toilets • Activities: Fishing • Elevation: 1782

Crystal Springs - ND GFD • Agency: State • Location: 11 miles W of Medina (limited services), 37 miles W of Jamestown • GPS: Lat 46.883918 Lon -99.446579 • Total sites: Dispersed • RV sites: Undefined • RV fee: Free • No water • No toilets • Elevation: 1765

Mercer

Heckers Lake - ND GFD • Agency: State • Location: 12 miles S of Mercer (limited services), 21 miles NE of Washburn • GPS: Lat 47.340357 Lon -100.676569 • Open: All year • Total sites: Dispersed • RV sites: Undefined • RV fee: Free • No water • Vault toilets • Activities: Fishing • Elevation: 1850

New Johns Lake - ND GFD • Agency: State • Tel: 701-328-6300 • Location: 19 miles SE of Mercer (limited services), 23 miles E of Washburn • GPS: Lat 47.322195 Lon -100.625979 • Total sites: Dispersed • RV sites: Undefined • RV fee: Free • No water • No toilets • Elevation: 1854

West Park Lake - ND GFD • Agency: State • Tel: 701-328-6300 • Location: 13 miles SW of Mercer (limited services), 16 miles NE of Washburn • GPS: Lat 47.360684 Lon -100.792094 • Open: All year • Total sites: Dispersed • RV sites: Undefined • RV fee: Free • No water • Vault toilets • Activities: Fishing, power boating, non-power boating • Elevation: 1841

Michigan

Michigan City Park Campground • Agency: Municipal • Tel: 701-259-2553 • Location: In Michigan (limited services), 36 miles E of Devils Lake • GPS: Lat 48.026277 Lon -98.128935 • Total sites: 4 • RV sites: 4 • RV fee: Free (donation appreciated) • Electric sites: 4 • Central water • Flush toilets • Activities: Golf • Elevation: 1516

Whitman Dam - ND GFD • Agency: State • Tel: 701-328-6300 • Location: 14 miles NE of Michigan (limited services), 34 miles SW of Park River • GPS: Lat 48.181859 Lon -98.056564 • Total sites: Dispersed • RV sites: Undefined • RV fee: Free • No water • No toilets • Elevation: 1499

Minnewauken

Devils Lake - Dumpground Landing - ND GFD • Agency: State • Location: 1 mile S of Minnewauken (limited services), 25 miles W of Devils Lake • GPS: Lat 48.049116 Lon -99.235197 • Total sites: Dispersed • RV sites: Undefined • RV fee: Free • No water • No toilets • Elevation: 1437

Mott

Castle Rock Dam - ND GFD • Agency: State • Location: 6 miles SW of Mott • GPS: Lat 46.336102 Lon -102.400595 • Total sites: Dispersed • RV sites: Undefined • RV fee: Free • No water • No toilets • Elevation: 2484

Mott Watershed Dam - ND GFD • Agency: State • Tel: 701-824-2230 • Location: 1 mile N of Mott • GPS: Lat 46.381397 Lon -102.324638 • Open: All year • Total sites: Dispersed • RV sites: Undefined • RV fee: Free • No water • No toilets • Activities: Fishing, power boating, non-power boating • Elevation: 2441

Mountain

Legion Campground • Agency: Municipal • Tel: 701-993-8723 • Location: In Mountain (limited services), 16 miles SW of Cavalier • GPS: Lat 48.688208 Lon -97.866271 • Total sites: 4 • RV sites: 2 • RV fee: Free (donation appreciated) • Electric sites: 4 • Elevation: 1066

Napoleon

Rudolph Lake - ND GFD • Agency: State • Tel: 701-328-6300 • Location: 14 miles E of Napoleon • GPS: Lat 46.503485 Lon -99.508178 • Open: All year • Total sites: Dispersed • RV sites: Undefined • RV fee: Free • No water • No toilets • Activities: Fishing, power boating, non-power boating • Elevation: 1886

West Lake Napoleon - ND GFD • Agency: State • Tel: 701-328-6300 • Location: 1 mile W of Napoleon • GPS: Lat 46.501149 Lon -99.788211 • Open: All year • Total sites: Dispersed • RV sites: Undefined • RV fee: Free • No water • No toilets • Activities: Fishing, power boating, non-power boating • Elevation: 1942

New Salem

Danzig Dam • Agency: County • Tel: 701-667-3363 • Location: 12 miles NW of New Salem (limited services), 37 miles W of Mandan • GPS: Lat 46.894725 Lon -101.602798 • Total sites: Dispersed • RV sites: Undefined • RV fee: Free • No water • Vault toilets • Activities: Fishing, power boating, non-power boating • Elevation: 2110

Fish Creek Dam • Agency: State • Tel: 701-667-3363 • Location: 17 miles SE of New Salem (limited services), 28 miles SW of Mandan • GPS: Lat 46.72977 Lon -101.236624 • Total sites: Dispersed • RV sites: Undefined • RV fee: Free • No water • Vault toilets • Activities: Fishing, power boating • Elevation: 1913

Sweet Briar Lake • Agency: County • Location: 11 miles NE of New Salem (limited services), 22 miles W of Mandan • GPS: Lat 46.873191 Lon -101.274162 • Total sites: Dispersed • RV sites: Undefined • RV fee: Free • Central water • Vault toilets • Activities: Fishing • Elevation: 1942

New Salem

Sweetbriar Lake - Southeast Ramp - ND GFD • Agency: State • Tel: 701-667-3363 • Location: 11 miles NE of New Salem (limited services), 21 miles W of Mandan • GPS: Lat 46.867832 Lon -101.263848 • Open: All year • Total sites: Dispersed • RV sites: Undefined • RV fee: Free • No water • Vault toilets • Activities: Fishing, power boating, non-power boating • Elevation: 1952

Sweetbriar Lake-Northwest Ramp - ND GFD • Agency: State • Tel: 701-667-3363 • Location: 9 miles NE of New Salem (limited services), 19 miles W of Mandan • GPS: Lat 46.874 Lon -101.277803 • Open: All year • Total sites: Dispersed • RV sites: Undefined • RV fee: Free • No water • Vault toilets • Activities: Fishing, power boating, non-power boating • Elevation: 1939

Noonan

Baukol-Noonan - East Mine Pond - ND GFD • Agency: State • Location: 3 miles SE of Noonan (limited services), 18 miles E of Crosby • GPS: Lat 48.875602 Lon -102.956138 • Total sites: Dispersed • RV sites: Undefined • RV fee: Free • No water • No toilets • Elevation: 2018

Baukol-Noonan- Spillway Pond - ND GFD • Agency: State • Location: 4 miles SE of Noonan (limited services), 18 miles E of Crosby • GPS: Lat 48.875765 Lon -102.948091 • Total sites: Dispersed • RV sites: Undefined • RV fee: Free • No water • No toilets • Elevation: 1975

Park River

Homme Dam-North Ramp • Agency: State • Tel: 701-328-6300 • Location: 4 miles NW of Park River • GPS: Lat 48.409967 Lon -97.804044 • Open: All year • Total sites: Dispersed • RV sites: Undefined • RV fee: Free • No water • Vault toilets • Activities: Fishing • Elevation: 1116

Powers Lake

Powers Lake South Ramp - ND GFD • Agency: State • Tel: 701-328-6300 • Location: 1 mile SE of Powers Lake (limited services), 28 miles NW of Stanley • GPS: Lat 48.549957 Lon -102.625277 • Total sites: Dispersed • RV sites: Undefined • RV fee: Free • No water • No toilets • Elevation: 2224

White Earth Dam - ND GFD • Agency: State • Tel: 701-328-6300 • Location: 12 miles SW of Powers Lake • GPS: Lat 48.457408 Lon -102.749373 • Open: All year • Total sites: Dispersed • RV sites: Undefined • RV fee: Free • No water • Vault toilets • Activities: Fishing, power boating, non-power boating • Elevation: 2178

Raleigh

Raleigh Reservoir - ND GFD • Agency: State • Tel: 701-328-6300 • Location: 3 miles W of Raleigh (limited services), 53 miles SW of Mandan • GPS: Lat 46.354445 Lon -101.37308 • Total sites: Dispersed • RV sites: Undefined • RV fee: Free • No water • No toilets • Elevation: 2228

Reeder

Cedar Lake - ND GFD • Agency: State • Location: 16 miles N of Reeder (limited services), 33 miles NE of Bowman • GPS: Lat 46.292905 Lon -102.966354 • Open: All year (closed to camping Tue-Wed) • Total sites: Dispersed • RV sites: Undefined • RV fee: Free • No water • No toilets • Elevation: 2700

Regent

Indian Creek Dam - ND GFD • Agency: State • Tel: 701-824-2515 • Location: 9 miles SW of Regent (limited services), 47 miles SE of Dickinson • GPS: Lat 46.340465 Lon -102.629694 • Open: All year (closed to camping Tue-Wed) • Total sites: Dispersed • RV sites: Undefined • RV fee: Free • No water • Vault toilets • Activities: Fishing • Elevation: 2569

Larson Lake - ND GFD • Agency: State • Tel: 701-328-6300 • Location: 2 miles NE of Regent (limited services), 41 miles SE of Dickinson • GPS: Lat 46.429642 Lon -102.515921 • Total sites: Dispersed • RV sites: Undefined • RV fee: Free • No water • No toilets • Elevation: 2470

Rhame

Spring Lake - ND GFD • Agency: State • Tel: 701-328-6300 • Location: 5 miles W of Rhame (limited services), 17 miles NW of Bowman • GPS: Lat 46.221136 Lon -103.739935 • Total sites: Dispersed • RV sites: Undefined • RV fee: Free • No water • No toilets • Elevation: 2959

Riverdale

Riverdale Spillway Lake - ND GFD • Agency: State • Tel: 701-328-6300 • Location: In Riverdale (limited services), 30 miles NW of Washburn • GPS: Lat 47.47581 Lon -101.403335 • Open: All year • Total sites: Dispersed • RV sites: Undefined • RV fee: Free • No water • Vault toilets • Activities: Fishing, power boating, non-power boating • Elevation: 1703

Robinson

Frettim Lake - ND GFD • Agency: State • Tel: 701-328-6300 • Location: 4 miles NE of Robinson (limited services), 54 miles SE of Harvey • GPS: Lat 47.162397 Lon -99.725249 • Total sites: Dispersed • RV sites: Undefined • RV fee: Free • No water • No toilets • Elevation: 1785

Jasper Lake - ND GFD • Agency: State • Tel: 701-328-6300 • Location: 8 miles N of Robinson (limited services), 50 miles SE of Harvey • GPS: Lat 47.241218 Lon -99.757619 • Open: All year • Total sites: Dispersed • RV sites: Undefined • RV fee: Free • No water • Vault toilets • Activities: Fishing • Elevation: 1821

Rogers

Ray Holland Marsh WMA • Agency: State • Tel: 701-328-6300 • Location: 7 miles NW of Rogers (limited services), 26 miles NW of Valley City • GPS: Lat 47.124433 Lon -98.255943 • Total sites: Dispersed • RV sites: Undefined • RV fee: Free • No water • No toilets • Elevation: 1421

Rolette

Island Lake - ND GFD • Agency: State • Tel: 701-328-6300 • Location: 12 miles SE of Rolette (limited services), 24 miles S of Rolla • GPS: Lat 48.573806 Lon -99.707837 • Open: All year • Total sites: Dispersed • RV sites: Undefined • RV fee: Free • No water • Vault toilets • Activities: Fishing • Elevation: 1594

Rolla

Armourdale Dam SGMA • Agency: State • Tel: 701-968-4340 • Location: 10 miles NE of Rolla • GPS: Lat 48.882493 Lon -99.418582 • Total sites: Dispersed • RV sites: Undefined • RV fee: Free • No water • No toilets • Elevation: 1650

Rugby

Sand Lake - ND GFD • Agency: State • Tel: 701-328-6300 • Location: 12 miles NE of Rugby • GPS: Lat 48.406267 Lon -99.798936 • Open: All year • Total sites: Dispersed • RV sites: Undefined • RV fee: Free • No water • Vault toilets • Activities: Fishing, power boating, non-power boating • Elevation: 1598

Rutland

Buffalo Lake - ND GFD • Agency: State • Location: 7 miles N of Rutland (limited services), 22 miles NW of Lidgerwood • GPS: Lat 46.138237 Lon -97.493833 • Total sites: Dispersed • RV sites: Undefined • RV fee: Free • No water • No toilets • Elevation: 1155

Silver Lake - ND GFD • Agency: State • Tel: 701-328-6300 • Location: 5 miles SW of Rutland (limited services), 24 miles NW of Lidgerwood • GPS: Lat 46.026095 Lon -97.570995 • Open: All year • Total sites: Dispersed • RV sites: Undefined • RV fee: Free • No water • Activities: Fishing, power boating, non-power boating • Elevation: 1227

Sprague Lake - North Ramp - ND GFD • Agency: State • Tel: 701-328-6300 • Location: 4 miles SW of Rutland (limited services), 9 miles SE of Forman • GPS: Lat 46.021426 Lon -97.54979 • Open: All year • Total sites: Dispersed • RV sites: Undefined • RV fee: Free • No water • No toilets • Activities: Fishing, power boating, non-power boating • Elevation: 1224

Sprague Lake - South Ramp - ND GFD • Agency: State • Tel: 701-328-6300 • Location: 4 miles SW of Rutland (limited services), 13 miles SE of Forman • GPS: Lat 46.016431 Lon -97.530483 • Open: All year • Total sites: Dispersed • RV sites: Undefined • RV fee: Free • No water • No toilets • Activities: Fishing, power boating, non-power boating • Elevation: 1214

Ryder

North Carlson Lake - ND GFD • Agency: State • Tel: 701-328-6300 • Location: 10 miles E of Ryder (limited services), 28 miles SW of Minot • GPS: Lat 47.920646 Lon -101.470654 • Total sites: Dispersed • RV sites: Undefined • RV fee: Free • No water • No toilets • Elevation: 2034

South Carlson Lake - ND GFD • Agency: State • Tel: 701-328-6300 • Location: 9 miles E of Ryder (limited services), 28 miles SW of Minot • GPS: Lat 47.918531 Lon -101.472908 • Total sites: Dispersed • RV sites: Undefined • RV fee: Free • No water • No toilets • Elevation: 2054

Scranton

Gascoyne Lake City Campground • Agency: Municipal • Tel: 701-275-6264 • Location: 4 miles SE of Scranton (limited services), 16 miles SE of Bowman • GPS: Lat 46.126946 Lon -103.091297 • Total sites: Dispersed • RV sites: Undefined • RV fee: Free • No water • Vault toilets • Elevation: 2749

Selfridge

Froelich Dam - SGMA • Agency: State • Tel: 701-328-6300 • Location: 10 miles N of Selfridge (limited services), 48 miles S of Mandan • GPS: Lat 46.160999 Lon -100.982314 • Total sites: Dispersed • RV sites: Undefined • RV fee: Free • No water • No toilets • Elevation: 2018

Solen

Breien Centennial Park • Agency: County • Tel: 701-667-3363 • Location: 7 miles W of Solen (limited services), 31 miles S of Mandan • GPS: Lat 46.383045 Lon -100.935132 • Total sites: Dispersed • RV sites: Undefined • RV fee: Free • No water • Vault toilets • Activities: Hunting • Elevation: 1700

St John

Gordon Lake - ND GFD • Agency: State • Location: 5 miles SW of St John (limited services), 10 miles NW of Rolla • GPS: Lat 48.916025 Lon -99.782751 • Total sites: Dispersed • RV sites: Undefined • RV fee: Free • No water • No toilets • Elevation: 2100

Jensen Lake - ND GFD • Agency: State • Tel: 701-328-6300 • Location: 13 miles NW of St John (limited services), 20 miles NW of Rolla • GPS: Lat 48.994733 Lon -99.927337 • Open: All year • Total sites: Dispersed • RV sites: Undefined • RV fee: Free • No water • Vault toilets • Activities: Fishing • Elevation: 2185

St Johns Lions Park (Lake Upsilon) • Agency: County • Tel: 701-477-3149 • Location: 8 miles NW of St John (limited services), 15 miles NW of Rolla • GPS: Lat 48.968761 Lon -99.831941 • Total sites: Dispersed • RV sites: Undefined • RV fee: Free • No water • No toilets • Elevation: 2123

Wakopa WMA - Dion Lake • Agency: State • Tel: 701-477-3149 • Location: 13 miles NW of St John (limited services), 20 miles NW of Rolla • GPS: Lat 48.980848 Lon -99.891317 • Total sites: Dispersed • RV sites: Undefined • RV fee: Free • No water • No toilets • Elevation: 2132

Wakopa WMA - Gravel Lake • Agency: State • Tel: 701-477-3149 • Location: 7 miles W of St John (limited services), 14 miles NW of Rolla • GPS: Lat 48.957155 Lon -99.838211 • Total sites: Dispersed • RV sites: Undefined • RV fee: Free • No water • No toilets • Elevation: 2149

Wakopa WMA - Hooker Lake • Agency: State • Tel: 701-477-3149 • Location: 10 miles W of St John (limited services), 17 miles NW of Rolla • GPS: Lat 48.961996 Lon -99.891668 • Total sites: Dispersed • RV sites: Undefined • RV fee: Free • No water • No toilets • Elevation: 2136

Wheaton Lake - North Ramp - ND GFD • Agency: State • Tel: 701-328-6300 • Location: 6 miles SW of St John (limited services), 11 miles NW of Rolla • GPS: Lat 48.922514 Lon -99.790491 • Open: All year • Total sites: Dispersed • RV sites: Undefined • RV fee: Free • No water • No toilets • Activities: Fishing, power boating, non-power boating • Elevation: 2132

Wheaton Lake - South Ramp - ND GFD • Agency: State • Tel: 701-328-6300 • Location: 6 miles SW of St John (limited services), 11 miles NW of Rolla • GPS: Lat 48.918503 Lon -99.787941 • Open: All year • Total sites: Dispersed • RV sites: Undefined • RV fee: Free • No water • No toilets • Activities: Fishing, power boating, non-power boating • Elevation: 2129

Stanley

Stanley Pond - ND GFD • Agency: State • Tel: 701-328-6300 • Location: In Stanley • GPS: Lat 48.32042 Lon -102.381927 • Open: All year • Total sites: Dispersed • RV sites: Undefined • RV fee: Free • No water • No toilets • Activities: Fishing, power boating, non-power boating • Elevation: 2234

Stanley Reservoir - ND GFD • Agency: State • Tel: 701-328-6300 • Location: 2 miles S of Stanley • GPS: Lat 48.292417 Lon -102.396133 • Open: All year • Total sites: Dispersed • RV sites: Undefined • RV fee: Free • No

water • No toilets • Activities: Fishing, power boating, non-power boating • Elevation: 2149

Strasburg

Cattail Bay • Agency: Corps of Engineers • Tel: 701-255-0015 • Location: 23 miles W of Strasburg (limited services), 30 miles SW of Linton • GPS: Lat 46.094604 Lon -100.591974 • Total sites: 13 • RV sites: 13 • RV fee: Free • Central water • Vault toilets • Activities: Fishing, power boating, non-power boating • Elevation: 1608

Langeliers Bay • Agency: County • Tel: 701-254-5491 • Location: 30 miles SW of Strasburg (limited services), 37 miles SW of Linton • GPS: Lat 45.978402 Lon -100.498645 • Total sites: Dispersed • RV sites: Undefined • RV fee: Free • No water • No toilets • Elevation: 1627

Rice Lake - ND GFD • Agency: State • Tel: 701-328-6300 • Location: 11 miles SE of Strasburg (limited services), 21 miles SW of Linton • GPS: Lat 46.029199 Lon -100.091974 • Open: All year • Total sites: Dispersed • RV sites: Undefined • RV fee: Free • No water • No toilets • Activities: Fishing, power boating, non-power boating • Elevation: 1791

Streeter

Streeter Lake - ND GFD • Agency: State • Tel: 701-328-6300 • Location: 1 mile S of Streeter (limited services), 46 miles SW of Jamestown • GPS: Lat 46.648868 Lon -99.365813 • Open: All year • Total sites: Dispersed • RV sites: Undefined • RV fee: Free • No water • No toilets • Activities: Fishing, power boating, non-power boating • Elevation: 1926

Sykeston

Sykeston City Park • Agency: Municipal • Tel: 701-984-2380 • Location: In Sykeston (limited services), 14 miles W of Carrington • GPS: Lat 47.466722 Lon -99.401634 • Total sites: 10 • RV sites: 10 • RV fee: Free • Electric sites: 6 • Water at site • No toilets • Activities: Fishing, swimming, power boating, non-power boating • Elevation: 1627

Sykeston Dam - ND GFD • Agency: State • Location: 1 mile N of Sykeston (limited services), 14 miles W of Carrington • GPS: Lat 47.476622 Lon -99.399952 • Total sites: Dispersed • RV sites: Undefined • RV fee: Free • No water • No toilets • Elevation: 1618

Tioga

Iverson Dam - ND GFD • Agency: State • Tel: 701-328-6300 • Location: 13 miles S of Tioga • GPS: Lat

48.226205 Lon -102.946104 • Open: All year • Total sites: Dispersed • RV sites: Undefined • RV fee: Free • No water • Vault toilets • Activities: Fishing • Elevation: 2188

Tioga Dam - ND GFD • Agency: State • Tel: 701-664-2563 • Location: 1 mile N of Tioga • GPS: Lat 48.410911 Lon -102.935535 • Open: All year • Total sites: 10 • RV sites: 4 • RV fee: Free • Electric sites: 4 • Central water • No toilets • Activities: Fishing, power boating, non-power boating • Elevation: 2284

Tokio

Wood Lake - ND GFD • Agency: State • Tel: 701-328-6300 • Location: 3 miles SW of Tokio (limited services), 16 miles S of Devils Lake • GPS: Lat 47.905687 Lon -98.846423 • Open: All year • Total sites: Dispersed • RV sites: Undefined • RV fee: Free • No water • Vault toilets • Activities: Fishing, power boating, non-power boating • Elevation: 1545

Tolna

Stump Lake - Tolna ramp - ND GFD • Agency: State • Tel: 701-328-6300 • Location: 3 miles N of Tolna (limited services), 34 miles SE of Devils Lake • GPS: Lat 47.867315 Lon -98.440077 • Open: All year • Total sites: Dispersed • RV sites: Undefined • RV fee: Free • Central water • Vault toilets • Activities: Fishing, power boating, non-power boating • Elevation: 1440

Tolna Dam • Agency: Municipal • Tel: 701-230-0356 • Location: 4 miles SE of Tolna (limited services), 40 miles SE of Devils Lake • GPS: Lat 47.802653 Lon -98.396111 • Total sites: 10 • RV sites: 10 • RV fee: Free (donation appreciated) • Electric sites: 4 • Vault toilets • Elevation: 1378

Tower City

Koldok WMA • Agency: State • Tel: 701-328-6300 • Location: 4 miles W of Tower City (limited services), 12 miles E of Valley City • GPS: Lat 46.929366 Lon -97.734213 • Total sites: Dispersed • RV sites: Undefined • RV fee: Free • No water • No toilets • Elevation: 1188

Towner

Towner City Park Campground • Agency: Municipal • Tel: 701-537-5834 • Location: In Towner (limited services), 19 miles W of Rugby • GPS: Lat 48.341221 Lon -100.405911 • Total sites: 4 • RV sites: 4 • RV fee: Free • Electric sites: 4 • Vault toilets • Elevation: 1483

Trenton

Missouri-Yellowstone Confluence Interpretative Center • Agency: State • Tel: 701-572-9034 • Location: 10 miles SW of Trenton (limited services), 21 miles SW of Williston • GPS: Lat 47.985026 Lon -103.988803 • Total sites: Dispersed • RV sites: Undefined • RV fee: Free (donation appreciated) • No toilets • Elevation: 1890

Trenton Lake RA • Agency: County • Tel: 701-572-8317 • Location: 1 mile SE of Trenton (limited services), 13 miles SW of Williston • GPS: Lat 48.064918 Lon -103.824446 • Open: May-Sep • Total sites: 18 • RV sites: 18 • RV fee: Free • Electric sites: 18 • Central water • Flush toilets • Elevation: 1850

Turtle Lake

Crooked Lake-North Landing - ND GFD • Agency: State • Location: 15 miles N of Turtle Lake (limited services), 27 miles S of Velva • GPS: Lat 47.696023 Lon -100.871598 • Total sites: Dispersed • RV sites: Undefined • RV fee: Free • No water • No toilets • Activities: Fishing, power boating • Elevation: 1915

Crooked Lake-West Landing - ND GFD • Agency: State • Location: 11 miles N of Turtle Lake (limited services), 28 miles S of Velva • GPS: Lat 47.659004 Lon -100.902106 • Total sites: Dispersed • RV sites: Undefined • RV fee: Free • No water • No toilets • Elevation: 1939

Lake Brekken - ND GFD • Agency: State • Tel: 701-448-2596 • Location: 3 miles N of Turtle Lake (limited services), 36 miles S of Velva • GPS: Lat 47.545498 Lon -100.906486 • Total sites: Dispersed • RV sites: Undefined • RV fee: Free • No water • Vault toilets • Activities: Fishing, power boating, non-power boating • Elevation: 1818

Lightning Lake - ND GFD • Agency: State • Tel: 701-328-6300 • Location: 2 miles NE of Turtle Lake (limited services), 39 miles S of Velva • GPS: Lat 47.527586 Lon -100.867837 • Open: All year • Total sites: Dispersed • RV sites: Undefined • RV fee: Free • No water • No toilets • Activities: Fishing, power boating, non-power boating • Elevation: 1821

Long Lake (McLean County) - ND GFD • Agency: State • Location: 21 miles N of Turtle Lake (limited services), 25 miles S of Velva • GPS: Lat 47.732402 Lon -100.852344 • Total sites: Dispersed • RV sites: Undefined • RV fee: Free • No water • No toilets • Elevation: 1923

Strawberry Lake - ND GFD • Agency: State • Tel: 701-328-6300 • Location: 20 miles N of Turtle Lake (limited services), 23 miles S of Velva • GPS: Lat 47.765159 Lon -100.860666 • Open: All year • Total sites: Dispersed • RV sites: Undefined • RV fee: Free • No water • No toilets • Activities: Hiking, fishing, swimming • Elevation: 1946

Tuttle

Cherry Lake - ND GFD • Agency: State • Tel: 701-867-2551 • Location: 11 miles SW of Tuttle (limited services), 18 miles N of Steele • GPS: Lat 47.056339 Lon -99.872134 • Total sites: Dispersed • RV sites: Undefined • RV fee: Free • No water • No toilets • Elevation: 1765

Lake Josephine - ND GFD • Agency: State • Tel: 701-328-6300 • Location: 3 miles N of Tuttle (limited services), 24 miles N of Steele • GPS: Lat 47.179056 Lon -99.999586 • Open: All year • Total sites: Dispersed • RV sites: Undefined • RV fee: Free • No water • Vault toilets • Activities: Fishing • Elevation: 1854

Valley City

Lake Ashtabula-Katie Olson's Landing - ND GFD • Agency: State • Tel: 701-328-6300 • Location: 16 miles N of Valley City • GPS: Lat 47.095033 Lon -98.029668 • Total sites: Dispersed • RV sites: Undefined • RV fee: Free • No water • No toilets • Elevation: 1322

Lake Ashtabula-Sibley Crossing - ND GFD • Agency: State • Tel: 701-328-6300 • Location: 22 miles N of Valley City • GPS: Lat 47.213625 Lon -97.964202 • Total sites: Dispersed • RV sites: Undefined • RV fee: Free • No water • No toilets • Elevation: 1257

Lake Ashtabula-Sundstorm's Landing - ND GFD • Agency: State • Tel: 701-328-6300 • Location: 11 miles N of Valley City • GPS: Lat 47.063779 Lon -98.047788 • Total sites: Dispersed • RV sites: Undefined • RV fee: Free • No water • No toilets • Elevation: 1322

Moon Lake - ND GFD • Agency: State • Location: 10 miles SW of Valley City • GPS: Lat 46.860436 Lon -98.164877 • Open: All year • Total sites: Dispersed • RV sites: Undefined • RV fee: Free • No water • Vault toilets • Activities: Fishing, power boating, non-power boating • Elevation: 1476

St. Marys Lake - ND GFD • Agency: State • Tel: 701-328-6300 • Location: 13 miles SW of Valley City • GPS: Lat 46.84296 Lon -98.16105 • Open: All year • Total sites: Dispersed • RV sites: Undefined • RV fee: Free • No water • No toilets • Activities: Fishing, power boating, non-power boating • Elevation: 1463

Velva

Velva Sportsmans Pond - ND GFD • Agency: State • Tel: 701-328-6300 • Location: 10 miles S of Velva • GPS: Lat 47.935064 Lon -100.970904 • Open: All year • Total sites: Dispersed • RV sites: Undefined • RV fee: Free • No water • No toilets • Activities: Fishing, power boating, non-power boating • Elevation: 1890

Washburn

East Arroda - ND GFD • Agency: State • Tel: 701-328-6300 • Location: 10 miles SW of Washburn • GPS: Lat 47.234544 Lon -101.22234 • Total sites: Dispersed • RV sites: Undefined • RV fee: Free • Central water • No toilets • Elevation: 1722

West Arroda - ND GFD • Agency: State • Tel: 701-328-6300 • Location: 11 miles SW of Washburn • GPS: Lat 47.23364 Lon -101.229301 • Total sites: Dispersed • RV sites: Undefined • RV fee: Free • No water • No toilets • Activities: Fishing • Elevation: 1736

Watford City

Summit (Dakota Prairie NG) • Agency: US Forest Service • Tel: 701-842-8500 • Location: 19 miles S of Watford City • GPS: Lat 47.539945 Lon -103.241835 • Total sites: 5 • RV sites: 3 • RV fee: Free • No water • Vault toilets • Activities: Hiking • Elevation: 2518

Williston

East Spring Lake Pond - ND GFD • Agency: State • Tel: 701-328-6300 • Location: 1 mile N of Williston • GPS: Lat 48.199385 Lon -103.616902 • Open: All year • Total sites: Dispersed • RV sites: Undefined • RV fee: Free • No water • Flush toilets • Activities: Fishing, power boating, non-power boating • Elevation: 1886

Little Muddy River - ND GFD • Agency: State • Tel: 701-328-6300 • Location: 1 mile E of Williston • GPS: Lat 48.152233 Lon -103.593504 • Open: All year • Total sites: Dispersed • RV sites: Undefined • RV fee: Free • No water • Vault toilets • Activities: Fishing, power boating, non-power boating • Elevation: 1873

Willow City

Willow City Campground • Agency: Municipal • Tel: 701-366-4545 • Location: In Willow City (limited services), 20 miles SE of Bottineau • GPS: Lat 48.605047 Lon -100.291084 • Open: May-Oct • Total sites: 2 • RV sites: 2 • RV fee: Free • Electric sites: 2 • Elevation: 1472

Wilton

Steckel Landing • Agency: County • Tel: 701-222-6455 • Location: 10 miles W of Wilton (limited services), 13 miles SE of Washburn • GPS: Lat 47.129343 Lon -100.937895 • Total sites: Dispersed • RV sites: Undefined • RV fee: Free • No toilets • Activities: Fishing • Elevation: 1690

Wing

Mitchell Lake - ND GFD • Agency: State • Location: 3 miles NE of Wing (limited services), 45 miles NE of Bismarck • GPS: Lat 47.170545 Lon -100.304549 • Total sites: Dispersed • RV sites: Undefined • RV fee: Free (donation appreciated) • Central water • Vault toilets • Activities: Fishing, swimming, power boating • Elevation: 1909

Woodworth

Barnes Lake - ND GFD • Agency: State • Location: 7 miles N of Woodworth (limited services), 22 miles SW of Carrington • GPS: Lat 47.230566 Lon -99.28571 • Total sites: Dispersed • RV sites: Undefined • RV fee: Free • No water • No toilets • Activities: Fishing • Elevation: 1821

Clark Lake - ND GFD • Agency: State • Tel: 701-328-6300 • Location: 8 miles NW of Woodworth (limited services), 31 miles SW of Carrington • GPS: Lat 47.181205 Lon -99.413804 • Total sites: Dispersed • RV sites: Undefined • RV fee: Free • No water • No toilets • Elevation: 1900

Wyndmere

Gateway CG • Agency: County • Tel: 701-439-2412 • Location: In Wyndmere (limited services), 24 miles W of Wahpeton • GPS: Lat 46.262728 Lon -97.125841 • Total sites: 12 • RV sites: 8 • RV fee: Free • Electric sites: 8 • Water at site • No toilets • Elevation: 1066

Zahl

Kettle Lake - ND GFD • Agency: State • Location: 6 miles NE of Zahl (limited services), 29 miles N of Williston • GPS: Lat 48.606454 Lon -103.625713 • Open: All year • Total sites: Dispersed • RV sites: Undefined • RV fee: Free • No water • Vault toilets • Activities: Fishing • Elevation: 1998

Oklahoma

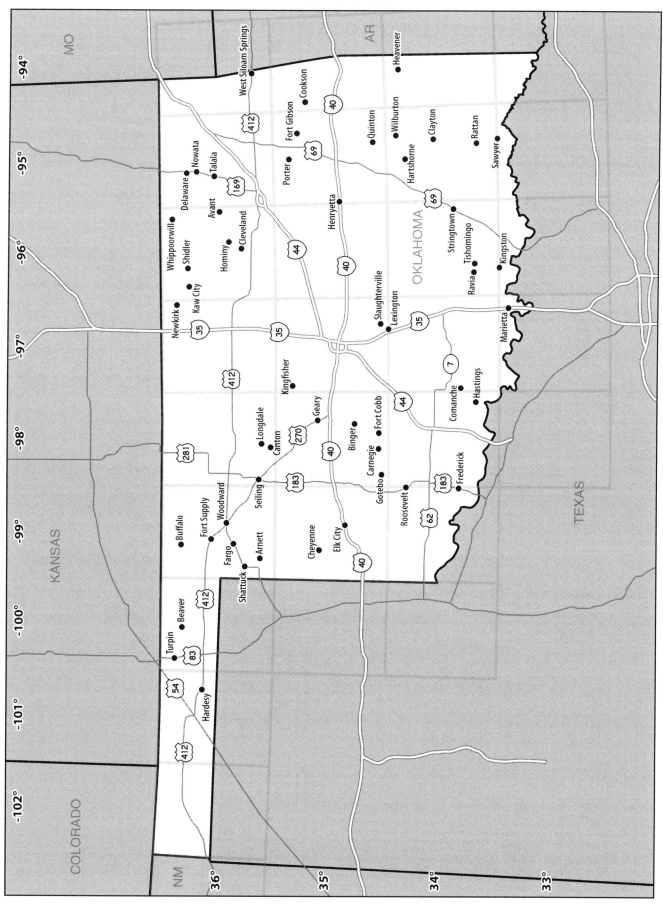

Oklahoma — Camping Areas

Abbreviation	Description
DWC	Department of Wildlife Conservation
NF	National Forest
NG	National Grassland
WMA	Wildlife Management Area
WMU	Wildlife Management Unit

Arnett

Ellis County WMA - Lake Vincent • Agency: State • Tel: 580-474-2668 • Location: 13 miles SW of Arnett (limited services), 13 miles SW of Shattuck • GPS: Lat 36.061597 Lon -99.924102 • Total sites: Dispersed • RV sites: Undefined • RV fee: Free • No toilets • Activities: Fishing, power boating, non-power boating • Elevation: 2280

Packsaddle WMA - Site 1 • Agency: State • Tel: 580-515-2030 • Location: 19 miles SE of Arnett (limited services), 34 miles SE of Shattuck • GPS: Lat 35.892049 Lon -99.709589 • Total sites: Dispersed • RV sites: Undefined • RV fee: Free • No water • No toilets • Activities: Fishing, hunting • Elevation: 2271

Packsaddle WMA - Site 2 • Agency: State • Tel: 580-515-2030 • Location: 19 miles SE of Arnett (limited services), 35 miles SE of Shattuck • GPS: Lat 35.897653 Lon -99.701232 • Total sites: Dispersed • RV sites: Undefined • RV fee: Free • No water • No toilets • Activities: Fishing, hunting • Elevation: 2219

Packsaddle WMA - Site 3 • Agency: State • Tel: 580-515-2030 • Location: 21 miles SE of Arnett (limited services), 36 miles SE of Shattuck • GPS: Lat 35.881014 Lon -99.692283 • Total sites: Dispersed • RV sites: Undefined • RV fee: Free • No water • No toilets • Activities: Fishing, hunting • Elevation: 2237

Packsaddle WMA - Site 4 • Agency: State • Tel: 580-515-2030 • Location: 24 miles SE of Arnett (limited services), 39 miles SE of Shattuck • GPS: Lat 35.868454 Lon -99.647074 • Total sites: Dispersed • RV sites: Undefined • RV fee: Free • No water • No toilets • Activities: Fishing, hunting • Elevation: 2208

Packsaddle WMA - Site 5 • Agency: State • Tel: 580-515-2030 • Location: 25 miles SE of Arnett (limited services), 40 miles SE of Shattuck • GPS: Lat 35.906274 Lon -99.604647 • Total sites: Dispersed • RV sites: Undefined • RV fee: Free • No water • No toilets • Activities: Fishing, hunting • Elevation: 2265

Packsaddle WMA - Site 6 • Agency: State • Tel: 580-515-2030 • Location: 25 miles SE of Arnett (limited services), 40 miles SE of Shattuck • GPS: Lat 35.917312

Lon -99.623134 • Total sites: Dispersed • RV sites: Undefined • RV fee: Free • No water • No toilets • Activities: Fishing, hunting • Elevation: 2316

Avant

Candy Creek WMA • Agency: State • Tel: 918-629-4625 • Location: 2 miles NE of Avant (limited services), 11 miles N of Skiatook • GPS: Lat 36.501369 Lon -96.033927 • Total sites: Dispersed • RV sites: Undefined • RV fee: Free • No water • No toilets • Activities: Fishing, hunting • Elevation: 705

Beaver

Beaver River WMA - Site 2 • Agency: State • Tel: 806-339-5175 • Location: 14 miles W of Beaver • GPS: Lat 36.816692 Lon -100.712931 • Total sites: Dispersed • RV sites: Undefined • RV fee: Free • No water • No toilets • Elevation: 2477

Beaver River WMA - Site 3 • Agency: State • Tel: 806-339-5175 • Location: 9 miles W of Beaver • GPS: Lat 36.814577 Lon -100.670977 • Total sites: Dispersed • RV sites: Undefined • RV fee: Free • No water • No toilets • Elevation: 2458

Beaver River WMA - Site 4 • Agency: State • Tel: 806-339-5175 • Location: 14 miles W of Beaver • GPS: Lat 36.831136 Lon -100.645256 • Total sites: Dispersed • RV sites: Undefined • RV fee: Free • No water • No toilets • Elevation: 2441

Beaver River WMA - Site 6 • Agency: State • Tel: 806-339-5175 • Location: 4 miles W of Beaver • GPS: Lat 36.829653 Lon -100.576397 • Total sites: Dispersed • RV sites: Undefined • RV fee: Free • No water • No toilets • Elevation: 2408

Binger

Ft Cobb WMA - Site 5 • Agency: State • Tel: 580-595-0347 • Location: 13 miles SW of Binger (limited services), 24 miles SW of Hinton • GPS: Lat 35.231226 Lon -98.506786 • Total sites: Dispersed • RV sites: Undefined • RV fee: Free • No water • No toilets • Activities: Fishing, hunting • Elevation: 1361

Ft Cobb WMA - Site 6 • Agency: State • Tel: 580-595-0347 • Location: 14 miles SW of Binger (limited services), 25 miles SW of Hinton • GPS: Lat 35.218697 Lon -98.503693 • Total sites: Dispersed • RV sites: Undefined • RV fee: Free • No water • No toilets • Activities: Fishing, hunting • Elevation: 1356

Ft Cobb WMA - Site 7 • Agency: State • Tel: 580-595-0347 • Location: 15 miles SW of Binger (limited services), 25 miles SW of Hinton • GPS: Lat 35.219189

Lon -98.485334 • Total sites: Dispersed • RV sites: Undefined • RV fee: Free • No water • No toilets • Activities: Fishing, hunting • Elevation: 1357

Ft Cobb WMA - Site 8 • Agency: State • Tel: 580-595-0347 • Location: 13 miles SW of Binger (limited services), 24 miles SW of Hinton • GPS: Lat 35.221138 Lon -98.482272 • Total sites: Dispersed • RV sites: Undefined • RV fee: Free • No water • No toilets • Activities: Fishing, hunting • Elevation: 1360

Buffalo

Cimarron Hills WMA • Agency: State • Tel: 405-990-7206 • Location: 27 miles NE of Buffalo • GPS: Lat 36.943824 Lon -99.362848 • Total sites: Dispersed • RV sites: Undefined • RV fee: Free • No water • No toilets • Activities: Fishing, hunting • Elevation: 1726

Canton

Canton WMA - Site 10 • Agency: State • Tel: 580-541-5319 • Location: 12 miles NW of Canton (limited services), 27 miles SW of Fairview • GPS: Lat 36.135845 Lon -98.707354 • Total sites: Dispersed • RV sites: Undefined • RV fee: Free • No water • No toilets • Activities: Fishing, hunting • Elevation: 1632

Canton WMA - Site 11 • Agency: State • Tel: 580-541-5319 • Location: 10 miles NW of Canton (limited services), 26 miles SW of Fairview • GPS: Lat 36.128212 Lon -98.688522 • Total sites: Dispersed • RV sites: Undefined • RV fee: Free • No water • No toilets • Activities: Fishing, hunting • Elevation: 1640

Canton WMA - Site 12 • Agency: State • Tel: 580-541-5319 • Location: 9 miles NW of Canton (limited services), 25 miles SW of Fairview • GPS: Lat 36.127425 Lon -98.675614 • Total sites: Dispersed • RV sites: Undefined • RV fee: Free • No water • No toilets • Activities: Fishing, hunting • Elevation: 1635

Carnegie

Ft Cobb WMA - Site 2 • Agency: State • Tel: 580-595-0347 • Location: 11 miles NE of Carnegie • GPS: Lat 35.207362 Lon -98.507335 • Total sites: Dispersed • RV sites: Undefined • RV fee: Free • No water • No toilets • Activities: Fishing, hunting • Elevation: 1353

Ft Cobb WMA - Site 3 • Agency: State • Tel: 580-595-0347 • Location: 12 miles NE of Carnegie • GPS: Lat 35.219532 Lon -98.513692 • Total sites: Dispersed • RV sites: Undefined • RV fee: Free • No water • No toilets • Activities: Fishing, hunting • Elevation: 1357

Ft Cobb WMA - Site 4 • Agency: State • Tel: 580-595-0347 • Location: 13 miles NE of Carnegie • GPS: Lat

35.231343 Lon -98.532534 • Total sites: Dispersed • RV sites: Undefined • RV fee: Free • No water • No toilets • Activities: Fishing, hunting • Elevation: 1365

Cheyenne

Black Kettle (Black Kettle NG) • Agency: US Forest Service • Tel: 580-497-2143 • Location: 10 miles N of Cheyenne • GPS: Lat 35.745318 Lon -99.714557 • Open: All year • Total sites: 12 • RV sites: 12 • Max RV Length: 27 • RV fee: Free • Central water • Vault toilets • Activities: Hiking, power boating, non-power boating • Elevation: 2100

Skipout (Cibola NF) • Agency: US Forest Service • Tel: 580-497-2143 • Location: 12 miles W of Cheyenne • GPS: Lat 35.635595 Lon -99.880054 • Open: All year • Total sites: 12 • RV sites: 12 • Max RV Length: 27 • RV fee: Free • Central water • Vault toilets • Activities: Hiking, power boating, non-power boating • Elevation: 2313

Spring Creek (Cibola NF) • Agency: US Forest Service • Tel: 580-497-2143 • Location: 19 miles NW of Cheyenne • GPS: Lat 35.772811 Lon -99.839531 • Open: All year • Total sites: 5 • RV sites: 5 • Max RV Length: 22 • RV fee: Free • Central water • Vault toilets • Activities: Power boating, non-power boating • Elevation: 2198

Clayton

Lake Nanih Waiya - DWC • Agency: State • Tel: 918-297-0153 • Location: 5 miles NE of Clayton • GPS: Lat 34.631234 Lon -95.301869 • Total sites: Dispersed • RV sites: Undefined • RV fee: Free • No water • No toilets • Activities: Fishing, power boating, non-power boating • Elevation: 610

Pushmataha WMA - Site 1 • Agency: State • Tel: 918-569-4329 • Location: 3 miles S of Clayton • GPS: Lat 34.550374 Lon -95.344653 • Total sites: Dispersed • RV sites: Undefined • RV fee: Free • No water • No toilets • Activities: Fishing, hunting • Elevation: 847

Pushmataha WMA - Site 2 • Agency: State • Tel: 918-569-4329 • Location: 5 miles S of Clayton • GPS: Lat 34.539216 Lon -95.359272 • Total sites: Dispersed • RV sites: Undefined • RV fee: Free • No water • No toilets • Activities: Fishing, hunting • Elevation: 1425

Cleveland

Cowskin Bay South (Keystone Lake) • Agency: Corps of Engineers • Tel: 918-865-2621 • Location: 10 miles SE of Cleveland • GPS: Lat 36.231445 Lon -96.364258 • Open: May-Sep • Total sites: 30 • RV sites: 30 • RV fee: Free • Vault toilets • Activities: Fishing • Elevation: 774

Comanche

Comanche Lake • Agency: Municipal • Tel: 580-439-6308 • Location: 4 miles E of Comanche • GPS: Lat 34.368838 Lon -97.894274 • Total sites: 13 • RV sites: 13 • RV fee: Free • Electric sites: 13 • Central water • Activities: Fishing, power boating, non-power boating, golf • Elevation: 1063

Cookson

Cookson WMA • Agency: State • Tel: 918-260-8959 • Location: 5 miles SE of Cookson (limited services), 18 miles SW of Stilwell • GPS: Lat 35.700074 Lon -94.860201 • Total sites: Dispersed • RV sites: Undefined • RV fee: Free • No water • No toilets • Activities: Fishing, hunting • Elevation: 904

Delaware

Oologah WMA - Site 2 • Agency: State • Tel: 918-629-5286 • Location: 3 miles E of Delaware (limited services), 8 miles NE of Nowata • GPS: Lat 36.786053 Lon -95.586232 • Total sites: Dispersed • RV sites: Undefined • RV fee: Free • No water • No toilets • Activities: Fishing, hunting • Elevation: 666

Elk City

Elk Lake Park • Agency: Municipal • Tel: 580-225-3990 • Location: 3 miles S of Elk City • GPS: Lat 35.366325 Lon -99.415865 • Open: All year • Total sites: 5 • RV sites: 5 • RV fee: Free • Electric sites: 5 • Water at site (no water in winter) • Notes: 4-night limit/30 days • Activities: Hiking, mountain biking, fishing, power boating, non-power boating, disc golf • Elevation: 1926

Fargo

Fort Supply WMA - Site 5 • Agency: State • Tel: 580-334-0343 • Location: 7 miles NE of Fargo (limited services), 10 miles W of Woodward • GPS: Lat 36.449965 Lon -99.590161 • Total sites: Dispersed • RV sites: Undefined • RV fee: Free • No water • No toilets • Activities: Fishing, hunting • Elevation: 2041

Fort Supply WMA - Site 6 • Agency: State • Tel: 580-334-0343 • Location: 8 miles NE of Fargo (limited services), 9 miles W of Woodward • GPS: Lat 36.449877 Lon -99.579164 • Total sites: Dispersed • RV sites: Undefined • RV fee: Free • No water • No toilets • Activities: Fishing, hunting • Elevation: 2040

Fort Supply WMA - Site 7 • Agency: State • Tel: 580-334-0343 • Location: 10 miles NE of Fargo (limited services), 11 miles NW of Woodward • GPS: Lat 36.481429 Lon -99.569903 • Total sites: Dispersed • RV sites: Undefined • RV fee: Free • No water • No toilets • Activities: Fishing, hunting • Elevation: 2038

Fort Cobb

Ft Cobb WMA - Site 9 • Agency: State • Tel: 580-595-0347 • Location: 10 miles NW of Fort Cobb (limited services), 23 miles NW of Anadarko • GPS: Lat 35.218736 Lon -98.476816 • Total sites: Dispersed • RV sites: Undefined • RV fee: Free • No water • No toilets • Activities: Fishing, hunting • Elevation: 1367

Ft Cobb WMA - Site 10 • Agency: State • Tel: 580-595-0347 • Location: 10 miles NW of Fort Cobb (limited services), 22 miles NW of Anadarko • GPS: Lat 35.204257 Lon -98.480572 • Total sites: Dispersed • RV sites: Undefined • RV fee: Free • No water • No toilets • Activities: Fishing, hunting • Elevation: 1354

Fort Gibson

Cherokee WMA • Agency: State • Tel: 918-931-0432 • Location: 15 miles SE of Fort Gibson • GPS: Lat 35.754124 Lon -95.046666 • Total sites: Dispersed • RV sites: Undefined • RV fee: Free • No water • No toilets • Activities: Fishing, hunting • Elevation: 694

Fort Supply

Fort Supply WMA - Site 1 • Agency: State • Tel: 580-334-0343 • Location: 5 miles S of Fort Supply (limited services), 17 miles NW of Woodward • GPS: Lat 36.517919 Lon -99.581923 • Total sites: Dispersed • RV sites: Undefined • RV fee: Free • No water • No toilets • Activities: Fishing, hunting • Elevation: 2016

Fort Supply WMA - Site 2 • Agency: State • Tel: 580-334-0343 • Location: 5 miles S of Fort Supply (limited services), 16 miles NW of Woodward • GPS: Lat 36.506973 Lon -99.586415 • Total sites: Dispersed • RV sites: Undefined • RV fee: Free • No water • No toilets • Activities: Fishing, hunting • Elevation: 2034

Fort Supply WMA - Site 3 • Agency: State • Tel: 580-334-0343 • Location: 7 miles S of Fort Supply (limited services), 15 miles NW of Woodward • GPS: Lat 36.492467 Lon -99.586641 • Total sites: Dispersed • RV sites: Undefined • RV fee: Free • No water • No toilets • Activities: Fishing, hunting • Elevation: 2041

Fort Supply WMA - Site 4 • Agency: State • Tel: 580-334-0343 • Location: 8 miles S of Fort Supply (limited services), 14 miles NW of Woodward • GPS: Lat 36.478452 Lon -99.585596 • Total sites: Dispersed • RV sites: Undefined • RV fee: Free • No water • No toilets • Activities: Fishing, hunting • Elevation: 2028

Hal and Fern Cooper WMA - Site 1 • Agency: State • Tel: 580-334-0343 • Location: 7 miles E of Fort Supply (limited services), 12 miles NW of Woodward • GPS: Lat 36.567543 Lon -99.507659 • Total sites: Dispersed • RV sites: Undefined • RV fee: Free • No water • No toilets • Activities: Fishing, hunting • Elevation: 1992

Hal and Fern Cooper WMA - Site 2 • Agency: State • Tel: 580-334-0343 • Location: 8 miles E of Fort Supply (limited services), 13 miles NW of Woodward • GPS: Lat 36.558015 Lon -99.494789 • Total sites: Dispersed • RV sites: Undefined • RV fee: Free • No water • No toilets • Activities: Fishing, hunting • Elevation: 2025

Hal and Fern Cooper WMA - Site 3 • Agency: State • Tel: 580-334-0343 • Location: 8 miles E of Fort Supply (limited services), 14 miles NW of Woodward • GPS: Lat 36.571479 Lon -99.496963 • Total sites: Dispersed • RV sites: Undefined • RV fee: Free • No water • No toilets • Activities: Fishing, hunting • Elevation: 1991

Hal and Fern Cooper WMA - Site 4 • Agency: State • Tel: 580-334-0343 • Location: 10 miles NE of Fort Supply (limited services), 18 miles NW of Woodward • GPS: Lat 36.597243 Lon -99.506319 • Total sites: Dispersed • RV sites: Undefined • RV fee: Free • No water • No toilets • Activities: Fishing, hunting • Elevation: 1972

Hal and Fern Cooper WMA - Site 5 • Agency: State • Tel: 580-334-0343 • Location: 9 miles NE of Fort Supply (limited services), 18 miles NW of Woodward • GPS: Lat 36.596762 Lon -99.489158 • Total sites: Dispersed • RV sites: Undefined • RV fee: Free • No water • No toilets • Activities: Fishing, hunting • Elevation: 1969

Frederick

Hackberry Flat WMA • Agency: State • Tel: 580-335-5262 • Location: 8 miles SE of Frederick • GPS: Lat 34.302043 Lon -98.975319 • Total sites: Dispersed • RV sites: Undefined • RV fee: Free • No water • No toilets • Elevation: 1187

Geary

American Horse Lake - DWC • Agency: State • Tel: 580-474-2663 • Location: 14 miles W of Geary • GPS: Lat 35.630467 Lon -98.506502 • Total sites: Dispersed • RV sites: Undefined • RV fee: Free • No water • No toilets • Elevation: 1663

Gotebo

Lake Vanderwork - DWC • Agency: State • Location: 8 miles NE of Gotebo (limited services), 19 miles SE of New Cordell • GPS: Lat 35.163116 Lon -98.825811 • Total sites: Dispersed • RV sites: Undefined • RV fee: Free • No

toilets • Activities: Fishing, power boating, non-power boating • Elevation: 1460

Hardesy

Optima WMA - Dispersed • Agency: State • Tel: 806-339-5175 • Location: 8 miles N of Hardesy (limited services), 13 miles S of Hooker • GPS: Lat 36.694232 Lon -101.180989 • Total sites: Dispersed • RV sites: Undefined • RV fee: Free • Elevation: 2785

Optima WMA - Highway 94 • Agency: State • Tel: 806-339-5175 • Location: 6 miles N of Hardesy (limited services), 11 miles S of Hooker • GPS: Lat 36.694551 Lon -101.203516 • Total sites: Dispersed • RV sites: Undefined • RV fee: Free • Elevation: 2783

Optima WMA - Optima Dam • Agency: State • Tel: 806-339-5175 • Location: 6 miles NE of Hardesy (limited services), 19 miles SE of Hooker • GPS: Lat 36.658472 Lon -101.132775 • Total sites: 19 • RV sites: 19 • RV fee: Free • Vault toilets • Elevation: 2724

Optima WMA - South • Agency: State • Tel: 806-339-5175 • Location: 5 miles NE of Hardesy (limited services), 17 miles S of Hooker • GPS: Lat 36.649354 Lon -101.158017 • Total sites: 67 • RV sites: 67 • RV fee: Free • Vault toilets • Elevation: 2783

Optima WMA - W Road • Agency: State • Tel: 806-339-5175 • Location: 6 miles NE of Hardesy (limited services), 15 miles S of Hooker • GPS: Lat 36.671798 Lon -101.164944 • Total sites: 51 • RV sites: 45 • RV fee: Free • Vault toilets • Elevation: 2807

Hartshorne

Eufaula WMA - Hickory Point • Agency: State • Tel: 918-617-1113 • Location: 8 miles NW of Hartshorne • GPS: Lat 34.932637 Lon -95.580332 • Total sites: Dispersed • RV sites: Undefined • RV fee: Free • No water • No toilets • Activities: Fishing • Elevation: 604

Hastings

Waurika WMA • Agency: State • Tel: 580-595-0347 • Location: 6 miles N of Hastings (limited services), 11 miles SW of Comanche • GPS: Lat 34.309725 Lon -98.106407 • Total sites: Dispersed • RV sites: Undefined • RV fee: Free • No water • No toilets • Activities: Fishing, non-power boating • Elevation: 970

Heavener

Ouachita WMA - Site 3 • Agency: State • Tel: 918-653-2012 • Location: 16 miles SW of Heavener • GPS: Lat 34.767965 Lon -94.760548 • Total sites: Dispersed • RV sites: Undefined • RV fee: Free • No water • No toilets • Activities: Fishing, hunting • Elevation: 922

Ouachita WMA - Site 4 (Crooked Branch Lake) • Agency: State • Tel: 918-653-2012 • Location: 12 miles SW of Heavener • GPS: Lat 34.793924 Lon -94.741811 • Total sites: Dispersed • RV sites: Undefined • RV fee: Free • No water • No toilets • Activities: Fishing, hunting • Elevation: 974

Henryetta

Nichols Lake • Agency: Municipal • Tel: 918-652-3348 • Location: 3 miles S of Henryetta • GPS: Lat 35.407829 Lon -95.974865 • Open: All year • Total sites: 7 • RV sites: 7 • RV fee: Free • Central water • No toilets • Elevation: 846

Hominy

Skiatook WMA - Site 1 • Agency: State • Tel: 918-629-4625 • Location: 6 miles SE of Hominy • GPS: Lat 36.377522 Lon -96.291154 • Total sites: Dispersed • RV sites: Undefined • RV fee: Free • No water • No toilets • Activities: Fishing, hunting • Elevation: 737

Skiatook WMA - Site 2 • Agency: State • Tel: 918-629-4625 • Location: 11 miles E of Hominy • GPS: Lat 36.399691 Lon -96.242026 • Total sites: Dispersed • RV sites: Undefined • RV fee: Free • No water • No toilets • Activities: Fishing, hunting • Elevation: 735

Skiatook WMA - Site 3 • Agency: State • Tel: 918-629-4625 • Location: 9 miles SE of Hominy • GPS: Lat 36.349137 Lon -96.259089 • Total sites: Dispersed • RV sites: Undefined • RV fee: Free • No water • No toilets • Activities: Fishing, hunting • Elevation: 738

Skiatook WMA - Site 4 • Agency: State • Tel: 918-629-4625 • Location: 14 miles E of Hominy • GPS: Lat 36.420083 Lon -96.224878 • Total sites: Dispersed • RV sites: Undefined • RV fee: Free • No water • No toilets • Activities: Fishing, hunting • Elevation: 761

Skiatook WMA - Site 5 • Agency: State • Tel: 918-629-4625 • Location: 14 miles E of Hominy • GPS: Lat 36.430053 Lon -96.215358 • Total sites: Dispersed • RV sites: Undefined • RV fee: Free • No water • No toilets • Activities: Fishing, hunting • Elevation: 726

Kaw City

Kaw WMA - Site 8 • Agency: State • Tel: 405-823-7936 • Location: 15 miles NE of Kaw City (limited services), 27 miles NE of Ponca City • GPS: Lat 36.828019 Lon -96.815381 • Total sites: Dispersed • RV sites: Undefined • RV fee: Free • No water • No toilets • Activities: Fishing, hunting • Elevation: 1049

Kingfisher

Lake Elmer - DWC • Agency: State • Tel: 580-474-2668 • Location: 5 miles NW of Kingfisher • GPS: Lat 35.882348 Lon -97.989181 • Total sites: Dispersed • RV sites: Undefined • RV fee: Free • No toilets • Elevation: 1138

Kingston

Fobb Bottom WMA - East (Lake Texoma) • Agency: State • Tel: 405-823-8383 • Location: 17 miles SW of Kingston • GPS: Lat 33.870695 Lon -96.845649 • Total sites: Dispersed • RV sites: Undefined • RV fee: Free • No water • No toilets • Activities: Fishing, hunting • Elevation: 641

Fobb Bottom WMA - West 1 (Lake Texoma) • Agency: State • Tel: 405-823-8383 • Location: 16 miles SW of Kingston • GPS: Lat 33.867057 Lon -96.869286 • Total sites: Dispersed • RV sites: Undefined • RV fee: Free • No water • No toilets • Activities: Fishing, hunting • Elevation: 632

Fobb Bottom WMA - West 2 (Lake Texoma) • Agency: State • Tel: 405-823-8383 • Location: 16 miles SW of Kingston • GPS: Lat 33.869519 Lon -96.870739 • Total sites: Dispersed • RV sites: Undefined • RV fee: Free • No water • No toilets • Activities: Fishing, hunting • Elevation: 632

Lexington

Lexington WMA - Dahlgren Lake • Agency: State • Tel: 405-527-6476 • Location: 11 miles NE of Lexington (limited services), 13 miles NE of Percell • GPS: Lat 35.056949 Lon -97.197902 • Total sites: Dispersed • RV sites: Undefined • RV fee: Free • No water • No toilets • Activities: Hiking, fishing • Elevation: 1132

Longdale

Canton WMA - Site 1 • Agency: State • Tel: 580-541-5319 • Location: 7 miles NW of Longdale (limited services), 15 miles SW of Fairview • GPS: Lat 36.157503 Lon -98.636656 • Total sites: Dispersed • RV sites: Undefined • RV fee: Free • No water • No toilets • Activities: Fishing, hunting • Elevation: 1626

Canton WMA - Site 2 • Agency: State • Tel: 580-541-5319 • Location: 7 miles NW of Longdale (limited services), 15 miles SW of Fairview • GPS: Lat 36.157055 Lon -98.649383 • Total sites: Dispersed • RV sites: Undefined • RV fee: Free • No water • No toilets • Activities: Fishing, hunting • Elevation: 1634

Canton WMA - Site 3 • Agency: State • Tel: 580-541-5319 • Location: 8 miles NW of Longdale (limited services), 16 miles SW of Fairview • GPS: Lat 36.155115 Lon -98.667562 • Total sites: Dispersed • RV sites: Undefined • RV fee: Free • No water • No toilets • Activities: Fishing, hunting • Elevation: 1633

Canton WMA - Site 4 • Agency: State • Tel: 580-541-5319 • Location: 11 miles NW of Longdale (limited services), 19 miles SW of Fairview • GPS: Lat 36.145296 Lon -98.675724 • Total sites: Dispersed • RV sites: Undefined • RV fee: Free • No water • No toilets • Activities: Fishing, hunting • Elevation: 1626

Canton WMA - Site 5 • Agency: State • Tel: 580-541-5319 • Location: 10 miles NW of Longdale (limited services), 18 miles SW of Fairview • GPS: Lat 36.149675 Lon -98.690432 • Total sites: Dispersed • RV sites: Undefined • RV fee: Free • No water • No toilets • Activities: Fishing, hunting • Elevation: 1632

Canton WMA - Site 6 • Agency: State • Tel: 580-541-5319 • Location: 13 miles NW of Longdale (limited services), 19 miles SW of Fairview • GPS: Lat 36.162317 Lon -98.727759 • Total sites: Dispersed • RV sites: Undefined • RV fee: Free • No water • No toilets • Activities: Fishing, hunting • Elevation: 1666

Marietta

Cross Timbers WMA • Agency: State • Tel: 405-823-9038 • Location: 17 miles NW of Marietta • GPS: Lat 33.977413 Lon -97.378004 • Total sites: Dispersed • RV sites: Undefined • RV fee: Free • No water • No toilets • Activities: Hunting • Elevation: 928

Hickory Creek WMA - Site 2 • Agency: State • Tel: 405-823-9038 • Location: 7 miles NE of Marietta • GPS: Lat 33.985075 Lon -97.059238 • Total sites: Dispersed • RV sites: Undefined • RV fee: Free • No water • No toilets • Activities: Fishing, hunting • Elevation: 788

Hickory Creek WMA - Site 3 • Agency: State • Tel: 405-823-9038 • Location: 7 miles NE of Marietta • GPS: Lat 33.988177 Lon -97.051748 • Total sites: Dispersed • RV sites: Undefined • RV fee: Free • No water • No toilets • Activities: Fishing, hunting • Elevation: 763

Hickory Creek WMA - Site 4 • Agency: State • Tel: 405-823-9038 • Location: 7 miles NE of Marietta • GPS: Lat 33.980224 Lon -97.053282 • Total sites: Dispersed • RV sites: Undefined • RV fee: Free • No water • No toilets • Activities: Fishing, hunting • Elevation: 749

Hickory Creek WMA - Site 5 • Agency: State • Tel: 405-823-9038 • Location: 10 miles NE of Marietta • GPS: Lat 33.991063 Lon -96.996273 • Total sites: Dispersed • RV sites: Undefined • RV fee: Free • No water • No toilets • Activities: Fishing, hunting • Elevation: 710

Love Valley WMA - Site 1 • Agency: State • Tel: 405-823-9038 • Location: 10 miles SE of Marietta • GPS: Lat 33.860814 Lon -97.020592 • Total sites: Dispersed • RV sites: Undefined • RV fee: Free • No water • No toilets • Activities: Fishing, hunting • Elevation: 638

Love Valley WMA - Site 2 • Agency: State • Tel: 405-823-9038 • Location: 12 miles SE of Marietta • GPS: Lat 33.852053 Lon -97.050565 • Total sites: Dispersed • RV sites: Undefined • RV fee: Free • No water • No toilets • Activities: Fishing, hunting • Elevation: 651

Newkirk

Kaw WMA - Site 1 • Agency: State • Tel: 405-823-7936 • Location: 11 miles NE of Newkirk • GPS: Lat 36.968166 Lon -96.957865 • Total sites: Dispersed • RV sites: Undefined • RV fee: Free • No water • No toilets • Activities: Fishing, hunting • Elevation: 1039

Kaw WMA - Site 2 • Agency: State • Tel: 405-823-7936 • Location: 7 miles E of Newkirk • GPS: Lat 36.903277 Lon -96.942033 • Total sites: Dispersed • RV sites: Undefined • RV fee: Free • No water • No toilets • Activities: Fishing, hunting • Elevation: 1051

Kaw WMA - Site 3 • Agency: State • Tel: 405-823-7936 • Location: 10 miles SE of Newkirk • GPS: Lat 36.854133 Lon -96.914677 • Total sites: Dispersed • RV sites: Undefined • RV fee: Free • No water • No toilets • Activities: Fishing, hunting • Elevation: 1069

Kaw WMA - Site 4 • Agency: State • Tel: 405-823-7936 • Location: 8 miles E of Newkirk • GPS: Lat 36.867604 Lon -96.930586 • Total sites: Dispersed • RV sites: Undefined • RV fee: Free • No water • No toilets • Activities: Fishing, hunting • Elevation: 1025

Kaw WMA - Site 5 • Agency: State • Tel: 405-823-7936 • Location: 12 miles NE of Newkirk • GPS: Lat 36.961053 Lon -96.935221 • Total sites: Dispersed • RV sites: Undefined • RV fee: Free • No water • No toilets • Activities: Fishing, hunting • Elevation: 1062

Kaw WMA - Site 6 • Agency: State • Tel: 405-823-7936 • Location: 7 miles E of Newkirk • GPS: Lat 36.897651 Lon -96.941726 • Total sites: Dispersed • RV sites: Undefined • RV fee: Free • No water • No toilets • Activities: Fishing, hunting • Elevation: 1068

Nowata

Big Creek Ramp (Oologah Lake) • Agency: Corps of Engineers • Tel: 918-443-2250 • Location: 7 miles NE of Nowata • GPS: Lat 36.729714 Lon -95.541055 • Open: All year • Total sites: 12 • RV sites: 12 • RV fee: Free • No water • Vault toilets • Activities: Fishing, swimming, power boating, non-power boating • Elevation: 666

Porter

Tullahasse Loop • Agency: Corps of Engineers • Tel: 918-682-4314 • Location: 6 miles NE of Porter (limited services), 9 miles NW of Wagoner • GPS: Lat 35.890397 Lon -95.447786 • Total sites: 6 • RV sites: 6 • RV fee: Free • No water • Vault toilets • Activities: Fishing, power boating • Elevation: 520

Quinton

James Collins WMA • Agency: State • Tel: 580-320-3178 • Location: 10 miles SW of Quinton (limited services), 25 miles NE of McAlester • GPS: Lat 35.043794 Lon -95.481059 • Total sites: 21 • RV sites: 21 • RV fee: Free • Central water • Vault toilets • Activities: Fishing, hunting • Elevation: 656

Rattan

Lake Ozzie Cobb - DWC • Agency: State • Tel: 918-297-0153 • Location: 4 miles NE of Rattan (limited services), 16 miles E of Antlers • GPS: Lat 34.244949 Lon -95.385046 • Total sites: Dispersed • RV sites: Undefined • RV fee: Free • No toilets • Elevation: 545

Ravia

Washita Arm WMA • Agency: State • Tel: 405-823-8383 • Location: 4 miles SW of Ravia (limited services), 8 miles W of Tishomingo • GPS: Lat 34.217535 Lon -96.800252 • Total sites: Dispersed • RV sites: Undefined • RV fee: Free • No water • No toilets • Activities: Fishing, hunting • Elevation: 676

Roosevelt

Mountain Park WMA - Site 1 • Agency: State • Tel: 580-595-0347 • Location: 6 miles SE of Roosevelt (limited services), 19 miles SE of Hobart • GPS: Lat 34.798908 Lon -98.972648 • Total sites: Dispersed • RV sites: Undefined • RV fee: Free • No water • No toilets • Activities: Fishing, hunting • Elevation: 1421

Mountain Park WMA - Site 2 • Agency: State • Tel: 580-595-0347 • Location: 7 miles S of Roosevelt (limited services), 22 miles SE of Hobart • GPS: Lat 34.796295 Lon -99.009199 • Total sites: Dispersed • RV sites: Undefined • RV fee: Free • No water • No toilets • Activities: Fishing, hunting • Elevation: 1422

Mountain Park WMA - Site 3 • Agency: State • Tel: 580-595-0347 • Location: 7 miles S of Roosevelt (limited services), 22 miles SE of Hobart • GPS: Lat 34.791809 Lon -99.007824 • Total sites: Dispersed • RV sites: Undefined • RV fee: Free • No water • No toilets • Activities: Fishing, hunting • Elevation: 1423

Sawyer

Lake Schooler - DWC • Agency: State • Tel: 918-297-0153 • Location: 7 miles N of Sawyer (limited services), 14 miles NE of Hugo • GPS: Lat 34.104633 Lon -95.371293 • Total sites: Dispersed • RV sites: Undefined • RV fee: Free • No water • No toilets • Activities: Fishing, power boating, non-power boating • Elevation: 548

Seiling

Canton WMA - Site 7 • Agency: State • Tel: 580-541-5319 • Location: 14 miles E of Seiling (limited services), 22 miles SW of Fairview • GPS: Lat 36.160228 Lon -98.746912 • Total sites: Dispersed • RV sites: Undefined • RV fee: Free • No water • No toilets • Activities: Fishing, hunting • Elevation: 1648

Canton WMA - Site 8 - Unmans Cutoff Lake • Agency: State • Tel: 580-541-5319 • Location: 14 miles E of Seiling (limited services), 22 miles SW of Fairview • GPS: Lat 36.160544 Lon -98.766575 • Total sites: Dispersed • RV sites: Undefined • RV fee: Free • No water • No toilets • Activities: Fishing, hunting • Elevation: 1646

Canton WMA - Site 9 • Agency: State • Tel: 580-541-5319 • Location: 10 miles E of Seiling (limited services), 32 miles SW of Fairview • GPS: Lat 36.144748 Lon -98.777079 • Total sites: Dispersed • RV sites: Undefined • RV fee: Free • No water • No toilets • Activities: Fishing, hunting • Elevation: 1658

Shattuck

Ellis County WMA - Site 1 • Agency: State • Tel: 580-515-2030 • Location: 15 miles S of Shattuck • GPS: Lat 36.069215 Lon -99.913917 • Total sites: Dispersed • RV sites: Undefined • RV fee: Free • No water • No toilets • Activities: Fishing, hunting • Elevation: 2269

Shidler

Kaw WMA - Site 9 • Agency: State • Tel: 405-823-7936 • Location: 11 miles NW of Shidler (limited services), 29 miles NE of Ponca City • GPS: Lat 36.862804 Lon -96.752098 • Total sites: Dispersed • RV sites: Undefined • RV fee: Free • No water • No toilets • Activities: Fishing, hunting • Elevation: 1054

Kaw WMA - Site 10 • Agency: State • Tel: 405-823-7936 • Location: 10 miles NW of Shidler (limited services), 29 miles NE of Ponca City • GPS: Lat 36.868854 Lon -96.750558 • Total sites: Dispersed • RV sites: Undefined • RV fee: Free • No water • No toilets • Activities: Fishing, hunting • Elevation: 1083

Kaw WMA - Site 11 • Agency: State • Tel: 405-823-7936 • Location: 10 miles NW of Shidler (limited services), 28 miles NE of Ponca City • GPS: Lat 36.865544 Lon -96.740841 • Total sites: Dispersed • RV sites: Undefined • RV fee: Free • No water • No toilets • Activities: Fishing, hunting • Elevation: 1074

Kaw WMA - Site 12 • Agency: State • Tel: 405-823-7936 • Location: 7 miles NW of Shidler (limited services), 22 miles NE of Ponca City • GPS: Lat 36.811197 Lon -96.770778 • Total sites: Dispersed • RV sites: Undefined • RV fee: Free • No water • No toilets • Activities: Fishing, hunting • Elevation: 1080

Slaughterville

Lexington WMA - HQ • Agency: State • Tel: 405-527-6476 • Location: 6 miles E of Slaughterville (limited services), 11 miles SE of Noble • GPS: Lat 35.085009 Lon -97.234597 • Total sites: Dispersed • RV sites: Undefined • RV fee: Free • No water • No toilets • Activities: Hiking, fishing • Elevation: 1230

Stringtown

Atoka WMA • Agency: State • Tel: 580-346-7664 • Location: 5 miles NE of Stringtown (limited services), 11 miles NE of Atoka • GPS: Lat 34.526087 Lon -96.026848 • Total sites: Dispersed • RV sites: Undefined • RV fee: Free • No water • No toilets • Activities: Fishing • Elevation: 712

McGee Creek WMA • Agency: State • Tel: 580-346-7664 • Location: 13 miles SE of Stringtown (limited services), 21 miles NE of Atoka • GPS: Lat 34.430511 Lon -95.888785 • Total sites: 20 • RV sites: 20 • RV fee: Free • No water • No toilets • Activities: Fishing, hunting • Elevation: 893

Stringtown WMA • Agency: State • Tel: 580-346-7664 • Location: 7 miles E of Stringtown (limited services), 14 miles NE of Atoka • GPS: Lat 34.460796 Lon -95.951031 • Total sites: Dispersed • RV sites: Undefined • RV fee: Free • No water • No toilets • Activities: Hunting • Elevation: 703

Talala

Oologah WMA - Goose Island • Agency: State • Tel: 918-629-5286 • Location: 7 miles SE of Talala (limited services), 16 miles S of Nowata • GPS: Lat 36.496046 Lon -95.621187 • Total sites: Dispersed • RV sites: Undefined • RV fee: Free • No water • No toilets • Activities: Fishing, hunting • Elevation: 652

Tishomingo

Blue River WMA - Site 1 • Agency: State • Tel: 580-443-5728 • Location: 10 miles NE of Tishomingo • GPS: Lat 34.322951 Lon -96.595895 • Total sites: Dispersed • RV sites: Undefined • RV fee: Free • No water • No toilets • Activities: Fishing • Elevation: 751

Blue River WMA - Site 2 • Agency: State • Tel: 580-443-5728 • Location: 10 miles NE of Tishomingo • GPS: Lat 34.327893 Lon -96.591978 • Total sites: Dispersed • RV sites: Undefined • RV fee: Free • No water • No toilets • Activities: Fishing • Elevation: 764

Blue River WMA - Site 3 • Agency: State • Tel: 580-443-5728 • Location: 11 miles NE of Tishomingo • GPS: Lat 34.319354 Lon -96.595491 • Total sites: Dispersed • RV sites: Undefined • RV fee: Free • No water • No toilets • Activities: Fishing • Elevation: 762

Blue River WMA - Site 4 • Agency: State • Tel: 580-443-5728 • Location: 11 miles NE of Tishomingo • GPS: Lat 34.322265 Lon -96.590192 • Total sites: Dispersed • RV sites: Undefined • RV fee: Free • No water • No toilets • Activities: Fishing • Elevation: 783

Tishomingo WMU - Site 1 • Agency: State • Tel: 405-823-8383 • Location: 3 miles SW of Tishomingo • GPS: Lat 34.217308 Lon -96.714289 • Total sites: Dispersed • RV sites: Undefined • RV fee: Free • No water • No toilets • Activities: Fishing, hunting • Elevation: 650

Tishomingo WMU - Site 2 • Agency: State • Tel: 405-823-8383 • Location: 4 miles S of Tishomingo • GPS: Lat 34.199009 Lon -96.694105 • Total sites: Dispersed • RV sites: Undefined • RV fee: Free • No water • No toilets • Activities: Fishing, hunting • Elevation: 655

Tishomingo WMU - Site 3 • Agency: State • Tel: 405-823-8383 • Location: 5 miles S of Tishomingo • GPS: Lat 34.191375 Lon -96.693959 • Total sites: Dispersed • RV sites: Undefined • RV fee: Free • No water • No toilets • Activities: Fishing, hunting • Elevation: 646

Tishomingo WMU - Site 4 • Agency: State • Tel: 405-823-8383 • Location: 4 miles S of Tishomingo • GPS: Lat 34.187993 Lon -96.695671 • Total sites: Dispersed • RV sites: Undefined • RV fee: Free • No water • No toilets • Activities: Fishing, hunting • Elevation: 651

Tishomingo WMU - Site 5 • Agency: State • Tel: 405-823-8383 • Location: 5 miles S of Tishomingo • GPS: Lat 34.183562 Lon -96.687456 • Total sites: Dispersed • RV sites: Undefined • RV fee: Free • No water • No toilets • Activities: Fishing, hunting • Elevation: 649

Turpin

Beaver River WMA - Site 1 • Agency: State • Tel: 806-339-5175 • Location: 10 miles SE of Turpin (limited services), 20 miles W of Beaver • GPS: Lat 36.813403 Lon -100.766717 • Total sites: Dispersed • RV sites: Undefined • RV fee: Free • No water • No toilets • Elevation: 2492

West Siloam Springs

Lake Frances • Agency: Municipal • Location: 5 miles S of West Siloam Springs (limited services), 5 miles SW of Siloam Springs, AR • GPS: Lat 36.129569 Lon -94.564398 • Total sites: Dispersed • RV sites: Undefined • RV fee: Free • No toilets • Elevation: 922

Whippoorwill

Hulah WMA - Site 1 • Agency: State • Tel: 918-349-2281 • Location: 15 miles NW of Whippoorwill (limited services), 28 miles N of Pawhuska • GPS: Lat 36.982451 Lon -96.295741 • Total sites: Dispersed • RV sites: Undefined • RV fee: Free • No water • No toilets • Activities: Fishing, hunting • Elevation: 784

Hulah WMA - Site 2 • Agency: State • Tel: 918-349-2281 • Location: 15 miles NW of Whippoorwill (limited services), 27 miles N of Pawhuska • GPS: Lat 36.992188 Lon -96.278065 • Total sites: Dispersed • RV sites: Undefined • RV fee: Free • No water • No toilets • Activities: Fishing, hunting • Elevation: 777

Hulah WMA - Site 3 • Agency: State • Tel: 918-349-2281 • Location: 15 miles NW of Whippoorwill (limited services), 27 miles N of Pawhuska • GPS: Lat 36.992244 Lon -96.250082 • Total sites: Dispersed • RV sites: Undefined • RV fee: Free • No water • No toilets • Activities: Fishing, hunting • Elevation: 782

Hulah WMA - Site 4 • Agency: State • Tel: 918-349-2281 • Location: 14 miles NW of Whippoorwill (limited services), 27 miles N of Pawhuska • GPS: Lat 36.998337 Lon -96.237826 • Total sites: Dispersed • RV sites: Undefined • RV fee: Free • No water • No toilets • Activities: Fishing, hunting • Elevation: 776

Hulah WMA - Site 5 • Agency: State • Tel: 918-349-2281 • Location: 13 miles NW of Whippoorwill (limited services), 26 miles N of Pawhuska • GPS: Lat 36.997736 Lon -96.226291 • Total sites: Dispersed • RV sites: Undefined • RV fee: Free • No water • No toilets • Activities: Fishing, hunting • Elevation: 763

Hulah WMA - Site 6 • Agency: State • Tel: 918-349-2281 • Location: 11 miles NW of Whippoorwill (limited services), 23 miles N of Pawhuska • GPS: Lat 36.974776 Lon -96.200691 • Total sites: Dispersed • RV sites: Undefined • RV fee: Free • No water • No toilets • Activities: Fishing, hunting • Elevation: 763

Hulah WMA - Site 7 • Agency: State • Tel: 918-349-2281 • Location: 11 miles NW of Whippoorwill (limited services), 23 miles N of Pawhuska • GPS: Lat 36.947994 Lon -96.221772 • Total sites: Dispersed • RV sites: Undefined • RV fee: Free • No water • No toilets • Activities: Fishing, hunting • Elevation: 758

Hulah WMA - Site 8 • Agency: State • Tel: 918-349-2281 • Location: 11 miles NW of Whippoorwill (limited services), 24 miles N of Pawhuska • GPS: Lat 36.946595 Lon -96.235018 • Total sites: Dispersed • RV sites: Undefined • RV fee: Free • No water • No toilets • Activities: Fishing, hunting • Elevation: 784

Hulah WMA - Site 9 • Agency: State • Tel: 918-349-2281 • Location: 6 miles NW of Whippoorwill (limited services), 22 miles N of Pawhuska • GPS: Lat 36.949015 Lon -96.184205 • Total sites: Dispersed • RV sites: Undefined • RV fee: Free • No water • No toilets • Activities: Fishing, hunting • Elevation: 751

Hulah WMA - Site 10 • Agency: State • Tel: 918-349-2281 • Location: 6 miles NW of Whippoorwill (limited services), 29 miles NE of Pawhuska • GPS: Lat 36.942024 Lon -96.181043 • Total sites: Dispersed • RV sites: Undefined • RV fee: Free • No water • No toilets • Activities: Fishing, hunting • Elevation: 751

Hulah WMA - Site 11 • Agency: State • Tel: 918-349-2281 • Location: 5 miles NW of Whippoorwill (limited services), 20 miles NE of Pawhuska • GPS: Lat 36.929676 Lon -96.188693 • Total sites: Dispersed • RV sites: Undefined • RV fee: Free • No water • No toilets • Activities: Fishing, hunting • Elevation: 745

Hulah WMA - Site 12 • Agency: State • Tel: 918-349-2281 • Location: 3 miles W of Whippoorwill (limited services), 20 miles NE of Pawhuska • GPS: Lat 36.914304 Lon -96.178821 • Total sites: Dispersed • RV sites: Undefined • RV fee: Free • No water • No toilets • Activities: Fishing, hunting • Elevation: 776

Hulah WMA - Site 13 • Agency: State • Tel: 918-349-2281 • Location: 2 miles NW of Whippoorwill (limited services), 21 miles NE of Pawhuska • GPS: Lat 36.922756 Lon -96.160123 • Total sites: Dispersed • RV sites: Undefined • RV fee: Free • No water • No toilets • Activities: Fishing, hunting • Elevation: 746

Hulah WMA - Site 14 • Agency: State • Tel: 918-349-2281 • Location: 15 miles N of Whippoorwill (limited services), 28 miles NE of Pawhuska • GPS: Lat 36.969822 Lon -96.149455 • Total sites: Dispersed • RV sites: Undefined • RV fee: Free • No water • No toilets • Activities: Fishing, hunting • Elevation: 780

Hulah WMA - Site 15 • Agency: State • Tel: 918-349-2281 • Location: 20 miles N of Whippoorwill (limited services), 33 miles NE of Pawhuska • GPS: Lat 36.934961 Lon -96.106867 • Total sites: Dispersed • RV sites: Undefined • RV fee: Free • No water • No toilets • Activities: Fishing, hunting • Elevation: 745

Hulah WMA - Site 16 • Agency: State • Tel: 918-349-2281 • Location: 20 miles N of Whippoorwill (limited services), 32 miles NE of Pawhuska • GPS: Lat 36.941934 Lon -96.105378 • Total sites: Dispersed • RV sites: Undefined • RV fee: Free • No water • No toilets • Activities: Fishing, hunting • Elevation: 752

Hulah WMA - Site 17 • Agency: State • Tel: 918-349-2281 • Location: 20 miles N of Whippoorwill (limited services), 33 miles NE of Pawhuska • GPS: Lat 36.937677 Lon -96.099104 • Total sites: Dispersed • RV sites: Undefined • RV fee: Free • No water • No toilets • Activities: Fishing, hunting • Elevation: 745

Hulah WMA - Site 18 • Agency: State • Tel: 918-349-2281 • Location: 9 miles N of Whippoorwill (limited services), 24 miles NW of Bartlesville • GPS: Lat 36.965562 Lon -96.097652 • Total sites: Dispersed • RV sites: Undefined • RV fee: Free • No water • No toilets • Activities: Fishing, hunting • Elevation: 736

Hulah WMA - Site 19 • Agency: State • Tel: 918-349-2281 • Location: 10 miles N of Whippoorwill (limited services), 25 miles NW of Bartlesville • GPS: Lat 36.968656 Lon -96.095785 • Total sites: 9 • RV sites: 9 • RV fee: Free • No water • No toilets • Activities: Fishing, hunting • Elevation: 746

Hulah WMA - Site 20 • Agency: State • Tel: 918-349-2281 • Location: 6 miles NE of Whippoorwill (limited services), 21 miles NW of Bartlesville • GPS: Lat 36.939941 Lon -96.077357 • Total sites: Dispersed • RV sites: Undefined • RV fee: Free • No water • No toilets • Activities: Fishing, hunting • Elevation: 732

Osage WMA • Agency: State • Tel: 918-349-2281 • Location: 10 miles SW of Whippoorwill (limited services), 16 miles NE of Pawhuska • GPS: Lat 36.846131 Lon -96.219653 • Total sites: Dispersed • RV sites: Undefined • RV fee: Free • No water • No toilets • Activities: Fishing, hunting • Elevation: 989

Wilburton

Yourman WMA • Agency: State • Tel: 918-569-4329 • Location: 10 miles S of Wilburton • GPS: Lat 34.821853 Lon -95.288018 • Total sites: Dispersed • RV sites: Undefined • RV fee: Free • No water • No toilets • Activities: Hunting • Elevation: 745

Woodward

Fort Supply WMA - Site 8 • Agency: State • Tel: 580-334-0343 • Location: 10 miles NW of Woodward • GPS: Lat 36.492562 Lon -99.567194 • Total sites: Dispersed • RV sites: Undefined • RV fee: Free • No water • No toilets • Activities: Fishing, hunting • Elevation: 2040

South Dakota

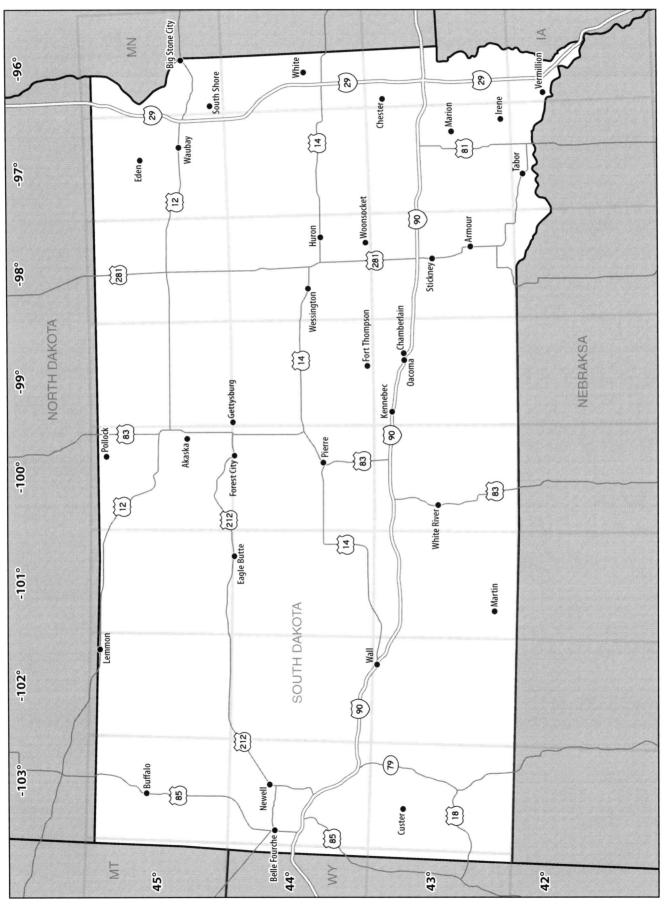

South Dakota — Camping Areas

Abbreviation	Description
GFP	Game, Fish and Parks
LUA	Lakeside Use Area
NF	National Forest
NP	National Park
NWR	National Wildlife Refuge
RA	Recreation Area

Akaska

LeBeau LUA - GFP • Agency: State • Tel: 605-765-9410 • Location: 12 miles SW of Akaska (limited services), 47 miles SE of Mobridge • GPS: Lat 45.277166 Lon -100.264837 • Total sites: Dispersed • RV sites: Undefined • RV fee: Free • No water • No toilets • Activities: Fishing • Elevation: 1614

Armour

Lions City Park • Agency: Municipal • Tel: 605-724-2245 • Location: In Armour (limited services), 18 miles N of Wagner • GPS: Lat 43.322246 Lon -98.343087 • Total sites: 10 • RV sites: 10 • RV fee: Free (donation appreciated) • Electric sites: 10 • Central water • Flush toilets • Elevation: 1522

Belle Fourche

Belle Fourche Reservoir • Agency: State • Location: 12 miles NE of Belle Fourche • GPS: Lat 44.726921 Lon -103.680355 • Total sites: Dispersed • RV sites: Undefined • RV fee: Free • No water • Vault toilets • Elevation: 2983

Big Stone City

Big Stone Rearing Ponds - GFP • Agency: State • Location: 4 miles N of Big Stone City (limited services), 13 miles NE of Milbank • GPS: Lat 45.337233 Lon -96.489682 • Open: All year • Total sites: Dispersed • RV sites: Undefined • RV fee: Free • No water • Vault toilets • Activities: Fishing, power boating, non-power boating • Elevation: 958

Buffalo

Picnic Spring (Custer Gallatin NF) • Agency: US Forest Service • Tel: 605-797-4432 • Location: 28 miles N of Buffalo (limited services), 99 miles N of Belle Fourche • GPS: Lat 45.874398 Lon -103.485574 • Open: May-Sep • Total sites: 8 • RV sites: 8 • Max RV Length: 30 • RV fee: Free • Central water • Vault toilets • Elevation: 3245

Reva Gap (Custer Gallatin NF) • Agency: US Forest Service • Tel: 605-797-4432 • Location: 20 miles E of Buffalo (limited services), 87 miles NE of Belle Fourche • GPS: Lat 45.525763 Lon -103.177222 • Total sites: 8 • RV sites: 8 • Max RV Length: 30 • RV fee: Free • Central water • Vault toilets • Activities: Hiking • Elevation: 3284

Chamberlain

Elm Creek LUA - GFP • Agency: State • Tel: 605-337-2587 • Location: 23 miles S of Chamberlain • GPS: Lat 43.559537 Lon -99.299058 • Total sites: 14 • RV sites: 14 • RV fee: Free • Central water • Vault toilets • Activities: Fishing • Elevation: 1365

Chester

East Brant Lake Access - GFP • Agency: State • Location: 2 miles N of Chester (limited services), 15 miles SE of Madison • GPS: Lat 43.915336 Lon -96.930083 • Total sites: Dispersed • RV sites: Undefined • RV fee: Free • No water • Vault toilets • Activities: Fishing • Elevation: 1608

Custer

Moon (Black Hills NF) • Agency: US Forest Service • Location: 30 miles NW of Custer • GPS: Lat 43.946136 Lon -104.009197 • Open: Jun-Nov • Total sites: 3 • RV sites: 3 • Max RV Length: 30 • RV fee: Free • No water • Vault toilets • Elevation: 6440

Eagle Butte

Foster Bay LUA • Agency: State • Tel: 605-223-7722 • Location: 35 miles SE of Eagle Butte (limited services), 60 miles NW of Pierre • GPS: Lat 44.733293 Lon -101.062565 • Open: All year • Total sites: 20 • RV sites: 20 • Max RV Length: 30 • RV fee: Free • Central water • Activities: Fishing, swimming, power boating, non-power boating • Elevation: 1647

Eden

Buffalo South LUA - GFP • Agency: State • Location: 5 miles E of Eden (limited services), 16 miles SW of Sisseton • GPS: Lat 45.607358 Lon -97.316093 • Total sites: Dispersed • RV sites: Undefined • RV fee: Free • No water • Vault toilets • Activities: Fishing, power boating, non-power boating • Elevation: 1821

Forest City

Sutton Bay LUA - GFP • Agency: State • Tel: 605-765-9410 • Location: 13 miles SW of Forest City (limited services), 44 miles N of Pierre • GPS: Lat 44.880015 Lon -100.358545 • Open: All year • Total sites: Dispersed • RV sites: Undefined • RV fee: Free • No water • Vault toilets • Activities: Fishing, power boating, non-power boating • Elevation: 1686

Fort Thompson

North Shore (Lake Sharpe) • Agency: Corps of Engineers • Tel: 605-245-2255 • Location: 2 miles W of Fort Thompson (limited services), 24 miles NW of Chamberlain • GPS: Lat 44.065188 Lon -99.475442 • Open: All year • Total sites: 24 • RV sites: 24 • RV fee: Free • Central water • Vault toilets • Activities: Fishing, power boating, non-power boating • Elevation: 1457

Old Fort Thompson (Lake Sharpe) • Agency: Corps of Engineers • Tel: 605-245-2255 • Location: 2 miles S of Fort Thompson (limited services), 22 miles NW of Chamberlain • GPS: Lat 44.059442 Lon -99.445538 • Open: All year • Total sites: 13 • RV sites: 13 • RV fee: Free • Central water • Flush toilets • Activities: Fishing, swimming, power boating • Elevation: 1358

Right Tailrace • Agency: Corps of Engineers • Location: 3 miles S of Fort Thompson (limited services), 24 miles NW of Chamberlain • GPS: Lat 44.036311 Lon -99.439985 • Total sites: Dispersed • RV sites: Undefined • RV fee: Free • Central water • Flush toilets • Activities: Fishing, power boating • Elevation: 1374

Gettysburg

Dodge Draw LUA - GFP • Agency: State • Tel: 605-765-9410 • Location: 26 miles NW of Gettysburg • GPS: Lat 45.176089 Lon -100.265146 • Open: All year • Total sites: Dispersed • RV sites: Undefined • RV fee: Free • No water • Vault toilets • Activities: Fishing, power boating, non-power boating • Elevation: 1614

East Whitlock LUA - GFP • Agency: State • Tel: 605-765-9410 • Location: 16 miles NW of Gettysburg • GPS: Lat 45.051772 Lon -100.247854 • Total sites: Dispersed • RV sites: Undefined • RV fee: Free • No water • Vault toilets • Activities: Fishing, power boating, non-power boating • Elevation: 1623

Forest City LUA - GFP • Agency: State • Location: 19 miles W of Gettysburg • GPS: Lat 45.026454 Lon -100.305012 • Open: All year • Total sites: 7 • RV sites: 7 • Max RV Length: 30 • RV fee: Free • No water • Vault toilets • Activities: Fishing, power boating, non-power boating • Elevation: 1627

Gettysburg City Park • Agency: Municipal • Location: In Gettysburg • GPS: Lat 45.007601 Lon -99.958985 • Stay limit: 3 days • Total sites: 3 • RV sites: 3 • RV fee: Free (donation appreciated) • Electric sites: 3 • Central water • Flush toilets • Elevation: 2057

Huron

James River Unit 1 LUA - GFP • Agency: State • Tel: 605-626-3488 • Location: 16 miles N of Huron • GPS: Lat 44.597209 Lon -98.239418 • Open: All year • Total sites: 4 • RV sites: 4 • RV fee: Free • No water • No toilets • Activities: Fishing • Elevation: 1257

Lake Byron Northwest LUA - GFP • Agency: State • Tel: 605-626-3488 • Location: 17 miles N of Huron • GPS: Lat 44.572554 Lon -98.159399 • Open: All year • Total sites: Dispersed • RV sites: Undefined • RV fee: Free • Central water • Vault toilets • Activities: Fishing, swimming, power boating, non-power boating • Elevation: 1250

Irene

Marindahl Lake LUA - GFP • Agency: State • Location: 10 miles SW of Irene (limited services), 15 miles NE of Yankton • GPS: Lat 43.036722 Lon -97.258659 • Open: All year • Total sites: Dispersed • RV sites: Undefined • RV fee: Free • No water • No toilets • Activities: Fishing, power boating, non-power boating • Elevation: 1316

Kennebec

Byre Lake - GFP • Agency: State • Location: 4 miles NE of Kennebec (limited services), 32 miles NW of Chamberlain • GPS: Lat 43.929533 Lon -99.836872 • Total sites: Dispersed • RV sites: Undefined • RV fee: Free • No water • Vault toilets • Activities: Fishing • Elevation: 1674

Lemmon

Hugh Glass LUA - GFP • Agency: State • Location: 18 miles S of Lemmon • GPS: Lat 45.736942 Lon -102.241285 • Open: All year • Total sites: 15 • RV sites: 15 • RV fee: Free • No water • Vault toilets • Activities: Fishing, power boating, non-power boating, equestrian area • Elevation: 2339

Marion

Hieb Memorial Park • Agency: Municipal • Tel: 605-648-2869 • Location: In Marion (limited services), 32 miles SW of Sioux Falls • GPS: Lat 43.426518 Lon -97.265049 • Total sites: 7 • RV sites: 7 • RV fee: Free • Electric sites: 3 • Water at site • No toilets (toilets/showers at pool) • Activities: Swimming • Elevation: 1430

Martin

Brooks Memorial Park • Agency: Municipal • Tel: 605-685-6330 • Location: In Martin (limited services), 45 miles NE of Pine Ridge • GPS: Lat 43.176314 Lon -101.730881 • Total sites: 4 • RV sites: 4 • RV fee: Free (donation appreciated) • Central water • Vault toilets • Elevation: 3317

Hodson Memorial Park • Agency: Municipal • Tel: 605-685-6330 • Location: In Martin (limited services), 45 miles NE of Pine Ridge • GPS: Lat 43.168892 Lon -101.731266 • Total sites: Dispersed • RV sites: Undefined • RV fee: Free (donation appreciated) • Elevation: 3327

Lacreek NWR - Little White River RA • Agency: US Fish & Wildlife • Tel: 605-685-6508 • Location: 12 miles E of Martin (limited services), 57 miles NE of Pine Ridge • GPS: Lat 43.171259 Lon -101.544933 • Total sites: Dispersed • RV sites: Undefined • RV fee: Free • No water • Elevation: 3018

Newell

Newell Lake LUA - GFP • Agency: State • Tel: 605-584-3896 • Location: 10 miles N of Newell (limited services), 34 miles NE of Belle Fourche • GPS: Lat 44.833311 Lon -103.389907 • Open: All year • Total sites: Dispersed • RV sites: Undefined • RV fee: Free • No water • Vault toilets • Activities: Fishing, swimming, power boating, non-power boating • Elevation: 2904

Oacoma

Dude Ranch - GFP • Agency: State • Location: 3 miles SW of Oacoma (limited services), 7 miles SW of Chamberlain • GPS: Lat 43.781235 Lon -99.425444 • Total sites: Dispersed • RV sites: Undefined • RV fee: Free • No water • Vault toilets • Activities: Fishing • Elevation: 1370

Pierre

Chantier Creek LUA - GFP • Agency: State • Tel: 605-223-7722 • Location: 17 miles NW of Pierre • GPS: Lat 44.478943 Lon -100.617426 • Open: All year • Total sites: Dispersed • RV sites: Undefined • RV fee: Free • No water • No toilets • Activities: Fishing, power boating, non-power boating • Elevation: 1608

De Grey LUA- GFP • Agency: State • Tel: 605-773-2885 • Location: 21 miles SE of Pierre • GPS: Lat 44.276823 Lon -99.926286 • Open: All year • Total sites: 10 • RV sites: 10 • Max RV Length: 25 • RV fee: Free • No water • Vault toilets • Activities: Fishing, power boating, non-power boating • Elevation: 1414

Joe Creek LUA - GFP • Agency: State • Tel: 605-773-2885 • Location: 36 miles SE of Pierre • GPS: Lat 44.145882 Lon -99.795614 • Open: All year • Total sites: 6 • RV sites: 6 • RV fee: Free • Central water • Vault toilets • Activities: Fishing, power boating, non-power boating • Elevation: 1414

North Bend LUA - GFP • Agency: State • Tel: 605-773-2885 • Location: 36 miles SE of Pierre • GPS: Lat 44.226169 Lon -99.684807 • Open: All year • Total sites: 10 • RV sites: 10 • RV fee: Free • No water • Vault toilets • Activities: Fishing, power boating, non-power boating • Elevation: 1417

Pollock

Shaw Creek LUA - GFP • Agency: State • Tel: 605-765-9410 • Location: 11 miles SW of Pollock (limited services), 33 miles N of Mobridge • GPS: Lat 45.798354 Lon -100.342976 • Open: All year • Total sites: Dispersed • RV sites: Undefined • RV fee: Free • No water • Vault toilets • Activities: Fishing, power boating, non-power boating • Elevation: 1647

South Shore

Round Lake LUA - GFP • Agency: State • Location: 1 mile E of South Shore (limited services), 20 miles SW of Milbank • GPS: Lat 45.108912 Lon -96.910668 • Open: All year • Total sites: 6 • RV sites: 6 • RV fee: Free • No water • Vault toilets • Activities: Fishing, power boating, non-power boating • Elevation: 1834

Stickney

Stickney City Park • Agency: Municipal • Tel: 605-732-4204 • Location: In Stickney (limited services), 27 miles SW of Mitchell • GPS: Lat 43.589261 Lon -98.441872 • Total sites: 2 • RV sites: 2 • RV fee: Free (donation appreciated) • Electric sites: 2 • Central water • Flush toilets • Activities: Swimming • Elevation: 1647

Tabor

Lesterville LUA - GFP • Agency: State • Location: 8 miles SE of Tabor (limited services), 13 miles W of Yankton • GPS: Lat 42.866643 Lon -97.586082 • Open: All year • Total sites: Dispersed • RV sites: Undefined • RV fee: Free • No water • Vault toilets • Activities: Fishing, non-power boating • Elevation: 1362

Vermilion

Lion's Park • Agency: Municipal • Tel: 605-677-7082 • Location: In Vermilion • GPS: Lat 42.786201 Lon -96.937992 • Open: Apr-Oct • Stay limit: 2 days • Total sites: 10 • RV sites: 10 • RV fee: Free • Electric sites: 10 • Central water • Flush toilets • Elevation: 1230

Wall

Badlands NP - Sage Creek • Agency: National Park Service • Tel: 605-433-5361 • Location: 17 miles SW of Wall (limited services), 51 miles SE of Rapid City • GPS: Lat 43.894115 Lon -102.414015 • Open: All year • Total sites: 18 • RV sites: 11 • Max RV Length: 18 • RV fee: Free • No water • Vault toilets • Notes: No open fires • Elevation: 2539

Waubay

Enemy Swim Lake - GFP • Agency: State • Tel: 605-882-5200 • Location: 9 miles N of Waubay (limited services), 19 miles NE of Webster • GPS: Lat 45.431029 Lon -97.281664 • Total sites: Dispersed • RV sites: Undefined • RV fee: Free • No water • Vault toilets • Activities: Fishing • Elevation: 1863

Waubay City Park • Agency: Municipal • Location: In Waubay (limited services), 11 miles E of Webster • GPS: Lat 45.341449 Lon -97.296812 • Open: All year • Total sites: 20 • RV sites: 20 • RV fee: Free • Electric sites: 5 • Central water • No toilets • Activities: Fishing, power boating, non-power boating • Elevation: 1795

Wessington

Rose Hill LUA - GFP • Agency: State • Tel: 605-626-3488 • Location: 13 miles SW of Wessington (limited services), 28 miles SE of Miller • GPS: Lat 44.313197 Lon -98.769217 • Open: All year • Total sites: Dispersed • RV sites: Undefined • RV fee: Free • Central water • Vault toilets • Activities: Fishing, power boating, hunting, non-power boating • Elevation: 1709

White

Lake Hendricks LUA -GFP • Agency: State • Tel: 605-627-5441 • Location: 12 miles NE of White (limited services), 27 miles NE of Brookings • GPS: Lat 44.480083 Lon -96.476875 • Open: All year • Total sites: 15 • RV sites: 15 • RV fee: Free • No water • Vault toilets • Activities: Fishing, power boating, non-power boating • Elevation: 1755

White River

White River City Park • Agency: Municipal • Location: In White River (limited services), 24 miles S of Murdo • GPS: Lat 43.564955 Lon -100.741975 • Open: All year • Total sites: 12 • RV sites: 12 • Max RV Length: 35 • RV fee: Free • Central water • Vault toilets • Notes: Call city clerk for permission to run 100' hose and 100' electric cord to your camper for free • Elevation: 2132

Woonsocket

Twin Lakes LUA - GFP • Agency: State • Tel: 605-256-5003 • Location: 9 miles SW of Woonsocket (limited services), 31 miles NW of Mitchell • GPS: Lat 43.965737

Lon -98.329677 • Open: All year • Total sites: 8 • RV sites: 8 • RV fee: Free • Central water • Vault toilets • Activities: Fishing, power boating, non-power boating • Elevation: 1326

Texas

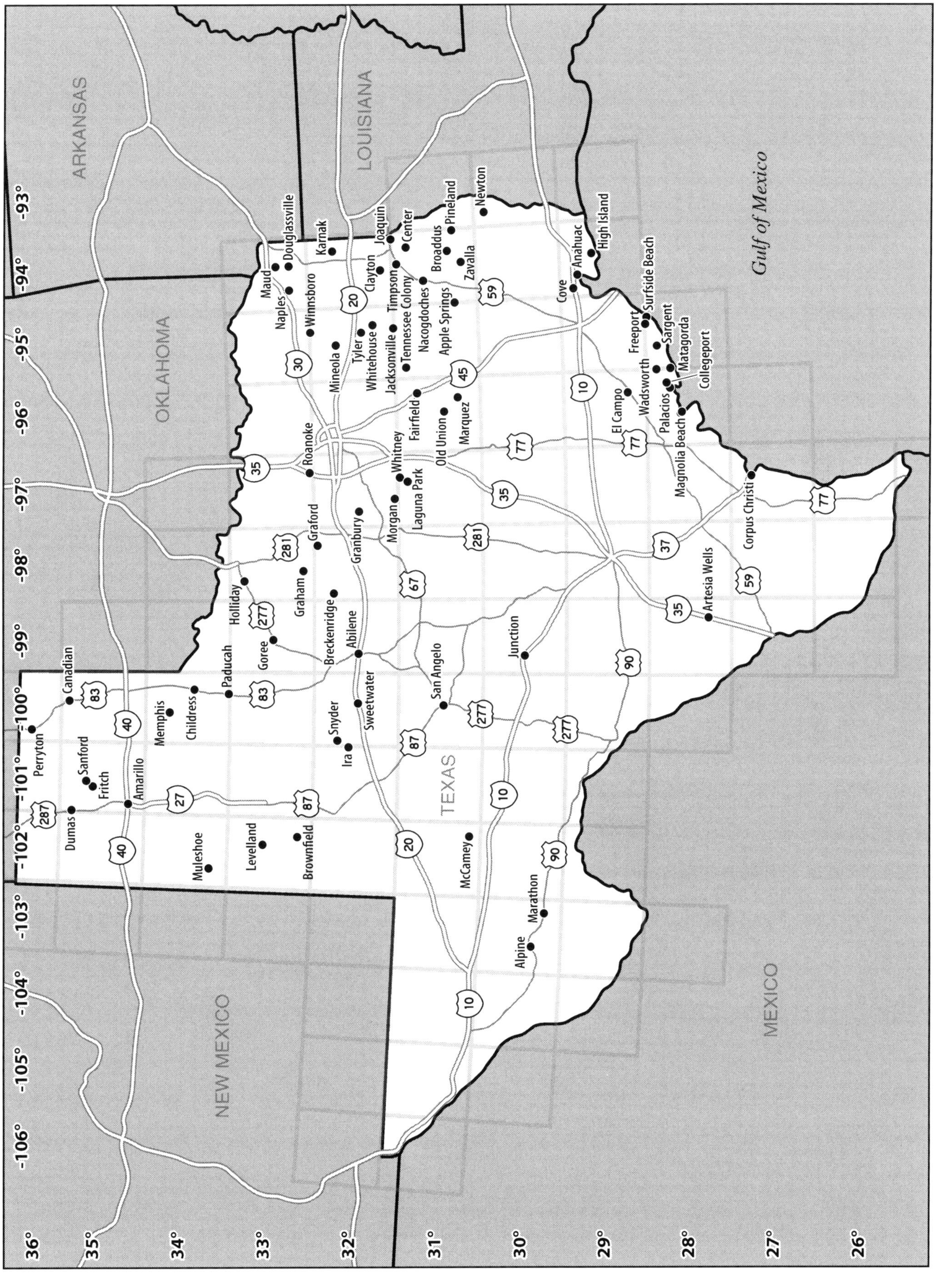
ARKANSAS
LOUISIANA
OKLAHOMA
NEW MEXICO
TEXAS
MEXICO
Gulf of Mexico
-93°
-94°
-95°
-96°
-97°
-98°
-99°
-100°
-101°
-102°
-103°
-104°
-105°
-106°
36°
35°
34°
33°
32°
31°
30°
29°
28°
27°
26°
Douglassville
Maud
Naples
Karnak
Winnsboro
Joaquin
Center
Clayton
Timpson
Tennessee Colony
Pineland
Newton
Broaddus
Zavalla
Nacogdoches
Apple Springs
Mineola
Tyler
Whitehouse
Jacksonville
Fairfield
Marquez
Old Union
Roanoke
Whitney
Laguna Park
Morgan
Granbury
Graford
Graham
Breckenridge
Holliday
Goree
Abilene
Paducah
Childress
Memphis
Canadian
Perryton
Sanford
Fritch
Dumas
Amarillo
Muleshoe
Levelland
Brownfield
Snyder
Ira
Sweetwater
San Angelo
Junction
McCamey
Marathon
Alpine
Anahuac
High Island
Cove
Surfside Beach
Freeport
Sargent
Matagorda
Collegeport
Wadsworth
El Campo
Palacios
Magnolia Beach
Corpus Christi
Artesia Wells
20
30
45
59
10
77
35
281
67
37
277
83
40
27
87
287
90

Texas — Camping Areas

Abbreviation	Description
BRA	Brazos River Authority
CRMWD	Colorado River Municipal Water District
LCRA	Lower Colorado River Authority
NCTMWA	North Central Texas Municipal Water Authority
NF	National Forest
NRA	National Recreation Area
NS	National Seashore
NWR	National Wildlife Refuge
PCFWD	Panola County Fresh Water District
TPWD	Texas Parks & Wildlife Department
WCTMWD	West Central Texas Municipal Water District
WMA	Wildlife Management Area

Abilene

Johnson City Park (Lake Fort Phantom Hill) • Agency: Municipal • Tel: 325-676-6217 • Location: 11 miles N of Abilene • GPS: Lat 32.613135 Lon -99.680363 • Stay limit: 2 days • Total sites: 5 • RV sites: 5 • RV fee: Free • No water • Flush toilets • Activities: Fishing, power boating, disc golf • Elevation: 1657

Seabee City Park • Agency: Municipal • Tel: 325-676-6217 • Location: 4 miles N of Abilene • GPS: Lat 32.538817 Lon -99.715444 • Stay limit: 2 days • Total sites: 4 • RV sites: 4 • RV fee: Free • Central water • No toilets • Activities: Fishing, power boating • Elevation: 1654

Alpine

Elephant Mountain WMA • Agency: State • Tel: 432-837-3251 • Location: 27 miles S of Alpine • GPS: Lat 30.040361 Lon -103.557309 • Open: All year • Total sites: 14 • RV sites: 14 • RV fee: Free • No water • No toilets • Notes: Permit required • Activities: Hiking, hunting • Elevation: 4342

Amarillo

Lake Meredith NRA - Rosita OHV • Agency: National Park Service • Tel: 806-857-3151 • Location: 21 miles N of Amarillo • GPS: Lat 35.472082 Lon -101.818789 • Total sites: Dispersed • RV sites: Undefined • RV fee: Free • No water • No toilets • Activities: Hiking, mountain biking, fishing, power boating, hunting, motor sports, equestrian area • Elevation: 3048

Anahuac

Job Beason • Agency: County • Tel: 409-267-2409 • Location: 8 miles S of Anahuac • GPS: Lat 29.655343 Lon -94.691658 • Open: All year • Stay limit: 3 days • Total sites: Dispersed • RV sites: Undefined • RV fee: Free • Central water • Flush toilets • Activities: Fishing, power boating, non-power boating • Elevation: 10

Whites Memorial • Agency: County • Tel: 409-267-2409 • Location: 5 miles NE of Anahuac • GPS: Lat 29.836529 Lon -94.652461 • Open: All year • Stay limit: 3 days • Total sites: Dispersed • RV sites: Undefined (RV's must be self-comtained) • RV fee: Free • Central water • Flush toilets (cold showers available) • Notes: Permit required • Activities: Fishing, power boating • Elevation: 27

Apple Springs

Alabama Creek WMA - FR 509 (Davy Crockett NF) • Agency: State • Tel: 936-569-8547 • Location: 10 miles SE of Apple Springs (limited services), 22 miles SW of Lufkin • GPS: Lat 31.176249 Lon -94.912795 • Open: All year • Total sites: Dispersed • RV sites: Undefined • RV fee: Free • No water • No toilets • Activities: Hiking, mountain biking, fishing, hunting, equestrian area • Elevation: 267

Alabama Creek WMA - FR 509C (Davy Crockett NF) • Agency: State • Tel: 936-569-8547 • Location: 5 miles SE of Apple Springs (limited services), 21 miles SW of Lufkin • GPS: Lat 31.183727 Lon -94.939797 • Open: All year • Total sites: Dispersed • RV sites: Undefined • RV fee: Free • No water • No toilets • Activities: Hiking, mountain biking, fishing, hunting, equestrian area • Elevation: 277

Alabama Creek WMA - Road 2262 (Davy Crockett NF) • Agency: State • Tel: 936-569-8547 • Location: 7 miles SE of Apple Springs (limited services), 19 miles SW of Lufkin • GPS: Lat 31.189052 Lon -94.887839 • Open: All year • Total sites: Dispersed • RV sites: Undefined • RV fee: Free • No water • No toilets • Activities: Hiking, mountain biking, fishing, hunting, equestrian area • Elevation: 269

Artesia Wells

Chaparral WMA • Agency: State • Tel: 830-676-3413 • Location: 6 miles W of Artesia Wells (limited services), 17 miles SW of Cotulla • GPS: Lat 28.294013 Lon -99.386904 • Open: Apr-Aug • Total sites: 15 • RV sites: 15 • RV fee: Free • No water • No toilets • Activities: Hiking, mountain biking, hunting • Elevation: 564

Breckenridge

Hubbard Creek Reservoir • Agency: Municipal • Location: 9 miles SW of Breckenridge • GPS: Lat 32.834943 Lon -98.974989 • Total sites: Dispersed • RV sites: Undefined • RV fee: Free • No water • Vault toilets • Activities: Fishing, swimming, power boating, non-power boating • Elevation: 1190

Lake Daniel • Agency: Municipal • Tel: 254-559-8287 • Location: 9 miles S of Breckenridge • GPS: Lat 32.646518 Lon -98.872551 • Open: All year • Total sites: Dispersed • RV sites: Undefined • RV fee: Free • No water • Vault toilets • Activities: Fishing, power boating, non-power boating • Elevation: 1322

Peeler Park - WCTMWD • Agency: Utility Company • Tel: 325-673-8254 • Location: 9 miles W of Breckenridge • GPS: Lat 32.768408 Lon -99.072778 • Open: All year • Total sites: Dispersed • RV sites: Undefined • RV fee: Free • No water • Vault toilets • Activities: Fishing, power boating, non-power boating • Elevation: 1201

Broaddus

Bannister WMA - Road 300 • Agency: State • Tel: 936-569-8547 • Location: 5 miles E of Broaddus (limited services), 24 miles SW of San Augustine • GPS: Lat 31.300402 Lon -94.201489 • Open: All year • Total sites: Dispersed • RV sites: Undefined • RV fee: Free • No water • No toilets • Activities: Hiking, mountain biking, fishing, hunting, equestrian area • Elevation: 318

Bannister WMA - Road 300A • Agency: State • Tel: 936-569-8547 • Location: 5 miles E of Broaddus (limited services), 24 miles SW of San Augustine • GPS: Lat 31.300388 Lon -94.209858 • Open: All year • Total sites: Dispersed • RV sites: Undefined • RV fee: Free • No water • No toilets • Activities: Hiking, mountain biking, fishing, hunting, equestrian area • Elevation: 282

Bannister WMA - Road 307A • Agency: State • Tel: 936-569-8547 • Location: 7 miles NE of Broaddus (limited services), 16 miles SW of San Augustine • GPS: Lat 31.340481 Lon -94.205887 • Open: All year • Total sites: Dispersed • RV sites: Undefined • RV fee: Free • No water • No toilets • Activities: Hiking, mountain biking, fishing, hunting, equestrian area • Elevation: 323

Brownfield

Coleman City Park • Agency: Municipal • Tel: 806-637-4547 • Location: In Brownfield • GPS: Lat 33.172692 Lon -102.275833 • Open: All year • Stay limit: 5 days • Total sites: 12 • RV sites: 12 • RV fee: Free • Electric sites: 12 • Water at site • No toilets • Activities: Swimming • Elevation: 3280

Canadian

Gene Howe WMA • Agency: State • Tel: 806-323-8642 • Location: 7 miles E of Canadian • GPS: Lat 35.910544 Lon -100.284254 • Open: All year • Total sites: Dispersed • RV sites: Undefined • RV fee: Free • No water • Vault toilets • Notes: Permit required. Open fires often prohibited • Activities: Hiking, mountain biking, fishing, hunting, equestrian area • Elevation: 2312

Center

Pinkston Dam (Lake Pinkston) • Agency: Municipal • Tel: 936-598-2941 • Location: 15 miles SW of Center • GPS: Lat 31.710211 Lon -94.363019 • Open: All year • Total sites: Dispersed • RV sites: Undefined • RV fee: Free • No toilets • Activities: Fishing, power boating • Elevation: 328

Sandy Creek (Lake Pinkston) • Agency: Municipal • Tel: 936-598-2941 • Location: 13 miles SW of Center • GPS: Lat 31.704905 Lon -94.336918 • Open: All year • Total sites: Dispersed • RV sites: Undefined • RV fee: Free • No toilets • Activities: Fishing, power boating • Elevation: 358

Childress

Childress Ramp (Lake Childress) • Agency: Municipal • Tel: 940-937-3684 • Location: 9 miles NW of Childress • GPS: Lat 34.466953 Lon -100.357585 • Open: All year • Total sites: Dispersed • RV sites: Undefined • RV fee: Free • No water • No toilets • Activities: Fishing, power boating, non-power boating • Elevation: 1818

Clayton

Rosie Jones Park - PCFWD (Lake Murvaul) • Agency: Utility Company • Tel: 903-693-6562 • Location: 5 miles S of Clayton (limited services), 13 miles SW of Carthage • GPS: Lat 32.045217 Lon -94.474727 • Total sites: Dispersed • RV sites: Undefined • RV fee: Free • Vault toilets • Elevation: 305

Collegeport

Oyster Lake • Agency: County • Location: 10 miles SW of Collegeport (limited services), 25 miles S of Palacios • GPS: Lat 28.610348 Lon -96.213754 • Total sites: Dispersed • RV sites: Undefined • RV fee: Free • No water • No toilets • Elevation: 10

Corpus Christi

Labonte Park • Agency: Municipal • Tel: 361-826-7529 • Location: 3 miles N of Corpus Christi • GPS: Lat 27.893821 Lon -97.631037 • Open: All year • Stay limit:

3 days • Total sites: 20 • RV sites: 20 • RV fee: Free • No water • No toilets • Notes: Obtain permit at City Hall • Activities: Fishing • Elevation: 10

Padre Island NS - North Beach • Agency: National Park Service • Tel: 361-949-8068 • Location: 12 miles S of Corpus Christi • GPS: Lat 27.439768 Lon -97.291089 • Open: All year • Stay limit: 14 days • Total sites: Dispersed • RV sites: Undefined • RV fee: Free • No water • No toilets • Notes: Beach camping, free permit required • Activities: Swimming • Elevation: 6

Padre Island NS - South Beach • Agency: National Park Service • Tel: 361-949-8068 • Location: 14 miles S of Corpus Christi • GPS: Lat 27.407587 Lon -97.304755 • Open: All year • Stay limit: 14 days • Total sites: Dispersed • RV sites: Undefined • RV fee: Free • No toilets • Notes: Beach camping, free permit required • Elevation: 13

Cove

Hugo Point • Agency: County • Tel: 281-576-2243 • Location: 3 miles S of Cove (limited services), 9 miles NE of Baytown • GPS: Lat 29.812548 Lon -94.796313 • Total sites: Dispersed • RV sites: Undefined • RV fee: Free • No water • Activities: Fishing, power boating, non-power boating • Elevation: 16

Douglassville

Armstrong Creek (Wright Patman Lake) • Agency: Corps of Engineers • Tel: 903-838-8781 • Location: 8 miles NE of Douglassville (limited services), 12 miles NW of Atlanta • GPS: Lat 33.226278 Lon -94.279362 • Open: All year • Stay limit: 14 days • Total sites: Dispersed • RV sites: Undefined • RV fee: Free • No water • No toilets • Activities: Fishing, power boating, non-power boating • Elevation: 244

Black Point • Agency: Corps of Engineers • Tel: 903-838-8781 • Location: 9 miles NW of Douglassville (limited services), 21 miles NW of Atlanta • GPS: Lat 33.258229 Lon -94.402746 • Stay limit: 14 days • Total sites: Dispersed • RV sites: Undefined • RV fee: Free • No water • No toilets • Activities: Fishing • Elevation: 236

Flatwoods (Wright Patman Lake) • Agency: Corps of Engineers • Tel: 903-838-8781 • Location: 6 miles NE of Douglassville (limited services), 18 miles NW of Atlanta • GPS: Lat 33.248267 Lon -94.310504 • Stay limit: 14 days • Total sites: Dispersed • RV sites: Undefined • RV fee: Free • No water • No toilets • Activities: Fishing • Elevation: 233

Jackson Creek Park (Wright Patman Lake) • Agency: Corps of Engineers • Tel: 903-838-8781 • Location: 7 miles NE of Douglassville (limited services), 13 miles NW of Atlanta • GPS: Lat 33.224198 Lon -94.302568 • Stay limit:

14 days • Total sites: 20 • RV sites: 20 • Max RV Length: 25 • RV fee: Free • No water • Vault toilets • Activities: Fishing, power boating • Elevation: 269

Thomas Lake (Wright Patman Lake) • Agency: Corps of Engineers • Tel: 903-838-8781 • Location: 14 miles NW of Douglassville (limited services), 26 miles NW of Atlanta • GPS: Lat 33.266835 Lon -94.470869 • Open: All year • Stay limit: 14 days • Total sites: Dispersed • RV sites: Undefined • RV fee: Free • No water • Vault toilets • Activities: Fishing, power boating, non-power boating • Elevation: 249

Dumas

Texoma City Park • Agency: Municipal • Tel: 806-934-0837 • Location: In Dumas • GPS: Lat 35.867101 Lon -101.979386 • Open: Apr-Oct • Stay limit: 1 day • Total sites: 12 • RV sites: 12 • RV fee: Free • Electric sites: 12 • Central water • Flush toilets • Notes: Near RR tracks • Elevation: 3665

El Campo

Hollywood Bottom Park - LCRA • Agency: Utility Company • Tel: 512-473-3366 • Location: 18 miles E of El Campo • GPS: Lat 29.161756 Lon -96.044552 • Total sites: Dispersed • RV sites: Undefined • RV fee: Free • No toilets • Activities: Non-power boating • Elevation: 85

Fairfield

Richland Creek WMA - Below Dam • Agency: State • Tel: 903-389-7080 • Location: 17 miles N of Fairfield • GPS: Lat 31.946267 Lon -96.096308 • Open: All year • Total sites: 12 • RV sites: 12 • RV fee: Free • No water • No toilets • Activities: Hiking, mountain biking, fishing, hunting, equestrian area • Elevation: 298

Richland Creek WMA - Zachry Lake • Agency: State • Tel: 903-389-7080 • Location: 17 miles N of Fairfield • GPS: Lat 31.980272 Lon -96.086737 • Open: All year • Total sites: 6 • RV sites: 6 • RV fee: Free • No water • No toilets • Activities: Hiking, mountain biking, fishing, hunting, equestrian area • Elevation: 254

Freeport

Bryan Beach • Agency: Municipal • Tel: 979-233-3526 • Location: 2 miles S of Freeport • GPS: Lat 28.912342 Lon -95.335597 • Open: All year • Total sites: Dispersed • RV sites: Undefined • RV fee: Free • No water • Vault toilets • Activities: Fishing, swimming • Elevation: 7

Fritch

Lake Meredith NRA - Bates Canyon • Agency: National Park Service • Location: 12 miles SW of Fritch • GPS: Lat 35.587504 Lon -101.706219 • Open: All year • Total sites: Dispersed • RV sites: Undefined • RV fee: Free • No water • Vault toilets • Activities: Hiking, mountain biking, fishing, power boating, hunting, motor sports, equestrian area • Elevation: 2942

Lake Meredith NRA - Fritch Fortress • Agency: National Park Service • Tel: 806-857-3151 • Location: 4 miles N of Fritch • GPS: Lat 35.681674 Lon -101.598428 • Total sites: 9 • RV sites: 5 • RV fee: Free • Central water • Flush toilets • Activities: Hiking, mountain biking, fishing, power boating, hunting, motor sports, equestrian area • Elevation: 3127

Lake Meredith NRA - Harbor Bay • Agency: National Park Service • Tel: 806-857-3151 • Location: 1 mile W of Fritch • GPS: Lat 35.648807 Lon -101.629296 • Total sites: Dispersed • RV sites: Undefined • RV fee: Free • No water • Vault toilets • Activities: Hiking, mountain biking, fishing, power boating, hunting, motor sports, equestrian area • Elevation: 3002

Lake Meredith NRA - McBride Canyon • Agency: National Park Service • Tel: 806-857-3151 • Location: 12 miles SW of Fritch • GPS: Lat 35.542784 Lon -101.732209 • Total sites: Dispersed • RV sites: Undefined • RV fee: Free • No water • Vault toilets • Activities: Hiking, mountain biking, fishing, power boating, hunting, motor sports, equestrian area • Elevation: 3071

Lake Meredith NRA - Mullinaw Creek • Agency: National Park Service • Tel: 806-857-3151 • Location: 15 miles SW of Fritch • GPS: Lat 35.526297 Lon -101.753324 • Total sites: Dispersed • RV sites: Undefined • RV fee: Free • No water • Vault toilets • Activities: Hiking, mountain biking, fishing, power boating, hunting, motor sports, equestrian area • Elevation: 3058

Goree

Miller's Creek Reservoir - NCTMWA • Agency: County • Tel: 940-422-4331 • Location: 11 miles SE of Goree (limited services), 18 miles SW of Seymour • GPS: Lat 33.409322 Lon -99.390768 • Total sites: Dispersed • RV sites: Undefined • RV fee: Free • No water • No toilets • Elevation: 1342

Graford

Possum Kingdom Reservoir - Bug Beach - BRA • Agency: Utility Company • Tel: 940-779-2321 • Location: 17 miles SW of Graford (limited services), 27 miles SE of Graham • GPS: Lat 32.875773 Lon -98.506107 • Total sites: Dispersed • RV sites: Undefined • RV fee: Free • Vault toilets • Activities: Fishing, power boating, non-power boating • Elevation: 1010

Possum Kingdom Reservoir - Downtown - BRA • Agency: Utility Company • Tel: 940-779-2321 • Location: 13 miles SW of Graford (limited services), 23 miles SE of Graham • GPS: Lat 32.891396 Lon -98.452397 • Total sites: Dispersed • RV sites: Undefined • RV fee: Free • Vault toilets • Activities: Fishing, power boating, non-power boating • Elevation: 1037

Graham

Possum Kingdom Reservoir - Westside Ramp - BRA • Agency: Utility Company • Tel: 940-779-2321 • Location: 22 miles SE of Graham • GPS: Lat 32.909814 Lon -98.495605 • Total sites: Dispersed • RV sites: Undefined • RV fee: Free • Vault toilets • Activities: Fishing, power boating, non-power boating • Elevation: 1011

Granbury

De Cordova Bend • Agency: Utility Company • Tel: 817-573-3212 • Location: 10 miles SE of Granbury • GPS: Lat 32.37756 Lon -97.69121 • Open: All year • Total sites: Dispersed • RV sites: Undefined • RV fee: Free • No water • Flush toilets • Activities: Swimming, power boating • Elevation: 722

Hunter Park - BRA • Agency: Utility Company • Tel: 817-573-3212 • Location: 3 miles N of Granbury • GPS: Lat 32.478053 Lon -97.794027 • Total sites: Dispersed • RV sites: Undefined • RV fee: Free • No water • Vault toilets • Activities: Fishing, power boating, non-power boating • Elevation: 715

Rough Creek - BRA • Agency: Utility Company • Tel: 817-573-3212 • Location: In Granbury • GPS: Lat 32.419495 Lon -97.786971 • Total sites: Dispersed • RV sites: Undefined • RV fee: Free • No water • No toilets • Activities: Fishing, swimming, power boating • Elevation: 718

Thorp Spring - BRA • Agency: Utility Company • Tel: 817-573-3212 • Location: 2 miles NW of Granbury • GPS: Lat 32.474008 Lon -97.814574 • Open: All year • Total sites: Dispersed • RV sites: Undefined • RV fee: Free • No water • Vault toilets • Activities: Fishing, power boating, non-power boating • Elevation: 715

High Island

High Island • Agency: State • Location: In High Island (limited services), 16 miles S of Winnie • GPS: Lat 29.549906 Lon -94.388151 • Open: All year • Total sites: Dispersed • RV sites: Undefined • RV fee: Free • No water • No toilets • Activities: Surfing, fishing, swimming • Elevation: 13

Holliday

Stonewall Jackson Camp • Agency: Municipal • Tel: 940-586-1313 • Location: 2 miles SE of Holliday (limited services), 11 miles SW of Wichita Falls • GPS: Lat 33.786211 Lon -98.679041 • Open: All year • Total sites: 25 • RV sites: 5 • RV fee: Free • Central water (no water in winter) • Vault toilets • Elevation: 1024

Ira

Bull Creek - CRMWD (Lake J B Thomas) • Agency: Utility Company • Tel: 432-267-6341 • Location: 15 miles W of Ira (limited services), 23 miles SW of Snyder • GPS: Lat 32.594919 Lon -101.172981 • Total sites: 7 • RV sites: 5 • RV fee: Free • No water • Vault toilets • Activities: Fishing, swimming, power boating, non-power boating • Elevation: 2260

Jacksonville

South Shore Park (Lake Jacksonville) • Agency: Municipal • Tel: 903-586-3510 • Location: 6 miles S of Jacksonville • GPS: Lat 31.901649 Lon -95.309308 • Open: All year • Total sites: Dispersed • RV sites: Undefined • RV fee: Free • No water • No toilets • Activities: Fishing, power boating • Elevation: 426

Joaquin

North Toledo Bend WMA Unit 615 • Agency: State • Tel: 936-569-8547 • Location: 8 miles SE of Joaquin (limited services), 32 miles SE of Carthage • GPS: Lat 31.912048 Lon -93.960561 • Open: All year • Total sites: Dispersed • RV sites: Undefined • RV fee: Free • No water • No toilets • Activities: Hiking, fishing, hunting, equestrian area • Elevation: 175

Yellow Dog • Agency: County • Location: 13 miles NW of Joaquin (limited services), 24 miles SE of Carthage • GPS: Lat 32.005105 Lon -94.092376 • Open: All year • Total sites: Dispersed • RV sites: Undefined • RV fee: Free • No water • No toilets • Activities: Fishing, non-power boating • Elevation: 180

Junction

Schreiner City Park • Agency: Municipal • Tel: 325-446-2622 • Location: In Junction • GPS: Lat 30.49065 Lon -99.76068 • Stay limit: 3 days • Total sites: Dispersed • RV sites: Undefined • RV fee: Free • Central water • No toilets (toilets/shower at nearby pool in summer) • Activities: Swimming • Elevation: 1696

Karnack

Caddo Lake WMA - Road 805 • Agency: State • Tel: 903-679-9817 • Location: 7 miles N of Karnack (limited services), 20 miles NE of Marshall • GPS: Lat 32.739562 Lon -94.167108 • Open: All year • Total sites: Dispersed • RV sites: Undefined • RV fee: Free • No water • Activities: Fishing, hunting, non-power boating, equestrian area • Elevation: 173

Laguna Park

Riverside (Whitney Lake) • Agency: Corps of Engineers • Tel: 254-622-3332 • Location: 2 miles NE of Laguna Park • GPS: Lat 31.868045 Lon -97.367785 • Total sites: 5 • RV sites: 5 • RV fee: Free • No water • Vault toilets • Activities: Fishing • Elevation: 512

Soldiers Bluff (Whitney Lake) • Agency: Corps of Engineers • Tel: 254-622-3332 • Location: In Laguna Park • GPS: Lat 31.862041 Lon -97.372373 • Open: All year • Total sites: 14 • RV sites: 14 • RV fee: Free • No water • Vault toilets • Activities: Fishing • Elevation: 574

Walling Bend (Lake Whitney) • Agency: Corps of Engineers • Tel: 254-622-3332 • Location: 7 miles N of Laguna Park • GPS: Lat 31.897572 Lon -97.397161 • Open: All year • Total sites: 10 • RV sites: 10 • RV fee: Free • No water • Vault toilets • Activities: Fishing, swimming, power boating, non-power boating • Elevation: 550

Levelland

Levelland City RV Park • Agency: Municipal • Tel: 806-894-0113 • Location: 1 mile S of Levelland • GPS: Lat 33.553607 Lon -102.374612 • Stay limit: 3 days • Total sites: 7 • RV sites: 7 • RV fee: Free • Electric sites: 7 • Water at site • No toilets • Notes: Beside runway • Elevation: 3504

Magnolia Beach

Indianola • Agency: County • Tel: 361-553-4689 • Location: 1 mile SE of Magnolia Beach (limited services), 11 miles SE of Port Lavaca • GPS: Lat 28.557244 Lon -96.527975 • Open: All year • Total sites: Dispersed • RV sites: Undefined • RV fee: Free • Central water • No toilets • Activities: Fishing, swimming • Elevation: 7

Marathon

Black Gap WMA • Agency: State • Tel: 432-364-2228 • Location: 57 miles SE of Marathon (limited services), 88 miles SE of Alpine • GPS: Lat 29.548704 Lon -102.934642 • Open: All year • Total sites: Dispersed • RV sites: Undefined • RV fee: Free • No water • Vault toilets • Notes: 51 primitive sites throughout WMA • Activities: Hiking, mountain biking, fishing, hunting • Elevation: 2526

Marquez

Limestone Lake Park • Agency: Corps of Engineers • Location: 10 miles N of Marquez (limited services), 20 miles SW of Buffalo • GPS: Lat 31.340133 Lon -96.309082 • Total sites: 20 • RV sites: 20 • RV fee: Free • Central water • Vault toilets • Notes: No campfires • Elevation: 385

Public Use Area #5 - BRA • Agency: Utility Company • Tel: 903-529-2141 • Location: 10 miles NW of Marquez (limited services), 20 miles SW of Buffalo • GPS: Lat 31.330985 Lon -96.308224 • Open: All year • Stay limit: 7 days • Total sites: Dispersed • RV sites: Undefined • RV fee: Free • No water • Vault toilets • Activities: Fishing, power boating, non-power boating • Elevation: 374

Matagorda

Jetty • Agency: County • Location: 6 miles S of Matagorda (limited services), 25 miles S of Bay City • GPS: Lat 28.595771 Lon -95.979466 • Total sites: Dispersed • RV sites: Undefined • RV fee: Free • No water • Flush toilets • Elevation: 8

River Bend Boat Ramp • Agency: County • Location: 2 miles S of Matagorda (limited services), 21 miles S of Bay City • GPS: Lat 28.670079 Lon -95.964521 • Total sites: Dispersed • RV sites: Undefined • RV fee: Free • No water • No toilets • Elevation: 10

Maud

Corely Area 2 (Wright Patman Lake) • Agency: Corps of Engineers • Tel: 903-838-8781 • Location: 7 miles SW of Maud (limited services), 23 miles SW of Texarkana • GPS: Lat 33.271756 Lon -94.404804 • Open: All year • Stay limit: 14 days • Total sites: Dispersed • RV sites: Undefined • RV fee: Free • No water • No toilets • Activities: Fishing, power boating, non-power boating • Elevation: 243

McCamey

Santa Fe City Park • Agency: Municipal • Tel: 432-652-3333 • Location: In McCamey • GPS: Lat 31.137967 Lon -102.216637 • Total sites: 4 • RV sites: 4 • RV fee: Free • Electric sites: 4 • Water at site • Notes: Permit required from City Hall • Elevation: 2474

Memphis

Memphis City Park • Agency: Municipal • Tel: 806-259-3001 • Location: In Memphis • GPS: Lat 34.711568 Lon -100.535574 • Open: All year • Total sites: 8 • RV sites: 8 • RV fee: Free • Electric sites: 8 • Water at site • No toilets • Notes: Obtain free permit at City Hall • Elevation: 2005

Mineola

Lake Holbrook - South Access • Agency: County • Tel: 903-569-6351 • Location: 4 miles NW of Mineola • GPS: Lat 32.688343 Lon -95.547376 • Open: All year • Total sites: Dispersed • RV sites: Undefined • RV fee: Free • No water • No toilets • Activities: Fishing, swimming, power boating, non-power boating • Elevation: 374

Lake Holbrook- West Access • Agency: County • Tel: 903-569-6351 • Location: 5 miles NW of Mineola • GPS: Lat 32.70043 Lon -95.557376 • Open: All year • Total sites: Dispersed • RV sites: Undefined • RV fee: Free • No water • Vault toilets • Activities: Hiking, fishing, swimming, power boating • Elevation: 390

Morgan

Steele Creek (Whitney Lake) • Agency: Corps of Engineers • Tel: 254-622-3332 • Location: 10 miles E of Morgan (limited services), 17 miles NW of Whitney • GPS: Lat 32.005741 Lon -97.451559 • Total sites: 21 • RV sites: 21 • RV fee: Free • Central water • Vault toilets • Activities: Fishing, swimming, power boating, non-power boating • Elevation: 551

Muleshoe

Muleshoe NWR • Agency: US Fish & Wildlife • Tel: 806-946-3341 • Location: 21 miles S of Muleshoe • GPS: Lat 33.95726 Lon -102.778768 • Open: All year • Total sites: Dispersed • RV sites: Undefined • RV fee: Free • No water • Vault toilets • Activities: Hiking • Elevation: 3758

Nacogdoches

Alazan Bayou WMA • Agency: State • Tel: 936-569-8547 • Location: 9 miles SW of Nacogdoches • GPS: Lat 31.496211 Lon -94.752927 • Open: All year • Total sites: Dispersed • RV sites: Undefined • RV fee: Free • No water • Vault toilets • Activities: Fishing, hunting, equestrian area • Elevation: 194

Naples

Mudd Lake (Blue Lake) • Agency: Corps of Engineers • Tel: 903-838-8781 • Location: 11 miles NE of Naples • GPS: Lat 33.291499 Lon -94.550663 • Open: All year • Stay limit: 14 days • Total sites: Dispersed • RV sites: Undefined • RV fee: Free • No water • No toilets • Activities: Fishing, power boating, non-power boating • Elevation: 248

Newton

Campbell Timberland Mgmt Unit 122 - East Site - TPWD • Agency: State • Location: 10 miles NE of Newton • GPS: Lat 30.913736 Lon -93.642973 • Open: All year • Total sites: Dispersed • RV sites: Undefined • RV fee: Free • No water • No toilets • Elevation: 302

Campbell Timberland Mgmt Unit 122 - West Site - TPWD • Agency: State • Location: 4 miles N of Newton • GPS: Lat 30.899381 Lon -93.749671 • Open: All year • Total sites: Dispersed • RV sites: Undefined • RV fee: Free • No water • No toilets • Elevation: 324

Old Union

Public Use Area #2 - BRA • Agency: Utility Company • Tel: 254-729-3810 • Location: 4 miles NE of Old Union (limited services), 14 miles SE of Groesbeck • GPS: Lat 31.431375 Lon -96.375103 • Open: All year • Stay limit: 14 days • Total sites: Dispersed • RV sites: Undefined • RV fee: Free • No water • Vault toilets • Activities: Fishing, power boating, non-power boating • Elevation: 308

Public Use Area #3 - BRA • Agency: Utility Company • Tel: 254-729-3810 • Location: 4 miles NE of Old Union (limited services), 14 miles SE of Groesbeck • GPS: Lat 31.448107 Lon -96.377503 • Open: All year • Stay limit: 14 days • Total sites: Dispersed • RV sites: Undefined • RV fee: Free • No water • No toilets • Activities: Fishing, power boating, non-power boating • Elevation: 390

Paducah

Matador WMA - Site 1 • Agency: State • Tel: 806-492-3405 • Location: 9 miles N of Paducah • GPS: Lat 34.117621 Lon -100.347928 • Open: All year • Total sites: 4 • RV sites: 4 • RV fee: Free • No water • Vault toilets • Notes: Permit required. Open fires often prohibited • Elevation: 1923

Matador WMA - Site 2 • Agency: State • Tel: 806-492-3405 • Location: 10 miles NW of Paducah • GPS: Lat 34.117177 Lon -100.356949 • Open: All year • Total sites: 10 • RV sites: 10 • RV fee: Free • No water • Vault toilets • Notes: Permit required. Open fires often prohibited • Elevation: 1910

Palacios

Carl • Agency: County • Location: 8 miles NE of Palacios • GPS: Lat 28.786322 Lon -96.150436 • Open: All year • Total sites: Dispersed • RV sites: Undefined • RV fee: Free • No toilets • Activities: Fishing, power boating, non-power boating • Elevation: 13

Perryton

Whigham Park • Agency: Municipal • Tel: 806-435-4014 • Location: In Perryton • GPS: Lat 36.390113 Lon -100.801923 • Stay limit: 2 days • Total sites: 10 • RV sites: 5 • RV fee: Free • Electric sites: 5 • Water at site • Flush toilets (closed in winter) • Notes: Get code for utilities from police • Elevation: 2946

Pineland

Moore Plantation WMA - Road 114 • Agency: State • Tel: 936-569-8547 • Location: 5 miles E of Pineland (limited services), 27 miles NE of Jasper • GPS: Lat 31.237988 Lon -93.918753 • Open: All year • Total sites: Dispersed • RV sites: Undefined • RV fee: Free • No water • Activities: Hiking, mountain biking, fishing, hunting, equestrian area • Elevation: 270

Moore Plantation WMA - Road 114B • Agency: State • Tel: 936-569-8547 • Location: 7 miles SE of Pineland (limited services), 24 miles NE of Jasper • GPS: Lat 31.206638 Lon -93.917599 • Open: All year • Total sites: Dispersed • RV sites: Undefined • RV fee: Free • No water • Activities: Hiking, mountain biking, fishing, hunting, equestrian area • Elevation: 228

Moore Plantation WMA - Road 152 • Agency: State • Tel: 936-569-8547 • Location: 7 miles E of Pineland (limited services), 29 miles NE of Jasper • GPS: Lat 31.265717 Lon -93.882713 • Open: All year • Total sites: Dispersed • RV sites: Undefined • RV fee: Free • No water • Activities: Hiking, mountain biking, fishing, hunting, equestrian area • Elevation: 333

Roanoke

Trophy Club Park (Grapevine Lake) • Agency: Municipal • Location: 3 miles NE of Roanoke • GPS: Lat 33.025964 Lon -97.176637 • Total sites: Dispersed • RV sites: Undefined • RV fee: Free • Vault toilets • Activities: Fishing, power boating, motor sports • Elevation: 564

San Angelo

Foster • Agency: County • Location: 12 miles SW of San Angelo • GPS: Lat 31.330414 Lon -100.639283 • Open: All year • Total sites: Dispersed • RV sites: Undefined • RV fee: Free • No water • Flush toilets • Elevation: 1983

Sanford

Lake Meredith NRA - Blue Creek Bridge • Agency: National Park Service • Tel: 806-857-3151 • Location: 10 miles NW of Sanford (limited services), 17 miles NW of Fritch • GPS: Lat 35.721641 Lon -101.663579 • Total sites: Dispersed • RV sites: Undefined • RV fee: Free • No water • Vault toilets • Activities: Hiking, mountain biking, fishing, power boating, hunting, motor sports, equestrian area • Elevation: 2986

Lake Meredith NRA - Blue West • Agency: National Park Service • Tel: 806-857-3151 • Location: 21 miles W of Sanford (limited services), 26 miles NW of Fritch • GPS: Lat 35.685389 Lon -101.629931 • Total sites: 50 • RV sites: 50 • RV fee: Free • No water • Vault toilets • Activities: Hiking, mountain biking, fishing, power boating, hunting, motor sports, equestrian area • Elevation: 3061

Lake Meredith NRA - Bugbee • Agency: National Park Service • Tel: 806-857-3151 • Location: 6 miles NW of Sanford (limited services), 13 miles NW of Fritch • GPS: Lat 35.714899 Lon -101.594138 • Total sites: Dispersed • RV sites: Undefined • RV fee: Free • No water • Vault toilets • Activities: Hiking, mountain biking, fishing, power boating, hunting, motor sports, equestrian area • Elevation: 2963

Lake Meredith NRA - Cedar Canyon • Agency: National Park Service • Tel: 806-857-3151 • Location: 4 miles W of Sanford (limited services), 6 miles N of Fritch • GPS: Lat 35.693944 Lon -101.572953 • Total sites: Dispersed • RV sites: Undefined • RV fee: Free • Central water • Flush toilets • Notes: Beach camping • Activities: Hiking, mountain biking, fishing, power boating, hunting, motor sports, equestrian area • Elevation: 2966

Lake Meredith NRA - Chimney Hollow • Agency: National Park Service • Tel: 806-857-3151 • Location: 22 miles W of Sanford (limited services), 29 miles NW of Fritch • GPS: Lat 35.692061 Lon -101.642041 • Total sites: Dispersed • RV sites: Undefined • RV fee: Free • No water • No toilets • Activities: Hiking, mountain biking, fishing, power boating, hunting, motor sports, equestrian area • Elevation: 2950

Lake Meredith NRA - Plum Creek • Agency: National Park Service • Tel: 806-857-3151 • Location: 24 miles SW of Sanford (limited services), 31 miles SE of Dumas • GPS: Lat 35.616004 Lon -101.757741 • Total sites: Dispersed • RV sites: Undefined • RV fee: Free • No water • Vault toilets • Activities: Hiking, mountain biking, fishing, power boating, hunting, motor sports, equestrian area • Elevation: 3018

Sargent

Chamber • Agency: County • Location: 5 miles SE of Sargent • GPS: Lat 28.770884 Lon -95.614622 • Total sites: 4 • RV sites: 2 • RV fee: Free • Central water • Flush toilets • Elevation: 20

West Moring Dock • Agency: County • Location: 6 miles SE of Sargent • GPS: Lat 28.763641 Lon -95.629686 • Total sites: Dispersed • RV sites: Undefined • RV fee: Free • No

water • Vault toilets • Activities: Fishing, swimming, power boating • Elevation: 13

Surfside Beach

Brazoria County Free Beach • Agency: County • Location: 4 miles NE of Surfside Beach • GPS: Lat 28.990096 Lon -95.237689 • Open: All year • Total sites: Dispersed • RV sites: Undefined • RV fee: Free • No water • No toilets • Activities: Surfing, fishing, swimming • Elevation: 4

Sweetwater

Lake Trammell Park • Agency: County • Tel: 325-235-4166 • Location: 8 miles S of Sweetwater • GPS: Lat 32.366417 Lon -100.431976 • Open: All year • Total sites: Dispersed • RV sites: Undefined • RV fee: Free • No water • No toilets • Activities: Hiking, mountain biking, fishing, power boating, non-power boating • Elevation: 2284

Tennessee Colony

Gus Engeling WMA - Highway 287 • Agency: State • Tel: 903-928-2251 • Location: 7 miles NW of Tennessee Colony (limited services), 19 miles NW of Palestine • GPS: Lat 31.910168 Lon -95.907486 • Open: All year • Total sites: Dispersed • RV sites: Undefined • RV fee: Free • No water • Vault toilets • Activities: Hiking, mountain biking, fishing, hunting, equestrian area • Elevation: 379

Timpson

Tinkle Park - PCFWD (Lake Murvaul) • Agency: County • Tel: 903-693-6562 • Location: 10 miles N of Timpson • GPS: Lat 32.020059 Lon -94.436527 • Total sites: Dispersed • RV sites: Undefined • RV fee: Free • No toilets • Elevation: 276

Tyler

Highway 64 Ramp (Lake Tyler) • Agency: Municipal • Tel: 903-939-2724 • Location: 8 miles SE of Tyler • GPS: Lat 32.278496 Lon -95.113168 • Open: All year • Total sites: Dispersed • RV sites: Undefined • RV fee: Free • No water • No toilets • Activities: Fishing, power boating • Elevation: 410

Wadsworth

FM 521 River Park - LCRA • Agency: Utility Company • Tel: 361-972-2719 • Location: 6 miles SW of Wadsworth (limited services), 14 miles S of Bay City • GPS: Lat 28.787518 Lon -95.996496 • Open: All year • Total sites: Dispersed • RV sites: Undefined • RV fee: Free • No water • Vault toilets • Elevation: 20

Whitehouse

Concession Park (Lake Tyler) • Agency: Municipal • Location: 3 miles SE of Whitehouse • GPS: Lat 32.211721 Lon -95.180071 • Total sites: Dispersed • RV sites: Undefined • RV fee: Free • No water • Vault toilets • Activities: Fishing, power boating • Elevation: 384

Hill Creek Park (Lake Tyler) • Agency: Municipal • Tel: 903-939-2724 • Location: 3 miles E of Whitehouse • GPS: Lat 32.233955 Lon -95.183367 • Open: All year • Total sites: Dispersed • RV sites: Undefined • RV fee: Free • No water • No toilets • Activities: Fishing, power boating • Elevation: 410

Old Omen Road Ramp - West (Lake Tyler) • Agency: Municipal • Tel: 903-939-2724 • Location: 10 miles E of Whitehouse • GPS: Lat 32.240437 Lon -95.136787 • Open: All year • Total sites: 6 • RV sites: 6 • RV fee: Free • No water • Vault toilets • Activities: Fishing, power boating • Elevation: 387

Whitney

Cedar Creek (Whitney Lake) • Agency: Corps of Engineers • Tel: 254-622-3332 • Location: 8 miles NW of Whitney • GPS: Lat 31.990085 Lon -97.373333 • Open: All year • Total sites: 20 • RV sites: 20 • RV fee: Free • Central water • Vault toilets • Activities: Fishing, swimming, power boating, non-power boating • Elevation: 558

Winnsboro

Lake Winnsboro North Park • Agency: County • Tel: 903-763-2716 • Location: 6 miles SW of Winnsboro • GPS: Lat 32.917961 Lon -95.355909 • Open: All year • Total sites: 15 • RV sites: 15 • RV fee: Free • Electric sites: 2 • Central water • No toilets • Activities: Fishing, swimming, power boating, non-power boating • Elevation: 443

Zavalla

Sandy Creek (Angelina NF) • Agency: US Forest Service • Tel: 936-897-1068 • Location: 18 miles SE of Zavalla (limited services), 30 miles SE of Huntington • GPS: Lat 31.099164 Lon -94.202327 • Total sites: 10 • RV sites: 10 • Max RV Length: 24 • RV fee: Free • Central water • Vault toilets • Activities: Fishing, power boating, non-power boating • Elevation: 200

Made in the USA
Columbia, SC
29 June 2020